OXFORD STUDIES IN SOCIOLINGUISTICS

General Editors:

Nikolas Coupland
Adam Jaworski
Cardiff University

Recently Published in the Series:

Discourse and Practice: New Tools for Critical Discourse Analysis
Theo van Leeuwen

Beyond Yellow English: Toward a Linguistic Anthropology of Asian Pacific America
Edited by Angela Reyes and Adrienne Lo

Stance: Sociolinguistic Perspectives
Edited by Alexandra Jaffe

Investigating Variation: The Effects of Social Organization and Social Setting
Nancy C. Dorian

Television Dramatic Dialogue: A Sociolinguistic Study
Kay Richardson

Language without Rights
Lionel Wee

Paths to Post-Nationalism
Monica Heller

Language Myths and the History of English
Richard J. Watts

The "War on Terror" Narrative
Adam Hodges

Digital Discourse: Language in the New Media
Edited by Crispin Thurlow and Kristine Mroczek

Leadership, Discourse and Ethnicity
Janet Holmes, Meredith Marra, and Bernadette Vine

Spanish in New York
Ricardo Otheguy and Ana Celia Zentella

Emotion in Interaction

Edited by Anssi Peräkylä

and

Marja-Leena Sorjonen

OXFORD
UNIVERSITY PRESS

OXFORD
UNIVERSITY PRESS

Oxford University Press is a department of the University of Oxford.
It furthers the University's objective of excellence in research,
scholarship, and education by publishing worldwide.

Oxford   New York
Auckland   Cape Town   Dar es Salaam   Hong Kong   Karachi
Kuala Lumpur   Madrid   Melbourne   Mexico City   Nairobi
New Delhi   Shanghai   Taipei   Toronto

With offices in
Argentina   Austria   Brazil   Chile   Czech Republic   France   Greece
Guatemala   Hungary   Italy   Japan   Poland   Portugal   Singapore
South Korea   Switzerland   Thailand   Turkey   Ukraine   Vietnam

Oxford is a registered trade mark of Oxford University Press in the UK and certain other countries.

Published in the United States of America by Oxford University Press
198 Madison Avenue, New York, NY 10016

© Oxford University Press 2012

Library of Congress Cataloging-in-Publication Data
Emotion in interaction / edited by Anssi Peräkylä and Marja-Leena Sorjonen.
p.   cm.—(Oxford studies in sociolinguistics)
Includes bibliographical references and index.
ISBN 978-0-19-973073-5 (alk. paper)
1. Emotive (Linguistics) 2. Language and emotions. 3. Sociolinguistics.
I. Peräkylä, Anssi. II. Sorjonen Marja-Leena.
P325.5.E56E46   2012
401'.9—dc23   2011041713

1 3 5 7 9 8 6 4 2

Printed in the United States of America
on acid-free paper

CONTENTS

Emotion in Interaction

CHAPTER 1

✿

Introduction

MARJA-LEENA SORJONEN AND ANSSI PERÄKYLÄ

Displays of emotion and affect are a central part of everyday actions and social relations.* During the last decades, emotions and emotional stance have been intensively discussed and studied in many fields, most notably in psychology (e.g., Manstead, Bem, & Fridja, 2000; Manstead, Frijda, & Fischer, 2004; Gross, 2007), social psychology (e.g., Harré & Parrott, 1996; Parkinson, Fisher, & Manstead, 2005), communication (e.g., Planalp, 1999), sociology (e.g., Scheff, 1997; Katz, 1999; Fineman, 2000; Turner & Stets, 2005; Hopkins et al. 2009; Sieben & Wettergren 2010), neuroscience (e.g., Damasio, 1994; Panksep, 2004), and linguistics (e.g., Wierzbicka, 1999; Harkins & Wierzbicka, 2001; Wilce, 2009). In spite of the fact that emotions in most cases are manifested and recognized when people interact with each other, they have usually been studied outside real interactions: in experimental settings, using written data, or using historical or theoretical materials.

On the other hand, an increasing number of studies are focusing on ways in which emotional stances are expressed and responded to in naturally occurring spoken interactions. The lines of research that have led to these studies have developed somewhat independently from each other, originating from, for example, conversation analysis, interactional linguistics, interactional sociolinguistics, linguistic anthropology, and discursive psychology. However, they all share the assumption that social interaction forms a key locus for the expression of emotion and, consequently, that a more comprehensive understanding of both the expression of emotion and the emotional underpinnings of activities carried out in everyday interactions requires an examination of the details of interaction.

This volume pays tribute to the importance of emotion in everyday interaction by offering a collection of studies that explore emotion in naturally occurring spoken interaction. The authors come from a range of disciplines, including sociology, social psychology, linguistics, and anthropology. Accordingly they use different research

*We wish to thank Betty Couper-Kuhlen for most helpful comments on this chapter.

frameworks and methods, but what unites them is an understanding of the expression of emotion and the construction of emotional stance as a process that both shapes and is shaped by the interactional context. All use conversation analysis (CA) as a key method.

The chapters in this volume examine verbal, vocal, and nonvocal resources for expressing emotional stance, the emotional aspects of action sequences and activities, and the role of emotions in institutional interaction and settings. They analyze how emotion is expressed and how its expression is responsive to the interactional context and embedded in sequences of action and structures of social interaction. The expression of emotion is constructed and managed as a collaborative process by the participants in interaction. The chapters here demonstrate how the sequential organization of action forms the key relevant unit for analyzing emotion in interaction: displays of emotion are located at specific sequential positions in interaction, and they are interpreted and responded to by reference to that context of occurrence.

In the area of interaction studies, conversation analysis has developed a rigorous methodology for analyzing how members of society create intersubjective understanding through ways of organizing actions and sequences of actions. In CA research to date, however, studies focusing directly on specific affects and emotions are scanty (but see e.g., Whalen & Zimmerman, 1998; Wilkinson & Kitzinger, 2006). More commonly, terms such as "affiliate," "display affiliation," and "display (affective) stance," or their counterparts—"disaffiliate" and so on—have been used to describe actions with which a recipient treats the preceding talk as affective, and supports the affective stance expressed by the prior speaker, or not (see Stivers, 2008; Couper-Kuhlen, 2009; Lindström & Sorjonen, in press). Affiliative turns at talk can, for example, be agreeing assessments, and disaffiliative turns, for example, challenging questions or accusations. The present volume tackles the topic of emotion in talk-in-interaction directly; its chapters not only contribute to explicating the emotional import of affiliative and disaffiliative responding actions, but also to exploring aspects of emotion in initiating actions.

Although the name of this volume is *Emotion in interaction*, the term "affect" is used in some of the chapters alongside "emotion." This is in part a reflection of differences in practices in different disciplines and traditions: the term "affect" is perhaps more common in linguistics and related areas such as linguistic anthropology, whereas in social sciences similar phenomena are often referred to by the term "emotion." Reflecting the terminology in different areas of linguistics and related fields, Ochs (1989, p. 1) states that the term "affect" is preferred over "emotion," as it "refers to expressed emotional dispositions or 'the experiential part of emotion'." In their influential review of the expression of affect through linguistic means, Ochs and Schieffelin (1989, p. 7) state that in their use affect is a broader term than emotion and includes "feelings, moods, dispositions, and attitudes associated with persons and/or situations" (see also e.g., Selting, 2010a). As the conceptualization of the area of the current volume, emotion in interaction, and ways of talking about it (including terminology) are in the process of developing, we as editors have considered it fruitful not to impose any one terminology on our contributors (see Wilce, 2009, pp. 28–32 on the treatment of the relationship between emotion and affect in a range of fields).

AFFECTIVE AND EMOTIONAL STANCE AND STANCE TAKING

Alongside the terms "emotion" and "affect," and partially interchangeably with them, the terms "emotional stance" and "affective stance" are used in the literature, and also in this volume. The term "stance" may be particularly appropriate for the CA enterprise, referring as it does to a positioning accomplished through conduct and thereby made publicly accessible. Research on stance taking is currently being pursued especially in linguistics (e.g., Kärkkäinen, 2003; Englebretson, 2007b; Jaffe, 2009b). Du Bois (2007, p. 169) defines stance "as a public act by a social actor, achieved dialogically through overt communicative means (language, gesture, and other symbolic forms), through which social actors simultaneously evaluate objects, position subjects (themselves and others), and align with other subjects, with respect to any salient dimension of the sociocultural field." Most common kinds of stance recognized in the literature include epistemic, evaluative, and affective stance, but for example Goodwin (2007) distinguishes five kinds of stances when analyzing the alignment of participants toward each other (instrumental, cooperative, espistemic, moral, and affective). At the moment, study of the kinds of stance indexed and their interactional and sociocultural role has a diverse expression in the literature (see Jaffe, 2009a, p. 4, for a synthesis of terms used in the literature to describe stance taking; also e.g., Englebretson, 2007a; Du Bois, 2007). One widely adopted distinction is made by Ochs (e.g., 1996), who has emphasized the privileged role of the expression of affective and epistemic stance in the constitution of social life (also Ochs & Schieffelin, 1989; Ochs, 1992) and the indexical character of stance displays. In the context of affiliative and aligning reception of storytelling, Stivers (2008) uses the term "stance" to describe the teller's affective treatment of the events she is talking about.

The chapters in this volume explore the indexing of emotional or affective stance. For example, chapter 2, by Goodwin, Cekaite, and Goodwin, on emotion as stance treats the display of emotion as a situated practice that is entailed in speakers' performance of affective stance through multisemiotic resources (intonation, gesture, and body posture). In investigating ways in which recipients affiliate or disaffiliate with the teller of a complaint story, Couper-Kuhlen analyzes linguistic (verbal and prosodic) resources that are used for expressing an affective stance such as anger or indignation. Hakulinen and Sorjonen's chapter shows sequential contexts in which an equivocal display of affective stance becomes relevant and is accomplished with a particular type of response cry.

RESOURCES FOR EXPRESSING EMOTION

As shown by an increasing number of studies and by the chapters in this volume, a variety of semiotic systems is made use of and mobilized in displaying emotion. The different types of resources and cues (cf. contextualization cues, Gumperz, 1982, 1992) work together in a given sequential context to express the speaker's emotive involvement and serve to index for the recipient the kind of emotional valence and intensity to be responded to, the response then going along with or changing the emotional ground constructed by the prior speaker.

Verbal resources for expressing emotion

In their early overview of verbal elements used for expressing affect in different languages and cultures, Ochs and Schieffelin (1989) state that affect permeates the entire linguistic system, not only the lexicon (see also Besnier, 1990; for an extensive treatment of affect in the grammar of one language, see Hakulinen, Vilkuna, Korhonen, Koivisto, Heinonen, & Alho, 2004). They differentiate between those linguistic features that modulate the affective intensity of utterances (e.g., quantifiers) and ones that specify a particular affect (e.g., the active verb voice in Malagasy to index negative affect), and show how the scope and position of "affect keys" (Gumperz, 1977) vary within and across clauses.

The interpretation of verbal resources as having emotional underpinnings is made in a context-sensitive fashion, not only in relation to the other morphosyntactic and lexical elements in the utterance but also, and perhaps more importantly, to its being part of an action produced at a specifiable place in the ongoing interaction. For example, verbal resources such as dense syntactic constructions, infinitival constructions, syntactic clause types containing copular verbs and predicate nominals with evaluative and intensifying elements (e.g., "Jeff made en asparagus pie = **it wz s::so: goo:d**," Goodwin & Goodwin, 1992), evaluative adjective phrases ("wonderful"), reported speech, and various forms of response have been shown to have a central role in constructing affective actions such as challenging, assessing, constructing the evaluative point of a telling, and affiliating in various ways (e.g., Steensig & Drew, 2008; Goodwin & Goodwin, 1987, 1992; Günthner, 1999; Holt & Clift, 2007; Wilkinson & Kitzinger, 2006; Hakulinen & Sorjonen, 2009; Jefferson 2002; Pomerantz, 1984b; Visapää, 2010; Selting, 2010a). The affective import of a verbal element is indexed in relation to, and inferrable from, its context of occurrence. Furthermore, the verbal displays of affect often form larger rhetorical units of talk (e.g., contrasts), which unfold temporally over the course of interaction.

The appreciation of lexical resources for expressing emotion has been furthered by studies that have focused on ways in which emotion terms contribute to actions done in the course of an interaction, for example, in blamings and in offering excuses or accounts (Edwards, 1997, pp. 170–201; see also Edwards & Potter, 1992; Edwards, 1999; Rae, 2008). The emotional meaning potential of different types of verbal resource forms a fruitful area for future research on interaction (cf. Hakulinen & Selting, 2005 on syntax and lexis in conversation).

The chapters in this volume add to research on verbal resources for displaying affect and emotion. For example, in analyzing complaint stories, Couper-Kuhlen discusses different verbal devices through which a recipient can respond affiliatively to the teller's displays of affective stance. Hakulinen and Sorjonen investigate the use of a two-word response type to display an equivocal affective stance, putting this response type in the context of a wider paradigm of structurally related affective response types.

Prosodic resources for expressing emotion

Within the last fifteen years research on prosody and phonetics has become one of the central areas of interaction studies (e.g., Couper-Kuhlen & Selting, 1996; Couper-Kuhlen & Ford, 2004; Barth-Weingarten, Reber, & Selting 2010; Local 1996; Local & Walker, 2008; see Selting, 2010b for an overview). This research has also started to specify the role of prosodic and phonetic resources in expressing emotion. It has shown that prosodic–phonetic features form bundles that work holistically to index affect and that there is no distinct prosody or phonetics of single affects. Instead, as Couper-Kuhlen (2009) states, the utterances in a given sequential place are examined with respect to a set of affects or emotions relevant for that place and the relevant affects are distinguishable from one another on a verbal and/or prosodic–phonetic basis. Similarly, Local and Walker (2008) emphasize that attributing a speaker state such as happy only on the basis of the phonetic details of talk is too simplistic and that, instead, a close analysis of the different aspects of talk (e.g., sequential organization, turn construction, lexis, phonetic detail) is required, together with evidence from how the talk is received by the coparticipants.

An example of this line of research is Selting's (1996) study of other-initiated repair, in which she shows that the presence of a certain type of prosodic marking on repair initiation indexes that the initiation has to do with a problem of expectation, and that the recipients interpret this as astonishment and respond to it accordingly. In his study on assessment sequences in conversation, Ogden (2006) shows how agreeing and disagreeing responsive assessments to the prior speaker's assessment have distinctive phonetic properties that are tied to the sequential environment of the turn (e.g., disagreement is conveyed with either phonetic upgrading or downgrading depending on the sequential context). The study also points to a ranking of types of resources in indexing stance such that the phonetic shape of the turn can override the verbal resources: with a certain type of phonetic shape a lexicogrammatically agreeing turn is treated as a disagreement. The affective character of types of responsive turns from a prosodic perspective is currently underway (e.g., Reber, 2008).

One important issue for future research is comparative work on the deployment of prosodic–phonetic versus verbal resources for conveying emotion in different languages. Couper-Kuhlen (2009) raises this question in relation to English and German response particles and suggests that German may rely more heavily on variation of particles for the display of affects, whereas English may rely on phonetic and prosodic variation of one and the same lexical item.

This volume develops the study of the role of phonetic–prosodic features in expressing emotion. Maynard and Freese analyze prosodic choices as a way of constructing the news as good or bad, and Couper-Kuhlen examines prosodic means for expressing affective stance and providing affiliative responses in the context of complaint stories. Prosodic displays also have a central role in the chapter by Good-win and her colleagues.

Nonvocal resources for expressing emotion

Also nonvocal resources of the body—posture, gesture, and facial expression—have been investigated in terms of the emotional work they do. In early work on family psychotherapy interaction, Scheflen (1973) explored the body postures taken up by participants as a means of conveying what we might call "affective stances" toward the ongoing activity (such as passive protesting, contending, or defending). The interplay of hand movements, gaze, head movements, and facial expressions in an episode of embarrassment was analyzed by Heath (1988), who showed that the seemingly chaotic gestures were "carefully designed with respect to the local circum-stances" (Heath, 1988, p. 143; cf. also Heath, 1989). Goodwin and Goodwin (2000; see also C. Goodwin, 2006) show how gestures such as pointing and animated replay-ing of the other's actions are used in accusations of misconduct by girls in a game of hopscotch, alongside vocal and verbal means. Recently, Selting (2010a) has pointed to the use of head nods and head shakes, as well as slashing and slapping hand ges-tures, in conveying anger and indignation in storytelling. The affective work done through the alignment of the bodies of participants to an interaction was further investigated by C. Goodwin (2007),who showed that actors can either align or mis-align with a proposed course of action through their body positions (in Goodwin's case, a father wanting to engage his child in doing the child's homework together). Choices in alignment are intimately tied to affect, with refusal to align one's body to a proposed action, for example, generating anger.

The facial expression of emotion is a classical theme in psychological research (see e.g., Ekman & Friesen, 1975/2003). However, relatively little research has been done on facial expression in social interaction. In her pioneering work, Chovil (1991; see also Bavelas & Chovil, 2000) suggested that one usage of facial expression in interac-tion is to convey the speaker's personal reaction to what is talked about (thus, for example, wrinkling one's nose when referring to "disgusting" food). More recently, Ruusuvuori and Peräkylä (2009; see also Peräkylä & Ruusuvuori, 2006) have investi-gated the use of facial expressions in assessments, showing how speakers can orga-nize their face and talk in different configurations to convey affective stance. Facial expression can foreshadow utterances that convey stance, it can cooccur with them, or it can follow them. Ruusuvuori and Peräkylä thus argue that one of the affor-dances of facial expression is to stretch the boundaries of action: to embody stance before and after it is verbally explicated.

In this volume, our understanding of the nonvocal resources used in conveying emotion in interaction is furthered in many chapters. The intertwining of emotions and the postures and alignment of bodies in the local geography of action is explored in chapter 2 by Goodwin and her colleagues, and in chapter 10 by and Heath and his colleagues. These chapters also examine the use of facial expression, which is then subjected to further scrutiny in the chapter by Peräkylä and Ruusuvuori.

On the whole, the contributions to this volume show that it is not single resources in isolation but the cooccurrence of resources from different modalities and levels of modality that display emotional stances and their intensity, and that these displays are interpreted and oriented to by the recipients of the displays at specifiable places in interaction.

DISPLAY OF EMOTION AND ACTIONS AND ACTIVITIES

In a conversation analytic perspective, verbal and nonverbal displays of emotion are understood in the context of actions that participants to interaction are involved in. However, we do not yet have a satisfactory understanding of the relation between action and emotion. On the one hand, they can be understood as separable. In a recent review of research on action formation, Levinson (forthcoming) points out that the primary action of any turn at talk involves "what the response must deal with in order to count as an adequate next turn" (p. 4). Alongside such primary action or actions, turns at talk may involve a "penumbra of less 'official' business that participants may intend to be recognized" (p. 5). In many cases, a display of emotion may be part of such less official business: something intended to be recognized alongside the primary actions such as questioning, requesting, offering, and so on. On the other hand, action and emotion can be considered as more closely intertwined. There are many categories of potential primary actions that seem to inherently involve an emotion, such as complaint (Heinemann & Traverso, 2008), assessment (Lindström & Mondada, 2009), and teasing (Drew, 1987): for example, a recognizable display of negative emotion might be a necessary design feature for an utterance to be understood as a complaint (see also Couper-Kuhlen, this volume, chapter 6). Perhaps the most intimate relation between emotion and action is to be found in displays of emotion that, at least in some contexts, can in themselves be considered actions. Laughing (e.g., Coates, 2007; Haakana, 1999, 2001, 2002; Glenn, 2003; Jefferson, Sacks, & Schegloff, 1987; Vöge & Wagner, 2010) and crying (e.g., Hepburn, 2004; Hepburn & Potter, 2007) are actions of that kind, and in this volume, they are taken up in contributions by Haakana, and Hepburn and Potter, respectively. As a whole, this volume is an effort to pave the way to more focused research on emotion and action in social interaction and the relation between them.

If an action can take place through a single turn at talk, activities are more complex entities that can consist of several actions. A number of earlier studies have explored activities where the expression of emotional stance plays a role. These include, for example, troubles telling (Jefferson, 1980, 1988; Coupland, Coupland, & Giles, 1991; Jefferson & Lee, 1992), other kinds of tellings (Stivers, 2008; Selting, 2010a; Heritage, 2011), accounting (Buttny, 1993, chapter 6), delivery and reception of good and bad news (Maynard, 2003), and conflictual request sequences in parent–child interaction (Wootton, 1997). This research demonstrates that rather than being locatable at one single point in interaction, the display of affect and emotion can be temporally unfolding, coconstructed by the participants as the interaction unfolds. Selting (2010a), for example, describes a trajectory of shared affectivity at the uptake of climaxes in storytelling: the uptake is organized in a sequence of two successive adjacency pairs, of which the first involves heightened affectivity, and the second weaker affectivity with subsequent exit from the shared affectivity. Jefferson (1980, 1988) shows how, in interactions between intimates, emotional reciprocity in troubles telling is regularly built up step by step: in the progression from exposition of the trouble by the troubles teller, via the affiliation shown by the troubles recipient, to an affiliative response with which the troubles teller is observably "letting go." In service encounters, by contrast, this reciprocity is normally missing, as professionals do not offer (and clients do not seek) affiliation (see Jefferson & Lee, 1992). An activity with another type of emotional display is studied by Kangasharju (2009), who examines serious disputes in three settings (private home, meeting, television reality show). She shows how the participants in the dispute display their heightened emotional involvement and oppositional positions through a variety of verbal and nonverbal practices (e.g., challenging questions, swearing, raised volume) and how in the three settings studied, different kinds of resources are used when seeking and moving to reconciliation.

All the contributions to this volume analyze the display of affect and emotion within specific activities and trajectories of action in them. Some, such as those by Peräkylä and Ruusuvuori (chapter 4), Hakulinen and Sorjonen (chapter 7), and Haakana (chapter 8), focus on a certain means of emotion display (facial expression, response cry, fake laughter) and relate this means to the larger ongoing activity in order to analyze the display of emotion as part of its activity context. Others, for example the chapters by Goodwin and her colleagues (chapter 2), Wootton (chapter 3), Couper-Kuhlen (chapter 6), and Maynard and Freese (chapter 5), analyze the display of emotion from the starting point of a larger activity (different types of conflict between children and their parents, complaint stories, news delivery sequences). Chapter 12, by Heritage and Lindström, traces the display of emotion through separate successive encounters between the same participants, the mother of a newborn child and a community nurse.

EMOTION IN DEVELOPMENTAL PERSPECTIVE

The importance of expressing emotional stance as part of language socialization and language-learning processes has formed one line of research for quite some time already. For example, the volume edited by Schieffelin and Ochs (1986) contains chapters that focus on an affect-loaded activity, teasing, in interactions in several different sociocultural contexts from the perspective of language socialization, and Ochs (1988, pp. 145–188) analyzes ways in which Samoan children come to know the organization of emotion in their culture through learning the norms and expectations associated with its verbal expression. More recently, Goodwin (M. H. Goodwin, 2006b), for example, has studied language and interactive practices that schoolgirls use to display emotional stances in seeking out conflicts through which they construct and reconstruct relationships, hierarchical positions, and membership in their social groups.

Interaction between preverbal infants and their caretakers is known to be highly emotional, employing rich prosodic, facial, and gestural resources (see e.g., Stern, 1985; Fonagy, Gergely, Jurist, & Target, 2002). There are good reasons to assume that the origin of many, if not all, prosodic and nonverbal practices of emotional expression in adults is to be found in early interaction. The conversation analytic exploration of this continuity has, however, yet to be done (but see Kahri, in preparation).

Two of the chapters in this volume deal with the display of emotion in interactions between children and their parents or other adults. Goodwin and her colleagues focus on multimodally organized interactional trajectories in which children refuse the directives by their parents. Wootton investigates the displays of distress by a child in interactions with her parents and extends the investigation to an exploration of interactional displays of distress by autistic children.

EXPRESSION AND REGULATION OF EMOTION IN INSTITUTIONAL INTERACTION

In studies on institutional interaction (e.g., Drew & Heritage, 1992; Heritage & Clayman, 2010; Drew & Sorjonen, 2011), it has been shown that in performing their institutional tasks, participants' actions are constrained by specific norms that concern, for example, their epistemic positions (e.g., patients holding back their ideas regarding the diagnosis in medical consultations [Gill, 1998; Peräkylä, 2002]) or the expression of opinion (e.g., journalists withholding overt expression of opinion in news interviews [Clayman, 1992; Clayman & Heritage, 2002]). The display of emotion is also subject to such institutional regulation. In his classic study, Parsons (1951) maintained that "affective neutrality" is a key component of modern professional behavior. The empirical study of institutional interaction has shown several facets of this neutralism, for example, in journalism (Clayman, 1992), mediation (Garcia, 1991; Heisterkamp, 2006), and psychiatry (Bergmann, 1992).

Institutional regulation of emotion is not, however, only about neutralizing affect displays. In institutions, there are specific places and procedures for affective expression. In a study on academic seminar interactions, Sandlund (2004) shows ways in which displays of frustration, embarrassment, and enjoyment are collaboratively managed. Ruusuvuori (2005, 2007) examines the ways in which professionals in general practice and homeopathy receive the patients' troubles tellings affiliatively (and thus non-neutrally), either through affiliating relevant response elements or through extended utterances in which they convey that they understand the patient's plight. This affiliation, however, is ordinarily short-lived, as it works "towards the closure of the sequence of troubles-telling and shifting back to [medical] problem-solving activity" (Ruusuvuori, 2007, p. 598). In some institutional settings, emotion displays and explicit talk about emotions are central for the main goal of the activity. Recently, the intricate organization of emotion displays has been taken up in research on psychotherapy interaction (see e.g., Peräkylä, 2008; Rae, 2008; Voutilainen, Peräkylä, & Ruusuvuori, 2010a, 2010b), revealing various practices through which therapists show that they recognize, validate, and empathize with their clients' emotion displays.

The contributions of this volume examine the institutional regulation of emotion in helpline calls (Hepburn and Potter, chapter 9), art galleries (Heath and others, chapter 10), psychotherapy (Voutilainen, chapter 11), and maternity health care (Heritage and Lindström, chapter 12). While Heath and his colleagues examine the ways in which gallery visitors design their emotion displays with reference to the presence of others, the other contributions analyze different practices in the display of empathy in professional responses to clients' emotion displays.

The earlier studies mentioned above bring out the importance of studying emotion as an interactional phenomenon. They emphasize the density of verbal and nonverbal resources for expressing emotion, as well as the subtleties of the interpretative work by the recipients of such expressions. However, the existing research is scattered and, more important, in many studies emotion forms a subordinate analytical theme rather than being the central topic addressed. The current volume zooms in on the expression of emotion and its reception in interaction from various angles. In doing so, it furthers the theoretical understanding of the role of emotion in constructing everyday interaction. Moreover, it presents a collection of original studies that contribute to the existing understanding of language and social interaction. The collection increases our understanding of emotion with respect to four questions:

1. How are emotional stances expressed and displayed verbally, vocally and nonvocally in social interaction?
2. How does the expression of emotional stance contribute to the organization of action sequences?
3. How is emotion regulated and managed in institutional encounters?
4. How does research on emotion contribute to understanding of language and social interaction?

ORGANIZATION OF THE VOLUME

To address the four questions outlined above, this volume offers a set of state-of-the-art studies on the expression and management of emotion and affective stance in naturally occurring interaction. The order of the chapters arises from several overlapping considerations. By and large, we proceed from interactions with children to interactions between adults; from interactions in noninstitutional settings to interactions in institutional settings; and from nonlexical means of expression to lexical means.

In chapter 2, Goodwin, Cekaite, and Goodwin offer and demonstrate a holistic, multisemiotic view on emotion. They explore the performance of affective stance through intonation, body postures, gestures, and facial expression in conflict situations. The chapter begins with a discussion of differences between an interactional view of emotion and conceptualizations that view emotions "as a set of universal, unintentional psychological states" residing within the individual; it also provides methodological tools for describing interactional moves that are done through bodily conduct. The main empirical part of the chapter examines children's responses to their parents' directives, ranging from bald refusals to compliance in interactions in the United States and in Sweden. The authors show that emotion and stance are not an add-on to an isolated individual action but, instead, an inherent feature of temporally unfolding sequences of social interaction.

In chapter 3, conflicts in interaction between a child, during her third year of life, and her parents are investigated by Wootton. He shows that particular distressed responses at this age arise from a parental breach of expectations regarding courses of action—an observation with important implications for developmental psychology as well as for a theory of emotion. Wootton also compares his observations on distressed responses in normally developed children with distress in autistic children, showing how the latter are particularly sensitive to breaches of routines rather than breaches in locally constituted expectations.

Facial expression of emotion is in focus in chapter 4, where Peräkylä and Ruusuvuori elaborate the intimate linkage between facial expression and verbal utterances, supporting the view of emotion as a multimodal co-constructed stance display. They examine the ways in which speakers, after having delivered stories or other tellings but not yet having received an affective response, use facial expressions to pursue affiliation from the recipient. The facial expressions at this sequential juncture can reinforce, explicate, or modify the stance initially expressed by verbal and vocal means during the telling. The authors elaborate their results in the light of recent psychological discussions on the regulation of emotion, suggesting that interactional and individual regulations are closely linked.

Chapter 5 by Maynard and Freese takes up prosody as a means for conveying emotion. They examine news delivery sequences, showing how the valence of the news (as good or bad news) is negotiated and established through prosodic choices in the deliverers' and recipients' utterances. Pitch level, range, and contour, as well as voice quality, loudness, and speech rate, are resources through which the participants display their orientation to the news as good or bad. Maynard and Freese show the moment-by-moment progression of such negotiation as a way of doing emotion work.

Prosody is also one of the foci in chapter 6 by Couper-Kuhlen. She analyzes the ways in which recipients of conversational complaint stories show affiliation with the teller's affective stance, specifically with displays of anger and indignation by the teller. It is shown that verbally affiliative responses are offered typically, but not always, by matching or upgrading the prosody of the teller, whereas disaffiliative responses are characterized by prosodic downgrading. The chapter explicates the verbal and prosodic resources through which the teller constructs her stance step by step, showing how the recipient's affiliation is made relevant at specific places in the course of the telling. The verbal responses range from claims of understanding, congruent negative assessments, and justifications of the stance initially displayed by the teller to response cries and sound objects.

In chapter 7, by Hakulinen and Sorjonen, response cries remain in focus. The authors take up an affective response type, the Finnish *voi että*, which consists of an interjection and a connective or particle, and which belongs to a larger paradigm of conventional affective response types initiated by an interjection. They show how this response type, which is "open" in that it lacks any explicit evaluative element, merely voicing a recognition of the coparticipant's prior turn as one that has made an affective response relevant, is used in contexts where an affective response is due, but the valence of the relevant affect is unclear. Hakulinen and Sorjonen also show how ambivalence regarding valence is intertwined with ambivalence in the sequential placement of a particular telling—*voi että* being able to accommodate both.

Laughter is taken up as a topic in chapter 8. Haakana discusses a particular variant or modification of it: fake laughter, in which the actor produces the tokens that are conventionally associated with laughter, such as *heh* and *hah*, as articulated lexical items, as "words." Haakana shows that fake laughter is used in interactional junctures where "real" laughter might be relevant, ranging from joking contexts to talk about delicate matters. Through fake laughter, the actor on the one hand shows that he or she recognizes the relevance of an emotion display at that precise place in interaction, and on the other, distances him- or herself from that display. The chapter sheds light on interactants' own knowledge concerning when affect is relevant in interaction and how it is conventionally displayed.

Like laughter, also crying is a prominent resource and form of action that is understood as conveying emotion. In chapter 9, Hepburn and Potter describe the expressive features of crying (e.g., tremulous voice quality and aspirations). Crying makes affiliative responses relevant; in empathetic responses the recipient goes on record by claiming understanding, while in sympathetic responses, the recipient displays emotion with nonpropositional means, through prosodic choices and/or response particles. The authors also make preliminary comparisons between responses to crying in ordinary conversation and in a particular institutional setting, helpline calls.

Chapter 10 by Heath, vom Lehn, Cleverly, and Luff offers an analysis of the interactional management of a distinct emotion, surprise, in a particular institutional setting, museums and galleries. Rather than treating surprise as an individual reaction to an unanticipated aspect of the setting, the chapter shows the intricate organization of visitors' orientations to the objects on display, and the coordination of their facial, postural, vocal, and lexical displays of surprise and accompanying emotions. The visitors can, for example, configure the others' bodily and visual orientation so as guide them toward being surprised, and they design their own displays of surprise so as to be observed and responded to by the coparticipants.

The interactional organization of emotion displays in psychotherapy is taken up by Voutilainen in chapter 11. In responding to the patient's disclosures of her negative emotional experiences, the cognitive therapist whose work Voutilainen analyzes combines two different orientations to therapeutic work: an empathizing orientation, and a more challenging orientation toward investigating the patient's underlying beliefs. In a single-session analysis included in the chapter, Voutilainen shows how these two orientations can sometimes be asynchronous, with the patient pursuing empathetic responses and the therapist offering investigative ones.

The final empirical chapter 11, by Heritage and Lindström, also addresses practices of empathy by a professional. In successive conversations between the mother of a newborn baby and a health visitor (community nurse), a trajectory of interaction unfolds in which the mother gradually discloses her anxiety regarding the lack of loving feelings toward her baby and the consequent experience of social and emotional isolation. The chapter shows how the health visitor attempts to build an empathetic union with the mother, and eventually succeeds in it when, instead of offering assurance with generalized statements, she makes a reciprocal self-disclosure regarding her own experiences as a mother.

In the epilogue, chapter 12, the core contributions of the volume are summarized and discussed. The main purpose of the epilogue is to contextualize the findings in the empirical chapters with respect to earlier psychological, sociological, and evolutionary conceptualizations of emotion. The psychological conceptualizations that are discussed have to do, for example, with arousal and valence as key components of emotion, the distinctiveness of basic emotions, cognitive aspects of emotion, and the subjective experience of emotions. The sociological conceptualizations have to do, for example, with emotional labor and the social construction of emotions. The evolutionary conceptualizations revolve around the advantages that emotions might have offered over evolutionary time. The core argument of the epilogue is that the studies in this volume, while arising from a distinctively different, interactional perspective, offer a new way of looking at many key phenomena in more traditional emotion research.

CHAPTER 2

ᴄⅤᴐ

Emotion as Stance

MARJORIE HARNESS GOODWIN, ASTA CEKAITE, AND CHARLES GOODWIN

In the midst of doing things together, participants display how they align them-selves toward other participants with whom they are interacting (as well as to their actions). In Goffman's (1981) terms, they display their stance, footing, or their "pro-jected selves." Ochs (1996, p. 410) defines affective stance as "a mood, attitude, feeling and disposition, as well as degrees of emotional intensity vis-à-vis some focus of concern."[1] In this chapter we develop the notion that the display of emotion is a situated practice entailed in a speaker's performance of affective stance through intonation, gesture, and body posture (Goodwin & Goodwin, 2000).

ANALYTIC FRAMEWORKS FOR INVESTIGATING EMOTION

The expression of emotions as an evolutionary and psychological process situated within the individual

Our analysis of emotion as stance is markedly different from the way in which emo-tion is theorized and investigated in much other contemporary research (Russell & Fernández-Dols, 1997).[2] In a tradition extending back to Charles Darwin (1872/1998) and given powerful life in the work of Ekman (1993, 2006; Ekman & Friesen, 1969), emotions are conceptualized as a set of universal, unintentional psychological states.[3] They are mediated by culturally variable display rules and made visible on the body of the actor expressing the emotion. The primary site where emotions are lodged is the interior psychological life of the individual actor, an interior that includes specific forms of muscle control (producing specific displays on the face) inherited from our primate ancestors. The environment around the actor is given no systematic analysis (except for variation in display rules among cultures). Indeed, it is argued that a defining characteristic of emotions, which differentiates them from other forms of expression, is that facial expressions as such do not reveal a seeable referent in the environment: "The angry expression does not reveal who is the target, nor can one know from the expression itself what brought forth the anger" (Ekman, comment, in Darwin, 1872/1998, p. 84).[4]

Though it is recognized that both sound and the face can display emotion, in practice almost all research has focused on the face. In research flowing from Ekman the face has been examined in two complementary ways: (a) through rigorous description of the muscles used to produce the specific facial displays that express emotion (a perspective in Darwin's original work that had its predecessor in the extraordinary use of photos by Duchenne of faces with different muscles stimulated by electricity); and (b) by asking members of different cultures to judge what emotion is shown by specific configurations of muscles on the face.

Despite the genuine rigor of this research, and the substantive findings it has produced, the perspective on emotion it adopts has an enormous lacuna. The investigative focus of research never moves beyond the face and underlying muscles of a single actor. In practice, a single face is examined in isolation from (a) the bodies of other actors; (b) other co-occurring sign phenomena such as prosodically indexed talk; and (c) the unfolding flow of action in interaction. However, there is no doubt that the scope of an emotion is *not* restricted to the individual who displays it. By virtue of their systematic expression on the face (and elsewhere, such as in prosody) emotions constitute public forms of action. Indeed, this is explicitly recognized by Ekman (afterword, in Darwin, 1872/1998, p. 373). However, Ekman argues that study of how emotional displays function as signals shifts focus away from study of the emotion itself (Ekman, afterword, in Darwin, 1872/1998, p. 372). For Ekman, its special status as involuntary rather than intentional action constitutes it as something that can be trusted in a special way: "We don't make an emotional expression to send a deliberate message, although a message is received" (Ekman, afterword, in Darwin, 1872/1998, p. 373).

The way in which a phenomenon is delimited at the beginning of a research enterprise creates an analytic geography with some phenomena being constituted as focal (the face, its muscles, and the interior psychological states thus expressed), while others are rendered invisible and beyond the pale of what should be studied (the interactive context, the social organization of emotional displays, other parts of the body.) There are also methodological advantages to constituting the field of study in this way. High-resolution photographs can easily be obtained of posed facial expressions, without having to be concerned with how to record spontaneous behavior unobtrusively, how much to record, and so on (Ekman, 2006, p. 189). Such theoretical and methodological choices have enormous consequences.

Imposing such a geography on the study of emotion is a choice. When Ekman proposed this form of research to Gregory Bateson, Bateson told him that he was being misled. According to Bateson:

> Use of the word expression directed attention away from the role of facial movements as communicative signals. It was a mistake to consider expression as tied to internal

sensations and physiological activity; *they were tied to the back-and-forth flow of conversation.* (Ekman, afterword, in Darwin, 1872/1998, p. 372, our emphasis added)

We agree with Bateson.

Emotion as Interactively Organized Stance

We will use the sequence in Figure 1 to investigate how emotion might be organized within the flow of ongoing interaction as a contextualized, multiparty, multimodal process. Four girls, who all attend the same "progressive" school, are eating lunch together at a table on the school grounds. Angela, sitting alone on the left is a scholarship student who has been excluded from the popular girls' in-group, despite her repetitive efforts for acceptance.[5] Indeed, her marginalization is to some extent visible in the way in which she is seated alone on one side of the table, while the other three girls form a tight inclusive group as they sit across from her. At the beginning of the sequence Angela, who is much poorer than the other girls, starts to eat her lunch without utensils. Lisa asks her to leave and go to another table (lines 1–3). Instead Angela turns away so that her face is not visible to the others. In line 10 Aretha describes what Angela is doing as "disgusting." As this word comes to completion Angela moves her body back so that she is again facing the girls across from her, and starts to eat by dipping her

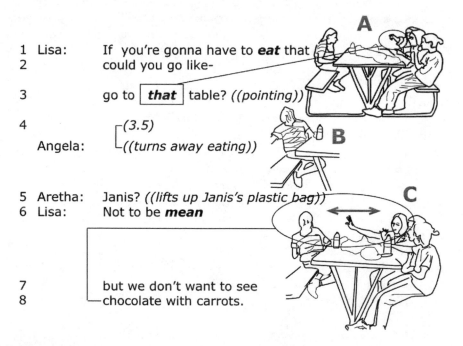

```
1  Lisa:     If  you're gonna have to eat that
2            could you go like-

3            go to │ that │ table? ((pointing))

4            ⌈(3.5)
   Angela:   ⌊((turns away eating))

5  Aretha:   Janis? ((lifts up Janis's plastic bag))
6  Lisa:     Not to be mean

7            but we don't want to see
8            chocolate with carrots.
```

Figure 1

9 Janis: ⌈Now *plea* (*::*) *se?*

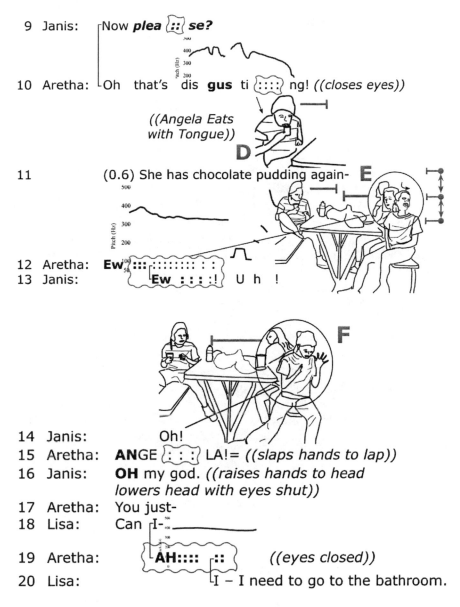

10 Aretha: ⌊Oh   that's   dis **gus** ti (*:::::*) ng! *((closes eyes))*

*((Angela Eats
with Tongue))*

D

11   (0.6) She has chocolate pudding again- **E**

12 Aretha: **Ew** ::: ⌈:::::::: : :
13 Janis: ⌈**Ew** : : : :!   U h !

F

14 Janis: Oh!
15 Aretha: **ANGE** (*: : :*) LA!= *((slaps hands to lap))*
16 Janis: **OH** my god. *((raises hands to head
          lowers head with eyes shut))*
17 Aretha: You just-
18 Lisa: Can ⌈I-

19 Aretha: ⌊**AH**:::: ⌈:::   *((eyes closed))*
20 Lisa: ⌊I – I need to go to the bathroom.

Figure 1 *(continued)*

tongue into the chocolate pudding container. When this happens the other three
girls turn their heads and upper bodies away from her while producing high-
pitched screams. These embodied displays escalate (see Figure 1, Image E), and in
line 20 Lisa, responding to what she has just seen, says that she needs "to go to
the bathroom."[6]

Emotion as Multiparty, Multimodal Stance.

Disgust as a Universal Emotion

One of the reasons that we have chosen the sequence in Figure 1 is that Ekman lists *disgust*, the term used by Aretha in line 10 to categorize her reaction to what Angela is doing, as one of the five distinct emotions universally agreed to be central to the human repertoire of emotions (Ekman, introduction, in Darwin, 1872/1998, p. xxx). Disgust has a central place in the analysis of both Darwin and the Ekman tradition. Indeed, what happens here is in strong agreement with Darwin's description of disgust. For Darwin "disgust . . . refers to something revolting, primarily in relation to the sense of taste, as actually perceived or vividly imagined" (Darwin, 1872/1998, p. 250). He notes that disgust is frequently accompanied by "gutteral sounds . . . written as *ach* or *ugh*;" and their utterance is sometimes accompanied by a shudder (see Figure 1, lines 13 and 14 and Image F), and is often accompanied "by gestures as if to push away or guard against the offensive object" (Darwin, 1872/1998, p. 256; see Figure 1, Images C and E). Darwin argues that the embodied actions used to express disgust are closely tied to processes such as vomiting, in which something treated as disgusting is forcibly expelled from the body. In line 20, after seeing how Angela eats, Lisa says "I need to go to the bathroom."

Moreover, for Darwin, *disgust* has very close ties to *scorn*, *disdain*, and *contempt*, in that "they all consist of actions representing the rejection or exclusion of some real object which we dislike or abhor" (Darwin, 1872/1998, p. 260). Through their displays of disgust that target Angela, the girls on the right side of the table are treating her as just such an abhorred object, and indeed the displays constitute a means of degrading her. For Darwin disgust can locate objects in the world, such as revolting food, and also constitute a social display that demeans other actors. Both of these processes are intertwined here.

Disgust Locates a Target

We are very impressed with how Darwin's observations, written almost a century and a half ago without any close examination of actual unfolding interaction, accurately draw attention to a number of relevant phenomena in Figure 1. However, the nature of Darwin's analysis renders problematic Ekman's definition of emotions as expressions that do not locate a target in the environment beyond the individual. For Ekman emotional displays have a special status and can be trusted precisely because they are "involuntary not intentional" (Ekman, afterword, in Darwin, 1872/1998, p. 372). Emotions "inform us that something important is happening inside the person who shows the emotion" (Darwin, 1872/1998, p. 372). Unlike phenomena such as hatred, envy and jealousy, emotions do "not reveal who is the target, nor can one know from the expression itself what brought forth the anger." (Ekman, comment, in Darwin, 1872/1998, pp. 83–4). By way of contrast Darwin continuously describes disgust as a response to something the person (or other animal) is encountering in the environment (revolting food, people to be abhorred, etc.). In Figure 1 a range of phenomena locate Angela quite explicitly as the target of the other girls' expressive behavior. These include both what they say (note the deictic "that's" that immediately precedes "disgusting" in line 10), and how they rapidly reorganize their bodies so as to avoid having to look at Angela. From a phenomenological perspective both the displays described by Darwin and what the girls do locate relevant intentional objects.

What difference does this make? If phenomena beyond an isolated actor's face are in fact relevant to the organization of expressions of disgust, and other emotions, analysis must take this expanded geography into account[7]. Using as primary stimuli static photographs of faces with different expressions renders phenomena in the actor's environment, such as relevant targets of the emotional expression, both invisible and irrelevant. This expanded perspective seems quite consistent with Darwin's original formulation of the issue. As already noted he typically describes not only the expression, but also what the expression is responding to. For example, the caption for a picture of a cat invoking a vivid display states "Cat terrified at a dog" (Darwin, 1872/1998, p. 127). The primary place where environmental response cannot be taken into account is Darwin's use of Duchenne's photographs of faces where electrical current was used to stimulate different muscles. These photographs are among the most striking produced in the entire nineteenth century. They should not, however, be used as methodological guidelines to delimit the parameters for subsequent research into emotion. In brief, we are proposing that emotional expressions be investigated within an environment of unfolding action being constituted in part through orientation to the bodies and actions of others.

Describing Interacting Bodies

Figure 1 and most of the later Figures in this chapter vividly illustrate the highly diverse ways that participants can use their bodies to take up stances, including emotional ones, toward other participants, proposed courses of action, and phenomena in their surround. How can such interacting bodies be transcribed in a way that is analytically relevant? Is it possible to accurately, indeed exhaustively, describe the configuration of a human body (Birdwhistell, 1970)? Thus in Figure 1 one can say that Angela turns around to her left in Image B and then back to her right in images D and E, or that front right girl in Image E moves her torso to her left while the rear girl moves her torso to her right. While accurate, such statements provide no relevant description of how these bodies are displaying affective stance.

To capture the variety of subtle ways that bodies in local circumstances are deployed to accomplish relevant action we are using line drawings, rather than linguistic descriptions. However, central to the phenomena being investigated in this chapter is how the body is used to display a stance toward someone else and a proposed course of action. To note this in the transcript we are annotating the images with simple symbols marking alternative alignments toward what others have just done, or are doing. A double-headed arrow ◄─── ► marks a *congruent alignment*. Thus in Image C Lisa has asked Angela to go somewhere else because of the way she is eating (lines 1–3). Angela doesn't leave the table, but does turn her body away so that her eating is not visible to others (and this, rather than simply moving her body to the left, is what is relevant as a form of embodied action). Over line 8 Lisa waves her hand toward Angela with a dismissive gesture (note Darwin's comments above about gestures showing disdain and contempt). Both Lisa's gesture and her talk openly insult Angela. However, by reorganizing her body to hide the activity the others find offensive, Angela is displaying a congruent alignment to the proposals made by Lisa, and thus participating in her own degradation. The configuration constituted through the mutual orientation of Lisa and Angela's bodies is thus annotated with a double arrow.

We use a horizontal arrow with a vertical line at the end toward the other ───┤ to mark an *oppositional alignment*. Thus in Image E Angela brings her face back into the gaze of Lisa and her friends, and shortly after this all three girls dramatically turn their faces and upper bodies away from Angela. These actions are thus annotated with oppositional arrows. We stress that these configurations are being defined not in terms of the behavior of a single isolated body, but instead with reference to how one actor's body aligns with others' bodies and proposed courses of action. Though the girls at each end of the bench turn their bodies in opposite directions, they are performing the same action with reference to the changes just made by Angela's body.

Prosody

While both Darwin and Ekman note that emotion can be displayed vocally, in practice most analysis in this tradition has focused on the face. However, prosody[8] is both pervasive and absolutely central to the organization of affective stance. Consider lines 12–13 in Figure 1. On seeing Angela eat with her tongue Aretha self-interrupts the talk in progress in line 11 (marked with a dash in *again-*), turns rapidly away from Angela while making a face and closing her eyes, and produces a cry with high sustained pitch. Note the Praat pitchtrack over the transcribed talk. Janis quickly joins her own voice to this cry.

The prosody that occurs here provides powerful resources for displaying affective stance. A number of its features will be noted. First, rather than simply expressing a single individual's internal state, it places something new in the public environment that is constituting the point of departure for the organization of the actions of the moment. Some evidence for the importance of the public organization of this display can be found in the way that Janis, in line 13, rapidly joins Aretha's cry. Rather than having an individual emotion, participants are situated within an environment structured in part by the public presence of hearable emotion.

Second, these prosodic displays are produced over talk that constitutes a form of emotive interjection or the response cry (Goffman, 1978) "<u>Ew::::.</u>" However, the prosody that occurs here in fact produces a more powerful and vivid display of affective stance than the production of the *emotion* word "disgusting" in line 10. Third, the display gets both its power and its intelligibility from its sequential placement, the way in which it is visibly organized as a sudden next move to what Angela has done (eating with her tongue). In this it is like the embodied alignments noted above. It requires an analytic framework that extends beyond the voice of the actor producing the prosody to encompass the target being responded to and operated on. It is an interactive, dialogic action rather than the expression of something internal to a single individual.

Fourth, unlike lexical items that can be abstracted from the stream of speech and transported to other settings and media, such as the transcript written here, prosody, like facial expression, is intimately tied to a particular actor's body performing consequential action at a specific moment. A person hearing it is thrust into the lived presence of another human being who is in the midst of experiencing something while taking up a powerful, embodied stance toward the phenomena that generated that experience.

Fifth, affective prosody can co-occur with other embodied phenomena. Here the turn-away and the prosody in lines 12 13 occur together as part of a larger ensemble of action. In light of this it might be argued that instead of focusing separately on the face, embodied movements, and prosody, one should analyze the entire action holistically. However, as they mutually elaborate each other, each of these modalities makes distinct and different contributions to the ensemble of emotion and stance that occurs here. Moreover, where relevant, participants can disassemble such structures, to build new forms of action through progressive transformation of distinct elements of a prior ensemble (C. Goodwin, 2011).

From a slightly different perspective the public organization of prosody provides the resources for socially complex alignment displays. When Janis joins Aretha in line 13, an individual display of affective stance is transformed into a shared, multiparty display of stance toward, and disgust with, Angela. One finds a situation of two against one, which is transformed into three against one a moment later when Lisa also turns away. Such coalitions in which within-group solidarity is cemented by shared opposition toward, and/or exclusion of, someone constituted as an outsider is central to not only human, but also primate organization in general. In the diagram to the right of Image E we have tried to indicate this graphically by combining lines of oppositional stance toward Angela with arrows of congruent alignment tying the three girls on the right together into a common framework of stance, opposition, experience, and emotion toward Angela. Prosody makes possible not only the display of experience, emotion, and stance, but provides the resources for constructing and organizing shared experience. Insofar as this is the case, it becomes a major locus for the constitution of embodied habitus (Bourdieu, 1977) within a dialogic framework (Linell, 2009), as separate individuals participate together in common verbal, prosodic, and embodied courses of action in ways that enable them to constitute shared affective stance toward relevant objects in their lifeworld. Some evidence for the *in situ* socializing power of these interactive environments for the constitution of affective stance and experience can be seen in the way in which Janis, the girl in the middle, starts to produce her embodied displays only after seeing what Aretha is doing.

Prosody will be extremely important in the examples in the rest of this chapter. The use of prosody frequently leads to particular kinds of phonetic selection. Sounds that can be produced with extended duration, such as vowels and nasals, but not stops, make extended prosodic displays possible. In the Jefferson transcription system such lengthening is marked with colons. Because this is so central to the phenomena that will be examined in this chapter we have decided to highlight such lengthening with gray boxes with wavy lines, such as are found in line 12. These boxes include not only lengthened sounds indicated with colons but also adjacent vowels and nasals (including a word such as "No"). This is a purely notational device that helps us to organize our transcripts to make relevant phenomena stand out as clearly as possible to the reader.

Summary

The interaction visible in Figure 1 provides materials for proposing a framework for the investigation of affective stance that conceptualizes such phenomena as dialogic and embedded within ongoing interaction within the lived social world. We have great respect for the work done by Ekman and his colleagues. The video materials we are using do not permit the close analysis of the face and its muscles that are central to his work. We are therefore very much in favor of the presence of diverse research traditions that can provide complementary analysis of important and complex phenomena such as emotion.

As part of a dialogue with other work on emotion we would like to note some distinctive ways that emotion emerges in unfolding interaction documented in our materials. First, rather than having its primary locus in the individual, it is dialogic both in the way in which it takes up a stance toward something beyond the individual, and in how it is organized within frameworks of temporally unfolding interaction. In constructing stance and emotion, participants perform operations on the displays, signs, and embodied materials produced by their coparticipants. Emotions arise in part from the world being encountered by local actors, and help to further shape both that world and the actions of others. Second, the use of interactive materials adds a strong temporal and sequential dimension to the study of emotion. The structured unfolding of interaction helps us to systematically investigate the rapid flow of emotion and the way in which mutable emotions are in a constant process of flux, something that has long been noted by poets such as Shakespeare and philosophers such as James and the phenomenologists. Third, a variety of different kinds of phenomena, such as facial expressions, prosody, embodied stances, and movements (for example, the girls turning away from Angela), are implicated simultaneously in the construction of specific displays of stance and emotion. The way in which action is built through the use of diverse materials that mutually elaborate each other

(C. Goodwin, 2000, 2011) enables actors to precisely adapt to local interactive environments by constructing a range of variable displays. This in fact seems consistent with Darwin's own interests in species as populations, rather than fixed types, with variability providing the resources necessary for both adaptation and change.

The approach to the study of emotion we are suggesting here requires particular kinds of materials. Most centrally we view emotions as dialogic phenomena, and this is certainly true for stance as well (Goodwin & Goodwin, 1987). Therefore, rather than focusing on the individual in isolation, we want to look at sequences in which one party is responding to, or in some other way performing operations on, actions produced by another. In the remainder of this chapter we will use as data sequences of family interaction recorded in the United States and Sweden in which one party, a child, is responding to a directive produced by another, a parent. Such interactively structured sequences provide environments where the dialogic organization of emotion can be systematically investigated.

CONTEXTUAL CONFIGURATIONS OF STANCE
DISPLAY IN DIRECTIVE SEQUENCES

In the midst of mundane activities, as family members take up various types of stances toward the actions in progress, they constitute themselves as particular kinds of social and moral actors (C. Goodwin, 2007). We examine the embodied practices that children make use of in response to directives: in particular, we are concerned with three basic types of next moves: bald refusals, moves that put off or avoid immediate compliance with parental directives, and compliance.

Directives constitute a form of *situated activity system*: "a somewhat closed, self-compensating, self-terminating circuit of interdependent actions" (Goffman, 1961, p. 96). As such, rather than being restricted to the verbal channel, frequently the focus of studies on directives, they require attention to next actions of participants, which entail fully embodied forms of participation (Cekaite, 2010; C. Goodwin, 2007; Goodwin & Goodwin, 2004; M. H. Goodwin, 2006a) in addition to talk. Kendon (2009, p. 363) argues, "Every single utterance using speech employs, in a completely integrated fashion, patterns of voicing and intonation, pausings and rhythmicities, which are manifested not only audibly, but kinesically as well." Indeed Bolinger (1989, p. 1) early described intonation as "part of a gestural complex" (one that includes the body as well as the face) for signaling attitudes. Both the way that talk and the body mutually elaborate each other and the ways that operations are performed vis-à-vis the other are part of the processes of mutual elaboration through which actions we studied are built.

Ervin-Tripp and Gordon (1984), in an early study of directives, were concerned with children's developmental acquisition of uses of verbal mitigation (through overt marking, justifying and allusion or hinting) to display deference to the addressee. Craven and Potter (2010) examine practices of moving from modal interrogative requests (ones showing concern with the hearer's willingness to comply, or "contingency") to upgraded parental directives displaying increasingly heightened speaker "entitlement" (Curl & Drew, 2008; Heinemann, 2006; Lindström, 2005) to control the recipient's actions. By way of contrast our interest is in the agency demonstrated in children's *responses* to directives, responses systematically shaped as affective stances toward the proposed course of action. As research exploring parent–child directive sequences that develop over time (a day, or a week) has demonstrated, children can exert a considerable degree of agency when formulating, revising or redefining parental terms for requested action (Aronsson & Cekaite, 2011).

Just as directives can take more "mitigated" or "aggravated" forms (Labov & Fanshel, 1977), so responses to directives can be formulated with various degrees of politeness or "impoliteness" (Bousfield, 2008; Mills, 2010). While Labov and Fanshel (1977, pp. 87–8) state that an unaccounted refusal can lead to a break in social relations, in the context of family interaction, as Blum-Kulka (1997, p. 150) has argued, "unmodified directness is neutral or unmarked in regard to politeness." In our data children's bald refusals constitute one possible response to directives. Alternatively, putting off a directive may be accomplished through actions such as ignoring the directive or pleading objections, which can lead to modifying or postponing the directive.

Ervin-Tripp, O'Connor, and Rosenberg (1984, p. 118) argue that speakers with high esteem have the right to receive verbal deference from others and can make control moves baldly, without offering deference to those who are lower in esteem. We find that through pleading objections children construct the parent as someone who is esteemed, but who nonetheless has obligations to attend to aspects of the children's emotional life. By way of contrast, children's bald refusals construct open confrontations and can lead to character contests (Goffman, 1967, pp. 237–8) in which parents and children negotiate relative positions of power (with children sometimes winning). Thus through their uptake to a directive children display a range of different perspectives, not only with regard to notions of obligation, but to notions of deference and demeanor as well. Across the data to be examined we find very different types of social order (Goffman, 1963, p. 8) developing from these alternative trajectories of action. Quite distinctive forms of ethos (Bateson, 1972) evolve as families overlay their activities with different forms of affect (M. H. Goodwin, 2006a, p. 516).

Data

The examples in this study are drawn from video recordings of naturally occurring interaction in families who were part of UCLA's Center on Everyday Lives of Families (CELF) and Sweden's sister project (SCELF). Approximately fifty hours of interaction were collected in thirty-two families over a week's time in the US and approximately thirty-seven hours for eight families in Sweden. Video-ethnographic methodology made it possible to record mundane talk (C. Goodwin, 1981), physical gestures (Streeck, 2009) and action (C. Goodwin, 2000), and routine activities (Tulbert & Goodwin,

2011), all within the household settings where people actually carry out their daily lives (Ochs, Graesch, Mittmann, & Bradbury, 2006). The age range of children recorded was one through eighteen, although in this chapter we deal primarily with children ages four through ten.

EMBODIED AFFECTIVE REFUSALS TO DIRECTIVES

Rather than delaying disagreement or a preference for agreement through hedges or pauses (Pomerantz, 1978), in the American data negation words often occur at the earliest possible place in response to (recycled) directives, at the beginnings of next moves to directives. In refusals ("No!") the most dramatic way in which opposition is expressed prosodically is through dramatic pitch leaps with rise–fall contours. Such defiant opposition turns exhibit acoustic features of emphatic speech style identified by Selting (1994, p. 375; 1996, p. 237): duration (the acoustic correlate of length)[9] or extended vowels and heightened fundamental frequency (the acoustic correlate of perceived pitch). Consider the following:

While children are watching television with Dad, Dad gives three directives to Jason (age four) to initiate actions to brush his teeth: "Here" ((extending toothbrush to Jason)), "Come on." and "Okay we gotta go" and Jason gives no response. Dad, himself, meanwhile, has remained on the couch avidly attending the television. When Dad gets up from the couch and delivers a fourth directive (line 1) Jason buries himself in the sofa. While speaking "We gotta go." Dad drags Jason from the couch toward the bathroom.

1 Dad: **Sorry** guys. (1.6) **Time** to turn it off.

2 Jason: **N O::::**   I'M   **NOT-**

3 Dad: We gotta **go. I told** you Jason.
4   A few **min**utes.
                . . .
5 Dad: Hailey g- go get the pair of shoes
6   you wanna wear. Also.
7 Dad: Let's **go**. We've gotta **go**.
8   Jason, do you want a piece of gum?

Figure 2

Three times Dad tells Jonah (age eight) to start getting ready for bed, and Jonah remains immobile, taking up a defiant stance with arms akimbo (line 3). Subsequently Jonah moves away from his father by going to the back door and begins looking out the back door. Father next gets up and moves to the back door and began massaging Jonah's shoulders (line 7)

1 Dad: **Go-** get a **book.**
2   For yours-
3 Jonah: **Ne**ver. *((defiant stance arms akimbo))*
4 Dad: How long is **ne**ver.

···
10 Seconds Later

5 Dad: **Lis**ten. You need to be in bed in twenty minutes.

6 Jonah: **N O   : : !**

7 Dad: If you're **not** in bed in twenty minutes
8   I will hunt down wherever your **game**boy is
9   And get it. (.) *h And it's be gone for the **week.**
10   So **hu**rry your harness.=okay?
11   Go brush your **teeth.**

massaging Jonah's shoulders

Figure 3

In response to Mom's refusal to let Emil (age five) brush his teeth on the couch Emil turns away from his Mom and begins dramatically flailing his arms in the air while crying out:

1 Mom: **Kom** nu höre du.
           Come on you.

2 Emil: Ma::a:h. Får man borsta tänderna härinne?
            Ma::ah. Can I brush my teeth in here?
            ((gestures protesting))

3 Mom: Ne:j. Det **får** du faktiskt inte.
            No:. You can't actually.

4 Emil: NE: U:::H m:::h

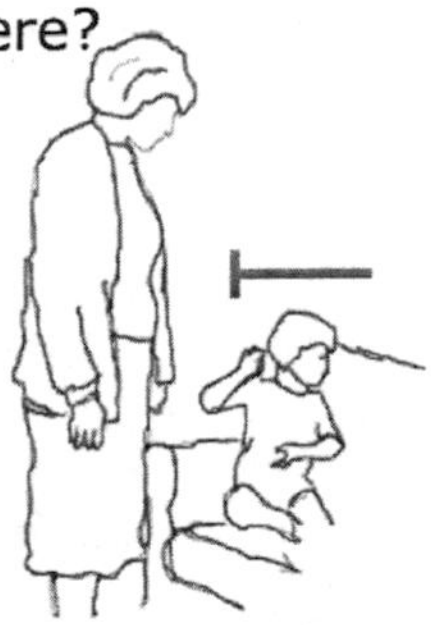

Figure 4

These defiant opposition turns exhibit acoustic features of emphatic speech style identified by Selting: (a) extended vowels (the acoustic correlate of length); and (b) heightened fundamental frequency (the acoustic correlate of perceived pitch):

	Vowel duration	Pitch height
Figure 2	580 msec.	750 Hz
Figure 3	860 msec.	612 Hz
Figure 4	673 msec.	663 Hz

In Figures 2–4 children protest over multiple turns the directives that are posed to them, and parents respond with upgraded responses: bribes (Figure 2) and threats (Figures 3–4). In Figure 2 Jason had to be bribed with gum (line 8) to dislodge him from the sofa where he hid his head to avoid going to the bathroom. Jonah in Figure 3 was threatened that he would have his Game Boy taken away (lines 8–9).

Rather than using threats or bribes, another possible parental response to a refusal is a metacommentary about the child's conduct. In Figure 5 below, in response to eight-year-old Alison's refusal to take a bath because she had done so yesterday, Mom responded: "It's not negotiable." (line 8).

Figures 2–4 show ways that children take up stances of defiance to their parent's directive. Both duration of the vowel (well exceeding 200 msec.) as well as the pitch height (above the 250 Hz normal pitch range for children) signal strong opposition. By way of contrast in Figure 5 the opposition that Alison produced was a softly produced, low-pitched "Uh uh" (going up only to 200 Hz, line 5). Her only bodily movement was a slight headshake. In response to Mom's ruling, Alison maintained a sullen face, and looked away from her mom, but she did not protest further. Mom closed down the sequence with her "It's not negotiable." Here disagreement was expressed silently, merely through the way Alison glanced away from her mother. When Mother declared that the act in

```
 1  Mom:    Alright. (4.0) It's twenty minutes to eight
 2           Even though it doesn't feel like it.
 3  Alison:  That says seven. ((pointing to the clock))
 4  Mom:     We have to get you in the bath.
```

```
 5  Alison:  Uh            uh.        ((shakes head))
 6           I had a bath yesterday.
 7               (0.8)
 8  Mom:     It's not negotiable. ((shakes head))
 9               (0.8)
10  Mom:     Okay?
11  Alison:  ((looks at mom, then turns head
12           away))
```

Figure 5

question was nonnegotiable, that ended the matter (line 10). When the family finished eating, Alison complied with her mom's directive and took a bath.

The examples presented in this section demonstrate a range of ways in which children use embodied language practices to take up oppositional stances toward parental directives. Different types of action trajectories can develop, depending on types of accounts, volume, intonation, and embodied actions used by coparticipants. Parents may bodily assist children in complying with a directive through shepherding (Cekaite, 2010), scooping them up in their arms (Figure 7), or even dragging them (Figure 2) toward the targeted location.

EMBODIED AFFECTIVE STANCES USED IN PUTTING OFF DIRECTIVES

In our data on directives in family life, we also find children's responses that put off the directives: in contrast to the dramatic moves of noncompliance (Figures 2–6), children can make appeals to take their position into account and ask to modify or postpone the directive. Pleading turns occur as responses to directives that clearly prescribe a specific course of action, expecting compliance, as in "Luke. Bath. (0.2) Come on."(Figure 6) or "I:ngella? You come here, because we've got to go to bed now." (Figure 8, below) or "Turn it off." (Figure 8) Grammatical forms used for these directives entail a range of resources: imperatives "Turn it off" (Figure 8) and "Come on" (Figure 6), second person declaratives (in Swedish used for indexing upgraded directives as in Figure 7), and noun phrases (Figure 6), that, together with prosody, provide for an unmitigated way of upgrading directives.

Verbal features of responses to such directive forms involve a range of resources, such as politeness terms ("please," address terms of endearment), and accounts (often prefaced by the sequential conjunction *but*) that argue that an action cannot be performed because it violates the child's personal desires. Putting off directive turns exhibit distinct prosodic contours, characterized by a high global pitch, rising–falling elongated glides on lengthened vowels as well as marked aspiration. Such features Günthner (1997b, p. 253), in her analysis of the contextualization of affect in reported speech in German, describes as a "plaintive tone of voice."

In Figure 6, eight-year-old Luke's pleading cries provide something other than an outright refusal. Covering himself up with a blanket on the sofa (see image below) Luke instead puts off the requested action (his mother's summons to take a bath), by stating "NO:: Not ye:::t!" (line 2) and "after piano" (lines 5, 12), and provides explanations for his lack of uptake through accounts such as "But I'm tired and I wanna go to slee-." (line 26). Throughout lines 1–17 he was curled up on the couch, hiding under a cover.

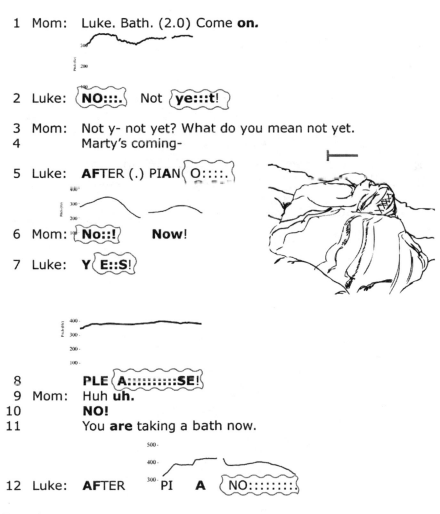

```
 1  Mom:   Luke. Bath. (2.0) Come on.

 2  Luke:  (NO:::.)  Not (ye:::t!)

 3  Mom:   Not y- not yet? What do you mean not yet.
 4          Marty's coming-

 5  Luke:  AFTER (.) PIAN(O:::::.)

 6  Mom:   (No::!)      Now!

 7  Luke:  Y(E::S!)

 8          PLE(A:::::::::SE!)
 9  Mom:   Huh uh.
10          NO!
11          You are taking a bath now.

12  Luke:  AFTER    PI   A   (NO:::::::::)
```

Figure 6

13 Mom: Nope.

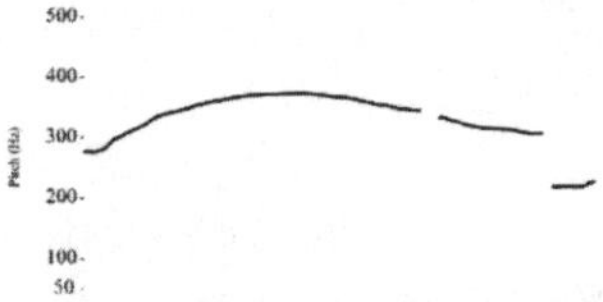

14 Luke: **Wh** ⟨ **y::::::::::::.** ⟩

15 Mom: **N OW::.**

16 Luke: **Pl** ⟨ **ea:::::se.** ⟩

17 Mom: By the time Marty- ((pulling blanket off Luke))
18   By ⌜the time you're
19 Luke: ⌞No.

20 Mom: No. By the time Marty's done
21   It's going to be ten thirty.⌜Come on.
22 Luke: ⌞**No::::::::.**
23 Luke: **PLE** ⟨ **A:::::SE.** ⟩
24 Mom: No. I'm counting to
25 Mom: three right now.

26 Luke: But I'm tired and I wanna go to **slee-**
27 Mom: And you're
28   And **you're** going to be even more tired.
29   Come on.=ONE,⌜TWO,
30 Luke: ⌞**PLE** ⟨ **A:::SE.** ⟩
31   **Please.**
32 Mom: NO! COME!
33 Luke: But I'm **t** ⟨ **i::red!** ⟩

Figure 6 (continued)

As Mom finishes eating dinner with other family members in the dining room, she initiates a directive to Luke (in the living room) to take a bath. Over numerous moves putting off the directive, Luke provides a series of dramatic rise–fall contours (lines 12, 14, 16, 26) with elongated vowels (some 1130 msec.) on the final falling syllables of utterances (lines 7, 8, 12, 14, 16, 22, 23, 26). Mom in this sequence insists that Luke comply, over seventy-five consecutive turns at talk, providing (continual) rationales for the directive (See M. H. Goodwin, 2006a, pp. 534–5, for a more complete analysis of this sequence). Providing a gloss of Luke's actions she states calmly, "I don't want to hear any more complaints please." Eventually, after a series of repeated directives from Mom and refusals and excuses from Luke, he walks to the bathroom to take a bath.

Utterances such as those in Figure 6 might be interpreted as forms of "appeals,"[10] described by Schieffelin (1990, p. 112) for Kaluli society as modalities of action strategically used to attempt to make others "feel sorry for" the speaker. The recipient of an appeal responds with compassion or assistance to the participant making the appeal, who is viewed as being helpless. In our data, pleading turns are used in second pair part accounts for noncompliance with a directive, implicitly casting the parent as someone who has obligations to take the child's feelings and position into account. The child's affective stance toward the requested action can be indexed through (turn-initial) response cries "E::H, AJ, UU:H" (signaling feelings of strong displeasure and indignation), crying sounds, sobbing that, in addition to the "pleading contour," signals the affective quality and intensity of objection.

In Figure 7 Mom demands that her five-year-old daughter, Ingella, who is in another room, go to bed right away in response to Mom's directive (line 1), Ingella, in a plaintive voice, directs her pleading appeal to Mom, with a turn-initial conjunction objecting to the prior turn (line 2). Mom, however, mockingly redirects the appeal to the daughter, employing herself a stylized pleading intonation contour. The daughter then upgrades her pleading with an account that features a strong display of sadness, namely, sobbing (lines 4–5). It is in response to this upgraded affective stance that Mom displays her coalignment with the daughter's position, and Ingella finally complies (approaching Mom).

Pleading objection turns exhibit distinctive acoustic features: duration/extended vowels, heightened fundamental frequency, and falling intonation on elongated final vowels (e.g. Günthner, 1997b, p. 253). Below are the durations and pitch heights of the vowels in selected sequences (including Figure 8):

	Vowel duration	Pitch height
Figure 6, line 2	560 msec.	350→300 Hz
Figure 6, line 12	529 msec.	410→300 Hz
Figure 7, line 2	530 msec.	400→200 Hz
Figure 8, line 9	380 msec.	400→200 Hz
Figure 8, line 11	558 msec.	480→200 Hz

1　Mom:　I:NGELLA? NU **KO**MMER DU, FÖR NU SKA VI **SO**VA.
　　　　I:NGELLA? YOU COME HERE, BECAUSE WE'VE
　　　　GOT TO GO TO BED NOW.

2　Ingella:　Me-(**ma**::mm=)
　　　　But mo: : m=

3　Mom:　=Men(**I:::::**n(gella.
　　　　=But I:::::ngella.

4　Ingella:　Huhh jag vill **so**(hhh)va
　　　　Huhh I want to slee(hhh)p

5　　　　där(hh)inn(hh)e, huhh huhh
　　　　the(hh)re, huhh huhh

6　Mom:　Jamen vi **ko**llar härinne.
　　　　We'll look in here.
　　　　((points at children's bedroom))

7　Ingella:　Jag ( ) inte. Jag är **trött**, heh heh
　　　　I ( ) not. I'm tired, heh heh
　　　　((runs to mom))

8　　　　((Ingella jumps up, mother
　　　　scoops her in her arms))

9　Mom:　Finns inte (.) nån plats hår.
　　　　Is there (.) any space here.
　　　　((carries daughter to the bedroom))

Figure 7

In our data, we find that the entire body is deployed to organize embodied stances toward the actions of others: such stances portray the children as being "unhappy," "helpless," or "tired," or otherwise unable to accomplish the request. In the following Figure 8, Mom tells her two daughters, Alma (eight years) and Saga (six years) to turn off the television and come to eat breakfast. Instead of complying with Mom's directive, the girls attempt to redefine the terms of the target action. In addition to prosody, the entire body, face, torso, and limbs, index a display of "unhappiness" (lines 9, 11). There is a sad, desperate look on Alma's face. She also leans back, stretching out both her head (turned a bit to the left) and her arms, arranging her body similarly to an iconic display of the Virgin Mary. Saga with her gesture covers her face.

1 Mom: **Tje**jer? Ni får stänga **a**v nu, och komma
         Girls? You've got to turn off now, and come

2   och äta frukost.
         and have breakfast.

3   (0.2)

4 Mom: Hör ni vad jag **sa**?
         Did you hear what I said?

5 Alma: Men jag vill-
         But I want-

6   (0.5)

7 Alma: Kan vi inte få äta **fru**kost häruppe?
         Can't we have breakfast upstairs?

8 Mom: Nej. Stäng av.
         No. Turn it off.

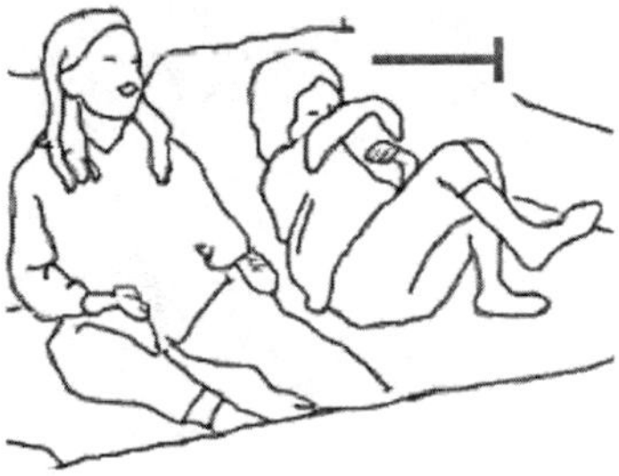

9 Alma: Sn(ä::lla mamma:::)

         Kind mom
         'Please mom'

10 Mom: Men ni har redan tittat nu. Stäng **av**.
         But you've watched it now. Turn it off.

Figure 8

500 -

400 -

300 -

200 -

11 Alma: Jag vill faktiskt verkligen **se:** på det (hä::r.)
            I want actually really see this.
            'I actually really want to see this.'

12   Det är faktiskt andra **gå:**ngen.
            It's the second time actually.

Figure 8 (*continued*)

When later, shown in Figure 9, Mom demands compliance by finally turning of the television herself, the girls' embodied responses—Alma's gesture of exasperation and Saga's slapping the couch, while looking at Mom—display their exasperation and frustration with Mom's action (lines 21, 22).

Children's pleading turns elicit specific types of responses: Parents may refuse to put off the directive (ignoring the pleading response, recycling it, or accounting for the

20 Mom: ((comes upstairs and turns off the TV))

606.6

318.8

21 Alma: (E::H)

352

22 Saga: Ma(**mma**::)
           Mom

23 Mom: A men ni har redan **ti**ttat på massvis.
           Yeah but you've already watched loads of this.

24   **Kom** nu.
           Come on now. *((follows girls downstairs))*

Figure 9

directive, Figures 6, 8, 9) or give in (modifying or postponing the initial directive, Figure 7). Affectively charged pleadings, harboring accounts for noncompliance, evoke parental rationales for directives and constitute a ground for the development of extended directive sequences.

EMBODIED TRAJECTORIES OF JOYFUL COMPLIANCE TO DIRECTIVES

While we have primarily been concerned with how directives are postponed or refused, alternative ways of responding are of course possible. Children do comply and can even enthusiastically spring into action following a directive.

In the examples below we find moves of joyful compliance. In Figure 10 at dinner the family had been discussing how eight-year-old Aurora might befriend a shy

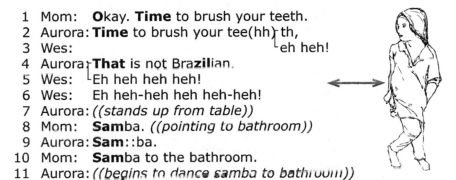

```
 1  Mom:    Okay. Time to brush your teeth.
 2  Aurora: Time to brush your tee(hh)┌th,
 3  Wes:                               └eh heh!
 4  Aurora:┌That is not Brazilian.
 5  Wes:   └Eh heh heh heh!
 6  Wes:    Eh heh-heh heh heh-heh!
 7  Aurora: ((stands up from table))
 8  Mom:    Samba. ((pointing to bathroom))
 9  Aurora: Sam::ba.
10  Mom:    Samba to the bathroom.
11  Aurora: ((begins to dance samba to bathroom))
```

Figure 10

Brazilian boy in her class by asking him about Brazilian samba; the conversation then shifted to a discussion of Brazilian Portuguese. When Mom states "Okay. Time to brush your teeth." Aurora, in a repair-like counter move (M. H. Goodwin, 1990b, p. 147), playfully challenging the directive, responds: "Time to brush your tee(hh)th, That is not Brazilian" (lines 2 and 4).

Rather than dealing with the pragmatic or referential meaning of the utterance, Aurora instead playfully challenges its form (line 4). Wes (aged five), Aurora's brother, displaying that he is joining in the humorous interpretation of Mom's talk, overlaps Aurora's talk with laughter (lines 5–6). As Aurora gets up from the table, and stands in a position indicating her willingness to carry out what has been asked of her, Mom (lines 8–10) then provides a directive that enters into the frame of play Aurora had initiated (lines 2 and 4), as she states, "Samba. Samba to the bathroom." Across a number of types of interactions these family members engage in wordplay and joyful exploration of their phenomenal world (M. H. Goodwin, 2007).

In Swedish families, we find similar directive trajectories keyed as playful endeavors. In figure 11 Mom's directives to go and clean the room before watching the TV show are designed as playfully embodied instructions. Mom helps her ten-year-old

1 Mom: A men du. (.) går du upp och så **plo**ckar
           Well but you. (.) go upstairs and then clean

2   lite på ditt **rumm**? Städa alla saker på
           your room a bit? Clean all things from

3   **bor**det. (0.3) Ska du göra det?
           the table. (0.3) You'll do that?
           ((turning the daughter around))

4 Marie: Ja.
           Yes.

5 Mom: Sen kan du komma och **se** det.
           Then you can come back and watch it.
           ((refers to TV show))

Figure 11

daughter pirouette, and Maria dancingly turns from the window toward the target activity-relevant location (i.e., the staircase that leads to the girl's room), while verbally confirming her compliance.

While most studies of directives in the family focus on the moves of parents, here we have investigated the ways in which children not only comply with but also resist actions proposed to them. In Figures 2–11 children display through their bodily behavior (e.g., arms akimbo) as well as their talk their stance toward the directive. Children can avoid entering any type of facing formation whatsoever vis-à-vis those who deliver the directive—hiding under a cover (Figures 6), burying their head in the couch (Figure 2), or turning away from parents (Figures 2, 5, 8, 9). Children can provide vivid portraits of the reluctant (Figures 6, 8–9) and defiant body (Figures 2–3) or, alternatively, assume a willing body, as, Aurora, and Maria (in Figures 10 and 11), displaying forms of cooperative semiosis (C. Goodwin, 2011). Figure 12 below demonstrates the pervasiveness of how the body is organized dialogically. A range of examples from two different societies all demonstrate how individuals organize their bodies with reference to the bodies of their cointeractants and the courses of actions they are pursuing together.

Discussing the special mutuality of immediate social interaction Park (1927, p. 738) argues that the individual in society lives "a more or less public existence in which all his acts are anticipated, checked, inhibited, or modified by the gestures and the intentions of his fellows." He argues that "it is this social conflict, in which the individual lives more or less in the mind of every other individual, that human nature and the individual may acquire their most characteristic and human traits."

Embodied stances exemplify such dialogic (Linell, 2009) public phenomena. While they are responsive to the prior action, simultaneously they are proactive: as a display of the speaker's alignment to another's action, they shape the hearer's

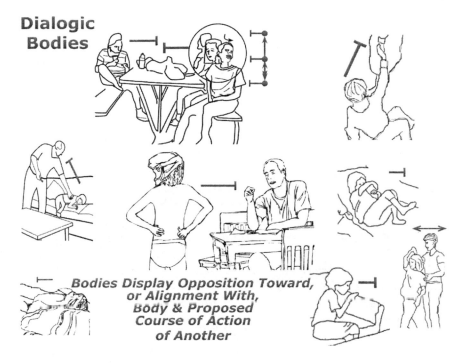

Dialogic Bodies

Bodies Display Opposition Toward, or Alignment With, Body & Proposed Course of Action of Another

Figure 12

response, constraining what will come next. Children's confrontational refusals result in little accommodation to the child; parents often recycle directives, and mention sanctions for noncompliance. The pleading mode, by way of contrast, is calibrated to invoke a parent's alignment with the child's position. Such multimodally organized directive trajectories thus show clearly that emotion and stance are not simply add-ons to an isolated individual action, but constitute an inherent feature of temporally unfolding sequences of social interaction.

CONCLUSION

In this chapter we have tried to develop a perspective for the analysis of emotion that focuses on how it is organized as social practice within ongoing human interaction.

Much analysis of emotion investigates its primary organization as being lodged within the psychology of the individual. One strong tradition, taking as its point of departure Darwin (1872/1998), focuses on the evolution of particular emotions, and organization of the muscles used to display emotion in the face. Our framework proposes a quite different geography. From our perspective it is necessary to take into account not only the psychology and facial expressions of the individual expressing the emotion, but also the relevant actions and bodily displays of the parties they are interacting with. We argue specifically that the body of the party producing an emotional display cannot be examined in isolation. Crucial to the organization of emotion as public practice is the way in which individuals display rapidly changing stances toward both other participants, and the actions currently in progress.

Methodologically it was therefore necessary to provide new ways of presenting relevant phenomena on the printed page: Because of the subtle way in which not just the face, but entire bodies are organized to display relevant stances, we found it appropriate to include images of bodies. The meaningfulness of bodily displays for indexing particular affective stances was constituted through how they were positioned within local activity frameworks, and vis-à-vis each other in the lived space of the habitual environments where interaction was occurring (i.e., homes with separate places for eating, watching television, and so on, and the tables on the playground). All of these phenomena were mobilized by interacting bodies in order to construct affective stance, and display locally relevant emotions.

Our focus on the analysis of emotion as situated interactive practice required particular kinds of data. Specifically, in order to examine how emotions were being mobilized with respect to the actions of others, we chose a particular sequential and multiparty environment. We focused our analysis on directives being given to children, and the responses made by these children, in both Sweden and the United States. All of these data demonstrate how emotion is organized as a multiparty phenomenon that mobilizes a range of different resources provided by both language and the body, including particular kinds of turn prefaces, and systematic use of prosody which showed similarities in the American and the Swedish data with respect to how bodies were mobilized to display either congruent alignment or opposition to the frameworks proposed by prior speakers. From our perspective both stance and emotion are not add-ons to action basically displayed through language structure. Instead they constitute central components of the situated actions participants build to carry out the mundane activities that make up the lived social worlds they inhabit together.

NOTES

This study is part of an interdisciplinary, collaborative research endeavor conducted by members of the UCLA Center on Everyday Lives of Families (CELF), under the direction of Elinor Ochs, and the Swedish counterpart (SCELF), under the direction of Karin Aronsson. CELF was generously supported by the Alfred P. Sloan Foundation program on the Workplace, Workforce, and Working Families, headed by Kathleen Christensen. We are indebted to the working families who participated in this study for opening their homes and sharing their lives. Diana Hill provided invaluable assistance and expertise in making the pitch tracts for this chapter. Katrina Laygo, Ian Dickson, and Erin Mays provided their artistic talents in the rendering of images. Malcah Yaeger-Dror and Christina Samuelsson provided invaluable help with understanding features of intonation. We thank Karin Aronsson for invaluable comments on an earlier draft and Anssi Peräkylä and Marja-Leena Sorjonen for helpful comments throughout the process of writing this chapter.
1. See also Jaffe (2009b) and Du Bois (2007) on stance.
2. Our focus on emotion as stance is, however, most relevant to the analysis emerging from neuroscience, of how emotions mark and inflect in a most consequential fashion

the events they are tied to (Damasio, 1999), which is relevant to phenomena such as the acquisition of complex skills, including becoming competent in a second language (Schumann et al., 2004).

3. In concert with work that views emotion as something that can be adequately described by restricting analysis to the individual, much work on emotion and language inspired by Wierzbicka (1995) has focused on her notion of semantic primitives. As Bamberg (1997, p. 210) defines it, "emotions to her are a semantic domain (1995, [p.] 235) to be investigated in a semantic metalanguage, i.e., in terms of indefinables or primitives (semantic universals) that are shared by all human languages." See Besnier (1990) and Wilce (2009) for reviews of language and emotion. See also Irvine (1982, 1990), Lutz and White (1986), Lutz and Abu-Lughod (1990), Matoesian (2005) Caffi and Janney (1994).

4. In 1998 Ekman prepared an edition of Darwin's original 1872 *The expression of the emotions in man and animals*, with his own introduction, afterword, and commentary. Thus many of the citations here that begin with Darwin's book are in fact quotes from Ekman. This is indicated in the in-text citation.

5. See M. H. Goodwin (2006b) for more extended analysis of the dynamics of this group and Angela's marginalization.

6. Talk is transcribed using a slightly modified version of the system developed by Gail Jefferson (see Sacks, Schegloff, & Jefferson, 1974, pp. 731 3). Talk receiving some form of emphasis (e.g., talk that would be underlined in a typewritten transcript using the Jefferson system) is marked with bold italics.

7. See also Fridlund's (1997) exposition of his "behavioral ecology view" of faces.

8. Reilly and Seibert (2003, p. 538) describe prosody as including "stress, intonation, loudness, pitch, juncture, and rate of speech. It is a suprasegmental feature in that prosody extends beyond the most basic linguistic unit, the phoneme."

9. The normal pitch range of preadolescent girls is between 250–350 Hz; any vowel longer than 200 milliseconds is considered extended (Yaeger-Dror, 2002; Richard Ogden, personal communication, 2010). Klatt (1976, p. 1209), writing about English, states that "the average (median) duration for a stressed vowel is about 130 msec. in a connected discourse." In Swedish the mean length of stressed vowels in connected discourse is 158 msec. and 103 msec. for short vowels (Elert, 1964).

10. Schieffelin (1990, p. 112) explains that she is using the term "appeal" to refer to a modality of action rather than a metalinguistic term in the Kaluli language.

CHAPTER 3

ᴖ

Distress in Adult–Child Interaction

ANTHONY J. WOOTTON

A focus of much research on children and emotion has been on how they and those who care for them talk about emotional states (for an overview see Carpendale & Lewis, 2006, pp. 214–20). Such talk can give clues as to how the child construes another person's mental life, a parameter of much interest to those investigating the child's "theory of mind": for example, the examination of talk between child and carer in which emotional states are topicalized can suggest discourse-based features which may contribute to the emergence of those cognitive parameters held to be germane to the child's understanding of emotion. Although there may be connections between such themes and what I shall have to say, connections that I will touch on later, my principal focus in this chapter is on the display of emotion rather than talk about it.

The display of emotion and talk about it are by no means coextensive. Long before children can predicate specific affects they can display them through a variety of linguistic and nonverbal techniques (Ochs, 1988, p. 185), and by the age of three there can be extensive communication of anger and aggression without any direct reference to emotional states (Miller & Sperry, 1988). There is a limited literature on the interactional dynamics of displays of emotion among young children. Some gives hints as to its distribution: for example, Dunn (1988, pp. 40, 194) argues that displays of anger and distress at eighteen to thirty-six months are associated with disputes over what she calls "rights," matters relating to the possession of things, sharing, taking turns, and fairness. But the emergence and shape of such disputes can take various forms, and their precise dynamics remain to be unraveled (though at older ages see Maynard, 1985; Goodwin & Goodwin, 2000). With regard to distress there is some suggestion that among young children breaches of expectation can be germane to distress onset. I'll give two examples of this. Fogel (1993, pp. 164–5) discusses this in the context of distressed reactions to the unexpected withdrawal of the nipple during breastfeeding. He points out that this withdrawal gains its significance to the child because the system of interaction between the child and nipple/mother is one of coregulation, one in which actions of both parties are shaped with reference to the relevant state of the other, so that unexpected withdrawal is a breach of a delicately organized ongoing system (see also Kaye, 1982). Between the ages of twelve and twenty-four months a different kind of breach can come to be relevant. Here children, and parents, become increasingly interested in objects which are broken, dirty, or out of place, or with mishaps which bear on such matters. While distress can occur in such circumstances the more standard emotional reactions appear to be milder ones involving the display of tension or worry (Kagan, 1981, pp. 47–9; Dunn, 1988, pp. 22–5; Cole, Barrett, & Zahn-Waxler, 1992), while on some occasions humor can be involved. In parentheses I should add that such mishaps and other kinds of untoward event are disproportionately represented in recollections about the past between parents and young children (see, for example, Miller & Sperry, 1988). There are, therefore, important links between the occurrence of events involving heightened emotion and later talk about such events, thus complicating the contrast that I made in my opening paragraph.

Breaches of expectation have also come to figure in my own explorations of emotional displays during a child's third year of life. My data were derived from a series of longitudinal video recordings made at about two-month intervals during this period (for details see Wootton, 1997, pp. 21–3). My line of interest was sparked off by finding striking examples of distressed behavior in certain kinds of interaction sequence, specifically request sequences. In such sequences one place in which distress can occur is when the child's request is turned down, and an example of this will be discussed later, but an intriguing feature of the cases which initially attracted my attention was that in them the child's displeasure seemed to be incurred in the course of parental attempts to grant the request. In the first section below I'll examine two such sequences, so as to identify some of the practices which inform the occurrence of such distress. The second section will compare sequences like this with those request sequences in which the child's request is turned down, especially with regard to the form that the distress takes. The third section compares some of my findings with what is known of the distribution of distress among children with autism. And the fourth section will examine the implications of what I have said for current ways of conceptualizing emotion in research on young children, and for the kinds of developmental enquiry which would seem to be suggested by these findings. In all this I am treating "distress" as roughly denoting those forms of tearfulness which have crying as their most extreme form of expression (for useful delineation of these forms of expression see Hepburn (2004); I adopt her transcription suggestion of using the tilde (~) to convey "wobbly voice"). Something of this, or the events immediately leading up to it, is evident within all my transcripts, but the exponents vary, and one of my main arguments will be that this variability is systematic, and connected to properties of the sequence that contains the distressed behavior.

REQUESTS AND DISTRESS

The kind of distress on which I want to focus initially can be found in Extract 1 (see also Figures A–D related to Extract 1, below). Here the child, Amy, aged 2;5 (two years five months), is sitting on her mother's knee. At line 1 she makes it clear that she would like some honey, "I want- I wanta- Get me (a) honey." The gist of the mother's reply at lines 2–4, 6, 9, and 12–13 is that Amy needs to have her hands washed first, but the implication is that she can have some honey when this has happened. At line 10 Amy says "You get it for me, (.) Put it on the:re for me," shifting onto the manner in which the honey is to be made accessible to her rather than whether or not she is going to have the honey, and thus revealing her expectation that the honey is to be forthcoming.

Extract 1
Amy (aged 2;5) is sitting on her mother's knee, having her socks pulled on. They have just been talking about a picture on the nearby blackboard. This is the first mentioning of the honey in this sequence. Her father is sitting just out of camera shot to the right, reading a newspaper. M is mother and F is father (who is also the author of this article). Superscript letters correspond with the images.

```
01   A:   I want- I wanta- Get me (a) honey.
02   M:   Get you the honey?=Well if you're going to have some
03        honey you're going to have to (.) have your hands washed
04        properly.
05        (.6)
06   M:   Cos your hands are all messy.
07        (1.0)
08   A:   [(           -)
09   M:   [All messy with chalk,
10   A:   You get it for me,(.) Put it on ᴬthe:re for me, ((points
11        to nearby stool during later part of this turn))
12   M:   Well you've got to go and have your hands all washed if
13        you're going to have honey,

14        ((F then brings a cloth and wipes A's hands while she is
15        still by her mother, prior to which there is also
16        discussion as to where she will put down some chalks she
17        is still holding: 45 seconds elapse in this omitted
18        segment))
19   A:   Now I'll have honey now (.) I'll sit (   )= ((moves
20        to sit in her chair))
21   M:   =You're going to sit there = that's the honey chair is it?
22   A:   Mm.
23        (1.0)
```

24 M: Right.
25 A: Here's the honey (   )?[B]((smiles as she says this, as F
26   comes into camera shot carrying the honey))
27 M: ((laughs)) Is this person ((pointing to A)) a bear really?=
28   ((by now F is also proffering the jar directly to A))
29 A: = No: No:[C] le:t mummy: ge:t i::t= ((with agonized voice
30   quality, sharp moves of head to face away to her right
31   and flailings of her arm in the direction of the
32   honey: by the end of her turn F, in reaction to this,
33   has passed the honey to M))
34 M: =Oh I've [[D]got it.
35 A: [NO:: NO:: (hh)(hh)= ((i.e., tearful voiced
36   outbreaths after the "no"s; arm flailings
37   co-occur with this turn))
38 M: =What d'you want me to do. =
39 A: = ~Ge::t it fro: [m the ta-~,
40 M: [I'll go and get it shall I.
41 A: Ge:t it fro:m ~the ta:[bl:e~?
42 M: [O:kay I'll go'n get it from the
43   table.((then M gets up and goes to table))
44   (5.0)
45 M: Uh:: loo:k I've found some honey (.) fancy that, ((all
46   done with "surprised" intonations))

A

Figure A related to Extract 1

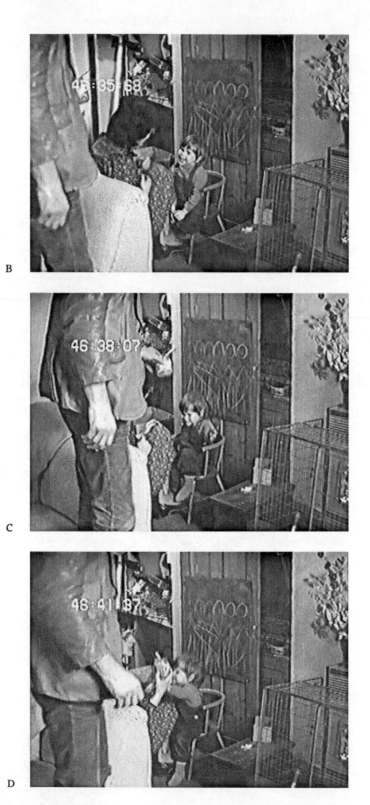

Figures B–D related to Extract 1

The handwashing then duly takes place and at line 19 Amy moves to sit in her own small chair to receive the honey, which is proffered to her by me, her father, at lines 27–8. Her distressed reactions to this are evident from line 29 onward. There it is clear that she is not happy with my passing her the honey, a matter that I promptly orient to by giving the honey to her mother, for her to give it to Amy. But this too is found unsatisfactory, at line 35, and after her mother's enquiry at line 38 Amy indicates at lines 39 and 41 that she wants the honey to be put back on the nearby dining table and her mother to transport it to her from that location. This the mother does at lines 43–5, and through "Oh:: loo:k I've found some honey (.) fancy that" she acts as though the honey is being topicalized for a first time, as though the prior sequence had not taken place.

In all this the child is clearly having problems with the manner in which the honey is being transported to her, problems being exhibited in a variety of ways which include the rejection of both my proffer (line 29) and that of her mother (line 35). A first point to make is that in such positions the child has available to her alternative ways through which she might have remedied the position in which she finds herself. Where there is a mismatch between what a request is seeking and what the parent does in response to it then children of this age have ways of engaging in repair which don't involve the kind of emotional turmoil that we have found in Extract 1. For example, on occasion, after the child has made a request it is clear that a parent is passing her something other than what she wanted. In such circumstances it can prove quite difficult to establish what the child really wanted, and such sequences can be prolonged and can involve various kinds of repair strategy on the child's part, efforts which usually involve attempts by the child to indicate the object that she really wants to be passed to her (Wootton, 1994). However, such sequences do not contain the kinds of distressed reaction that we've found in Extract 1, which raises the question of what makes those rather few sequences like Extract 1 run off so differently from the more standard forms of repair that we find in both request sequences and other sequence types? Eventually, after the end of Extract 1, the child finds it perfectly acceptable to receive the honey from her mother, so what is it about the shape of this sequence which lays the basis for her rejecting such a solution at lines 34–5? To answer this we need to look at the relationship between the child's original request and the parents' efforts to grant it.

A key point in this regard is that the father's attempt to grant the request at line 28, by proffering the honey to the child, is identifiable as deficient according to any strict interpretation of what has earlier taken place. After her original request for the honey at line 1 she later specifies who is to give it to her with "You get it for me" at line 10, identifying her mother as the one to be involved in conveying the honey to her; and even though it is her father who subsequently wipes her hands, the child still has this earlier basis for expecting that her mother will take the primary role in actually giving her the honey. From the child's behavior as her father approaches with the honey it seems that she would have been happy for her father to have initially passed the honey to her mother, for her to give it to the child—at line 25 (see Figure B related to Extract 1) her face is a picture of happiness as her father comes into camera shot holding the honey jar. What prompts the initial distress is her father's proffer of the honey directly to her, an act which she has a basis for treating as in breach of an agreement as to how events are to proceed. This basis, as noted above, is one that has been overtly established within the prior interaction, and an important feature of those distraught incidents which resemble Extract 1 is that they also contain within them such an earlier basis for the child to identify a breach of expectation.

Extract 2 contains another example of this kind of phenomenon (see also Figures A–D related to Extract 2). In the course of organizing a pretend game of shops, which involves her mother being the shopkeeper, Amy, at line 3, directs her mother to sit in a particular chair. In that vicinity there are in fact two chairs, one a small child's chair, the other an adult armchair. Between lines 10 and 21 Amy's gaze and attention are bound up with exchanges with her coshopper, her father, and it is not until line 23 that she turns to look at her mother again. What she sees prompts the immediate charged negative response that we find at line 24, and a variety of further actions that I'll address later.

Extract 2
Father (F), mother (M), and Amy (aged 2;9) are close to the dining table. There has already been discussion about playing shops, and Amy carries a bag that she has fetched for this purpose. F has just suggested to A that M be the shopkeeper.

```
01   A:   C-c-c-come ᴬ o:n? ((to M, as A moves across room))
02   M:   ((laughs)) =
03   A:   =You sit o:n- o:n this: chair (mis [ter) shopkeeper. ((to M))
04   F:                                  [Ye:::s.
05   F:   Ye:s. ((then chuckles))
06   M:   I'm going [to sit the:re am I, ((then M gets up to move
07            towards [a chair))
08   F:              [Yes ((then laughs))
09        (5.7)
10        ((in this pause M goes to the chair and F moves other chairs))
11   F:   Ye::s the shopkeeper should sit (   way).
12        (1.7)
13   A:   No.hh no: you ca::nt sit 'ere.ᴮ ((to F, as she picks up a
14        bag that has just fallen from a chair to the floor; at 13
15        A is inferring that F had placed the bag on the chair with
16        a view to then sitting in it))
17   F:   We:ll I'm just putting this:-, ((said as he moves another
18        chair under the table))
19        (4.2)
20   F:   ((A passes the shopping bag to F)) Ye:s I know I've got to
21        hold tha:t.
22        (2.1)
23        ((A turns for the first time to see where M is seated))
24   A:   NO: NO: ↑NOᶜ::::::::::::::↑~NO::::::::::::::~. =
25        ((to M; stamping and moving around room as these words
26        are said; at the end of this turn A takes hold of M's
27        hand))
```

28   M: =£^DWhe:re do I sit the:n.£
29   A: ↑NO::::::. ((pulling at M's arm to get her up, M laughing))
30   (.)
31   A: ~(GE::T U::P)~,   ((though by now M is up))
32   M: Whe:re do I si:t? ((being pulled across the room, out of
33   camera shot from here on))
34   A: ~GO: AWA:::::Y~,
35   M: Oh: dea::r I sat on the wrong seat I think.
36   ((A has now taken M into an adjacent room, out of
37   camera shot))

A

B

Figures A and B related to Extract 2

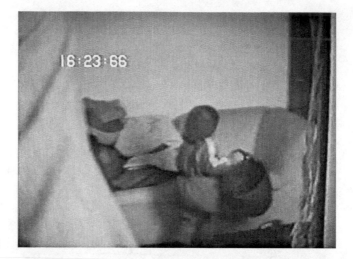

C

D

Figures C and D related to Extract 2

At line 24, it would have been within Amy's capabilities simply to correct her mother by saying something like "No, not that chair, this chair." Indeed, within this very same sequence we can see her engaging in one form that such remedial action can take. At line 13 she appears to be treating the fact that her father has placed his shopping bag on the seat of a nearby dining chair as an indication that he was going to sit there, when going on to engage in the shopping game as her coshopper. The bag falls off this chair, and as she stoops to retrieve it and stands up again she says "No.hh no: you ca::nt sit 'ere," thus correcting something that she felt was about to happen, and in doing so displaying a reading of her father's intentions from the disposition of the chair and bag, the occurrence of these features in this sequential location, and so on. What occurs from line 24 is very different from such low-key corrective action. What seems to lie at the heart of this outburst is the seating position that has been adopted by her mother at lines 6–10 in response to the child's request at line 3—an analysis later confirmed by the mother's "Whe:re do I sit then" at line 28, which treats the location of where she is sitting as the main problem, and her later "Oh: dea::r I sat on the wrong seat I think" at line 35. What has been breached is an expectation that the child could feel had been established within the earlier interaction. On turning to her mother at line 23 she finds that her mother is sitting in a different chair from the one she had meant for her to sit in, the small chair rather than the armchair, one incommensurate (for the child) with what she could feel entitled to expect on the basis of the prior exchange at lines 3–7.

In both Extracts 1 and 2 the timing and nature of the child's emotional reaction appears sensitive to the existence of a prior basis that the child has for expecting events to unfold in a different way. And, in addition, in both cases, after this basis has been established, the child has engaged in further activities which are in some sense preparatory to, and predicated on, the projected course of action taking place. In Extract 1 the various hand-wiping and seating preparations noted at lines 12–21 are in anticipation of the honey being given to Amy. In Extract 2 the exchanges between Amy and her father at lines 11–21 also prepare the way for these two people to begin the shopping activity, most obviously through the father being given a shopping bag at line 20. It is not, then, that the child just has a basis for expecting events to unfold in a particular way; after that basis has been established further moves have taken place which anticipate the eventual granting of the child's request.

THE SHAPE OF THE DISTRESS

These incidents involving distress have, as we've seen, emerged from a distinctive kind of interaction scenario, one which provides a sequential basis for the child to find later parental actions to be deficient, as out of line with the projectable sequence trajectory. In such circumstances simple corrective remedies prove not to be ones which the child employs, the deficient parental act is treated as spoiling the course of events in more radical ways. In Extract 1 my remedial action of passing the honey jar to Amy's mother (line 33) for her to give it to Amy proves unacceptable. Given this it seems possible that Amy's "let mummy: ge:t i::t," at line 29, is already an indication that the remedy needs to involve more than just her mother being passed the honey jar. Be that as it may, it is certainly clear from line 39 onward that what is now being sought is some kind of replay by the mother of the whole activity of fetching the honey from the table—"Ge:t it fro:m the ta:bl:e" (line 41). Therefore a feature of the child's solution to the state of affairs she finds herself in is to restore the status quo ante, to have things now proceed along the lines they should originally have done.

In other sequences such as Extract 2 the infringement of the child's sequential expectation can have even more radical consequences. During her prolonged and tearful

"Nos" at line 24 the child stamps around the room in an agitated state, eventually taking her mother's hand and then dragging her out of the chair on which she has been sitting. Rather than then guide her to the chair that she wanted her to sit in she instead pulls her mother out of the room into an adjacent room, shuts the door on her, and returns to the room where the shopping was to have taken place. In effect she treats her mother's action of sitting in the incorrect chair as destroying the viability of the projected activity.

In these sequences, therefore, we find a combination of features. By reference to the child having a basis for expecting the course of action to take a particular form then parental actions can be identified as untoward. This untowardness appears not susceptible to remedy through simple repair, through engaging in the kind of correction of which elsewhere the child has shown herself to be capable. Through treating the situation as now in need of more radical restoration she treats the parents as having in some way spoiled or disrupted the course of events. And it is in this context that we find her displaying the verbal and nonverbal signs of distress noted in the transcripts. In this kind of sequence it is also of note that the distress itself has features which make it different from that which can be found in other sequences, and at this point I'll try and bring this out through comparison with another kind of request scenario in which distress can be generated, namely one in which the parent is not able to grant the child's request.

In Extract 3, which takes place near bedtime, Amy indicates that she wants to play farms—"Wanta play fa:rms" (line 1). Initially I respond to this with clarification checks at lines 2 and 5, a type of decision-postponing action that characteristically foreshadows a nongranting alignment on the part of the person to whom the request is being made (Wootton, 1981). Such an alignment becomes more overtly exposed at lines 10–11, by which time I have begun to move the various toys, which include ones that might be used to play farms, from the floor into the toy basket, an action recognizable as preparing to put the toys away prior to bedtime. It is from this point onward, lines 12 and 13, that Amy begins to exhibit distress, hearable within her exhalations and within several of her variously produced versions of the word "No." This negation word is used to reject and oppose my attempts to move the focus and action on to other matters, and eventually, at line 31, this all gives way to full blown crying.

Extract 3
Amy (aged 2;5) is being carried by her father into the room where the camera is when she makes the first request below:

01   A: Wanta play fa:rms.
02   F: You wanta do what?
03   (.)
04   A: Play fa:::rms.
05   F: Pla:y fa:rms?
06   A: Yea::h,   ((F puts A on floor as this is said))
07   F: But we started playing farms and you stopped? ((then he

```
08        picks up toy basket))
09        (.)
10   F:   Come on these things are going away now    [=you help me
11        put them away,                             [
12   A:                                       [(  )n:o::,
13   A:   No (hh hh) ((i.e., voiced, upset breathiness)) No: I-
14        (.)  I::,=    ((during this turn she sits on the floor and
15        begins to handle her toys))
16   F:   =We've had our game (.) we've played our-we've had
17        [the game of farms.
18   A:   [No:: No ↑::::(hh hh hh). ~No::::::::::~.
19        ((i.e., voiced, upset exhalations after second "no";
20        gazing at F for most of this time))
21   F:   We've got a lot of things to do yet [Amy we're-we're
22        going to be very very busy,        [
23   A:                                  [~No:::: ooh~.
24        ((upset intonation; looking at F))
25        (.)
26   A:   [~No::~.   ((not looking at F; plays with her toys))
27   F:   [We- we've got lots of things to put away in the other
28        room as we:ll and we've got to go upstai::rs and we've
29        got to,.hh
30        (1.0)
31   A:   ~ehNo: [: (hh hh) no:.~. ((then full blown crying))
32   F:          [Do all sorts of things,
```

Several contrasts can be drawn between the nature of the child's distressed behavior in Extract 3 and that which occurs in incidents like our earlier Extracts 1 and 2. The first concerns the position in which it emerges and the character of this emergence. Where distress is generated in nongranting sequences like Extract 3 then characteristically it gradually emerges in the course of the child's oppositional behavior, only reaching its peak at some later phase of the sequence. In Extract 3 a type of upset breathiness is detectable at line 13; the intonations become more recognizably upset in lines 18 and 23; eventually at line 31 we have crying proper. In Extracts 1 and 2, however, there is evidence of distress in the child's initial reaction to the carer's egregious act. In Extract 1 the child's face changes from one of pleasure in Figure B to distraughtness in Figure C, and this change is accompanied by the agonized voice quality and sharp head and arm movements described in lines 29–32. In Extract 2 the child immediately exhibits her strong opposition to what her mother has done when she first turns to look at her (lines 23–7), and, in the course of this, tearfulness immediately becomes apparent within her voice quality. Whereas the escalation of distress can be gradual in sequences like Extract 3 this is not the case in those sequences like 1 and 2.

A second differentiating feature concerns the nature of the distress. Whereas various kinds of tearfulness are the predominant exponents of this in Extract 3, other exponents become apparent in 1 and 2. In Extract 1 the reactions of the child from line 29 onward, especially the nonverbal features described in lines 29–37, also convey a sense of indignation and frustration with her mother and father; their line of action is not just being treated as not to the child's liking but as egregious in some way. In Extract 2 this egregiousness is displayed even more vividly, through the loud and prolonged "Nos" at line 24 and the punitive action of removing her mother to the adjacent room.

Third, in extracts like 1 and 2 we find the child deploying remedial solutions to her predicament of a kind never found in nongranting sequences like Extract 3. In Extract 1 her solution, as we've seen, hinges around the idea of restoring the situation to the preceding status quo, having her mother pass her the honey jar from the table. In Extract 2 the parental action is similarly being treated as spoiling the projected course of events, only in this case the action prompts the child to abandon, at least temporarily, the line of action, the shopping game, that was being prepared for.

These various observations suggest that the shape and nature of the child's distress is discriminable as between different sequence types, in this case between the kinds of sequence exemplified in Extracts 1 and 2 and nongranting sequences like Extract 3. The details of this distress are, then, linked to those distinctive features of the interaction configuration that we have found in these sequences.[1] For example, the sudden onset of the distress display found in Extracts 1 and 2 is clearly linked to the fact that the child can then recognize that there has been a breach of some earlier understanding, an understanding that we have been able to trace within the earlier interaction. This kind of configuration is not exclusive to request sequences. Elsewhere I have also shown that it can also be found within offer sequences, where similar distress reactions can occur to those we've found in Extracts 1 and 2 (Wootton, 1997, pp. 113–24). Where the child has made it clear that she wants to do something herself, where, that is, she has a basis for expecting the trajectory of a sequence to proceed in a particular way, carer attempts to "help" her by doing the act for her can be met by similar expressions of indignation, and by attempts to restore the situation to the preceding status quo.

SCRIPTS, AUTISM, AND DISTRESS

Quite often in the literature on young children, episodes of conflict are identified as centering on household routines, where the implication is that conflict arises from a breach of expectation as to how such routines should proceed (Shantz, 1987; Dunn, 1988). On the face of it our Extract 1 takes place in similar circumstances, in which a routine event, the giving and taking of food, becomes the focus of dissent. Closer inspection has revealed things to be more complex than this. What is being breached here is not a generic, transcontextual procedure as to how this event should proceed—in this house there was no rule or set procedure as to who should pass the child honey, nor one governing where someone should sit when engaged in pretend play of the kind being prepared for in Extract 2. Instead, we've seen that the distress which transpires is linked to local understandings which the child has a basis for treating as having been established in the recent past. With certain other children, however, especially those with autism and similar, if less severe, pragmatic "disorders" such as Asperger's syndrome, there is various evidence suggesting that distress *does* appear to have a special association with the breach of more standard script-like patterns.

The special attachment of these children to routines is so well known that this forms a dimension of diagnostic instruments for these conditions (American Psychiatric Association, 1994; Bishop, 1998). One corollary of this attachment is that when such routines are altered, even in quite minor ways, then serious upset can arise. Howlin and Rutter write that many children with autism:

> become very distressed by minor changes in their environment, such as a door left in a slightly different position, or an ashtray moved a few inches out of its normal place or any redecorating in the house. A typical example of this was Stevie's distress when his parents removed a large fitted cabinet from the kitchen while he was away at school. On his return he screamed incessantly for two days, but finally, on the third night, much to his parents' relief he settled quietly. Only on waking the next morning did they discover their new paintwork completely ruined by a life size drawing of the original cupboard in indelible ink on the kitchen wall. (1987, p. 83)

The actual detail of such interactions is rarely presented in this literature, but in Extract 4 we have part of an incident involving a boy with autism which has similar features. We'll call this fluent and articulate twelve-year-old James. One of his school teachers, Fred, is visiting James's home, together with a camera operator. They are discussing another of James's teachers, Miss Chalmers, who is going to be away from school the following day. Her forthcoming absence has already been discussed on the video record made earlier that same day, and within that record there is every indication that there has also been other discussion of this matter prior to this. In the previous video segment James has become very distressed at the prospect of this teacher's absence:

Extract 4
There is a cut in the tape and we switch to a new location in the house, with James (J) sitting at the top of some stairs, elbows on his knees, hands by his ears. Fred (F) stands at the bottom of the stairs with the camera person behind him; the transcript below begins at the beginning of this filmed section:

```
01   J:    ((his hands move to cover ears fractionally prior to turn
02         beginning)) We'll see Miss Chalmers tomorrow = .hsh:::::::::
03         ((latter sound is lateralized bilabial fricative on long
04         single inbreath + coordinated harder pressing of hands
```

```
05          over ears + strained, tight closing of eyes))
06          (1.6)
07    F:    ((quiet and brief clearing of his throat))
08                    ((During the silence, J continues to hold his posture,
09                    though in this pause he opens his eyes and then closes
10          (4.6)     them; timing of F's next turn may be sensitive
11                    to a brief movement of J's hands away from, and
12                    back to his ears, as though checking whether
13                    there is any sound))
14    F:    James I kno:w [you're upset.
15                       [(((J's hands tighten on his ears + opens his
16                       eyes, gazing at F, then twice takes his hands
17                       quickly away from his ears, as though trying to
18          (2.5)       time their return to the ear when F shows signs
19                       of speaking; when F next speaks the hands do
20                       briefly flick back towards the ears, but the full
21                       movement is stalled, and his hands are away from
22                       the ears when F is speaking))
23    F:    Why you keep plugging your ears up ((J's gaze shifts away
24          from F after end of turn; hand position changed in the
25          later part of this turn, so that both are now brought
26          together in front of his mouth))
27          (.8)
28    F:    You don't want to hear what I'm saying? ((J's gaze returns
29          to F at turn beginning))
30    J:    Yea:::h. ((then takes his hands to his ears, where his
31          hands are held momentarily in position before he moves
32          them to a front of mouth position))
33          (.9)
34    J:    [(((as F begins to speak J moves his hands about half way to
35          [ears; at F's repair they are then moved to cover the
36          [ears))
37    F:    [Well you have to-you're gonna have to-
38          (1.4)
39    F:    [Accept it Jamie.
40    J:    [(((J's hands begin to move from his ears; in front of his
41          face again by F's next turn))
42          (.7)
43    F:    That's the way things go sometimes.
44          (2.7)
45    F:    You'll see Miss Chalmers      [soo::n.
46    J:                                  [(((J's hands go fast to his ears;
```

47   held there for 1.8 seconds; then moved to a side
48   of face position + he looks intently at F))
49   (3.4)
50 J: Tomorrow,((as he says this he puts his hands back over his
51   ears, and keeps them there and still looks at F))
        ((then some nonverbal signal from F in response, probably a headshake,
        prompts J to start crying again))

As with the anecdotal case from Howlin and Rutter mentioned earlier, it seems that it is a change in standard practice that lies at the heart of these events, in this case the absence from school of a teacher who is normally present. James's way of dealing with this predicament is to act as though the teacher will actually be present, as though the situation will not depart from the normal status quo—see especially "We'll see Miss Chalmers tomorrow" at line 2, and "Tomorrow" at line 50. And in a variety of ways he attempts to protect this possibility from the projectable skepticism of his recipient: by covering his ears and eyes in positions where such skepticism is expectable (lines 1–5, just ears at lines 50–51); by keeping his hands in a position, throughout the sequence, so as to prevent, rapidly, his hearing talk which runs contrary to his preference (e.g., at line 46 he quickly covers his ears so as not to hear words after "Chalmers"), and so on. The point, then, is not just that for him the breach of a normal arrangement occasions his distress but that reinstating the normal arrangement is the key to his solution for remedying matters—just as it was for Stevie in dealing with the absence of the cabinet.

Among children with autism and related conditions certain forms of sequential skill are often preserved (Ochs & Solomon, 2005, pp. 153–6), but there is, at the same time, every suggestion that generic patterns and scripts play an unusually prominent role in structuring their involvements (Wootton, 2002/3; for relevant data see also Sterponi, 2004), and this, as we have seen, also applies to those domains of action which incur distress. By contrast, we have found that the workings of episodes involving distress with Amy, a typically developing child, turn on local understandings and expectations, ones where the formation of the expectation that has been breached can be traced to the particular content of verbal interaction in the recent past. At this stage one implication needs to be brought out. The literature on children's development that gives more prominence to environmental input in shaping the emergence of children's skills has often placed much emphasis on the transmission of scripts and shared cultural presuppositions in accounting for how the child comes to incorporate his or her surrounding culture (e.g. Bruner, 1983; Valsiner, 1987). In the light of what has been argued, it is evident that the careful regard paid to generic patterns within social life in some ways fits rather better the practices of children with autism and related conditions than it does that of the typically developing child. The mastery of generic patterns and practices does not guarantee modes of involvement in online interaction which are characteristic of typically developing people. For example, Rutter and Bailey write that "it is a commonplace observation in the social skills training of autistic adults that often they are quite adept at saying what they should do in particular circumstances, but are quite hopeless in doing what is needed when they actually encounter such circumstances" (1993, p. 493). Taken together these points give caution to accounts of the early social development of typical children which place centre stage the acquisition of generic knowledge pertaining to scripts, rules, cultural presuppositions, and the like.

TWO THEMES

In this final section I examine connections between what I have said and two kinds of literature on children: the functionalist analysis of emotion and developmental themes.

Functional Analysis of Emotion

In recent years what is termed a "functionalist" view of emotions has come to be influential in research on children (for an overview see Saarni, Campos, Camras, & Witherington, 2006). Within this framework emotions do not precede actions but are generated via events impinging on the goal that a person is pursuing. Events which are appraised as impeding attainment of a goal tend to induce negative toning: for example, sadness is associated with having to relinquish a goal, frustration or anger with having obstacles placed to goal attainment. But the identification of emotion in the behavior of the person whose goal is, in one way or another, thwarted is held to be complicated because the emotion cannot be "read off" the child's response, off the shape of the behavioral display. This is most obviously so once children's reactions are shaped by "display rules", which constrain the expression of emotions. So, on this view, in order to identify emotions various information needs to be taken into account, notably the type of action being engaged in, inferences regarding what the person's goal is or was and inferences as to the relation of the action in question to the goal's realization.

This framework has been used to make sense of various findings on children's emotion and is loosely compatible with the data that I've presented above. In extract 1, for example, we have evidence regarding the immediate goal of the child, obtaining the jar of honey for the purpose of eating it. There is then an obstacle to this goal being immediately realized, and it would not seem far fetched to describe the child's reaction as containing a mixture of anger and frustration, along lines consonant with the framework above. However, this framework does not arise from the analysis of particular episodes of interaction like extract 1; indeed, "the question of how specific emotion actions emerge during specific emotion episodes remains largely unaddressed by the functionalist framework" (Saarni et al., 2006, p. 234). An analysis of the kind that I have presented places the sequencing of action center stage, and it may be useful to draw out some of the implications that this may have for this functionalist framework.

Working with actual, online interactional data permits more ready ways of handling issues addressed within the functionalist framework. The matter of the type of action being engaged in, which also speaks to the objective of the action, can be addressed more directly, through close attention to the design of the action, its sequential positioning and the manner in which it is treated by the immediate recipient(s). In these ways the need for analytic inference which goes beyond the immediate behavioral display is much reduced. A second point is that if one proceeds in this way it remains a more open question as to whether and how analysis needs to go beyond the behavioral displays of emotion found within particular sequences. Once actions are examined within the context of the sequences which form their natural home then systematic connections with sequence types may come to be evident. This is suggested by Dickson, Walker, and Fogel's (1997) research in which they show that the design of twelve-month-old's smiles is associated with the nature of the activity in which the child is engaged with her parents. And it is suggested by my earlier observations concerning the differential shape of the child's distress in sequences where her request is being turned down (Extract 3) compared with those in which a parental act was taken as in breach of an expectation (Extracts 1 and 2). Note that all three incidents took place in a request sequence, a linked action series initiated by a child request, so in order to discriminate between these displays of distress along the lines that I have it was necessary to locate more specific action configurations within such sequences. Working along these lines, and in the light of what we know about the operation of such sequences, it would seem premature to exclude the possibility that differential exhibitions of distress are associated with particular sequence types and configurations of action within sequence types. And, by extension, the same point would hold for the examination of any kind of emotion display. This is not to say that particular actions within particular sequences will always tend to attract the same kind of emotional display. For example, when children omit a "please" from their request the parent will sometimes attempt to elicit this item, perhaps by saying "Pardon?" or "What do you say?" or "Ple-." If and when the child then produces a "please" features of its prosody can be used by the child to convey variable emotional quality. For some children the "please" can be produced in a sullen way, as though this is a disagreeable task that is being expected of them, while others can imbue their "please" with forms of prosodic creativity which treat the action as more fun and game-like (see Wootton, 1984, p. 151; 2007, p. 196 and note 10 therein).

My third point concerns the nature of what one finds when inspecting the sequential realization of emotion displays. In my initial Extracts 1 and 2 we found a variety of phenomena in some way associated with the displays of distress, action packages rather than singular displays. For example, as well as the display of tearfulness and indignation various actions also occurred which showed that for the child the course of the sequence was not normally progressable, that the parental action had spoiled the shape of the emerging course of action—this action being abandoned in Extract 2 and needing to be rerun in Extract 1. Once examined within actual stretches of interaction such systematic practices associated with the display of distress can become evident, practices which, as I have shown, are by no means uniform across the expression of all forms of distress, even just among those occurring in request sequences. In these ways the examination of emotion *in situ* is likely to throw up collections of action packages, the properties of which will both specify and shed light on the analysis of emotion displays as systems of action.

Finally, it would seem useful to make explicit an important corollary of these various arguments. If it is the case that emotional displays are in some sense built for particular sequential positions, and if these displays are shaped so as to display a sensitivity to these positions, then there is a strong case for treating these sequential positions and their associated behaviors as the primary units for the analysis of emotion, rather than the units of sadness, anger, and so on, which are taken as primes both within the functionalist framework and much other literature on emotion.

Developmental Matters

If, as argued above, our focus is on identifying the practices that are involved in the composition of emotional displays then it follows that it is the development of these practices around which developmental enquiry needs to revolve. Many of the practices involved in this will be generic ones, ones not exclusive to episodes in which emotion displays are recognizable. Thus the child's orientation to the salience of understandings arrived at earlier in the sequence can be traced through various facets of this child's communicative conduct after the age of 2;0, as well as in cases like Extracts 1 and 2. For example, at 2;3, two months before the appearance within her transcripts of episodes like Extracts 1 and 2, I've shown that this same child's frequent usage of the word "actually" is bound up with the making of contrasts between what has earlier been agreed and what she is now stating to be the case (Wootton, 2010). And I've shown that at a similar and slightly later age her selections between those request forms that are available to her (notably imperative, declarative, and various designs of interrogative request) are similarly informed by the shape of the local interactions in which they occur (Wootton, 1997). There is every sense, therefore, that these sequential skills inform many aspects of the child's conduct at this age, that they form one component among those that make up what Levinson (2006b) has described as the "interaction engine", the set of components required to account for various features of human interaction as we know it.

If this component is of generic significance then it is likely to play a role in shaping the development of children's interactional practices through time. In my own work I've explored this mainly in the context of request development, showing how the process of linguistic differentiation is intimately connected to one of social differentiation, to locally distinctive interactional scenarios which have systematic connections with the deployment of various standardized linguistic formats for making requests (Wootton, 1997, chapter 4; 2005), a line of research that is paralleled in similar recent enquiry into adult interaction (e.g., Heinemann, 2006; Curl & Drew, 2008). In this work it is recognized that the operation of these practices has psychological entailments, indeed one thing I hope to have shown is that they make possible those particular kinds of emotional expression that we have found in Extracts 1 and 2, forms which are not present in the recordings of this child prior to her second birthday. But these forms of analysis differ from much developmental research in that they do not place the mind and its properties center stage. When I speak of the salience of local understandings I am basing this on identifiable connections that can be made at any given time between the child's current behavior and alignments that have been taken up in the prior interaction sequence. This demonstrable connectedness suggests that the child is taking this earlier material into account in the design of her action, and it is this salience, for her, which leads me to use the term "understanding" to describe it (see also Wootton, 1997, pp. 24–6). By contrast, within much developmental work the generic feature under investigation is most commonly some characterization of the capacities of the child's mind. The literature relating to "theory of mind" is the most influential current strand of such work, indeed within this work social understanding is largely taken as equivalent to how children understand themselves and others as psychological beings (Carpendale & Lewis, 2006, p. 5, though for qualification see pp. 225–7). While this is not the impetus behind my own line of research there are, nevertheless, potential connections between these two forms of enquiry. In Extracts 1 and 2 the child organizes her conduct so as to take into account alignments that have been taken earlier in the interaction. So in the course of constructing lines of action early in her third year of life she is routinely taking into account what people have agreed to, what they know, what their preferences are, and so on (for a different type of further evidence which also suggests this within request sequences, see O'Neill, 2005). If this is so then it seems reasonable to suppose that for those with an interest in how cognitive skills emerge, such as psychologists interested in theory of mind, the distinctive ways in which the child participates in sequences of interaction can offer important clues as to how such skills come into being (for recognition of which see Tomasello, 1999; Lohmann, Tomasello, & Meyer, 2005). In this sense there are also likely to be ontogenetic connections between those practices associated with, for example, exhibitions of distress and the ways in which the child comes to make inferences regarding the emotional states of other people, though in thinking about this ontogenesis we need to resist the temptation to see it as principally powered by the structure of the child's psychological capacities (Hutchins, 2006, pp. 392–4). Structures of social interaction, as we have seen, can play their own distinctive role in shaping up psychological propensities.[2]

Looking forward in time to ages beyond three, one complication to the analysis of emotional displays is the emergence of "display rules," forms of self-control which can involve the suppression and concealment of emotional expression, and even the feigning of appearance so as to convey a particular impression to recipients. These features form a central component of the vision of social life disclosed within the writings of Goffman (1959), and Sacks (1980) develops these themes in the context of children's behavior. For example, in the game of passing the button he shows how the practices of the game can encourage children to recognize that their own appearance can matter (e.g., how they appear to the person who is guessing where the button is when they themselves are trying to conceal it) and that they can exercise a degree of control over that by, for example, deliberately acting as though they are holding the button when, in fact, they are not. Within such a game children have, therefore, a motivation to invent, and practice, actions in which there is an embedded recognition that what they know to be true of the world can be different from what another person believes to be the case. This kind of game is probably playable among children from about five years onward, but has not been subjected to the kinds of empirical enquiry suggested by Sacks's remarks. Experimental analysis of gift giving suggests that some children younger than this, under four years old, are capable of producing smiles, or at least certain types of smile, in sequences where the gift giver is present and where the nature of the gift is designed to engender disappointment (Saarni, 1979, 1999). Another kind of event which is likely to be revealing in this regard is the child's engagement in some kind of culpable action. There is now a variety of evidence that in this context, and well before three years of age, children can design their actions so as to take account of whether their actions are seen, how they are seen, and how they can shape the reactions of other people to these actions (Dunn, 1988, chapter 2; Kidwell, 2003; Kidwell & Zimmerman, 2006). The examination of the actual organization of conduct in these kinds of sequence is likely to expose children's mastery of a much wider range of social skills than previously envisaged. Locating the ontogenesis of those practices which make an orientation to "display rules" possible will add a further dimension to the ways in which the analysis of emotional expression can be taken in new directions through the examination of naturalistic interaction.

ACKNOWLEDGMENT

I would like to thank the editors for their careful reading of the text and for their helpful input into its final formulation.

NOTES

1. The shape of the child's behavior in Extract 3 may also be connected with further features of the design of turns. After the child has made a request the recipient can select from various response designs to convey an unwillingness to grant the request, ranging from an outright "No" to clarification requests, deferred grantings like "Not yet" or "You can have it later," and so on (see Wootton, 1981, for an outline of this range for children aged just four years). Examination of these sequences suggests that where recipients do not initially select an overt rejection, such as "No," then this appears to form a basis for children of this age to engage in various behavior designed to have the recipient alter their negative stance. In more technical terms, where the recipient's turns are designed initially to display a preference for granting the request then the child's subsequent actions treat such turns as leaving open the negotiability of the recipient's stance. The development of such sequences is a site that has the capacity to generate various florid forms of emotional display by the child (for examples see Wootton, 1981, Extracts 49 and 50). In Extract 3 the child's request at line 1 is initially met with a clarification request which delays the production of her recipient's negative stance, and which thereby exhibits a preference for granting. And here also in her subsequent turns the child finds ways of challenging this stance.

2. If we extend this approach to children with autism then we should be examining the emergence of those interactional precursors that inform these children's concern with sameness, with continuity in the shape and character of the scenes in which they are involved. Here there is no difficulty in locating earlier interactional histories which show radical forms of communicative departure from those of typically developing children: things like delay in language onset, low levels of speech initiation once speech is available, persistent preoccupation with certain topics and themes, much repetition of the talk of others (echolalia). But in recent years the majority of ontogenetic research relating to these children has been shaped by theories as to the cognitive deficit involved in this condition, theories which principally treat the interactional features as a screen shaped by underlying cognitive processes. This is least true of the approach of Hobson (1993, 2002), which anchors autism in the disruption of the child's earlier relationship with others rather than some inbuilt cognitive deficit. But at this stage, although we can say that an orientation to sameness is consistent with many other characteristics of children with autism, the details of how such an orientation comes to emerge within actual interactional practice is not known (for some further observations on this see Wootton, 2002/3). This matter is made more complex by the fact that recent research by Stribling (2007) suggests that when interaction is examined closely some of the characterizations which have been made of children with autism may prove to be misleading. For example, although such children, in their early years, may initiate rather little in the way of conventional communication they may use other ways to initiate encounters with other people.

CHAPTER 4

⌒

Facial Expression and Interactional Regulation of Emotion

ANSSI PERÄKYLÄ AND JOHANNA RUUSUVUORI

Among the channels of expression in multimodal interaction, the face is special because it is, arguably more than the other channels, specialized in one task. This task is to convey emotion (see Ekman, 2009, p. xxii). Other channels of expression— be they lexical choices, syntactic structures, prosody, gestures, spatial movements, or the like—can be used in this task (see e.g., Besnier, 1990, and this volume, intro- duction), but they also perform a multitude of other tasks. Facial expression pre- dominantly conveys what we feel about something. In this chapter, we will explore ways in which facial expression of emotion is organized in relation to another mo- dality, spoken utterances, at a particular juncture of social interaction: at a closure of a story, anecdote, or other kind of telling. In our examination of facial expression, a key issue for us is *regulation of emotion*—one of the hot topics of current psychological emotion research (see e.g., Gross, 2007; Vandekerckhove, von Scheve, Ismer, Jung, & Kronast, 2008).

REGULATION OF EMOTION IN INTERACTION

Usually, the regulation of emotions is conceived as an individual competence, in- volving "the process by which individuals influence which emotions they have, when they have them, and how they experience and express these emotions" (Gross, 1998, p. 275). According to Gross and Thompson (2007, pp. 10–16) this process has five facets. *Situation selection* involves seeking or avoiding occasions that might arouse emotions, *situation modification* involves efforts to change such situations, *attentional deployment* involves directing one's attention in ways that influence emotions, *cognitive change* has to do with the ways in which individuals appraise the emotional meaning of the situation at hand, and *response modulation* involves efforts to change the physiological, experiential or behavioral responses to the situation.

The view of Gross and Thompson (2007), as well as most other research on emotion regulation, is individual-centered, focusing mostly on the ways in which individuals influence their own emotions. But emotion regulation can also be seen from a more sociological perspective. Without using the emotion regulation vocabulary, Hochschild (1979) had already in the 1970s elucidated the social dimension of regulatory phenomena, by suggesting that in social situations, individuals apply culturally derived *feeling rules* to adjust their emotions to what is understood as appropriate in a given situation or setting. Likewise, in their theory of facial expression of emotion, Ekman and Friesen (1969) suggested that culture-specific *display rules* influence the way in which individuals, in presence of others, modify the biologically given facial expressions of different emotional states. Hochschild, and Ekman and Friesen (whose theories otherwise are far apart) thus agree on the view that sociocultural factors influence the way in which individuals regulate their emotional experience and/or its expression. (See also Bloch, 2008; Mesquita & Albert, 2007; Poder, 2008; Trommsdorff & Rothbaum, 2008.)

Our conversation analytical conceptualization of the role of facial expression in the regulation of emotion differs from both the psychological and the sociocultural views. Rather than tracking the ways in which individuals influence their own emotions, or the cultural and social motivators of regulation, we examine *interactional* regulation (cf. Beebe & Lachmann, 2002). This involves the ways in which participants in interaction influence *each others'* emotions *in situ*. We focus on the ways in which the expressions of emotion are on the one hand regulated by the contingencies of the social situation, and how they on the other hand influence the unfolding of that situation.

Although our basic understanding of emotion regulation is different from the psychological, individual-centered view and the cultural view, we believe that our findings complement rather than contradict these other approaches. In terms of the emotion-regulation process model of Gross and Thompson, our primary focus is in response modulation. By examining the interactional dynamics of the facial expression, we will show some ramifications of the modulation of what Gross and Thompson would call behavioral emotional response. However, as we will show in the concluding discussion of the paper, our findings also contribute to the understanding of other facets of emotion regulation process: situation modification, attentional deployment and cognitive change.

PURSUING A RESPONSE TO TELLING

Stories, anecdotes, and other kinds of telling usually involve a display of stance by the teller to what is being told, and make relevant the recipient's affiliation or disaffiliation with that stance (Jefferson, 1988; Maynard, 2003; Maynard & Freese, this volume, chapter 5; Couper-Kuhlen, this volume, chapter 6). A stance qualifies the telling with a positive or negative valence, depicting what is being told, for example, as funny or sad. In this chapter we explore the ways in which facial expressions convey stance: how they show the storyteller's own stance toward her telling and give hints to the recipient about an appropriate way to receive the story through an assessment or other stance display.

Our interest lies in a specific type of moment of the telling sequence: occasions where a story or a telling is coming to its closure and a response is due, but it is delayed. This is an environment that potentially threatens the maintenance of alignment and shared understanding as well as the existing level of intimacy between the participants (cf. Jefferson, Sacks, & Schegloff, 1987). Consequently, the interactional regulation of emotion is dense in these occasions. As we will show, facial expression is a key means for emotion regulation here.

Anita Pomerantz (1984a) has examined a conversational sequence similar to ours in telephone calls. She examined the lack of recipient uptake to what she, in quite broad terms, called "assertions," and showed how the speakers may deal with the lack of response. Typically, the speakers clarify or revise the telling, whereby they, in Pomerantz's terms, "pursue response." This offers a point of comparison with the phenomenon that we examine in face-to-face conversations. By examining the facial expressions of the participants at the closure of tellings, such as complaints, anecdotes, and self-blaming remarks, we show what sort of particular relevancies facial expression can create for the upcoming response. In this way, we hope to bring to view an instance of what we call the "interactional regulation of emotions."

DATA AND METHOD

Our data consist of five video recordings of conversations over lunch in dyads of female friends. Out of these recordings, we found forty instances of the phenomenon under scrutiny: an interlocutor has made an assertion (a story, an anecdote, a remark) that makes relevant the recipient's response, the response has been delayed, and the interlocutor observably changes her facial expression, slightly turning her head toward the recipient. We call this combination of movements within the above-mentioned sequential location *facial pursuits*.

The recordings were made in a cabinet of a student refectory, where we invited the participants to have their ordinary daily lunch. They were seated half-toward each other, one at the end of the table, the other at the side of it (see Figure 1). This way they were able to notice if the other participant made a gesture, such as a head-turn to seek engagement, even when gazing away from the coparticipant (Goodwin, 1986).

Figure 1
The setting

In what follows, we will explicate the interactional work that facial expressions do when response to a telling with a stance is delayed. By specifying some ways in which facial pursuits of response differ from verbal pursuits, we seek to show the specific affordances of face as means of pursuit of response.

We will start by showing an example of *verbal* pursuit of response to a story.

PURSUING RESPONSE VERBALLY

Consider the following example.

Extract 1

01	B:	*£Hemmetti mää oon jo ihan sillai .hh nyrkki* [*ojossa*
		£Bloody hell I'm already like kind of.hh shaking my [fist
02	A:	[*ehhe*
03	B:	*siellä£ mutta tota,*
		there£ but like,
04		(1.0)

05   B: *Se vilahti just jonneki lattian rakoon nyt täytyy* [*alottaa*
            It just rushed somewhere to a slit in the floor now I must [start

06   A: [Mmm,

07   B: *uus sota ilmeisesti.*
            a new war I suppose.

08   A: *Mm/**Fig2**/m.*

09   →   (1.5)

10   B: *Hit* [*to vie semmonen joku uus yhdyskunta./Fig3/*
      →   Da [mn it some sort of like a new colony./**Fig3**/

11   A: [*Mmm,*

12   (2.2)

13   A: °*Niih*° *no >ku niil on< (0.4) päämajana se mun viemäristö*
            °Right° well >as they have< (0.4) their headquarters in that sewer
            of mine

14   *n*[*i ne on varmaan sieltä £putkia myöten tullu£..hhhmth*
            s[o they must have crawled from there £along the pipes£..hhhmth

15   B: [*hhmh*

Prior to the extract, B has been telling a story about how she has tried to get rid of
bugs in her sewer—with no real success. The story seems to have entailed two different stances toward the events described: on the one hand the teller has been
laughing at her "warfare" against the bugs, while on the other, she has been telling
about a real problem (see Ruusuvuori & Peräkylä, 2009). During the production of
the story, A has appreciated its humor by laughing and smiling (Ruusuvuori & Peräkylä, 2009; see line 2). At the completion of the story, however, she remains rather
silent, producing only two acknowledgement tokens (lines 6 and 8). At most, this
constitutes a very minimal reciprocation of emotional stance at the completion of
the telling.

There then follows a gap (line 9), after which B adds an exclamation-like closing
element to her story (line 10). With this element, emphasizing perhaps more the
troublesome than the humorous nature of her experience, she verbally pursues a further uptake of her story. Following a gap of 2.2 seconds, A continues the topic by offering a humorous explanation to B's continuing problem, thereby more fully
reciprocating the stance of the telling.

The two frames, Figures 2 and 3, show the participants' facial expression before
and during the verbal pursuit (lines 8 and 10). In all frames, participant A is on the

left, and participant B on the right. At the end of the story in Extract 1, the recipient withdraws her gaze from the teller (see Figure 2).

A   B

Figure 2
08   A: Mm/**Fig2**/m.

During the verbal pursuit and the subsequent silence, the participants are disengaged from one another, gazing at their food. Their faces are straight, without observable emotional expression (see Figure 3).

A   B

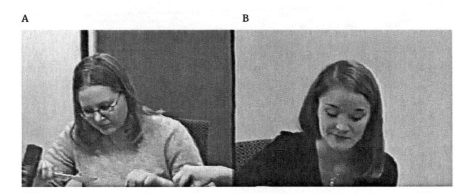

Figure 3
10   B: Da̠[mn it some sort of like a new colony. /**Fig3**/

Thus, in this case, the pursuit of response to a story occurs predominantly, if not only, through verbal means.

In the following we will present variations of facial pursuits in a location comparable to the one where the facial pursuit occurred in Extract 1. First, we will examine segments of interaction where the facial expression *reinforces* the stance displayed in the telling, then a case where the facial expression *explicates* emotional stance that in the telling is left implicit, and finally, we will examine a case where the facial expression *modifies* the emotional stance displayed in the telling.

REINFORCING STANCE THROUGH FACIAL EXPRESSION

Consider Extract 2, in which facial pursuit reinforces the emotional stance of a troubles telling. At the beginning of the extract, B is coming toward the end of a story in which she tells about her failure to get an appointment at the student health center. The complaining stance of the story (see Drew, 1998) unfolds as the telling proceeds. The temporal references in the story (lines 6–9) implicate the time of the telling, which is at the end of November.

B's story is hearably at its completion in line 9, through an utterance in which B reports, using a mocking voice (Günthner, 1997a; Holt, 1996; Haakana, 2007), the answer she got from the representative of the organization. The recipient, however, does not produce an immediate response (lines 10–12). But after the gap, she gives an affective evaluation of the story (line 13).

Extract 2

```
01  B:    >Mä en< ehtiny sillon soittaa sit mä ajattelin et mä soitan
          >I didn't have< time to call then so I thought I'll call

02        maanantaina,
          on Monday,

03  A:    Mmm,

04        (0.7)

05  B:    Soitin maanantaina varmaan joskus yheksäl/Fig4/tä
          I called on Monday about like ni/Fig4/ne o'clock

06        aamul?   .mthhhh   @Joo   kaikki   tota   joulukuun   ajat
          morning+in         yes    all      PRT    December's   times
          in the morning?.mthhhh @yes all like appointments for December

07        on        jo                menny   että   .hhh   odota   tonne
          have      already           gone    PRT           wait    there
          are taken already so that.hhh wait until around

08     → joulukuun   [puoleen väliin       ja   soita   sitte   ja /Fig5/ koita  varata
          December's  [half+to distance+to  and  call    then    and       try   to+book
          mid-December and call then and /Fig5/try to make
          [((A withdraws her gaze))
```

09 → *tammikuulle se* [*ai°ka°.@/Fig6/*
       January+to the [appointment
       the appointment for <u>January.@</u>/**Fig6**/
             [((A returns her gaze))

10 → (1.3) /**Fig7**//**Fig8**/

11 B: *.mthhh*

12   (0.5)

13 A: *Siis* /**Fig9**/*voi pliis oikees*/**Fig10**/*ti,*
       Like /**Fig9**/c'm<u>o</u>n really no/**Fig10**/w,

14   (0.7)

15 B: <u>M</u>*mmm. hhe*

We shall now examine the intensive facial work that the participants are engaged in. The storyteller has maintained her gaze toward the recipient through the final part of the narrative, without any lapse from the end of line 5 (see Figure 4).

A   B

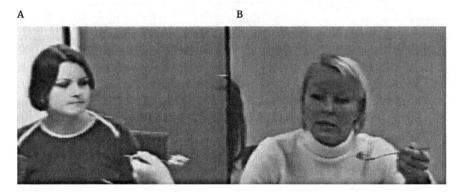

Figure 4
05 B: I called on Monday about like ni/**Fig4**/ne o'clock

A, the recipient, however withdraws her gaze (after the word "December") for a moment during the citation which serves as a story climax (see lines 8 and 9). During her disengagement, she gestures in an ambiguous way, bringing her right hand, fingers bent, in front of her mouth, and moves them as if she were scratching her upper lip (see Figure 5). While the postural disengagement incorporates lack of engagement in the story (during its climax), the gesture on the other hand can be received as conveying emotional stance, treating what is being told as ridiculous.

A   B

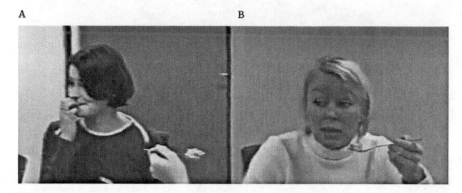

Figure 5
08   B: call then and **/Fig5/** try to make the appointment

By the final word of the reported answer (line 9), A has returned her gaze to the story teller. She does not, however, initiate any talk, and her face is non-affective (see Figure 6).

A   B

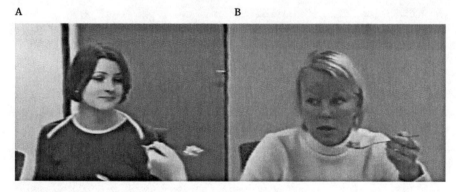

Figure 6
09   B: the appointment for January.@ **/Fig6/**

At the completion of her utterance (line 9), and during the silence that ensues (line 10) B produces an animated facial expression (observe the change from Figure 5 to Figure 6), conveying an affect which might be formulated like "this is appalling and unbelievable" (see Figures 6 to 8).

This expression serves as a pursuit of response. B leaves her mouth open, as it was at the end of her last word *aika* ("appointment"). Then, while continuously gazing at A, she turns her head in two phases more directly toward A. B's mouth remains open and a bit round, her eyebrows are up and eyes become bigger and "round" (Figure 7). In response, A (who maintains her gaze at B) raises her eyebrows (Figure 8). During the change in A's expression, the affect display on B's face seems to get more intensive; the impression is probably due to her second head movement toward A, and the way in which she maintains the same expressive features over a period of time (Figures 7–8). Toward the end of the silence in line 10, B withdraws her gaze from A and breaths in (line 11). After a gap, A, who maintains her gaze at B, then starts a verbal,

affective evaluation of the story (line 13; Figure 9). During the last word of her evaluation (*oikeesti*, "really"), A also withdraws from visual orientation toward the coparticipant (see Figure 10).

A   B

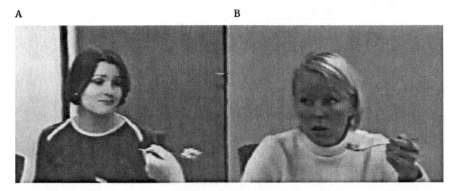

Figure 7
Silence in line 10

A   B

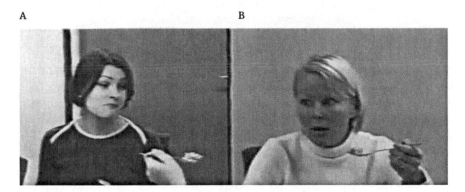

Figure 8
Silence in line 10

A   B

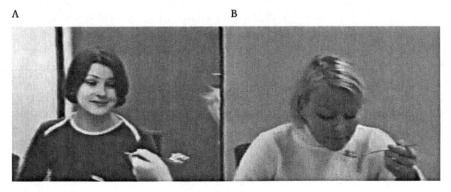

Figure 9
13   A: Like **/Fig9/** c'mon really now,

A   B

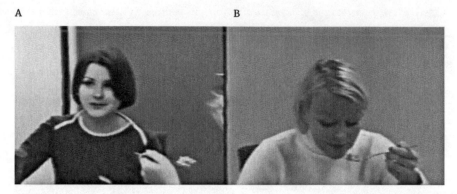

Figure 10
13   A: Like c'm<u>o</u>n really no/**Fig10/** w,

The two cases we have now seen are similar in many respects, but yet contrastive. In Extract 1, at the hearable completion of the story, the teller and the recipient are *disengaged in terms of gaze*. In absence of adequate response from the recipient, the teller pursues response through adding a new verbal element—which preserves the emotional stance of the telling—to the narrative. In Extract 2, the participants are *in mutual orientation* at the completion of the story. In absence of adequate response, the teller pursues response through maintaining and intensifying the facial expression that was on her face at the completion of the telling and by making her facial expression more available to the coparticipant by turning her head further toward her. The facial expression preserves the emotional stance that was embodied in the telling. So, we see two ways of pursuing an emotional response to a telling.

In a verbal pursuit, the teller produces a new unit of talk—a new turn construc- tional unit (Sacks, Shegloff, & Jefferson, 1974)—thereby also creating a new transi- tion relevance place (Sacks et al., 1974) after the pursuit, where the recipient's response is relevant. Place for response is thus, as it were, postponed, and created anew. The response to be produced in the new transition relevance place is a response not only to the telling as it initially was (i.e., the telling as it was before the first transition relevance place) but it is a response to the talk that has been revised through the new element. We can see this in Extract 1: B's response, as it eventually comes forth in lines 13–14, does not focus on the activities of A, which were the focus at the first possible completion of the story in lines 5 and 7 ("n<u>o</u>w I must st<u>a</u>rt a new war I suppose"), but rather, on the properties and whereabouts of the bugs, which was the focus of the verbal pursuit in line 10: "D<u>a</u>mn it some sort of like a n<u>e</u>w colony". Thus, in pursuing the response through verbal means, the speaker inevi- tably invites response to a transformed telling.

The place and relevancies for response in facial pursuits are different. As the teller does not add anything to her talk, she also maintains, more than in verbal pursuits, the initial relevancies regarding the response. As we have argued elsewhere (Peräkylä & Ruusuvuori, 2006; Ruusuvuori & Peräkylä, 2009), the facial pursuit of response *stretches the boundaries of action*. This means that in a facial pursuit, the initial sequential place for launching the next action is maintained. The facial pursuit reinforces, explicates, or modifies the stance of the initial telling, but it does not change the verbal telling per se. In consequence, the response, when it eventually occurs, is a *response to the telling as it was initially delivered*. Thus, in Extract 2, when A eventually responds in line 13 by saying "Like c'm̲on really now", she is hearably commenting upon what the student health center receptionist said, as mockingly cited by B in lines 6–9.

So, the choice between verbal pursuit and facial pursuit might also entail a choice between inviting a response to talk that the verbal pursue has somehow renewed, and a response to the talk as it initially was. The latter choice may sometimes have interactional benefits: it gives the recipient an opportunity to show affiliation with and understanding of the stance of the telling earlier in the sequential time, at the very transition relevance place where it initially is made relevant. If the participants take up this trajectory, they may preserve their joint action and the shared stance toward the object of evaluation with minimal rupture to the progressivity of the interaction.

In Extract 2, the facial pursuit maintained and intensified the affective stance that the speaker had displayed in her preceding utterance, response to which was pursued. In Extract 3 below we see a parallel case. As Extract 2, it also involves troubles telling. In Extract 3, however, the facial pursuit does not alone manage to elicit an affective response.

A is talking about a commitment she gave to an organization to produce a piece of research in a given time, pointing out how the commitment made her feel tied. The telling is part of a larger set of A's narratives all describing her difficulties in coping with her writing tasks. In response to B's affectively dense description (see the word choices "horrified," "help," and "completely tied") of her helplessness in lines 1–2, the recipient produces two somewhat delayed *mm*-tokens (line 4). The response is less than fully engaged, albeit the soft voice quality and even intonation in especially the latter token make it hearable as minimally empathizing. A's narrative about this particular piece of research reaches a point of completion in line 3: she discontinues her sentence "now I'm like", and after a 0.3 second pause, produces an idiomatic expression describing an untoward situation, *tässä sitä ny ollaan* (literal translation, "here we are now"). The idiom brings the telling hearably to completion (see Drew & Holt, 1988) and makes display of affiliation by the recipient relevant (see also Jefferson, 1988). After the closure of the telling, a gap ensues, whereafter B offers in line 5 a response token *nii* (line 6). The voice quality and the intonation contour of the *nii* are close to those in the latter *mm*-token in line 4, but as lexical choice, *nii* is arguably more affiliative than *mm* (Sorjonen, 2001, chapter 6). B does not, however, offer any more elaborate verbal display of understanding the trouble (cf. Ruusuvuori, 2005; Voutilainen, Peräkylä, & Ruusuvuori, 2010a; Heritage, 2011). A does not treat the minimal display of affiliation as sufficient, as she enters into verbal pursuit (line 7) through an incremental element that clarifies when her anxiety started, thereby treating the lack of response as a problem of unclear reference (cf. Pomerantz, 1984a). The recipient remains rather passive (line 8) and only after the narrator has made further verbal pursuits in which she shifts her position (cf. Pomerantz, 1984a) to a more normalizing one (lines 9, 11, and 13) does the recipient launch a more elaborate response (lines 14–15) in which she seems to reciprocate primarily the normalizing stance.

Extract 3

01 A: *No   sitte   mulle   tuli   siitä   semmone jotenki   /Fig11/   hirvitys*
        PRT   then   me+to   came   it+from   such   somehow   horror
        Well then it made me sort of **/Fig11/**horrified

02   *että   apua että   ny[t   mä oon   ihan   sidottu sii[hen   että   /Fig12/*
          PRT   help PRT   no[w I   am   completely   tied   th[at+to PRT
          that help that no[w I am completely tied to th[at so **/Fig12/**
                               [((A gazes at B))   [((mutual gaze))

03   *nyt [mä oon niinku (0.3) e[ttä   tässä sitä ny   ollaan./Fig13/*
          now[I   am   PRT   [PRT here PRT now   are+we
          now[I am like (0.3) [so that here we are now.**/Fig13/**

04 B: *[Mmm.*   *[Mmmm,*

05   (1.2) **/Fig14//Fig15/**

06 B: *Nii,   /Fig16/*
        Yeah, **/Fig16/**

07 A: *Ku mä niinku lähetinne/Fig17/pe°rit°.*
        As I sent the **/Fig17/** pa°pers°.

08 B: *Mmm[mm mm.*

09 A: *[Niinku /Fig18/↑MÄ oonki.*
              [So **/Fig18/**↑I am indeed.

10 B: *Mmmmm [mmmm.*

11 A: *[Mikä ei sinänsä se[n pitäs olla niinku*
                    [Which isn't in itself i[t should be like

12 B: [.hhhh

13 A: *positiivin[en juttu. .mt   Mutta.]*
        A positi[ve   thing. .tch   But.]

14 B: *[.mt Nii nii et se sitoo sua]*
                    [tch Yea yea so it ties you]

15   *tekemään[ki   mutta.*
          also to   [do   it but.

16 A: *[Nii.*
                    [Yeah.

We'll focus our analysis of the facial expression right after the completion of the telling. At the beginning of the extract, the participants are posturally disengaged, both gazing down (Figure 11).

A   B

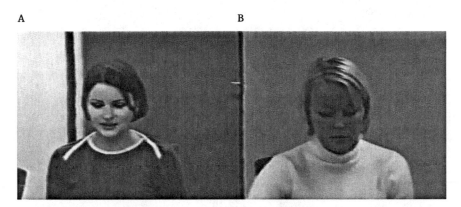

Figure 11
01   A: it made me sort of **/Fig11/** horrified

When approaching the completion of the telling, in line 2, A shifts her gaze to B, who reciprocates the gaze at word *siihen*, "to that," and mutual engagement is thus established (Figure 12).

A   B

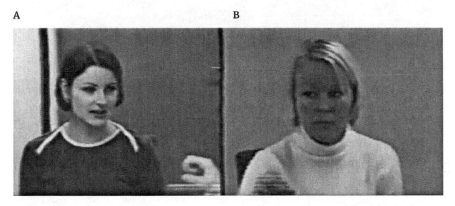

Figure 12
02   A: I am completely tied to that so **/Fig12/**

A produces the completion of the telling with a neutral face. Mutual orientation is maintained. At the closure of the telling (end of line 3), the participants are still gazing at one another. A's face remains affectively neutral while B is stroking her hair and purses her lips (appearing to be swallowing) (Figure 13).

A   B

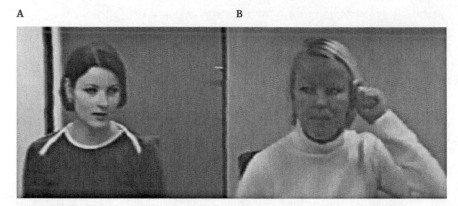

Figure 13
03   A: so that here we are now. **/Fig11/**

A silence (line 5) with intensive facial and gestural work ensues. After finishing her hair stroke, B tilts her head to right (Figure 14). Immediately thereafter, A raises her eyebrows, horizontal wrinkles appear to her forehead, she closes her mouth, bringing its corners slightly down, and tilts her head slightly forward toward the recipient (Figure 15).

A   B

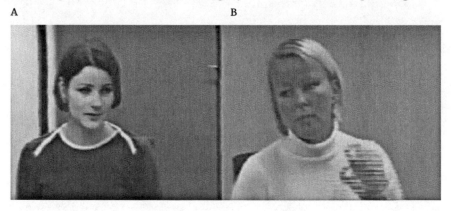

Figure 14
Silence in line 5

A   B

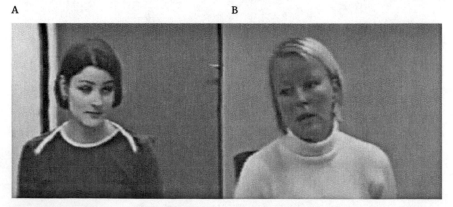

Figure 15
Silence in line 5

A's facial expression serves as pursuit of response, and as in the previous example, the accompanying head move toward the recipient seems to make the face more available and prominent. Albeit clearly affective, A's expression appears not to convey a distinct, unambiguous emotion. In terms of Ekman and Friesen's (1975/2003) classificatory system, her expression has some affinity to sadness (Ekman & Friesen, 1975/2003, pp. 119–121) and, on the other hand, to what they call questioning (Ekman & Friesen, pp. 13, 39). The head tilt forward, and the consequent gazing of the coparticipant from a "lower" position, together with the raised brows, creates an impression of remorse or begging for understanding—something we might call appealing. As a whole, we might say, her expression creates a strong relevance for responsive action and the response that is elicited is marked as somehow affiliating with A's negative affect (conveyed by face in Figure 15, as well as the preceding utterance in lines 1–3).

In response to A's gesture, B produces her affiliating response token *nii* (line 6); A preserves her facial expression and posture while B produces the *nii* (Figure 16).

A   B

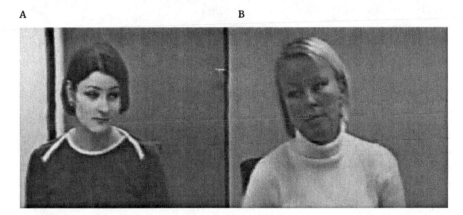

Figure 16
06   B: Yeah, **/Fig16/**

Her head position and brows remain in this position even when she produces the first verbal pursuit (line 7; Figure 17).

A   B

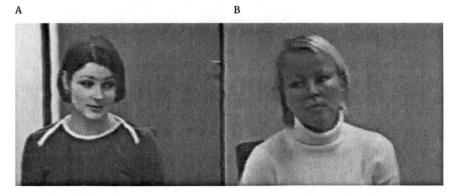

Figure 17
07   A: As I sent the **/Fig17/** pa°pers°.

Only at the outset of her second verbal pursuit (line 9) her facial expression changes, as she tilts her head to left and starts to smile through her talk (Figure 18).

A   B

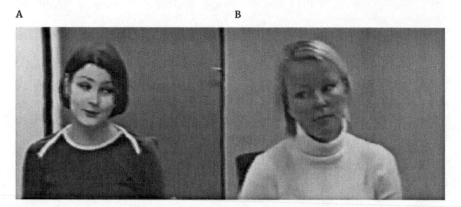

Figure 18
09   A: [So **/Fig18/** ↑I am indeed.

In Extract 3, the verbal design of A's first utterance (word choices *hirvitys*, "horrified," *apua*, "help," and the use of the idiomatic exclamation *tässä sitä ny ollaan*, "here we are now"), as well as the position of the utterance as a completion of troubles telling, constitute the utterance as conveying negative emotion, characterizable as anxiety, helplessness, and self-blame. The postcompletion facial expression by A maintains this emotional stance and succeeds in eliciting a minimal, affiliating response to it. The response B gives after the facial pursuit is not, however, treated by A as sufficient, and she launches new verbal pursuits.

EXPLICATING STANCE THROUGH FACIAL EXPRESSION

In Extracts 2 and 3, the facial pursuits of response to tellings preserved an affective stance that was there already in the tellings. In a number of other cases, the relation between the facial stance display, and the telling, is somewhat more complex. In this section, we will examine an example of cases where the facial expression *explicates* a stance that was not quite manifestly put forward during the telling itself. The explication of stance through face seems to be a practice particularly apt to humorous tellings.

Consider Extract 4. A and B have just been talking about the recommendations that some employers have given to trainees for dress-code at work. They have laughed at a conservative employer who—according to a mutual acquaintance— prohibits male employees from wearing jeans (lines 1–2). After this, B in lines 4–6 shares something that she has heard about the dress code for women by this particular employer. After the informing there follows a delay of 1.2 seconds (line 7), after which A responds with a token of disbelief *eh:* (line 8). An approximate English translation could be "No:". B starts a series of laugh tokens in overlap with A's response, and after B's laughter, A produces yet another vocalization *öhhh* (line 10) which resembles the first one but it uttered with more emphasis and perhaps through the change of vowel conveys stronger evaluative stance. A's response tokens (lines 8 and 10) convey that she considers what was told as foolish or unbelievable.

Extract 4

01 B: *Suorat housut vaa.*
      Straight trousers only.

02 A: *eh heh hehh he* [*he*

03 B: [*.hh Sit< tuon mie kuulin ihan Samilta itteltään*
                [.hh then< that I heard right from Sami himself

04   *mutta (0.4) mie en muista se oli si-joku muu joka oli sanonu*
      but (0.4) I don't remember it was the- someone else who had said

05   *et siel niinku suositellaan naisillekki*
      that there they also recommend to women

06   *et ne* [*käyttäis /**Fig19**/ham°etta°.*
      that they [should wear /**Fig19**/a °skirt°.
        [mutual gaze

07   (1.2)/**Fig20**/ / Fig21/ Fig22/

08 A: *e* [h/**Fig23**/:

09 B: [*hmh hmh hmh hmh hmh hmh .hmhhhh*

10 A: *.hhh öhhhh*

11   (0.3)

12 B: *Sellasta me£noa£.*
      That sort of bu£siness£

Toward the end of the informing (by the word *käyttäis*, "should wear"), the participants establish mutual gaze, B first turning to A, and A responding almost immediately by shifting her gaze to B. At this point, both participants have "straight faces", without observable emotional expression (see Figure 19). The facial neutrality persists to the end of the announcement.

A   B

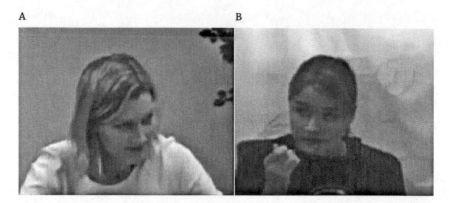

Figure 19
06   B: that they should w<u>ea</u>r **/Fig19/** a °skirt°.

During the silence that follows (line 7), however, B starts to smile, simultaneously as she puts the spoon in her mouth (see Figure 20): the corners of her mouth get drawn up, and her cheeks appear to be raised. While taking the spoon away from her mouth, she turns her head toward A and the smile gets more intensive (Figure 21), after

A   B

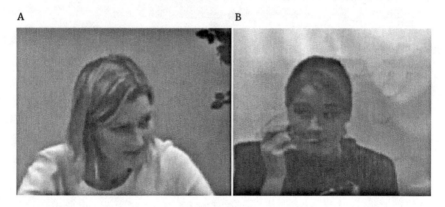

Figure 20
Silence in line 7

A   B

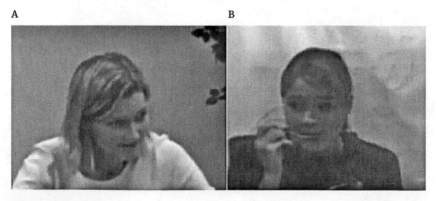

Figure 21
Silence in line 7

A   B

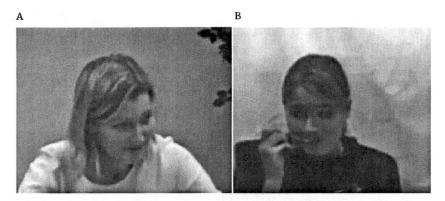

Figure 22
Silence in line 7

which she tilts her head slightly forward, and eventually (still during the silence in line 7), A starts to reciprocate the smile as the corners of her mouth raise (Figure 22).

Almost immediately after the change in the expression in her face, she begins to produce her first vocal response (line 8, Figure 23).

A   B

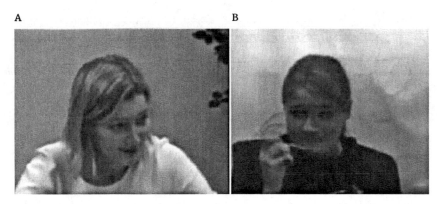

Figure 23
08   A: e[h **/Fig23/** :

B's smile, accompanied by the head moves toward the recipient, in Extract 4 serves as pursuit of response to the telling. It is in response to this smile that A, the recipient, begins to smile, and eventually produces the evaluative and appreciative vocal response to the telling in line 8. They achieve a shared stance to the telling as something foolish or ridiculous first through their reciprocated smiles (see especially Figure 22) and thereafter through aligned vocalizations (lines 8–10).

The context of the telling strongly suggests that the teller may consider that what she is reporting is foolish or ridiculous: just before, the participants have laughed at *male* dress code in the same workplace. However, in the actual delivery of the announcement in lines 5–6, B seems to be avoiding emotional expressions: she offers no lexical cues for stance, her face is nonaffective, and her tone of voice also appears to be neutral. Therefore, her stance is implicit rather than explicit at the moment of the telling. This indeed seems to be one conventionalized way of making humorous remarks: to deliver them in a matter-of-fact way, leaving it to the recipient to infer the humor. As the recipient in Extract 4 does produce an immediate response, the teller starts to smile after the completion of the telling, thereby *explicating* the affective stance of her short anecdote. She now openly indicates what kind of response she is after.

Finally, we might ask, as in the earlier extracts, why was the pursuit here made with the face, and not by adding a new verbal element to the telling? In lines 3–6, B tells a potentially and implicitly funny anecdote, with neutral face, without indicating then and there that it is meant to be funny. The fun in the announcement needs to be inferred, as it were. Should she pursue affective response verbally, especially if she then would somehow explicate the fun for example by an evaluation, her line of action would be compromised, as it would become evident that the recipient did not get the concealed humor in the announcement. Therefore, facial expression that stretches the boundaries of action and thereby gives the recipient a new chance to react, and to evaluate the story at the right spot, may serve in preserving the initial line of action in an optimal way, while still accomplishing the pursuit.

MODIFYING STANCE THROUGH FACIAL EXPRESSION

The third type of facial pursuit of response transforms or modifies the emotional stance that there was in the telling. In these cases, the initial expression does display a stance—as in cases where the facial expression reinforces such stance, see Extracts 2 and 3—but instead of reinforcing the initial stance, the facial expression modifies it. This usage of facial expression seems to be apt in tellings involving self-criticism. Consider Extract 5. The participants are having a meal, and at the beginning of the extract, B completes a sequence of assessments of the first course that they have just finished. In line 3, she begins a new topic and activity by making a noticing: she has spilled water on the table. The noticing is made in a neutral tone of voice. However, as it points out a slight misconduct by the speaker, it is hearable as involving self-criticism. The self-critical stance is also incorporated in the lexical choice, as B says "I've *already* spilled the water"—thus presupposing that spilling water is something she would be expected to do. A silence of one second ensues, whereafter the recipient, A, briefly laughs (line 6), thereby treating the matter as nonserious.

Extract 5
01   B: *Se oli oikke hyvää.*
          That was very good.

02   (3.0)

03   B: *Mä oon jo kaatanu /**Fig 24**/ve°det° /**Fig 25**/.*
          I've already spilled /**Fig 24**/the wa°ter° /**Fig 25**/.

04   (1.0) / **Fig 26/**

05   B: *hh/**Fig 27**/h*

06   A: *mhi hi̱* **/Fig 28/**

07   (?):   *.hhhh*

08   (0.3)

09   B: *Kaadettiin niin* **/Fig 29/***tä°ydet°, krhm*
            We poured them so /**Fig 29**/°full°, krhm

10   A: *M̱mmm.*

11   (0.5)

12   A: >*Mu̱l on tänään tota*< (0.7) *mä hu̱omaan et mul on tosi* (0.3)
            >I have today like< (0.7) I re̱alize that I have a real (0,3)

13   *ho̱mejuustopäivä ko,*
            blu̱e cheese day as,

The shift from the teller's self-criticism to the recipient's laughter is orchestrated through the participants' visual conduct. Through her utterance in line 3, B is gazing down, toward her tray, with neutral face. Likewise, A is gazing down (Figure 24) until she,

A   B

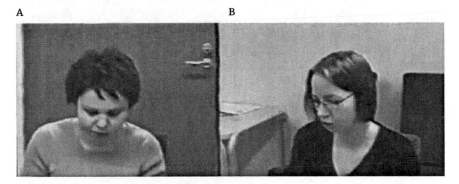

Figure 24
03   B: I've already spilled **/Fig24/** the wa°ter°.

A   B

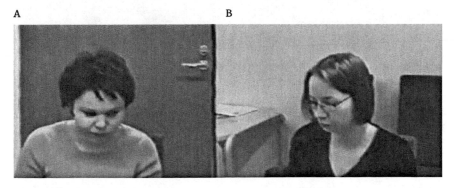

Figure 25
03   B: I've already spilled the wa°ter° **/Fig25/**

during the last word of B's utterance, shifts her gaze toward B's glass (Figure 25)—thus making available for herself what B's noticing was about.

Silence of about 0.5 seconds ensues, during which the participants maintain their positions: A looking at the glass, B looking down. A is chewing her food, and both participants maintain neutral faces. Then B starts to shift her gaze toward A, moving her head slightly up and to the recipient, who almost immediately responds by a corresponding move to B. Simultaneously with her gaze shift, B starts to smile (see Figure 26). Her smile gets more intensive as she breathes out (Figure 27).

A   B

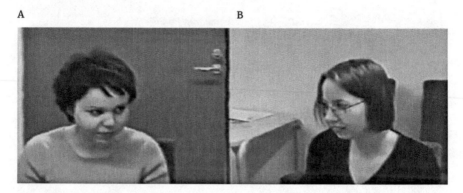

Figure 26
Silence in line 4.

A   B

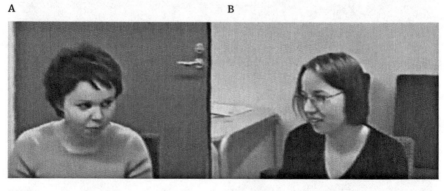

Figure 27
05   B: *hh/**Fig27**/ h*

At the end of B's outbreath, A withdraws from mutual orientation, starts to smile, and shakes her head strongly to the left (Figure 28) and then back. During the head-shake, she also produces two laugh tokens (line 6). B withdraws her gaze from A quickly after the coparticipant's gaze withdrawal. Gazing down, she maintains her smile through lines 6–9 in the transcript. In line 9, while both participants are again gazing down, B smilingly gives an account of her misconduct (Figure 29). A new topic and action are started by A in line 12.

A   B

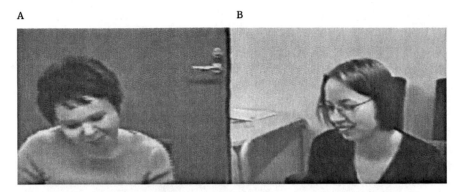

Figure 28
06   A: *mhi hị* **/Fig28/**

A   B

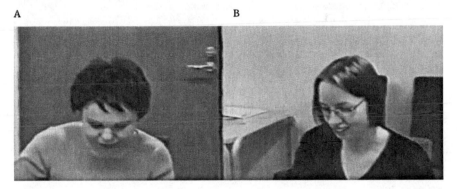

Figure 29
09   B: we poured them so **/Fig29/** °full°, krhm

B's gaze and smile in lines 4 and 5 (Figures 26 and 27) modify the stance of the teller when facing a delayed response. They occur while the recipient of a noticing is silent. Given the lack of mutual gaze during the notification (Figures 24 and 25), it may not, at the time of its production, have involved a strong invitation for a response (see Stivers & Rossano, 2010). However, as the speaker shifts her gaze to the recipient and smiles, a response is made relevant. Simultaneously, the emotional stance of the notification gets modified. During its occurrence, it observably involved the speaker's (at least mild) self-criticism; any humor possibly involved in the noticing was concealed and not oriented to by the recipient either. B's smile makes the stance light and humorous. It is this modified stance that the recipient orients herself to and reciprocates, through her laugh tokens, smile, and headshake, which as a *Gestalt* convey that the "misconduct" is amusing and nothing to worry about.

In Extract 5, the modification of stance through facial expression seems to serve as means for managing the complex relevancies of response to self-criticism. The preferred response to self-criticism is disagreement (Pomerantz, 1984b). In Extract 5, however, the speakers' notification that conveys self-criticism is hard to deny (unlike in assessments of appearances, for example): the water undeniably is there on the table, and the recipient is gazing at it (see Figure 25). Thus, the recipient is in an awkward situation where the preference organization would encourage her to distance herself from the speaker's notification, but her visible orientation to the environment does not afford that. A facial pursuit that modifies speakers' stance toward their telling from a self-blame into a laughable assertion efficiently saves the recipient from this awkward situation.

Our analysis has shown some variations of what we have called "facial pursuits of response." These consist of a particular combination of an observable change of the facial expression of the speaker and a head turn toward the coparticipant. Such facial pursuits can be found in a particular sequential location: at the closure of a telling with a stance, when response is delayed. We saw three types of semantic operations that were performed by the facial pursuits: reinforcing, explicating, and modifying the stance of the preceding telling. We also saw how such facial pursuits were reciprocated, providing the recipient was gazing at the speaker to observe the change in her facial expression. As compared with verbal pursuits, facial pursuits were different in one important respect. They could be situated within the transition space between turns of talk, adding a clarifying or modifying element to it *without* verbally respecifying and in this way slightly altering the focus of the action. In this way, facial pursuits were capable of retrieving an affiliating response from the coparticipant without overtly marking the preceding turn of talk as a trouble-source of some kind—they were capable of "stretching the boundaries of the ongoing action" (see also Peräkylä & Ruusuvuori, 2006; Ruusuvuori & Peräkylä, 2009).

DISCUSSION

At the beginning of this chapter, we pointed out that the face is special among the multimodal means of communication, as it is arguably specialized in the expression of emotion. This paper has shown that in spite of this specialized task, the face does not work on its own. We examined the intimate linkages between facial expression and the actions—such as storytelling, complaining, or self-criticism—carried out through spoken utterances. Our examples showed how facial expression of emotion was part of the multimodal organization of action at its particular junction. Our findings give further support to Goodwin & Goodwin's (2000; see also this volume, chapter 2) conceptualization of emotion as multimodal stance display.

Facial pursuits display the stance of the speaker at the closure of a telling and give cues for a relevant way to respond to the telling. They facilitate an affiliating response, a reciprocal display of emotion. They emerge *in situ*, as a device to regain affective balance when facing possible disaffiliation and increased distance between the participants. With facial pursuits, the speaker thus regulates her immediate affective environment.

The facial expressions that we examined in this chapter have much in common with the verbal pursuits examined by Pomerantz (1984a) in nonvisual settings. As compared with verbal pursuits, one interactional advantage of the facial pursue arises from the capacity of the facial expression to stretch the boundaries of action. The facial pursuit, more than a verbal pursuit, leaves the initial action intact, as no new unit of talk is added to it. The teller does not have to explain or give grounds for her stance, when she reinforces, clarifies, or even modifies it through facial expression. Therefore, facial pursuit minimizes the rupture of progressivity of interaction and the breach of the affective relation between the participants.

In future studies, it would be worthwhile to compare systematically the uses of facial and verbal pursuits. Pomerantz's (1984a) study suggests that there is a relative ordering between the different types of verbal pursuit: clarifying referent encodes orientation to the least serious problem and hence, it can be the first choice of pursuit; while reviewing common knowledge and revising opinion orient to more of a problem, and they are resorted to only if clarifying reference fails or is not relevant. Our observations suggest the possibility that there might be similar sorts of relative ordering between facial and verbal pursuits: due to their capacity to preserve the prior action, and to minimize the nonprogressivity, facial pursuit might be something to be tried first. That was indeed the case in Extract 3: the facial pursuit was the speaker's first effort to pursue response, and as it failed, the speaker resorted to verbal pursuits. More systematic comparison of facial and verbal pursuits could clarify the matter.

Our observations lend themselves for elaborating some of the key ideas of regulation of emotion. For Gross and Thompson (2007, pp. 10–16), emotion regulation has five facets: situation selection, situation modification, attentional deployment, cognitive change, and response modulation. Each of these can be investigated from the point of view of an individual actor. However, it appears that interactional research such as that reported in this chapter can elaborate what these facets might involve. Our results address all but the first facet (situation selection).

The most obvious linkage concerns *response modulation*, which for Gross and Thompson (2007, p. 15) involves "influencing physiological, experiential or behavioral responding." An individual's means of response modulation vary from drugs, exercise, and relaxation to reflection and verbalization of the emotional experience. The picture of emotional response modulation becomes rather different if we focus on interaction process rather than on individual. We showed that a key aspect of what Gross and Thompson would call "behavioral response", that is, facial expression of emotion, is very intimately linked to the organization of interaction. The interactants timed their facial expression in relation to turn transition (at the completion of utterances) and the organization of larger activities (at the end of activities such as storytelling, troubles telling, complaining). In producing these expressions, they were attentive to their recipient's actions, producing facial pursuits when the recipients had not reciprocated the teller's stance. Thus, response modulation was adapted to the momentary contingencies of the interaction process. We also showed that facial expression was there to elicit consequences in the cointeractant. Thus, modulation of emotional expression is not only as it were looking backward (downregulating or upregulating an emotional response to a trigger) but it is also looking forward, in inviting the cointeractant into relevant emotional activity, in this case, to reciprocate the stance of the telling.

Interaction is also consequential to issues pertaining to *situation modification*, which involves efforts to change some features in a situation that triggers emotions in individuals. Gross and Thompson (2007, p. 12) point out that emotional expressions can in themselves modify the situation: crying, for example, halting an escalation of anger. Our observations are in line with this. We showed how the emotional relevance of a situation is modified moment by moment through the subtle choices that the interactants make in designing their vocal and nonvocal actions. The first speakers (the tellers) in our data extracts were monitoring the recipient actions at the completion of the telling and designed their further actions accordingly (pursuing response through facial expression if the recipient had not reciprocated the stance of the telling). Thus, for the first speakers, the recipient action was a key feature of the situation. Then, if an affiliating response did not occur at the moment where it would be expected, the first speakers reinforced, explicated, or modified their own stance displays, thereby modifying the situation to be responded to by the second speaker. Our observations demonstrate how the situation modification is a thoroughly reflexive process, as the interactants' momentary actions constitute the situation for the cointeractants.

Our observations also speak to *attentional deployment*, which for Gross and Thompson (2007, p. 13) involves the ways in which "individuals direct their attention within a given situation in order to influence their emotions." Attention can be shifted away from emotion-eliciting stimuli, or it can be drawn to them. A recurrent feature in our extracts incorporates interactive attentional deployment. In producing their facial pursuits of response, the interactants regularly moved their heads toward the recipients while changing their facial expression. In Extract 5, the head move co-occurred with the speaker turning her gaze to the recipient, but in most cases the speaker and recipient had already established mutual orientation when the speaker produced the facial expression couched by the head movements. Our case-by-case analysis does not warrant any conclusions, but it is a sensible hypothesis that these systematic head movements toward the recipient, concomitant with facial expressions, served to intensify the attention that the gazing recipients pays to them. Thus, our observations suggest that the tellers were at key moments (at the completion of a telling that had not received stance reciprocation) not only displaying affect through their face, but they were also engaged in a particular activity, head movement, to draw their recipients' attention to that display. Attentional deployment, as part of the interactional regulation of emotion, is thus a momentarily unfolding collaborative achievement.

Cognitive change is yet another facet of emotion regulation that our observations address. In Gross and Thompson's terms (2007, p. 14) it involves "changing how we appraise the situation we are in to alter its emotional significance." Interactional management of cognitive change was taking place in cases where the first speakers *explicated* (Extract 4) or *modified* (Extract 5) the emotional valence of their telling through their postcompletion facial expressions. The facial expressions served as invitations for the recipient to reconsider, at that very moment, the stance attached to the telling just completed. By their responses, the recipients then showed the corresponding "reappraised" stance—in Extract 4, unambiguously, and in Extract 5, ambiguously. So, also cognitive change can be seen as an interactional achievement.

In existing literature, the concept of emotion regulation is predominantly used to refer to regulatory processes *within* individuals. As conversation analysts, we are not investigating individuals but interactions. However, as the discussion above shows, there seem to be sensible linkages and parallels between the way in which the individual-centered process of emotion regulation is understood, and our findings on interactional regulation of expressions of emotion. Individual regulation and interactional regulation may be two sides of the same coin. That is what Beebe and Lachmann (2002, p. 22) suggest: there is "an intimate connection between self-and interaction regulation." Basically, they argue that the same behaviors that entail interactional regulation of emotion, also serve for self-regulation, and that the interactional regulation and the self-regulation for that reason comprise a system.

Our data as such do not give us access to self-regulation, as they show only interactional regulation. But the parallels between our findings and the way in which researchers have broken down the concept of individual regulation of emotion are in line with the "systemic" argument put forward by Beebe and Lachmann. From the point of view of interaction research, it appears that the practices of the interactional regulation of emotion can serve as the springboard of the self-regulatory processes. Situation modification, attentional deployment, cognitive changes, and response modulation take place in and through interaction, and these interactive processes may be the substrate from which the individuals' emotion regulation arises.

CHAPTER 5

ᐧᔪᐧ

Good News, Bad News, and Affect

Practical and Temporal "Emotion Work" in Everyday Life

DOUGLAS W. MAYNARD AND JEREMY FREESE

When we deliver or receive bad and good tidings, however mild or extreme, it momentarily disrupts involvement in a social world whose contours and features we may otherwise unthinkingly accept. Along with this disruption, more or less strong emotions may be evoked. In this respect, episodes of bad and good news in interaction demonstrate the relation "between common understanding and affects" that Garfinkel (1967, p. 50) discusses. In and through the delivery and reception of news, common understandings and taken-for-granted orientations undergo more or less profound change, and participants experience a kind of interruption or *epoché* as they begin to realize and realign to a transfigured social world (Maynard, 2003). In so doing, participants may undergo and produce a variety of emotional reactions and displays. Our concern in this chapter is with how participants in interaction organize these experiences and reactions according to the unfolding of news delivery sequences.

Sociology and the social psychology of emotions provide a number of approaches to understanding the role of affect[1] in everyday life. They range from objectivist, structural theories that posit relations between sociodemographic status characteristics or social positioning and emotion (Kemper 1984; Kemper & Collins 1990), to subjectivist psychodynamic ones that draw on Freud and promote an understanding of how social functioning requires adequate (rather than blocked) processing of emotions related to loss or other experiences (Scheff, 1997, 2000). In between these approaches, and most relevant for our investigation, are two ways of studying emotion that help in distinguishing our road to the social organization of affect and emotion in everyday life. One approach involves social constructionism and the other draws on dramaturgy and discusses emotion "work" as the effort to bring displays of affect in line with the social rules governing their appropriate expression. In relation to these approaches, we develop notions of *co*-construction and the collaborative accomplishment of the emotions involved in bad and good news. And, by exploring of issues of conversational sequencing, we show that the social organization of affect involves "work," but not in a strictly rule-bound manner whereby participants align their emotions with abstract strictures for expression. Rather, there is the unfolding practical and temporal matter of action and reaction in real time as deliverer and recipient both cue and handle the cues of the other as to the *valence* of the news—the evaluative and affective stance deliverer and recipient take toward some reported event. To the degree that this stance may comport with emotion rules, that comportment is an outcome of embodied concrete practices rather than something effected by the rules or adherence to them as such.

SOCIAL CONSTRUCTIONISM: PROCEDURAL AND PRACTICAL EMOTION

Social constructionism involves the idea that features of social worlds are not inherent in those worlds, but instead are assemblages that participants produce and define. If affect and emotions as features are constructed, it contradicts the idea that they are natural responses flowing from a person's reaction to events or experiences, and it implies that they may be contingent upon specific social practices that may vary in specific groups, cultures, or societies. Constructionists who discuss emotion often cite the research by Schacter and Singer (1962), which showed that when experimental subjects were given an injection of epinephrine, but were not told about the physiological arousal the injection would cause, confederates could manipulate subjects' emotions by exposing them to expressions of anger or happiness. Similarly, Becker's (1953) classic research on marijuana usage suggested that neophytes' experiences and whether they feel "high" or something else depend on the interpretations that members of the peer group offer to the person.

Later versions of social constructionism propose turning attention away from the relation between physiological states and imposed definitions to focus almost entirely on participants' *use* of emotion vocabularies or ascriptions. Discursive psychologists, for example, examine emotion vocabularies and refer to emotion discourse as a "way of talking" (Edwards, 1999, pp. 277–8). "Instead of asking the question, 'What is Anger?'," Harré (1986, p. 5) writes, "we would do well by asking, How is the word 'anger' . . . actually used in this or that cultural milieu and type of episode?" Coulter (1986, p. 127) likewise suggests that the linkages between situations and emotional states are conventional rather than deterministic or biological, and ascriptions (emotion vocabularies) can be present even when feeling states or arousals are not. Witnesses to displays of affect who cannot find a meaningful ascription to describe it may make imputations about the social competence of the individual and suggest hallucinations, illness, or other sources for the display.

This focus on vocabularies, ascriptions, and the like is taken up in Whalen and Zimmerman's (1998) study of 9-1-1 emergency calls. They argue that the emotion category "hysteria" is neither something inherent in a person's behavior, nor something they necessarily feel, nor what people uniformly ascribe to a behavior independent of context. Concretely, an emotion word like hysteria is assigned to a helpline caller when he or she cannot facilitate the verbal and form-filling tasks that are necessary to the call-taker's task of dispatching emergency personnel. Within that task, the word is an organizational designation in the sense of providing an account for the inability to assemble an actionable textual record.

Certainly there can be "feelings" or internal states experienced in association with displays (Stets, 2003, p. 310), but our research on bad and good news shares the constructionist commitment to studying displays of emotion in interaction and remaining agnostic about the existence of internal accompaniments to such displays. Also consistent with the constructionist tradition, we regard the valence of news as determined not by some intrinsic goodness or badness that a reported event-in-the-world may have. Rather, valence develops according to the actions of deliverer and recipient as they take an evaluative stance through a four-part news delivery sequence (Maynard, 1997; 2003, chapter 4). That is, participants orient to announcements of information in terms of its novelty as well as its perceived affective significance.

Participants to a news delivery can display valence by way of lexical items, as in preannouncement forecasts (e.g., "I have some *bad news* for you"), or, more frequently, postannouncement assessments (e.g., "Oh that's *terrible*"). Another way of ascribing the valence of the news is through prosody, which is the focus of this chapter. Prosody here is used loosely to collect aspects of talk such as pitch, intonation, loudness, and speech rate, as well as more properly paralinguistic features such as voice quality (Szczepek Reed, 2011). As participants work through a news delivery sequence and deploy prosody, we explore how their methods are embedded parts of the interaction. That is, the social constructionism we explore means attending to ways in which speakers design their talk and action to take into account how a coparticipant potentially may or actually does respond in the course of an utterance's production. How an event in the world comes to be news with a particular valence and affective quality depends on collaborative, concerted action and interaction.

Attention to prosody for its role in coproduction can draw on conversation analysts (Couper-Kuhlen & Ford, 2004; Couper-Kuhlen & Selting, 1996; French & Local, 1983; Goodwin & Goodwin, 2000; Local, Kelly, & Wells, 1986; Szczepek Reed, 2011; Selting, 1992) who have greatly advanced our understanding in this area. We draw on this research to demonstrate that the social constructionist approach to emotion—where that has referred to affective displays "embedded in local contexts of social actions" (Whalen & Zimmerman, 1998, p. 158)—can be advanced through an ethnomethodological and conversation-analytic approach that emphasizes the concreteness of both the practical and temporal aspects of participants' methods.

PRACTICAL AND TEMPORAL "EMOTION WORK": THE NEWS DELIVERY SEQUENCE

In a well-known study about the social ordering of affective experience, Hochschild (1979) developed the notion of "emotion management" as consonant with the work needed to deal with emotion rules. Participants must engage in this work to bring feelings in line with what is appropriate to display in social situations. While Hochschild's (1979, 1983) studies concerned flight attendants and other service workers who manage their own and their clients' feelings, the notion of "emotion work" has been extended to other settings such as public ones that users of wheelchairs may inhabit (Cahill & Eggleston, 1994), medical schools where students deal with training experiences (Smith & Kleinman, 1989), and others.

Although it has not been noted before, the concept of emotion work fits with what Sacks (1984a) has suggested about "doing being ordinary," "entitlement to experience," and how one's emotional perception of an event is conditioned by access to that event, whether directly by immediate involvement or indirectly (as a recipient of story from someone with such involvement). In his lectures, Sacks (1984a; 1992, vol. 2, pp. 242–8) proposes that entitlement to experience has to do not so much with rules but with the *practices* by which one shows, through positioning a story in conversation or other devices, just what sort of experience a particular reported event was for the speaker. For example, a teller can display the importance of a story and the experience it embodies by delivering the story sooner rather than later in a conversation. Other practices include telling the story in such a way as to highlight what anyone who has similar involvements usually or commonly feels, rather than claiming exceptional or superlative experience (Sacks, 1984a, pp. 428–9). For their part, recipients of stories about difficult life events exhibit secondary access to what the teller has undergone. Accordingly, for analyzing the social regulation of emotional experience, it is possible to examine actual design features of members' methods and conversational practices rather than abstract rules and norms.

Taking this cue, and drawing on Hochschild's concepts of emotion management and work, we extend a strong analytic base for investigating news deliveries, which occupy a recurrent sequential form. Sacks (1992, vol. 2, p. 572) discusses this form in terms of the consecutive occurrence of "news announcement – surprise" and "news development – sympathy" pairs in bad-news deliveries, and Jefferson (1981, p. 62) reframes the "prototype" news delivery as a four-part sequence. Maynard (1997, 2003) refined these observations into a general News Delivery Sequence (NDS) that provides for instances of both good and bad news (as well as other kinds). The NDS is a four-part sequence comprising, (1) a News Announcement. (2) an Announcement Response, (3) an Elaboration, and (4) an Assessment.

The canonical four-turn NDS is subject to innumerable orderly transpositions in the course of actual conversation, including the condensation of the four parts into two or three turns, and the extension of the sequence through a series of appended elaborations and assessments. Each of the NDS parts can be manipulated prosodically to display affect regarding the news, which means that in and through the NDS, there is practical temporal work to manage displays of emotion in conjunction with other devices whereby participants establish the valence of the news across the four turns.[2] "Practical" means that there are practices, devices, or members' methods (Garfinkel, 1967) by which participants assemble a news delivery including its affective features. And "temporal" refers to the work by which participants build the news delivery in a sequential, step-by-step manner in real time. And finally, to the extent that emotion is a social construction, we treat it as collaboratively managed on a turn-by-turn basis in association with the social action that a sequence of talk implements. In face-to-face encounters, gesture, gaze, and posture all can be involved. In this chapter, we deal with telephone conversations and focus on the talk and its prosody, through which ascriptions of valence and affect are displayed across the four turns of the prototypical NDS.

PRACTICAL AND TEMPORAL WORK: AN ILLUSTRATION

Before our systematic description of prosodic phenomena associated with bad and good news, an illustration using an episode of good news can further demonstrate what we mean by the practical temporal work involved in emotion displays, and clarify our social constructionist position. The following extract is from a conversation telephone call between two friends, Andi and Betty. They live in different parts of the United States, and call one another periodically for purposes of updating one another on family and other events. The extract begins just after they have been talking about riding in minivans on long distances, and how difficult the sitting can be on "bottoms." At line 1, referencing this previous talk, Andi, in a prototypical "pre-pre" device (Schegloff, 1980) that can foreshadow the delicacy of forthcoming news, asks whether Betty is "sitting do::wn." She then preannounces some "surprising" news (lines 3 and 5)[3]. After Betty's "go ahead" signals, which ask for (line 4) and then urge the "telling" (line 6), Andi produces the announcement at line 7.

Extract 1 [PND3:18]
```
01   Andi:    Well, speaking of bottoms, are you sitting do::wn?
02   Betty:   Yea::h
03   Andi:    Well we have some news for you.
04   Betty:   What?
05   Andi:.   hhh that may come as a bit of a surprise ehhh!
06   Betty:   I see- what are you telling me?
07   Andi:    hhhh! Bob and I are going to have a baby.
08   Betty:   Oh my good↑ness hhow-(1.0) did you have a reversal-he have
09            a reversal?
10   Andi:    Yea:h.
11               (1.0)
12   Andi:    .hhh [::::::::::]
13   Betty:        [↑whe::n.]
14   Andi:    tch eyup. Last ↑March.
15               (0.4)
16   Andi:    .mhhh ((sniff))
17   Betty:   O↑H [↓MY  ↑G:OOD]↑↑NESS:
18   Andi:        [And  (ituh)    ]
```

```
19  Andi:    It was [very    succe̲s̲sful,]   [v̲ery quickly] hh::h  .hhh
20  Betty:         [↑OH  I'M   SO]  [↑H̲A̲P̲PY.  ]
```

As subsequent questioning by Betty (lines 8–9) reveals, Andi's husband Bob had had a vasectomy. This was something well known by their friends, including Betty. Hence, when she first hears the news, it can be, according to the way the news was preannounced, very surprising indeed, as her "Oh my good↑ness" (line 9) displays in part through its rise–fall–rise prosodic contour. In Figure 1(a), we can observe the "Oh" registering at about 200 Hz (which is the approximate level of Betty's line 6 utterance also), the "my" falling to 70 Hz, and "goodness" escalating to around 300 Hz.[4] As indicated by her subsequent question about whether Bob had a "reversal" (lines 6–7), Betty does not yet know what Andi's announcement means or how to appraise the news. After Andi confirms that Bob did have a reversal (line 10) and responds (line 14) to a further question about its timing, Betty produces, in crescendo-like fashion, another "oh my goodness" utterance (line 17) but with both increased pitch and volume (Figure 1(b)).

With such contrasting prosody and amplification, Betty thereby displays what she goes on to claim at line 20—she is "so happy," which utterance she also speaks with elevated volume, rising intonation, and stress on the focal word (line 20, Figure 1(c)). This is a dramatic celebration and affect-laden show of positive regard for the news.

The practical, temporal, interactional work involved in managing the news includes how, in real time, Betty responds to Andi's pregnancy announcement by an expression of surprise (line 8) that withholds assessment. Only subsequent to Andi's elicited and incremental elaborations of the news (lines 10, 13), which contribute to the understanding of just what sort of news it is, does Betty at line 17 use the same utterance type[5] as employed at line 8, but now in a more expressive fashion (compare Figure 1 (a) and (b)) to adumbrate a good news assessment that is then lexically expressed with Betty's claim of being "so happy" at line 20. Accordingly, we can observe the social construction of affect—here, toward a pregnancy—that the talk heralds. Methodically, participants deploy announcement, response, elaboration, and assessment turns in a news delivery sequence along with prosodic manipulations. They do so in a temporal fashion—that is, through synchronized, progressive, interactional practices—to display emotional features of the event.

It has been said that bad and good news are not about events as fixed and existing objectively in the outside world. Rather, in ordered increments of interactively

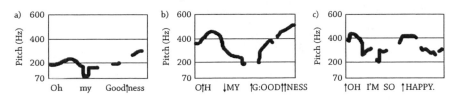

Figure 1
Responses by Same Speaker to News Delivery and Elaboration (Extract 1), a: line 8; b: line 17; c: line 20

produced talk, participants accord events-in-the-world their *in situ* newsworthy status and their *in vivo* valence as favorable or unfavorable happenings (Maynard, 1997, 2003). Along with achieving the newsworthiness and valence of some event-in-world, participants also may coproduce affective features and displays of emotional experience that the event may entail for them.

By "experience," we do not mean some internal emotional state. Rather, consistent with the pragmatist notion of "return to experience," we eschew the bifurcation between consciousness and embodied conduct (or more generally, mind and nature) and mean to capture the concreteness of practices through which participants engage courses of conduct and exhibit the sensuous quality of such conduct.[6] That they may socially construct the event in these ways does not mean they regard themselves as manufacturing the event and its qualities. Indeed, participants' sense may be that the news is inherently bad or good, as the case may be, and that their displays of affect emanate from within and are not under their control. Such a stance is not incompatible with the orderliness that turns up by way of close inspection of the practices of talk and interaction. In any case, prosody is a particularly important vehicle for coproduction, and we now can specify some of the artful ways that prosody is used to ascribe affect and valence in each of the four turns of the NDS. Afterward, we discuss how prosodic manipulations may not only contribute to the establishment and affective evaluation of news, but also provide a means for showing what sort of experience of the event coparticipants are permitted to display during its conveyance depending on their situated identities as deliverer and recipient.

PROSODIC CHARACTERISTICS OF GOOD AND BAD NEWS

The data for this chapter are approximately 100 good and bad naturally occurring conversational news deliveries assembled from several available corpora of American and British telephone conversations.[7] The first author compiled these deliveries as part of a larger ethnomethodological and conversation analytic study (Maynard, 2003), and they were the basis of an earlier paper (Freese & Maynard, 1998). When we compared lexically transparent good and bad news deliveries, certain prosodic patterns could be identified as recurrent within deliveries of each valence. The patterns were often capable of pairing such that a phenomenon prevalent in good news deliveries would have its opposite in bad news deliveries. Recurrent features were present across the course of the delivery and marked the speech of both deliverers and recipients. The orderliness of these phenomena suggested their methodic use by conversationalists.

Prosodic differences between good and bad news are summarized in Table 5.1.[8] The prosodic characteristics of good and bad news deliveries closely resemble what has been identified in previous research as expressive of positive and negative emotions more generally (Couper-Kuhlen, 1986, pp. 173–87; Goudbeek & Scherer, 2009). As a result, the characteristic structures may be heard to display "enjoyment" in the telling and receiving of good news and "regret" in telling and receiving bad news,

Table 5.1 CHARACTERISTIC PROSODIC STRUCTURES OF GOOD AND BAD NEWS.
The Features can be Compared to the Table of Prosodic Correlates of various emotions provided by Couper-Kuhlen (1986, p. 181), especially the Prosodic Structure of "Happiness" and "Sorrow."

	Good news	Bad news
Pitch level	High	Low, excepting displays of surprise at the start of Announcement Responses
Pitch range	Increased, wide	Narrow
Contour	Frequent, sharp, and often abrupt steps-up and rises; announcement responses sometimes produced with a high onset and with a sustained high contour	Stretched vowels with pronounced falling pitch
Voice quality	Normal	Often breathy or creaky
Loudness	Very loud on key words	Key words sometimes quieter
Speech rate	Fast; tending to speed up as the utterance progresses	Slow; tending to slow down as the utterance progresses

although it is prosody in combination with turn design and sequential organization rather than prosody abstractly or independently that matter for the ascription of affect (Local & Walker, 2008). Still, these patterns are consistent with previous observations that conversationalists asymmetrically value good news over bad (Maynard, 2003, chapter 6), as some of the prosodic differences appear to accentuate good news and diminish bad. For example, the faster speech rate and increased pitch range associated with good news can be heard to indicate "eagerness" and "excitedness," while the reduced speech rate and constricted pitch range of bad news may indicate the "reluctance" or "difficulty" with which it is presented. Couper-Kuhlen and Selting (1996) argue that intonation assists in contextualizing, and we suggest that prosody, in conjunction with other resources of talk, helps enact a systematic valuation of good news over bad.

It must be emphasized, however, that none of the features listed in the table occur in all good or bad news deliveries or only in news deliveries; prosodic devices are highly multifunctional and achieve their significance through systematic relationships with lexical, sequential, and situational information. One can therefore never claim a deterministic relationship between prosody and meaning, but rather can only note the utility of particular prosodic structures when employed in particular sequential environments. When an utterance is a constituent of a news delivery, prosodic manipulations may act to make the utterance further recognizable as proposing the news to be good or bad and with particular affect. As a result, abstract descriptions of a characteristic structure cannot by themselves illuminate how participants use prosody, and instead the task requires a close analysis of real interactional data.

VALENCE ASCRIPTION IN NEWS DELIVERY SEQUENCES

We will examine the four turns of the News Delivery Sequence for the detail involved in how each turn can be involved in the display of affect.

Initiating turns

News Announcements may be produced in response to another's inquiry (Button & Casey, 1984), may follow a preannouncement of the speaker's (Terasaki, 2004 [1976]), or they may initiate a delivery sequence.[9] Although news inquiries and pre-announcements of course can be involved in the display of affective features associated with news, in this chapter we concentrate, although not exclusively, on the NDS itself, starting with the news announcement.

By building ascriptions of valence into their first turn, deliverers can more insistently dramatize the forthcoming news and sequentially implicate a response that aligns with the proposed valence. Ascriptions made in the News Announcement turn implicate acceptance much more strongly than ascriptions in news inquiries, although there are instances of "problematic presumptiveness" (Maynard, 2003, p. 113), when the valence proposed in a news inquiry is rejected in the next turn by the deliverer. Conversely, nowhere in our corpus did a recipient fail to align with a deliverer's valence proposed in the Announcement turn. Indeed, it seems possible that prosodic ascriptions in Announcements provide recipients with a valuable resource for interpreting implications of the reported news:

Extract 2 H13G [Holt:1988:2:4:1]
```
01   Carrie:   I: ↑thought you'd li↑ke to know I've g↑ot a lit'l
02             ↓ gran'daughter
03   Leslie:   ˙thlk ↑Oh: how love↓ly.
```

In Extract 2, the birth of a new granddaughter is accomplished as good news, beginning with the deployment of several prosodic markers of positive valence in the News Announcement turn: rises on "thought," "like," and "got," as well as increased speed near the end of the utterance. The prosody is therefore upbeat and provides for an immediate positive assessment of the news, which Leslie produces with a sustained high contour that moves from the high onset of the surprise token through the assessment, before dropping on the final syllable. Deliverers use prosody in the Announcement turn to propose a valence for the entire sequence, and these ascriptions structure the interpretation of the presented information in a way that enables recipient alignment in the next turn.

Announcement Responses

Announcement Responses do regularly align with the proposed valence of the preceding turn. By incorporating aligning ascription into responses, recipients display their understanding of the news as consistent with that of the deliverer. This is true whether the news is bad or good, and here we illustrate with an episode of good news.[10] In Extract 3, Robbie's Announcement (line 2) has markers of positive valence: a rushed speech rate, raised amplitude, and a sharp upward movement on "two" (Figure 2).

Extract 3 H05G (retranscribed)
01   Leslie: ↑Did um (.) ˙tch (.) ↑Did <u>uh</u> you get that ↓book back↓
02   Robbie: ↓I've got ↑<u>two</u> books f'you:,
03   Leslie: Have ↑↑<u>YOU:</u> OH <u>goo</u>hhd

Then, the middle two syllables of Leslie's response (line 3 above, Figure 3 below) are produced at a pitch that is much higher than ordinary female speech. Additionally, the utterance is performed with raised amplitude and a faster speech rate. Leslie's response is clearly produced with a prosodic structure indicative of good news, and includes a lexical assessment of positive valence as well. Leslie's response thus embellishes or accentuates the valence and display of affect that Robbie initiated in her previous turn.

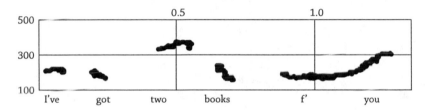

Figure 2
Extract 3, line 2

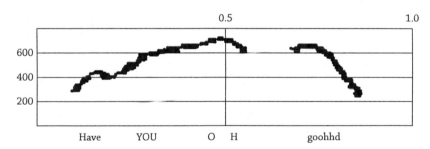

Figure 3
Extract 3, line 3

While prosodic ascriptions in the Announcement Response turn were very common in the corpus, lexical ascriptions were much less so. Of eighty-nine deliveries in the corpus, sixty-one featured a hearable prosodic ascription of valence in the Announcement Response, while only thirty-two employed some sort of lexical ascription. Lexical ascriptions of valence, such those occurring in "oh"-prefaced assessments (i.e., "oh good" or "oh how terrible") or assessments preceded by a Newsmark, as below in Extract 4, appear to help organize the preceding information as a potentially complete item of news (Heritage, 1984b). Although more details can be (and usually are) provided in subsequent Elaboration turns, no more is needed for the information to be assessable in its own right, and the deliverer may choose to move on to another topic or item of news:

Extract 4 H3G [Holt:X(C)1:2:7:8]

```
01   Leslie:   We had a ↑very nice evening at the(k) (0.3) Ditchit-(0.2)
02             Old Time Musi[c Ha:ll.]
03   Mum:                   [↑O h::] ↓did ↑you ↓that's goo↑[:d
04   Leslie:                                              ['hhh An'
05             Gordon went to watch Big Country las' week at um the
06             Sharring Pavillion (Chetsham Mallet)?
```

When prosodic ascriptions in the Announcement Response turn are not accompanied by a lexical assessment, they can have a more provisional character. While an alignment is made, the recipient indexes her understanding that the deliverer will provide more information before the sequence is complete.

Extract 5 H15B [Holt:M88:1:5:28]

```
01   Leslie:   'hhh ↑Well: th:this ↑is eh why I'm not ↑quite ↓so well at
02             th'moment I'd though I'd got t'the: bottom a'my ↑allergies but
03             I came out'n most ↑terr↓ible rash last week.hhh [h h
04   Robbie:                                                 [↑Oh: [↓:
05   Leslie:                                                      [An' I wz
06             telling th'm all at school how m'ch better I wa:s but I: think
07             it might have been: um primulas I touched.
08                         (.)
09   Robbie:   ↑Oh you poor ↑↑thi::ng.
```

The Announcement Response above (line 4) follows a delivery of news that has the design of a "surprise source" (Wilkinson & Kitzinger, 2006), in which Leslie reveals a discrepancy between the expected improvement of her allergy condition and the actual outcome. As Leslie draws an inbreath (line 3), Robbie's "Oh" (line 4) allows for Leslie's continuation, and she moves without delay to an Elaboration. Here, as indicated by the arrows,[11] the "Oh" displays the high onset and rising–falling contour indicative of surprise, and may thereby encourage Leslie's Elaboration (lines 5–7), rather than discourage it as may be usual with freestanding "oh"-tokens. After the elaboration, Robbie produces a sympathetic lexical assessment (line 9).

Elaborations

By the first Elaboration turn, an ascription of valence has sometimes been offered by one party and ratified by the other. Consequently, an ascription in the Elaboration can be more an affirmation of a valence that has already been mutually established than an independent appraisal in its own right. This is not interactionally redundant, however; by providing the same ascription as the recipient in the previous turn, the deliverer also confirms that the recipient's displayed understanding of the news and its valence align to the affective trajectory adumbrated in the announcement or any preannouncement. In the corpus, ascriptions of valence were done in the Elaboration turn using the same collection of prosodic devices that were used to ascribe valence in previous turns of the delivery sequence, but there were no instances in which a lexical ascription was made in a first Elaboration.

A news delivery will often have more than one Elaboration–Assessment pair. These pairs may all reiterate the valence established in the News Announcement and Announcement Response:[12]

Extract 6 Extension of Extract 2

```
01    Carrie:   I: ↑thought you'd li↑ke to know I've g↑ot a lit'l
02              ↓gran'daughter
03    Leslie:   ˙thlk ↑Oh: how love↓ly.
04    Carrie:   ↓Ye:s bo:rn th's early hours'v this ↓morning.
05    Leslie:   ˙k↑Oh: joll[y goo:d, [h
06    Carrie:              [↓Ye:s  [↑Christi:ne ↓Ru [th.
07    Leslie:                      [˙hhhhh ↑hOh:: that's
08              ↓ni::ce:.h What a nice name.
```

The positive valence of this delivery is established in the first two turns (see Extract 2). Although Carrie does not provide her own lexical evaluation in the first Elaboration turn (line 4), her "Yes" aligns with Leslie's positive assessment, and the Elaboration also provides a positive prosodic ascription through the use of a wide-ranging, animated pitch, which has an almost songlike quality, after which Leslie proposes an "oh"-prefaced lexical characterization of affect, "jolly good." Carrie also provides a confirming "Yes" at the beginning of her second Elaboration (line 6), which is produced with an intonation highly similar to the first, and the positive trajectory is sustained by Leslie's third lexical assessment in lines 7–8. Thus, elaborations are each heard as assessable in their own right while preserving the strongly positive valence of the delivery as a whole.

An issue emerges here as to whether it is possible retrospectively to cast bad news as something different—as good news, for instance—in a way that displays what has been called the "benign order of everyday life" (Maynard, 2003, chapter 6). In the context of telling troubles, Jefferson (1988) shows, speakers may produce "optimistic projections" as devices that have closure implicativeness, and Holt (1993) reports that, after a bad news delivery, participants regularly perform a "bright side sequence" or exchange of turns in which they assume a positive stance toward some aspect of the event, as happens in Extract 7, where Leslie tells her Mum that Philip Cole's mother had died (line 4). A first move toward a bright-side sequence occurs just after that telling and Mum's "ah::::," which is produced with a downward intonation

contour. Leslie goes on to report that the death had occurred "in the week very peace-
fully" (line 6), and further elaborates (lines 8–9) to suggest the mode of death was
like falling "asleep," which Mum registers with a change of state token (line 10) and
"nice way t'go" assessment (line 13).

Extract 7 H07B [Holt 1993]

```
01   Leslie:   D'you remember-You know Philip Cole? You ↑know 'e had this
02             u-very good ˙hhhh very busy little mother that was always
03   Mum:      ↑Oh:: ↓yes
04   Leslie:   busy doing thin:gs (.) 'nd (.) She die:d.
05   Mum:      Ah↓:::.
06   Leslie:   eh-in the week very peacefully:
07   Mum:      Yes.
08   Leslie:   She just didn't recover from a stroke, she
09             ju[st sort'v fell asleep.
10   Mum:      [Oh:.
11                 (1.0)
12   Leslie:   A:[nd  u h ]
13   Mum:      [Well tha]t's a nice ↓way t'go↓ [isn't it?]
14   Leslie:                                   [Y e: s  ],
15   Leslie:   tha[t's right.
16   Mum:      [(     ),
17                 (0.6)
18   Leslie:   An' an' ↑people had a chance to say cheerio t[o her
19   Mum:                                                    [Yes
20   Leslie:   ='n the vicar came 'n you know 'n i-it wz all very
21             peaceful
22   Mum:      Yes,
23                 (.)
24   Mum:      How   nice
25                 (0.3)
26   Leslie:   So they're ↑not going to have a dis↓mal funeral↓ they said
27             they're goin t' have r::eally a thanksgiving for her=
28   Leslie:   =li[:fe
29   Mum:      [for her ↓life. Yes that's [right.]
30   Leslie:                              [Mm: ]
31                 (0.5)
32   Mum:      ↑Hm:
33                 (0.6)
34   Mum:      That's ni:ce
```

With the trajectory for a bright side mutually established, the remaining pronounce-ments in this delivery (lines 18, 20–21, 26–8) including the lexical assessments are all positively valenced, and all receive affirmations from Mum, including the additional assessments, "How nice" (line 24) and "That's nice" (line 34).

It is possible to wonder if the delivery is properly characterized as bad news at all, or if the bright-side sequence organizes a cooperative revision in which the news is trans-formed from bad to good. When the prosody is examined more closely, however, it becomes clear that the positive prosodic ascriptions are continually tempered in a way that preserves the original negative ascription and display of affect, even while lexically a positive stance is constituted toward its elaborating details. The turns are produced at a pitch that is markedly lower than in good news deliveries between these same partic-ipants; fragments of two of Leslie's utterances in this delivery are shown in Figure 4. Leslie also makes ample use of the breathy voice quality and stretched, falling vowels that are more characteristic of negative valence. The entire segment of Figure 4a is done with a softened voice, and the turn also has a very constricted pitch range with that of the good-news deliveries presented in this chapter. In Figure 4b, it is noticeable that the intensifier "very" is said with a flat contour, while in a good-news delivery the pattern is for a sharp upstep between the two syllables of the word.

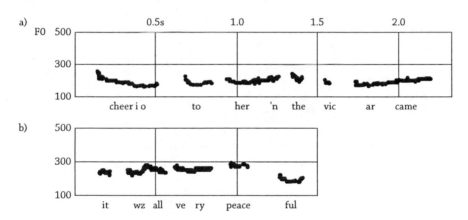

Figure 4
Extract 7, a) lines 18, 20, b) lines 20–21

The utterances are also produced with a reduced speech rate that is more consis-tent with bad news. That is, falling pitch, breathy voice quality, and slower pacing may display sadness or regret on the part of deliverer. Although the lexical ascriptions of positive valence are perhaps more prominent, the presence of clearly depressed pro-sodic features shows that bright-side sequences are not transformations of valence. It is not that Leslie and Mum have changed their stances and are now pleased by the death of Philip's mother, but that they have collaboratively found positive aspects to focus on in the face of the overall unfortunate nature of the event embodied in their initial displays of regret and sympathy. Consequently, the sequence evinces an asym-metrical valuation of good news over bad—a benign order—rather than a reversed sentiment toward the news. Accordingly, in line with what Sacks (1984a) has proposed about entitlement to experience, reporting a death may involve practices whereby the sadness of the event is conveyed and not yielded even though deliverer and recipient can converge on a post-news bright side.

Assessments

In the collection, the majority of first lexical ascriptions were made in either the Assessment turn or in a combined Announcement Response / Assessment turn (53 of 75[13] deliveries, or 61 percent). As noted, prosodic ascriptions are initiated earlier in the NDS, and participants regularly, through their practices as temporally constituted, establish a mutual orientation to valence by the time a recipient produces a lexical assessment. There were no instances in the corpus in which the valence of the previous turn was contradicted in the Assessment. Although the valence a recipient exhibits in the Assessment turn thus appears strongly determined by preceding utterances, this slot still features the most intense prosodic, and often the only lexical, ascriptions in the entire delivery, and it may be the sequential slot in which displays of affect also are exacerbated, marking the sequential, in-time movement from a provisional to an accountably confirmed valence and display of affect associated with the valence. This pattern differs from that which Selting (2010a) documents for storytelling, where the elaboration of the story's climax displays less affect than the climax itself, at least in part because the elaboration suggests exit from the sharing of affectivity. Also, her data involve stories encompassing anger or indignation. It can be proposed that although entitlement to experience is strongest when it is the speaker's own, the emotional expressions of stance toward that experience in practical ways depend on the type of action (news delivery versus storytelling) and the type of affect being evinced.

However, the intensified nature of Assessment turns was part of a more general trend. Recipients' turns in news deliveries, something like strongly agreeing second assessments (Ogden, 2006, pp. 1761–2), tended to employ more dramatic prosody than deliverers'. This difference may be partially attributed to differences in the shapes of the turns; deliverers' turns are constructed as sentential units that evaluate the news in and as its reporting, while recipients' turns are compact phrases or even single words that are more exclusively dedicated to the task of evaluating the news. Because deliverers are producing information-as-news, they have more complex turn-design tasks, whereas recipient turns can attend more narrowly to emotive displays. Yet, this explanation is necessarily partial in that it does not account for an important pattern among the cases; namely, that the differences in intensity between deliverers' and recipients' prosody are most extreme when deliverers present news about themselves.

Differing Intensities of Delivery and Receipt

Both deliverers and recipients employed the prosodic conventions for attributing valence to news summarized in Table 5.1, but recipients appeared to use the conventions more strongly in forty-nine out of seventy-one cases in the corpus.[14]

The disparity in the prosody of deliverers and recipients appears to be greatest when the deliverers are presenting good news about themselves, that is, when the deliverer is the main consequential figure in the delivery (Maynard 2003, chapter 5). In these instances, valence markers used by the deliverer are subdued (if not absent), while the recipient's assessment is stronger than usual.[15] For example, in Extract 8, Gordon is responding to a news inquiry from Susan about his efforts to study in France. His response constitutes a narrative with several different turn constructional units, each of which could be construed as constituting good news, at least by the completion of the turn. Gordon presents his news with the prosody of positive valence only after several opportunities for recipient assessment are bypassed:

Extract 8 H19G [Holt:SO88:1:5:3]

```
01   Gordon:   =˙p An:d e-she wrote-(0.2) back well she eshly phoned ˙hh
02             a:n' said h ˙hhh (.) that uh she wz very impressed by the
03             letter,❶ hhh So thank your dad for that an' uh:°that-
04             (0.4) she actually had somebody over there this ↓year
05             unfortunately↓ but uh: ˙hhh she wanted me to come over
06             another yea:r ❷ (.) ˙hhh u-uh 'nd she said if:: it wasn't
07             possible that (0.3) you know I c'd stay with her. she c'd
08             always find ˙hhh friends'v hers:: who could (.) put me up.❸
09             hhh An' ↑al↓so: ˙hhh her: (0.3) u-husband i:s an
10             architect.hh °hhhhhh A:n:[:d uh
11   Susan:                             [You're kidding [me.
12   Gordon:                                            [nNo: ↓n[o.
13   Susan:                                                     [Oh:: G[od.
14   Gordon:                                                            [An'
15             she said that uh (.) if I (.) if I decided after the third
16             year that I wanted to do: my year of practice in-: ↓Paris
17             ˙hhhh then it (0.2) would be completely acceptable b'cz all
18             the family speak about half a dozen languages, hh ˙hhh So: I
19             c'd work for hi:m.
20   Susan:    Oh brillian:t. Oh that's good news.
21   Gordon:   It's really good.
```

At each of the numbered points, Gordon completes the production of a turn constructional unit. Although the first of these is relatively unequivocal in comprising good news, the second and third start out on a possibly disappointing note, but end with a positive cast and as candidate good news. At each point he pauses, breathes in or out, or produces some other perturbation in talk; these provide a possible space for a continuer or a positive assessment of the news. Susan bypasses each opportunity, leaving Gordon to resume his narrative. At line 9, though, the next narrative component has increased stress and rising pitch on the "al" in the word "also" (going from about 70 Hz on "An'" to 183 Hz on "al"). Gordon stresses the tail end of "also" such that both syllables of the word end up with increases[16] and may more overtly signal still more forthcoming good news; grossly put, the "also" sounds upbeat.

After Gordon completes the Announcement (lines 9–10), with an emphasis on "architect." Susan responds with a newsmark (line 11) displaying astonishment (Selting, 1996), and, following Gordon's confirmation at line 12, produces an "Oh:: God" appreciation of his news (line 13). The newsmark and appreciation both have sustained high pitch, dramatic emphases, and a "gasping" voice. Accordingly, whereas Susan forgoes previous opportunities for turn transition, Gordon's prosody at lines 9–10 may be more strongly implicating a response and, specifically, soliciting the positive display of appreciation and affect Susan subsequently produces at line 13. After this, Gordon further elaborates the news (lines 14–19), whereupon Susan produces strong lexical assessments (line 20). Gordon then agrees (line 21), although in a mitigated fashion. Here, practical temporal emotion work involves how there may be concrete efforts situated in and through the unfolding of a news delivery to cue and solicit a display of affect from a recipient fitted to the deliverer's projections. When that display is provided, it is stronger than what the deliverer exhibited in successive utterances whose design had already implicated affective uptake from the recipient.

Intensity is more equal when the deliverer presents news about a third party. Below, Leslie and a nursing home employee provide comparably intense ascriptions in discussing the health of one of Leslie's distant relatives:

Extract 9 H2G [Holt:X(C)1:2:2:3]
```
01   Leslie:   Well ↑how's Missiz Wood↓chamber getting on:
02                        [ . . . . . . ]
03   Ward:     ·hh W'she's (0.2) she's doin' very well actually um: she's
04             inde↑pendent.
05                        (.)
06   Leslie:   Oh she ↓is.
07   Ward:     Ye:s she's walking arou::nd uh: washing 'n dressing herse:lf?
08   Leslie:   Oh ↓good.
```

In answering Leslie's news inquiry, Ward precedes her announced news "she's independent" with a preassessment of this information—"she's doin' very well actually" (line 3). This Announcement also employs intonational devices indicative of good news, most conspicuously the sharp rises on "well" and "inde↑pendent." Ward's combination of lexical and strong prosodic ascription assumes a much more overtly positive stance toward the news she delivers than did Gordon's Announcement in Extract 8. Meanwhile, Leslie's response, while positive, is not emphatically so: the Announcement Response is slightly delayed, and both it and the Assessment turn (line 8) are produced at normal amplitude with mid-range pitch. Compared to Susan's "You're kidding me" and "Oh God" responses in Extract 8, Leslie's reaction may be characterized as tepid.

The increased intensity of deliverers when giving news about others suggests that they may be suppressing their use of valence markers and displays of affect in news deliveries about themselves, which we noted above to be prosodically subdued. Similarly, decreased intensity of recipients' utterances in deliveries about third parties suggests that they may be intensifying markers of valence when assessing news about the deliverer. Pomerantz (1978) identifies a system of self-praise avoidance within conversation, in which parties tend to minimize praise of their own feats and maximize praise of their fellow interactants (see also Freese, 1997, and Leech, 1983, pp. 131–8). For deliverers, insofar as presenting good news about themselves may be hearable as "bragging," they may orient to the system by presenting news neutrally or with minimal positive valence. Gordon's Announcement in Extract 8 contains only minimal markers of positive valence in the production of his good news narrative. And Andi's "surprising" and (as it turns out) happy pregnancy news in Extract 1 also is minimized in its prosodic contours. In subsequent turns, recipients may upgrade the valence and display of affect, using more intense prosody to do so (Pomerantz, 1978). We saw this in Extract 1, and in Extract 8, Susan's strong appreciation and assessment of the news may be the proper counterpart to Gordon's exhibited "modesty." Even after her "Brilliant. Oh that's good news," Gordon's agreement is tempered.

While Pomerantz's observations on constraints against self-praise are here only applicable to instances of good news, the data suggest a similar injunction may exist against strong displays of regret when presenting bad news about oneself. Whereas self-praise avoidance can be seen as preventing the appearance of the sanctionable behavior known as "bragging," subdued deliveries of bad news about oneself may exhibit stoicism (Maynard, 2003, chapter 5) and ward off potential accusations of "whining." Moreover, just as recipients exhibit an orientation toward ensuring that the prosperity of others is properly recognized, so too do they display a concern for others' woes. Examples of bad news about the deliverer, as in Extract 5, feature stronger displays of sadness by the recipient than the deliverer. In deliveries of either bad or good news, then, the prosody of valence ascriptions displays sensitivity to the relationship of the parties to one another and their relative positions as consequential figures in the news. Practical and temporal emotion work involves the practices whereby deliverers and recipients exhibit a certain kind of entitlement to experience in relation to what sort of news is reported and whose news it is. At least for some deliveries of news, and contrary to storytelling about indignities a speaker has undergone, paradoxically the one who is most entitled to the experience displays less affective intensity. Consequently, the social construction of affect and emotion in the delivery of good and bad news, as reflected in participants' practical and temporal work, can be said to incorporate disparate kinds of orientation, not only to the epistemics of experience but also to matters of restraint, modesty, and the like.

CONCLUSION

Previous studies on the sociology of emotions are wide-ranging. We have focused on two perspectives as related to the research in this chapter. One perspective is that of social constructionism, which avoids treating emotions as some outward expression of an inner state, and substitutes the idea that participants in the social world produce the sense of an affective state by way of definition and attribution. Our approach is meant to extend the possibility of social construction by showing how affective experiences associated with bad and good news are coproductions or collaborative achievements existing in the concreteness of what participants say to and do with one another. Even when they do not formulate or define their emotions, and even when they may confront bad and good news as emotional experiences associated with joy and sadness over which they have no control, participants are methodic in their expressions. Our attention to the practices and temporality of coproduction does not imply an ironic take on experience, but only that its expression has overt, orderly, and deeply interactional components. In this sense, our study is consistent with the American pragmatist tradition, aiming to avoid the bifurcation of internal and external or mind and body and instead to convey the seamlessness of affective experience and the displays by which it is realized for coparticipants in the concreteness of conduct (Emirbayer & Maynard, 2011).

We follow previous research that has identified a strong connection between prosody and the expression of emotion; for example, Bolinger (1989, p. 1) argues that "even when it interacts with such highly conventionalised areas as morphology and syntax, intonation manages to do what it does by continuing to be what it is, primarily a symptom of how we feel about what we say." Here, we found that there were systematic differences in the prosody of good and bad news deliveries and responses, and that these differences are consistent with those associated with the expression of joy and sorrow. At the same time, our goal has not been to identify correlates of prosody and emotional display, but to show how participants use prosody as a semiotic resource for converging upon a shared evaluative orientation toward an item of news. We find that parties make prosodic ascriptions of valence throughout the four turns of the prototypical News Delivery Sequence, and that explicit lexical ascriptions and displays of affect in a delivery are often only concretizations of a valence that has already been mutually established prosodically. Moreover, by noting differences in the intensity with which participants use prosody in displaying their orientation toward a reporting, we suggest that prosody also serves the reconstitution of parties' relationships to one another and their consequential positioning in the news. To the degree that participants mirror one another's stances as the delivery and reception of news progresses, they may reproduce a more or less close or intimate association with one another. Not fully explored here for reasons of space, relationship constitution is another facet of social construction in bad and good news (Maynard, 2003, chapter 5).

The sociologically evocative phrase "emotion work" has referred to the effort required to conform emotion displays to rules about the types, extent, and duration of expression in social settings. As Hochschild (1979, p. 561) has illustrated emotion work, it is captured in verb forms such as:

> I *psyched myself up*. . . . I *squashed* my anger down. . . . I *tried hard* not to feel disappointed. . . . I *made* myself have a good time. . . . I *tried* to feel grateful. . . . I *killed* the hope I had burning. . . . I *let myself* finally feel sad. [original emphasis]

Possibly because much of this research involves interviews and observations, analysis relies on post hoc accounts like these, and has not given us much purchase on the practices and temporal or in-course real-time patterns by which participants fashion displays of affect in interaction with one another. Where the concept of emotion work does refer to "evoking or shaping, as well as suppressing" (Hochschild, 1979, p. 561) affective experiences in accordance with rules, our study suggests also that with bad and good news, notions of rule-governed expressions can be supplanted or embellished. Participants perform or enact the valence and affective quality of news in interaction by way of devices that have emotional features according to the in-time placement of such devices relative to utterances (including gestures, when participants are copresent) and the sequences these utterances comprise. While prosodic manipulations provide one set of resources available to participants in the interactional production of the affect and valence of news, we have attempted to demonstrate their operation within organized sequences of actions that are developed on a moment-by-moment basis. Emotion work, in other words, involves practices through which participants affectively orient to tidings in particular ways in the here and now of actual interaction.

NOTES

1. In sociology, affect is considered to be a general category (Smith-Lovin, 1995, p. 118; Stets, 2003, p. 310) with emotion (along with sentiments and mood) being a subset of affect. However, the terms affect and emotion are often used interchangeably. As reviewed by Selting (2010a, pp. 229–30), this is consistent with other literatures (Besnier 1990; Ochs & Schieffelin, 1989) although the term "stance" often is equated with or, as in Local and Walker's treatment (2008), subsumes "affect." Couper-Kuhlen (2009, p. 95) has observed the difficulty of establishing "a reliable taxonomy of affect and emotion." We take the approach outlined in previous conversation analytic work (Couper-Kuhlen, 2009, p. 96; Goodwin & Goodwin, 2000, p. 239; Selting, 1996) regarding affect and emotion as embodied displays (including those in talk), situated in analyzable sequences of action and interaction, and thereby context-bound and context-sensitive.
2. In his lectures, Sacks (1992, vol. 2, pp. 572–3) seems to imply that ascribing valence is recipients' work, and that it is done only at the end of delivery sequences.
3. See also Wilkinson and Kitzinger's (2006, pp. 158–9, 176–7) discussion of this extract.
4. Pitch diagrams were constructed using Praat and Adobe Photoshop. Original pitch diagrams from Freese and Maynard (1998) were developed from SoundEdit 16, Photoshop, and with the help of Kenneth DeJong of Indiana University.
5. See Local and Walker (2008) on the "interplay of sequential and phonetic resources" whereby the "same" utterance with the "same" phonetic design ("wow" is the target of their study), used by different speakers, can be produced in very different sequential environments (bad news and good news). Here the "same" utterance by the same speaker (the news recipient) takes on different prosody in its distinct sequential environments and both constitutes and deals with progressive realizations of the news. Not only is there no "straightforward mapping between phonetics and stance, and vice versa" (Local & Walker, 2008, p. 737), but the mapping between utterance type and stance or affect also is contingent.

6. For discussion, see Emirbayer and Maynard (2011).
7. Differences between British English and American English intonation are sketched by Bolinger (1989). None of these differences is considered consequential for the discussion here. That is, episodes could not be distinguished in terms of their prosodic patterning in the delivery or receipt of news.
8. For details, pitch diagrams, and illustrative extracts, see Freese and Maynard (1998, pp. 198–205).
9. Terasaki (2004 [1976]) shows that news deliveries may also begin with a preannouncement sequence, but these sequences are not analyzed in this chapter. See also Schegloff (2007, p. 169–80) on topic proffers.
10. For an example of bad news and its aligning announcement response, see Excerpt 14 in Freese and Maynard (1998, p. 208).
11. See also Freese and Maynard (1998, p. 207, Figure 4c).
12. This delivery actually goes on much longer than the excerpt provided, with at least eight positive Elaborations and Assessments across turn of the entire delivery.
13. This number counts only those deliveries that follow the two- or four-part structure of the News Delivery Sequence.
14. This number does not count instances in which the party using the stronger prosody could not be discerned.
15. Again, this differs from Selting's (2010a) study of storytellings involving anger or indignation: tellers' displays of affect either exceeded or were simply matched by recipients, rather than recipients displaying stronger affect.
16. Uhmann (1996) identifies in German this configuration as a "beat clash" that adds to the intensity of an utterance when done in the context of a news delivery.

CHAPTER 6

⚬⟋⟍⚬

Exploring Affiliation in the Reception of Conversational Complaint Stories

ELIZABETH COUPER-KUHLEN

This chapter investigates the linguistic resources deployed by recipients of conversational complaint stories to show affiliation (or not) with the teller, affiliation being understood as the display of support and endorsement for a conveyed affective stance, here typically anger and/or indignation. Among the verbal means for affiliative reception are claims of understanding, congruent negative assessments and by-proxy justifications, while factual follow-up questions, minimal responses, and withholdings are shown to be nonaffiliative. As a rule, affiliative verbal devices are accompanied by prosodic matching or upgrading, while nonaffiliative ones have prosodic downgrading. The affiliative import of response cries is shown to depend even more heavily on prosodic matching or upgrading, although the transitoriness of prosody makes verbal reinforcement a desideratum. All in all, the data discussed here present a complex picture of what it takes to come across as affiliative in response to a conversational complaint story, but one not lacking in systematicity.

ON STORY RECEPTION IN CONVERSATION
Affiliation versus alignment

In a recent contribution to the literature on conversational storytelling, Stivers (2008) distinguishes two types of story reception: "alignment" and "affiliation." Alignment involves supporting the asymmetric distribution of roles which characterizes the storytelling activity: for example, positioning oneself as story recipient and refraining from coming in while the telling is in progress. Misaligning involves, for example, competing for the floor during the telling or failing to treat a story as in progress or, on its completion, as over. Alignment is thus a structural dimension of the activity of story reception. It can be achieved among other things through the use of vocal continuers (*mm hm, uh huh,* and *yeah*) during story production.

Affiliation, on the other hand, is a social dimension in story reception. Stivers describes it as "the hearer displays support of and endorses the teller's conveyed stance" (2008, p. 35), "stance" being understood as "the teller's affective treatment of the events he or she is describing" (2008, p. 37). How do storytellers convey stance? For one, story *prefaces* (e.g., "something very very cute happened last night" or "I'm broiling about something") inform recipients about the sort of response which the teller is seeking on story completion (Sacks, 1974). But stance can also be conveyed through *prosody*, for example, in reported speech (Couper-Kuhlen, 1999; Günthner, 1999), and through various forms of "embodiment" (Niemelä, 2010; Goodwin et al., this volume, chapter 2). Furthermore, the (sequential) *context* of the telling can offer clues; for instance, in a medical visit a telling is likely to be conveying a trouble or problem (Stivers, 2008). It is through resources such as these that story recipients are provided with access to the teller's stance.

Affiliation is generally agreed to be the preferred response in storytelling. Stivers argues that it is achieved by "the provision of a stance toward the telling that mirrors the stance that the teller conveys having . . . [. . .] whether that is as funny, sad, fabulous, or strange" (2008, p. 33). Stance mirroring can be done, according to Stivers, through assessments ("That's fantastic") and other full-turn responses ("I see"), but also—at least in midtelling position—through head nods. On story completion, by contrast, simple head nods do not provide sufficient affiliation, while assessments and congruent second stories do.

One of Stivers's most important findings in this study is that a single resource, the head nod, can be affiliative during the telling of a story but can display a lack of affiliation upon its completion. This is intriguing because it suggests that response types are not intrinsically affiliative or nonaffiliative; instead, what counts as affiliative depends crucially on *where* the response is placed in the sequential or interactional context. The present chapter explores further resources which are either affiliative or nonaffiliative at particular locations in storytelling, here specifically at climaxes and high points in conversational complaint stories.[1]

Complaint stories as a rule concern some (nonpresent) third party whose behavior (often toward the teller) is perceived as blameworthy. They are typically produced in order to account for why that person's behavior should be considered morally reprehensible (Drew, 1998) but also serve a primordial impulse to share experienced feelings. Many complaint stories are prefaced in ways which project that the teller was angry, mad, annoyed, or aggravated by the behavior in question: "I was so upset," "I'm so mad at that painter," "well I really was cross," "I'm broiling about something," "I don't know what there is about it that annoys you." In addition to reconstructing their aggravation and the motivation for it in the story world, tellers may also make *in situ* displays of anger and indignation in the here and now. This study now asks the following questions: (a) When affect-laden displays of anger, indignation, or annoyance —be they reconstructed or *in situ*—are made in the course of a complaint story, what kinds of uptake count as affiliative? (b) What kinds of response count as nonaffiliative in these contexts? The focus will be on verbal (lexicosyntactic) and vocal (prosodic–phonetic) resources, with visible (gestural–kinesic) dimensions being taken into consideration where relevant. The data base is a collection of thirty-six strong displays of affect, as a rule by the teller, in fifteen different British and American complaint story episodes, nine taken from audio recordings of everyday telephone conversation and six from video recordings of face-to-face conversation. The results are intended to cast light on the recipient's task in storytelling: how to come across as affiliative, or nonaffiliative as the case may be, in the given context?

Distinguishing affiliative from nonaffiliative reception

Storytellers have a vested interest in knowing whether their recipients are affiliating with the story as told and the stances as conveyed. This information is crucial not only for assessing the emotional resonance they are achieving but also, quite mundanely, for determining what to do next. As Jefferson's (1978, 1988) work has shown, storytellers make different next moves depending on how their stories are being received. This provides their recipients (and analysts) with important clues concerning the emergent interaction. In particular, what the teller does next, after points in the story where responses have been made relevant, equips analysts with a ready tool for determining whether these responses were taken by participants to be affiliative or nonaffiliative.

To see how storytellers' next actions reflect recipients' behavior, let us compare the sequential development of two episodes involving complaint stories. The first is organized around a story told by Lesley to her friend Joyce on the telephone. With this story she is "letting off steam" about the behavior of a mutual acquaintance, referred to as Mr. R., whom she accidentally ran into at a vicarage sale:[2]

Extract 1 "Something for nothing"[3] (Holt: Christmas 1985: Call 4)

```
01  Les:      oh:;
02      →     hh y- uhm you ↓know i=i i'm BROILing about something;
03            heh°   [heh°]
04  Joy:             [WH]A::T;
05  Les:      well thA:t ↓SA:LE. (0.2)
06            at_at (.) the VICarage;
07            (0.6)

08  Joy:      oh ↓ye[s:,
09  Les:            [t
10            (0.6)
11  Les:      u (.) yOur friend_n_MI:NE was the:re,
12            (0.2)
13  ( ):      (h[h hh)
14  Les:        [mister: R:,
15  Joy:      oh (ye:s XXX)
```

```
16              (0.4)
17   Les:       and em:
18              <<p> ↑we (.) ↑rEally didn't have a lot of CHA:NGE that (.) day,
19              because we'd BEEN to ↓bAth;
20              and we'd BEEN: chrIstmas shOppin:g,
21              (0.5)
22   Les:       but we thOUght we'd bEtter go along to the SALE;
23              and dO what we COULD;
24              (0.2)
25   Les:       we hAd↑n't got a lOt (.) of e⁷ rEady cash to ↑SPE:ND.
26              (0.3)
27   Les:       t[hh
28   Joy:        [mh;
29   Les:       in ANy case we thought the thIngs were vEry ex^PENsive;
30   Joy:       oh DID you;
31              (0.9)
32   Les:       And uh ↑we were lOoking round the ↓STA:LLS;
33              and poking aBOUT;
34              and hE came UP to me,
35              and he said;
36      →       Oh:, <<aspirated> H>ELlo lEsley,(.)
37      →       <<h> stIll trying to bUy something for NOTHing,>
38   Joy:       ((click)) °HAH:::
39              (0.8)
40   Joy:       OO[:: (lesley)            ]
41   Les:          [↑OO: ehh heh ↑heh]
42              (0.2)
43   Joy:       ↓i:s  [n't    ]      [↓he
44   Les: →     <<f,h> [↑what] dO ↑y[ou!↑SA:Y!.>
45              (0.3)
46   Joy:       <<p> ↓oh isn't hE ↓DREA:Dful;>
47   Les:       <<pp, h> YE:S,>
48              (0.6)
49   ( ):       <<p> ((click))>
50   Joy:       what_n AW::ful MA:: [N;]
51   Les:                          [eh] heh heh ↑heh
52   Joy:       OH:: hOnestly;
53              I cannot stAnd the mAn;
54              it's just    [(XXX XXX)]
55   Les: →                 [i thOUght ] well i'm gonna tell JOYCE thAt;
56              ehh[heh    ]
```

```
57  Joy:      [(  )]
58  Les:      =[heh-heh he-e]  uh:    ↑e[h eh hhhhh  ]
59  Joy:      =[OH::;        ]  i        [i DO think he]'s DREADful;
60  Les:      <<pp> ((click))> OH: dEar;

61  Joy:      OH: he r[eally  (i]:s;)
62  Les:             [↑he dra⁊]
63     →      he (.) took the WIND out of my sails comPLETEl(h)y;
64            (.)

65  Joy:      i KNOW;
66            the (AWKward/AWful) thing is you've never got a rEady A:NS [wer;
67  Les:                                                                [no:

68  Joy:      have ↓you. that's ri:ght;   ]
69  Les:      i thought of lots of ready a]nswers A:Fterward  [s;]
70  Joy:                                                      [ye]s thAt's RI::GHT;=
71  Les:      =yE:s-
72            (.)

73  Joy:      but you can nEver think of them at the TI: [ME.
74  Les:                                                 [nO: [NO;]
```

((talk about ready answers continues))

Where is the teller's stance conveyed in this story? Where are affiliative responses made relevant? Importantly, Lesley's stance is foreshadowed here in the story preface, "I'm broiling about something" (line 2)[4]. This preface alerts her recipient, as the story unfolds, to a turning point that could have motivated Lesley's anger. That turning point, as it transpires, is Mr. R.'s remark to her at the vicarage sale: "oh:, hello Lesley, (.) still trying to buy something for nothing," (lines 36–7). Here then is a climactic point in the story with a displayed affective dimension, making a subsequent affect-related recipient response relevant. In Heritage's (2011) terminology, it constitutes an "empathic moment," a point in time when recipients are under some moral obligation to affiliate empathically.[5]

How is Lesley's stance made accessible here? For one, she performs the encounter as a dramatic scene, enacting the voices of the *dramatis personae* with reported speech and thought and thereby enabling an overlay of her own voice to display her evaluation (see also Günthner, 1999). The antagonist Mr. R.'s remark is delivered as an oxymoron and cast as an unanswerable question (line 37). This converts a potentially innocent greeting into an occasion of verbal aggression. Mr. R.'s voice is animated with hyperarticulation and a sharp, spikey voice quality, symbolic of the stabs it is portrayed to be making against Lesley's character. Such rhetorical and prosodic devices add heightened emotive involvement to the climactic moment by embodying Lesley's (reconstructed) anger at her aggressor. Joyce responds by producing an initial click followed by a sharp inbreath (line 38), suggestive of sudden shock. After a short pause, she continues with "oo:: Lesley" (line 40) and then an exclamation, "i:sn't he" (line 43), discontinued when Lesley now comes in.[6]

The teller's next turn is a high-pitched, loud "what do you sa:y" (line 44). With this turn, Lesley evaluates the climactic event in a here-and-now perspective. At the same time, her turn elevates the specific situation being reported to a more general level: "what does one say when these things happen?" This turn is also heavily marked for affect through its exceptionally high pitch and peaked contours (see Figure 8, p. 142), affording another opportunity for Joyce to respond affiliatively. Joyce now produces three separate negative evaluations of Mr. R: "oh isn't he drea:dful." (line 46), "what_n aw::ful ma::n;" (line 50) and "oh:: honestly; I cannot stand the man;" (lines 52–3).[7] At this point Lesley moves to exit the storytelling episode with "I thought well i'm gonna tell Joyce that;" (line 55). After further negative evaluations of Mr. R from Joyce, the episode is brought to a close with an idiom "he (.) took the wind out of my sails completel(h)y" (line 63) (see also Drew & Holt, 1998), where-upon turn-by-turn talk, here concerning ready answers, resumes.

All in all, the story in Extract 1 is a neatly circumscribed package consisting of pref-ace (line 2), setting (lines 5–6, 11, 14), background (lines 18–29), precipitating events (lines 32–6), climax (line 37), and here-and-now evaluation (line 44).[8] Following mul-tiple affect-laden responses from the recipient, the storytelling exit is accomplished in an orderly fashion. All of this suggests a relatively unproblematic trajectory, one that appears all the more unproblematic when compared to the next extract, where a com-plaint story goes awry. The following fragment comes from a face-to-face conversa-tion in which Jessica is telling her two flatmates, Tricia and Bridget, about a long-distance phone call she had the day before with her boyfriend, Andy.

Extract 2 "Goodbye to Andy" (Housemates_Boulder_1997)[9]

```
01   Bri:       <<all> so have you talked to ANDy lately?>
02              (0.6)
03   Jes:       <<h> mHM,>
04              tAlked to him YESterday.
05              (1.6)
06   Bri:       REALly?
07              (0.5)
08   Bri:       [how was THAT.
09   Jes:       [YEAH;
10   Jes:   →   it was good;
11          →   but then-
12              (1.5) uh::
13              i kInd of like (0.2) drEw: out the goodbye: for a lOng time,
14              (0.5)
15   Jes:       <<p> and I was like>
16              ((clears throat))
17              (0.7)
18   Tri:       n hn hn
19              (0.4)
20   Jes:       <<p i was like> <<h, stylized> O:KAY::;
```

```
21              ¹⁰| <<h, stylized> swEEt dreams;
                  | ((gazes at Tricia))
22              <<h, stylized> he's like OKAY- yOU TOO- = >
23              =i'm like (0.7)

24              <<h, stylized>   | talk to you SOON:,>
                                 | ((gazes at Bridget))

25    Bri:      | [heh
                | ((slight smile))
26    Jes:      [he's like (0.4) <<f, stylized> OKAY::;>
27              and i'm like (0.7) mhm <<f, stylized> i love you:=>
28              =he's like i love you <<f, stylized> too:>
29              and then- (0.3)
30              | i'm like <<h, f, stylized> see(h) ya(h) LA(h)ter;>
                | ((smiling))
31        →     he goes ↑Okay;

32        →     and he just   | hangs UP.
                              | ((hand gesture of hanging up))
33              (0.2).h (0.1)

34        →     and⁷ (0.2) ⁷I   [we hadn't said   | ^!BYE:! yet.
                                                   | ((eyebrow flash))
                                                   | ((gazes at Bridget, then Tricia))
35    Tri:                      [O::H:;

36    Bri:      ^O | [H::;
37    Tri:         | [^MM::;
                   | ((brief exchange of glances between Bridget and Tricia))
38              (0.6)

39    Jes: →    it's ↑rEAlly COMmon to be like;
40              <<sung>   | da↑↑DA:da;da↑DA:da;daDA::dada>
                          | ((weaving hand and head back and forth))

41              bye;=
42              =bye.
43              (0.7)
44    Jes: →    | right? (0.3)
                | ((gazes at Tricia))
45              <<p, l> click.>
46              (0.7)
47    Jes: →    and sO: he⁷
48              i'm like <<h, stylized> see you LAters;>
49              (0.4)
50    Jes:      | i said <<h, stylized> see ya LAter;>=
```

```
                 | ((hand raised in telephone gesture))
51               =he's like <<h, stylized> MHM - >
52               (0.4)

53   Jes:        it was mO[re like he said <<all> MHM,>
54   Bri:             [hehh
55   Jes:        ((click))

56   →           <<p, all> and I was all>   |<<f>!↑↑HEY:!>=
                                            | ((bared teeth))

57   Bri:        =<<all> did you> [call him back?
58   Jes:                         [and so I called him back[( )
59   Bri:                                                  |[<<f, stylized> HAH HAH>
60   Tri:                                                  |[<<f, stylized> HAH HAH>
                                                           | ((Bridget & Tricia exchange
                                                              glances))
```

((Lines 61–75: Story expansion continues))
((Lines 76–91: Here-and-now explanation and pursuit of response))

```
92   Jes: →      =.t and so:;
93               (1.0)
94   Tri:        [uh::

95   Jes: →      [i was like ↑we're   |rEAlly fAr away:;=
                                      | ((raised eyebrows))

96               =<<p> it's important,=

97               =to b hAve lIke nIce  |(0.8) closure. on the phOne.>
                                       | ((eyebrow flash))

98               |(1.5)
                 | ((Jessica gives post-completion shoulder shrug))

99   Tri:        <<p> clOsu [re:..>
100  Bri:                   [it ↑is.
```

In this case the story being told has been solicited by one of the participants: Bridget asks Jessica whether she has spoken to Andy recently (line 1) and what it was like (line 8). From its inception Jessica's story is projected to be about something negative which happened to mar an otherwise "good" event (lines 10–11, "but then-"). As it turns out, the negative event transpires during the drawn-out closing of the call, when Andy "just hangs up" (lines 31–2).

The climax of the story is enacted gesturally: during the delivery of "and he just hangs up" (line 32), Jessica makes a rapid hanging-up gesture with her hand to index the precipitousness of Andy's action. Yet there is no immediate response from her recipients (line 33).[11] So she clarifies the problem in what is cleverly designed as a turn extension with "and": "and⁷ (0.2) ⁷I we hadn't said bye: yet" (line 34). This line is delivered with unmistakable signs of heightened emotive involvement: the word "bye" has a strong rising–falling pitch accent and is accompanied by an eyebrow flash. At the same time Jessica gazes first at Bridget and then at Tricia, as if to elicit a response.

Bridget and Tricia briefly exchange glances now and respond with "oh::" and "mm::" (lines 36–7).[12] Yet unlike Lesley in Extract 1, Jessica does not now provide an affect-laden evaluation of the point of her story. Instead she treats her recipients as not having understood the point, giving a matter-of-fact explanation of the norm in telephone closings (lines 38–45) and then recycling the climax of the story (lines 47–56). The second version of the climax contains an even more dramatic performance of Andy's hanging up and her emotive reaction to it: "!hey:!" visibly directed at Andy through the telephone receiver with an angry voice and face. Bridget responds by rather prosaically inquiring what happened next: "did you call him back?" (line 57), implying that if the phone call was abruptly ended, the logical thing to do would be to reestablish the connection.

Jessica now adds another story component (not shown here), detailing what happened when she called Andy back. This story component also receives little uptake, whereupon Jessica provides even more explanation and engages in further pursuit of response from her recipients. She finally launches the story exit by enacting her parting remark to Andy, performed now with vocal, facial and gestural cues displaying not anger, but sadness and resignation: "I was like we're really far away:; it's important, to b have like nice (0.8) closure. on the phone" (lines 95–7). Her recipients, however, remain immune to this renewed display of affect: Tricia gazes down and echoes the word "closure" under her breath, Bridget nods and then produces an agreeing "it is," which because of its delay comes off as somewhat pro forma (lines 99–100).

The trajectory that the complaint story in Extract 2 takes is thus strikingly different from that in Extract 1. First, the storytelling episode itself (from story preface to story exit) is almost twice as long as that in Extract 1. Second, following the climax, the teller in Extract 2 does not move into an affect-laden evaluation of the point but rather into (a) an explanation and recycling of the climax, (b) a story expansion, and then (c) more explanation and pursuit of response. With the story exit in Extract 2 there is a shift from a display of anger to one of sadness and resignation, yet this new stance does not receive support or endorsement from the recipients either. Compared with the unremarkable development of the storytelling episode in Extract 1, the trajectory in 2 is convoluted and indicative of problematic story reception. In fact, approximately ten minutes after the fragment shown in Extract 2, Jessica complains to her flatmates about their behavior during her talk about Andy.[13]

In the following I propose to use the teller's behavior subsequent to affect-laden displays of stance (typically at story climaxes and thereafter) as a gauge in determining which kinds of recipient behavior are perceived to be affiliative and which nonaffiliative in the aftermath of conversational complaint stories. As an even cursory comparison of the recipient responses in Extracts 1 and 2 will show, there is no simple answer to the question of what counts as affiliative reception in conversational complaint stories. Whereas a change-of-state token such as "oh" might be thought more indicative of a supportive stance than, say, the avoidance of words altogether, it is significant that the purely nonverbal click and inbreath in line 38 of Extract 1 are more affiliative than the "oh" in line 36 of Extract 2, judging from the trajectory that each storytelling episode takes.

AFFILIATIVE RESPONSES

Verbal devices

What counts as an affiliative response to a teller's display of anger and indignation in a conversational complaint story? The following fragment from a telephone conversation between two friends, Dinah and Bea, is instructive in this respect. Dinah's story concerns a mutual friend, Marty, who is a compulsive money borrower:

Extract 3 "Money borrower" (SBL 1:1:11)
```
01  Din:    ( ) er:   gets me pai:d.
02          i don't  [knO:w i]h(h)aven' GOT it yet. =
03  Bea:             [ah hah ]
04  Din:    but at lea:st she SAID something abou:t i[t.
05  Bea:                                            [oh: uh hu:h,
06          (0.3)
07  Bea:    y(h)eah th(h)at m(h)akes you feel EA:sie(h)r. hh[h hh
08  Din:                                                    [we:ll
09          i[: wasn'
10  Bea:    [(   )
11          (.)
12  Din:    wasn't worried abou:t the fI:ve ↑DOLlars;=
13          =only⁷ ↑i do[n't know what there i]:s a↓b(h)Out it that
14  Bea:                [I: know what          ]
15          (0.2)
16  Din:    ^an!NOYS! you: to think that=
17  Bea:    =well that's what I MEA:N.
18          it isn't the (.) MONey as [much as       ]
19  Din:                              [no MONey doe:s] didn't mean
            anything,
20          or i'd do it for ^MARty only.
21          ((creak)) it's: it's jUst this: uh:: (0.7)
22          °h ↑you KNO:W,=
23          =now for instance wu⁷ she: used to BORrow from me;=
24          =she borrowed TWICE (.) from me once;
25  Bea:    uh_HUH
26  Din:    °h an:: (.) pf° (0.3)
27          oh i was sitting in her HOU:SE,
28          'n: re:j oakley came_n de↑LIVERED something.
29          an_she: w °h said she didn't hAve the chΛ:nge;
30          would i loan her the money to PAY him;
```

31		an_she'd pay me LATER:;
32		an_i: said well you already BORrowed from me twIce:,
33		an_never offered to PA:Y,
34	Bea:	uh_HUH [:]
35	Din:	[°h]and ↑shE prodU:ced money (.) enou:gh to pa:y rej
		oakley and me !BO:TH!.
36	Bea: →	°h (.) uh i:!↑KNO:W!;
37	→	there's it's a!↑QUI:RK:!;
38	→	there's SOMEthing the:re,
40	Din:	becuz she <<h> she did
41		it ↑WASN'T becuz she'd> have n:Eeded to borrow the money
		from mE:,
42	Bea:	mh'_ hm',
43		(0.6)
44	Bea:	mh_[hm]
45	Din:	[I ↑don]'t know ↑WHAT it <<creaky> i:s,>>
46		(.)
47	Bea:	i don't Either;
48		(0.2)
49	Din:	but <<creaky> it's it so it> jus:t left you kind_of feeling
		FUNny,
50		no:t that (.) it (.) rEa:lly made any DIFfere:nce,
51		so i_d_v in↓VI:ted her_n tAken her;
52		n_d °h would have thought NOTHing of it;
53	Bea:	hm_[MH

This story is triggered by talk about a loan that Dinah has apparently made to Marty but which is still outstanding. Bea responds to Dinah's implicit complaint (lines 2, 4) by suggesting that if Marty has mentioned it, Dinah can feel more confident about getting the money back (line 7). Dinah, however, resists the implication that she is worried about the money (lines 8–9, 12). Instead, she remarks with reference to their friend's behavior "I don't know what there i:s ab(h)out it that (0.2) an!noys! you:" (lines 13, 16). After Bea now insists that that was what she meant (lines 17–18), Dinah proceeds to tell an exemplifying story, whose climax is "and she produ:ced money (.) enou:gh to pa:y Rej Oakley and me !bo:th!" (line 35). Bea's response to this is to say: "I: !kno:w!" (line 37).

Interestingly, the phrase "I know" in this context does not mean that Bea knows Dinah's story, but rather that she recognizes the type of situation Dinah is talking about. In other words, Bea is claiming to *understand* Dinah's objection to their friend's egregious behavior. Understanding is, in Goffman's words, not merely a matter of cognition: "To quickly appreciate another's circumstances (it seems) is to be able to place ourselves in them empathetically" (1978, p. 798).[14] Claims of understanding are then one way to mark affiliation with a storyteller's displayed stance of anger and/or indignation.

But Bea not only claims to understand, she now goes on to show, or exhibit this understanding (Sacks 1992, vol. 2, p. 252) by offering assessments that are congruent with Dinah's implied stance toward their friend's behavior: "there's it's a !qui:rk!" (line 37) and "there's something the:re" (line 38). Although not intrinsically negative, these qualifying descriptions, in the context of a complaint story and in the context of "I know," are heard as assessments with negative overtones—and thus as agreeing with the teller's implied negative stance toward their friend's behavior. Because they generalize from the reported event to other, similar occasions, Bea's assessments are furthermore heard as documenting an independent epistemic position (Heritage & Raymond, 2005), which in this context increases her implied support of Dinah's negative stance.

If stance-congruent assessments from an independent epistemic position are a second way to demonstrate understanding and thereby signal affiliation with a teller's angry or indignant stance, a third is to formulate, by proxy, a motivation for it. This is what happens in the following episode, extracted from another telephone conversation between Lesley and her friend Joyce (see also Holt 1996, 2000). In this episode, Joyce is complaining to Lesley about a mutual acquaintance, Nancy, who volunteered her au pair to help out at a charity event but then at the last minute asked Joyce to do it instead:

Extract 4 "Like dirt" (Holt Oct 1988:1:8)
```
42   Joy:        but THEN: you see:,
43               at the LAST minute;
44               she SUDdenly thought-
45               well she's a BIT inexPErienced;=and °h
46               she said i wOndered if YOU: uhm:-
47               you know as you're exPERienced;
48               could DO it; °h (.)
49               and i

50               i was <<h> sO:!CRO:SS!> les that    [i    ]
51   Les:                                           [YES;]

52   Joy:        well i'm TERribly sO[rry but     ]
53   Les:   →                        [wE:ll YES;  ]    because NO:Rmally it's the
                 sort of thIng she'd a:sk you <<h> ^AN[yways::  ];=
54   Joy:                                             [exACTly;]

55   Les:   →    =uh wEeks   [^beFO:::RE;]>
56   Joy:                    [ex!ACT!ly;  ]

57   Les:        <<h> YE:S;>  [°hh]
58   Joy:                     [and] i (.)((creak))
```

59		she said oh i DID come round to sEe you uhm:: (about)((creak))
60		a couple of WEEKS ago,
61		and i said Oh yes we were aWA:Y, °h
62		she said then I was away lAst week;
63		and sUddenly it's All On ME;
64		and <<acc> [this that and] the Other,>
65	Les:	[eh: he: he: he]
66	Joy:	and i s_↑well i'm TERribly sOrry;=
67		=al↑thOUgh i shall be cAlling IN;
68		i'm [: [you know i'm [(now)]
69	Les:	[°hh[hh [oh ↑gOod] [for YOU:;]
70	Joy:	[i C]A:N'T
71	Les:	gOod for ↓YOU;:
72	Joy:	↑well what ^HONestly (.) les;
73		she treats us All lIke (.)↓DI:RT.

Joyce has prefaced her story with "well I really was cross:" (not shown here), so that when Lesley hears "and I I was so:!cr:oss! Les that I (. . .) well I'm terribly so-" (lines 49–50, 52), Lesley can anticipate that the climax is near and that Joyce has rejected Nancy's last-minute request.[15] Lesley furthermore has both direct and indirect evidence of Joyce's affective stance: Joyce not only says that she was angry, she does so in a high, loud, and tense voice that nearly breaks on the word "cross." Lesley now shows her support for and endorsement of Joyce's stance by justifying it, for and on behalf of Joyce, in her next turn: "we:ll yes; because no:rmally it's the sort of thing she'd a:sk you anyways::; uh weeks befo:::re;" (lines 53, 55).

The reason that Lesley gives here is designed with a free-standing "because" clause: in syntactic terms there is no explicit main clause, either before or after, to which it could be said to be "subordinate." Yet on semantic and pragmatic grounds, this "because" clause can be said to be accounting for the stance that Joyce has just made accessible (see also Couper-Kuhlen, 2011).[16] Lesley portrays this account as something she knows independently of the incident Joyce is describing: with it she implies that she knows on her own account that Nancy's behavior is egregious and that Joyce is justified in becoming angry.[17] This kind of by-proxy accounting is a third way to mark affiliation with an interlocutor's stance.[18]

Timing and prosodic matching

So far the argument has been that claims of understanding, stance-congruent negative assessments, and by-proxy justifications are all verbal devices for signaling affiliation with a teller's display of anger or indignation. Yet the timing of the turns that implement these actions and their prosodic formatting are not irrelevant to their affiliative import. For instance, in Extract 3, the affiliative expression of understanding (line 36) is produced with only minimal delay.[19] The stance-congruent negative assessments in lines 37–8 follow immediately. In Extract 4 the by-proxy justification beginning in line 53 actually comes in overlap with the ongoing (but projectable) turn unit: its point of onset is carefully timed to come after Joyce has indicated that she rejected the request. By contrast, Bridget's agreeing but nonaffiliative turn in line 100 of Extract 2, "it is," is produced after a 1.5 second delay. So prima facie, responding in a *timely* or even *early* fashion to a teller's display of anger or indignation is more supportive of that stance than responding with delay—and this by virtue of timing alone.[20]

Furthermore, the affiliative claims of understanding, stance-congruent assessments, and by-proxy justifications in Extracts 3 and 4 are delivered with prosodic features which *match* or *upgrade* those of the prior affect-laden turn. In Extract 3, for instance, Dinah produces high rising–falling peaks on "she" and "both" in line 35, and these are matched by similar peaks from Bea on "know" (line 36) and "quirk" (line 37). The intensity level of Dinah's climactic turn is increased in Bea's response to it. (See Figure 1 below.)

Two terms have been proposed in the interactional phonetic literature to describe such cases: (a) "prosodic orientation" (Szczepek Reed, 2006), and (b) "phonetic upgrading" (Ogden, 2006). Whereas "prosodic orientation" refers most frequently to the *matching* of one or more prosodic features from a prior turn in a response to that turn and would account nicely for the pitch design of Bea's turn, "phonetic upgrading" refers among other things to *increases*, for example in amplitude, in a second turn vis-à-vis a first, and would seem a more appropriate label for the way intensity is handled in Bea's response (lines 37–8 of Extract 3).

Prosodic peak matching is also evident in Lesley's affiliative response to Joyce in Extract 4: Joyce reaches a peak of 500 Hz and more on "so cross" and Lesley produces similar 500 Hz peaks in her response (see Figure 2 (a) and (b) respectively).

Prosodic matching and upgrading of this sort in responses to affect-laden displays of anger and indignation in complaint stories make small displays of congruent affect themselves: they signal vocally—that is, nonverbally—that the recipient shares the stance conveyed in prior turn. And they do so precisely because they are not merely claiming understanding and affiliation with words, but are showing, or exhibiting it with the voice in ways which suggest that the affect is being experienced vicariously. This is perhaps the primordial form of expressing empathy.[21]

NONAFFILIATIVE RESPONSES

Verbal devices

What counts as a nonaffiliative response to displays of anger or indignation in conversational complaint stories? Extract 2, an instance of nonaffiliative story reception, offers a number of instructive examples. For instance, following Jessica's enactment of her angry performance toward Andy on the telephone, "and I was

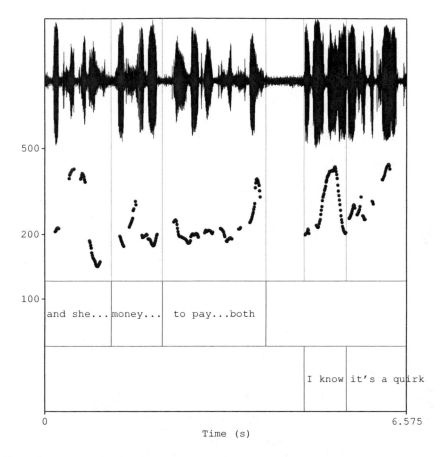

Figure 1
Waveform and pitch track for lines 35–7 in Extract 3.

all !hey:!" (line 56), Bridget does not respond with a display of congruent affect but asks a factual follow-up question: "did you call him back?" (line 57).[22] This move addresses the sequence of events in the story (what happened next), but it does not deal with the storyteller's manifest stance toward the story events. As is evident from the way Jessica's narrative unfolds subsequently, Bridget's response is not perceived to be affiliative with the stance conveyed.

If factual follow-up questions lack affiliation because they do not engage empathically with the display of affect the teller has made, uncommitted minimal responses are just as nonaffiliative. This can be seen from the following episode, where Shirley is telling her friend Geri about how a mutual friend, Cathy, who is under the legal age for drinking, finagled a strong rum-and-coke drink in the bar where Shirley was working.[23]

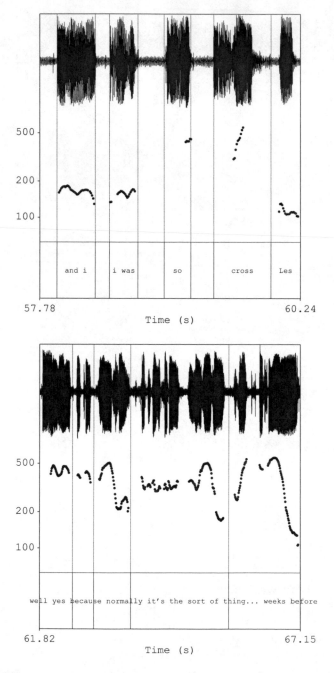

Figure 2(a) (b)
Wave forms and pitch tracks for lines 50, 53, 55 in Extract 4

Extract 5a Shmucky kid (Frankel, Geri and Shirley)

36	Shi:	°hh so lAter on i walked out on the PAtio;.
37		'n she was sitting OUT there with some friends of hers;
38		°hhh so (0.7) one of the uh BOUNcers cAme up to me=
39		=this NEW guy;
40		an_he said °h tEll me he said do you KNOW that gIrl?
41		°h an_i said SURE; (.)
42		i said you know I knOw her,
43		°h an_he said WELL? (0.3)
44		h'said she's drinkin rUm_n cOke out of a WAter glass;
45		(1.3)
46	Shi:	he said NOW;
47		he said °h YOU decide what you do since she's yOur friend;
48		(0.7)
49	Shi:	((click)) °h so i WALKED up to cAthy;
50		an_i said ^OH you're drinking a cOke.
51		can i HAVE a sip?
52		(0.5)
53	Ger:	hm_mh,
54	Shi:	((click)) °h you KNOW;
55		((click)) °h so i took a SIP of it;
56		(.)
57	Shi:	°h <<f>!EIGHTY>> prOo:f!.
58		(.)
59	Ger: →	°mh_mh
60	Shi:	=i couldn't belIEVE it;–
61		=jimmy pOurs bacardi_n_CO:KE.
62		°h she had some GUY go get it for her,
63		((click)) °h so i looked a'
64		i took the DRINK;
65		an_i DRANK out of it; (.)
66		an_i LOOKED at her.
67		(0.4)
68	Shi:	((click)) °h i said CAthy.
69		i said you must think the people who work here are rEally STUpid.
70		(1.0)
71	Shi:	you KNOW,
72		(0.4)
73	Ger: →	°YEAH°.
74	Shi:	i said <<all> you don't> HONestly think;(.)

```
75              that we are all gonna just STAND here;
76              °h an_watch you break the ^LA:W.
77              (0.4)
78    Shi:      you KNO:W,
79              (0.4)
```

Shirley has introduced her story with the preface "Listen, something very very cute happened last night at the Warehouse" (not shown here), so as the story proceeds Geri is monitoring its progress for an event that would merit the label "cute," used here ironically, at which point a recipient response will be relevant next. One of the first of these empathic moments comes at a point where the teller details how she discovered what Cathy was drinking: this moment is constructed as climactic through the high granularity of the description ("so I walked up to Cathy. . .; [. . .] so I took a sip of it," lines 49, 55. . .) and the dramatic formulation of the discovery, delivered with loud and sharply contoured prosody: "!eighty proof!." Yet Geri's response is a barely audible "mh_mh" (line 59).

That this response is perceived as lacking in affiliation can be seen from what Shirley does next. Like the storyteller in Extract 2, she backs up to give an explanation (in this case of how Cathy was able to finagle the drink) and then recycles the climax with even greater granularity ("I took the drink; and I drank out of it; and I looked at her," lines 64–6[24]). This produces another point at which a recipient response is relevant, whereupon, in the face of Geri's silence (line 70), the teller actually solicits a response (line 71) but receives merely a bland "yeah" (line 73).

Shirley now reformulates and expands on the last story event and then adds another story component detailing how the bouncer came to support her and how she morally upbraided Cathy (not shown here). This segment of the story also culminates in an affect-laden highpoint making a recipient response relevant next, but here too Shirley must solicit a comment from Geri (line 108), receiving only a noncommittal "yeah" (line 110) in return:

Extract 5b, Shmucky kid, cont'd.
```
99    Shi:       °hh i said not only THA:T,
100              °h but the fAct remains that it IS against the law,
101              an_that you're JEOPardizing;
102              °hh NOT only jAck's lIquor license,
103              °hh but Also (.) his means of (.) of Income;
104              °h an_everybody ELSE's means of income;
105              who WORKS here.
106              (0.4)
107   (S):       ((click)) °hh
108   Shi:       you KNOW,
109              (0.3)
110   Ger:  →    Y[E:AH;]
```

Thus, repeatedly in this part of the storytelling episode, the recipient declines affect-laden empathic moments set up by the storyteller by producing only minimal responses and doing so only once they have been requested. This leads to the storyteller expanding the story even more, thereby creating more opportunities for affiliation.

Just as indicative of nonaffiliation, if not more, is the withholding of any reaction at all when a recipient response has been made relevant during storytelling by a display of anger or indignation, be it reconstructed or *in situ*. This is what happens in the following part of Extract 5:

Extract 5c, Shmucky kid, cont'd.

```
141   Shi:        °h i TOLD hEr;
142               if you ever drink !ANY!thi:ng.
143               °h you are gonna g
144               don't _WOrry.
145               ha_ha_ha
146               (.)
147   Ger:        ((click)) Oy::°hh
148   Shi:        <<h> such a !sh::mUcky KI:D!.>=you knO:w?
149        →       (0.6)
150   Shi:        °h <<h> i was really !AG!gravated.>
151        →       (0.7)
152   Shi:        ((click)) °h but ANYway;
153               i made a LOT of money last night;
154               <<p> so i'm happy about THAT;>
155               (1.0)
156   Shi:        <<h> and that's all that's NEW- >
157               (0.6)
158   Shi:        oKAY?
```

At the conclusion of her story, Shirley delivers a high-pitched, affect-laden evaluation of Cathy the antagonist: "such a shmucky kid you know?" (line 148) but Geri withholds any response at all (line 149). When Shirley next formulates her affective stance toward the events explicitly, again with high pitch and heavy affect, "I was really !ag!gravated" (line 150), Geri once more passes the floor (line 151). In the light of these nonaffiliative responses, it is hardly surprising that the teller now recasts her story as having a bright side to it (lines 153–4) and closes down the episode shortly thereafter.

Delays and prosodic downgrading

Factual follow-up questions, minimal responses and withholdings all owe their non-affiliative import to the fact that they ignore the affect or stance displayed in a prior turn and its relevancies for an empathic response. Nonaffiliative minimal responses

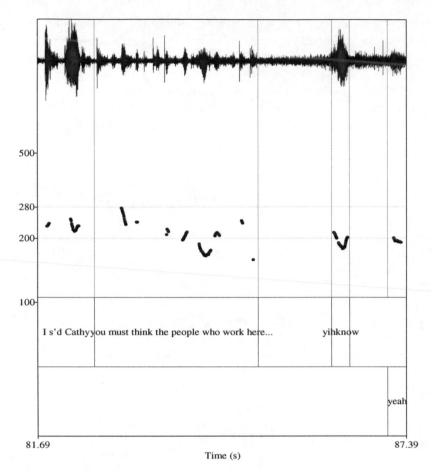

Figure 3
Waveform and pitch track for lines 68–73 in Extract 5a

are also typically delayed and prosodically downgraded vis-à-vis the prior turn. This exhibits on a purely vocal level that the recipient is not endorsing the stance conveyed. For instance, in Extracts 5a and 5b delays are evident before and after the storyteller's pursuit of response (lines 71 and 108, respectively). In addition, Geri's "yeah" tokens on these two occasions do not match, much less upgrade the pitch peaks of Shirley's prior turns and come off as breathy and weak compared with the storyteller's intensity and voice quality. See Figures 3 and 4.[25]

Summarizing the discussion so far, we have seen that claims of understanding, stance-congruent negative assessments, and by-proxy justifications are used in responding affiliatively to displays of anger and indignation in complaint stories, while factual follow-up questions, minimal responses, and withholdings are found in nonaffiliative responses. The affiliative devices are deployed as a rule with timely or early onsets and prosodic matching or upgrading, while the nonaffiliative forms, especially minimal responses, have delayed onsets and are prosodically downgraded.

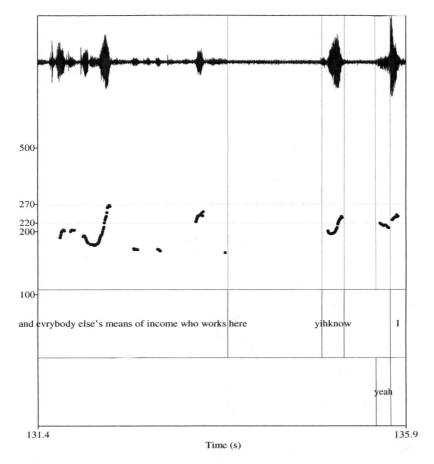

Figure 4
Wave form and pitch track for lines 104–110 in Extract 5b

Yet not all verbal forms used to respond to affect displays in complaint stories are as unambiguously affiliative or nonaffiliative as these. Some are intrinsically ambivalent as to whether they are marking affiliation or not. This is the case of response cries and sound objects.

VERBALLY AMBIVALENT RESPONSES AND PROSODY

The term "response cry" was first introduced by Goffman (1978) to refer to forms such as *brr!, oops!, eeuw!, ouch!, wheee!,* and the like, which are commonly thought of as "blurted out" on occasions when the self undergoes some untoward event. Goffman argues, however, that response cries are produced in social gatherings and consequently strategically selected for the particular occasion on which they occur. The forms Goffman describes are typically ritualized and often have a standard orthographic representation, although they lack lexical meaning. For this reason, he refers to them as "semi-words" (1978, p. 810).

Yet response cries are not the only nonlexical vocalizations encountered in everyday interaction. A perusal of Jefferson's transcripts, for instance, reveals any number of other vocal sounds and noises[26]—some partly conventionalized, others much less so—including *.t,.p, .tch, oo, wuhh, clok, klk, hhrhh, .plhhp, .p.lak, phhh.gnk,.tl*.[27] A number of these, for instance *.t,.p* and *.tch*, which represent clicks, have been shown to be recurrent and systematic in specific sequential environments (Wright, 2005, 2007; Reber, 2008). The term "sound object" is used here to refer to this larger set of sounds and vocalizations (Reber & Couper-Kuhlen, 2010).

As Heritage (2011) points out, response cries and the like are ambivalent markers of empathy. In the case of sound objects, this may be due to their nonword status. Lacking full word status, they also lack referential meaning and consequently are not accountable in the same way as words are. Response cries, and sound objects more generally—especially if they are sonorant[28]—do, however, carry prosody and this makes them particularly effective in signaling emotive stances (Goodwin & Goodwin, 2000).

To see how response cries and sound objects work in complaint stories, let us examine the continuation of Extract 4, shown in Extract 6 below. In this fragment Lesley is now telling her friend Joyce about how Nancy, after learning that Joyce could not help out at the charity event, then called up Lesley to ask for help:

Extract 6 "Supply person" [Holt Oct 1988:1:8]

```
74   Les:          and ↑then she rAng me UP;
75                 and said that (.) J:OYCE suggested that I [normally](hel)
76   Joy:   →                                              [AHHH::::]

77   Les:          ↑huh  [hah huuh↑
78   Joy:   →            [OHHH:::::::.

79   Les:          huhuhu °hh    [↑so] I sAid um- ((click))°h
80   Joy:                        [(   )]
81   Les:          well i'm sOrr[y i'm] TEACHing;
82   Joy:                       [(   )]

83   Les:          she said °hh
84                 <<hh> OH::; (.)
85                 ↑Oh my dEar;
86                 well how lOvely that you're invOlved in ↑↑TEACHing;>
87                 a[nd ↓I: thOught; °h
88   Joy:          [ohh:
89   Les:          <<h> ↑well al↑RIGHT then,>
90                 perhaps i'd like to suggest << ☺ > ↑↑YOU for the nExt
                   supplY pe(h)ers [(h)on;>=
91   Joy:   →                      [UH:::[::h heh                    ]
92   Les:                               =[heh uh heh uh heh uh huh]
```

Lesley's point in this story continuation is that Nancy's excuse for calling Lesley was that Joyce had suggested it, this constituting another instance of reprehensible behavior on Nancy's part.[29] In line 75 Lesley's negative stance toward Nancy's manipulation is conveyed phonetically by a lengthening of the initial consonant on "Joyce"[30] and prosodically through a pronounced rise–fall contour. Joyce now expresses her congruent negative stance by producing two affiliative response cries "ahhh::::" and "ohhh:::::::" in overlap with Lesley's turn as it dissolves into laughter. The second of these response cries is somewhat more prominent and is pitched at roughly the same level as Lesley's "Joyce." It is stretched to be coextensive with Lesley's laughter but once in the clear, slowly glides downward. This response cry then is carefully calibrated to "fit" Lesley's affect-laden turn: it is produced concurrently and done in a way which matches the pitch and timing of the turn to which it is responsive.

By way of evaluation, Lesley now reports what she thought to herself in response to Nancy, whose expressed enthusiasm over teaching (lines 85–6) Lesley treats as overdone and insincere: "Well alright then perhaps I'd like to suggest YOU for the next supply person" (lines 89–90). Joyce again responds with an affiliative vocalization "UH::::h" (line 91), this time one which matches the pitch of Lesley's focal accent on "you" but upgrades the overall loudness of her turn. (See Figure 5, where the

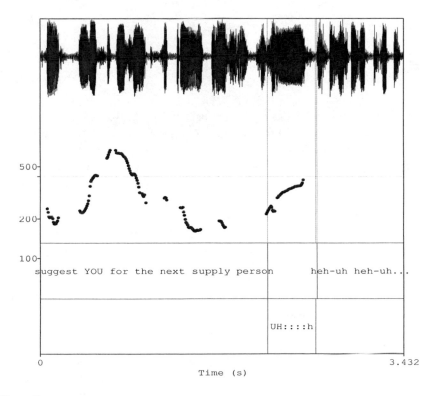

Figure 5
Waveform and pitch track for lines 90–92 of Extract 6

dotted line marks the peak of Lesley's "you" and that of Joyce's "uh:::h.") Although "uh:::h" is not a conventionalized response cry (it would qualify here as a sound object), it serves the purpose of allowing Joyce to convey strong vocal affiliation with Lesley's stance.

Response cries and sound objects which are delivered with prosodic matching and/or upgrading are thus another set of devices for responding affiliatively to displays of anger and indignation in complaint stories. However, the same tokens can convey lack of affiliation if they are delivered in a way that downgrades the prosody of the turn they are responding to. To see this, we return to Extract 2 for a closer analysis of the climax of Jessica's story and her recipients' subsequent responses:

Extract 7 "Goodbye to Andy" (from Extract 2)

```
31              he goes ↑Okay;
32              and he just  | hangs UP.
                             | ((hand gesture of hanging up))
33              (0.2).h (0.1)
34      →   and⁷ (0.2) ⁷I  [we hadn't said  | ^!BYE:! yet.
                                             | ((eyebrow flash))
                                             | ((gazes at Bridget, then Tricia))
35  TRI:                    [O::H:;
36  BRI:  →  ^O | [H::;
37  TRI:  →      | [^MM::;
                 | ((brief exchange of glances between Bridget and Tricia))
```

Recall that the response tokens which Bridget and Tricia produce after the climax of Jessica's story (line 32) and the clarification of her point (line 34) are treated by the teller as lacking in affiliation: rather than initiating a round of affect-laden evaluations, Jessica begins to explain prosaically why the event which constitutes the climax of her story is a departure from the norm, or in other words why her story is tellable.

The fact that Bridget's and Tricia's responses (lines 35–37) come off as nonaffiliative is due in large part to the way they are produced. In terms of timing, Tricia's first "O::H:" (line 35), delivered in overlap with line 34, is a delayed reaction to the climax in line 32.[31] The next responses, Bridget's "OH::" and Tricia's partially overlapping "MM::" (lines 36-7), are even more delayed vis-à-vis the climax in line 32: they come only once the teller has elaborated the point (line 34). Moreover, although both "oh::" and "mm::" are delivered with pitch contours which echo the strong rise–fall of Jessica's "BYE:" in line 34, these contours are significantly lower and flatter in pitch and also quieter in volume (see Figure 6).

Coinciding with the brief exchange of glances between Bridget and Tricia, which suggests an element of collusion (M. H. Goodwin, 1990a), this prosodic downgrading contributes to a lack of displayed affiliation and arguably accounts for why the storytelling episode subsequently develops the way it does.[32]

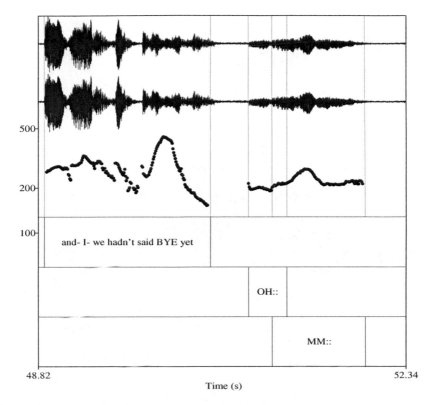

Figure 6
Waveform and pitch track of lines 34–7 in Extract 7

In contrast to the verbal devices examined in earlier sections of this chapter for doing affiliation—claims of understanding, congruent negative assessments and by-proxy justifications—the response cries and sound objects considered in this section, "ahhh::::," "ohhh:::::::," "uh::::," "oh::," and "mm::," are more heavily dependent for their affective value on prosodic realization. Their affiliative or nonaffiliative import depends crucially on how their timing, pitch, and/or loudness relate/s to that of the prior turn. In cases of prosodic matching and/or upgrading, the affective value of these response cries and sound objects is affiliative; where prosodic matching or upgrading is lacking, their affective value also lacks in affiliation.

RESPONSE CRIES AND VERBAL REINFORCEMENT

If response cries and sound objects are inherently ambivalent means of affiliating, their import being largely dependent on how they are delivered prosodically in relation to the turn they are responding to, they are also inherently less accountable than words. This means that their effect vanishes relatively quickly if they are not followed up by some type of lexical reinforcement. It is arguably for this reason that a verbally more explicit indication of the recipient's stance typically follows a purely vocal display of affiliation.

To see this, let us return briefly to Extract 1:

Extract 8 "Something for nothing" (from Extract 1)

```
32   Les:          And uh ↑we were lOoking round the ↓STA:LLS;
33                 and poking aBOUT;
34                 and hE came UP to me,
35                 and he said;
36                 Oh:, <<aspirated> H>ELlo lEsley,(.)
37                 <<h> stIll trying to bUy something for NOTHing,>
38   Joy:         ((click)) °HAH:::
39                 (0.8)
40   Joy:         OO[:: (lesley)            ]
41   Les:              [↑OO: ehh heh ↑heh]
42                 (0.2)

43   Joy:         ↓i:s   [n't   ]           [↓he
44   Les:         <<f,h> [↑what]    dO ↑y[ou!↑SA:Y!.>
45                 (0.3)

46   Joy:   →     <<p> ↓oh isn't hE ↓DREA:Dful;>
47   Les:         <<pp, h> YE:S,>
48                 (0.6)
49   ():          <<p> ((click))>

50   Joy:   →     what_n AW::ful MA::[N;]
51   Les:                           [eh] heh heh ↑heh

52   Joy:   →     OH:: hOnestly;
53          →     I cannot stAnd the mAn;
```

Recall that on completion of Lesley's story in line 37, Joyce produces first a sound object in the form of a click and an audible, prolonged inbreath (line 38). Then a split second later she delivers another sound object, represented here as "oo::," followed by the vocative "Lesley." Importantly, these sound objects are not left to stand on their own. Instead, following a brief pause, the story recipient moves to "put into words" the stance she has been displaying vocally: in line 43 she begins with "i:sn't he" and at the next opportunity recycles this to "oh isn't he drea:dful" (line 46). In her next turns two more, differently worded negative assessments follow: "what_n aw::ful ma::n" (line 50) and "oh:: honestly; I cannot stand the man" (lines 52–3). So following her "spontaneous" reaction to the climax of Lesley's story, achieved nonlexically through sound objects, Joyce takes every opportunity offered thereafter to reinforce her stance verbally.

It is thus the *combination* of sound object and verbal reinforcement that leads to the story reception in Extract 1 coming off as affiliative.[33] Response cries and sound objects which are left to stand on their own run the risk of losing their affiliative import in the aftermath. This is what happens in the following fragment, where Norma has been complaining to her friend Bea on the telephone about a painter she hired to fix up her bathroom. She prefaces her first complaint story with "I'm so ma:d at that (0.2) p:ainter:;" (not shown here). The second complaint story, which concerns her bathroom cabinet, goes as follows:

Extract 9 "Medicine cabinet" [SBL 2:1:8:R]

24	Nor:		an_then (.) this morning i got mad aGAIN,
25			becuz i GOT up;°hh
26			and was TRYing to saw the Edge;=
27			=i thought MAYbe it was: uh:: (.) stUck;
28			(1.2)
29	Nor:		uhm::
30			(0.6)
31	Nor:		rubbing at the TO:P.
32	Bea:		YE:S.
33	Nor:		so i had my little case_n i was_n i was UP there,
34			sawing aWAY,
35			and i discOvered that °hh
36			I: had a pIece of this: uh: (0.7) °h SHELF paper;(.)
37			stUck on the tOp of that (0.7) uh: ↑MEDicine chest-
38			and he'd painted right Over it.
39			(0.3)
40	Bea:	→	Oh [f:]
41	Nor:		[and the] little Edge had curled Up_n was showing RE:D.
42			(0.4)
43	Bea:	→	[oh for goodn]
44	Nor:		[and i thought gEez whiz] what's THI:S;
45			(0.3)
46	Bea:		ah_ h [a]
47	Nor:		[and_i] (.) rEached out TOWARD it,
48			an_he'd pAinted <<f> ↑RI:GHT> Over it.
49			(0.3)
50	Bea:	→	for gOodness [(xxx)]
51	Nor:		[an then he pUt]uh he mO:ved a LA:TCH,
52			uh:: so i can't lATCH my DOO::R,
53		→	(1.4)
54	Nor:		a::nd uh
55		→	(1.2)
56	Nor:		well he's coming BA:CK;

```
57                    n i'm gonna tEll him i: had unkInd THOUGHTS about him.
58                    (.)
59    Bea:    →       uh_huh_huh_huh °h_°h yes°;
60                    (0.6)
61    Nor:            SO[: uh    [i've b]een: (.) fUssing with THA:T.
62    Bea:               [°h    [well ]
63    Bea:            <<ff> It'll get strAightened OUT;>
64                    (0.2)
65    Nor:            ah:_HA:,
66                    (0.4)
67    Bea:            ↑dOn't get up↓SET about it.
```

On completion of Norma's first climactic line "and he'd painted right over it" (line 38), Bea begins a response cry "oh: f:,"[34] which, however, she discontinues when Norma rather unexpectedly adds on another climactic line: "and the little edge had curled up'n was showing re:d" (line 41). Once again Bea launches a response cry: "oh for goodn-," cut off when Norma again goes on, now animating the climactic moment when she discovered the painter's transgression: "and I thought geez whiz what's thi:s" (line 44). The last rendition of the climax "and I (.) reached out toward it, an_ he'd painted ri:ght over it" (lines 47–8) is dramatic and delivered with prosodic marks of heightened affect: sudden loudness and high, sharp pitch peaks. See Figure 7.

Pursuant to Norma's display of indignation in line 48, Bea's response cry in line 50 is pitched at a level which approximates the height of Norma's final pitch accent: see the dotted line in Figure 7, which passes through the peak of Norma's "over" and that of Bea's "goodn-."

Yet when Norma proceeds to extend her complaint to include another of the painter's transgressions (lines 51–2), Bea does not take the next opportunity to lexically reinforce the vocal stance she displayed earlier. Instead she withholds a response in line 53 and again in line 55. Norma next delivers a here-and-now evaluation of her story (lines 56–7), but Bea again passes up the chance to make an affiliative stance verbally explicit. Instead, she merely produces a string of inarticulate laugh particles (line 59).

The withholding of verbally articulated responses as a follow-up to purely vocal response cries ultimately leads to less than affiliative story reception in Extract 9. Evidence for the perceived lack of affiliation is to be found in what happens next: the storyteller now moves to close the episode, playing down the anger reconstructed and displayed earlier in her story and downgrading it to something trivial that she has been "fussing with" (line 61). The story recipient optimistically projects the situation will get "straightened out" (line 63) and advises the teller not to get "upset" about it (line 67). Rather than empathize with the indignation that Norma has been displaying, Bea's subsequent turns effectively sanction it and convert the complaint into an occasion for advice-giving.[35]

Verbal reinforcement of a stance displayed initially with vocal means only is important for another reason. It can obviate the need for prosodic matching or

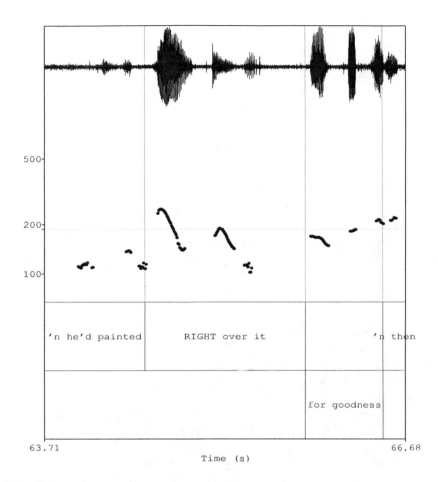

Figure 7
Waveform and pitch track for lines 48–51 in Extract 9

upgrading on these more substantive turns altogether. This will be seen by taking a closer look again at Extract 1:

Extract 10 "Something for nothing" (from Extract 1)

```
32   Les:       And uh ↑we were lOoking round the ↓STA:LLS;
33              and poking aBOUT;
34              and hE came UP to me,
35              and he said;
36              Oh:, <<aspirated> H>ELlo lEsley,(.)
37              <<h> stIll trying to bUy something for
                NOTHing,>
38   Joy:       ((click)) °HAH:::
39              (0.8)
```

```
40    Joy:        OO[:: (lesley)            ]
41    Les:           [↑OO: ehh heh ↑heh]
42                (0.2)

43    Joy:        ↓i:s   [n't    ]        [↓he
44    Les:   →    <<f,h> [↑what] dO ↑y [ou!↑SA:Y!.>
45                (0.3)

46    Joy:   →    <<p> ↓oh isn't hE ↓DREA:Dful;>
47    Les:        <<pp, h> YE:S,>
48                (0.6)
49    ():         <<p> ((click))>

50    Joy:        what_n AW::ful MA::[N;]
51    Les:                          [eh] heh heh ↑heh

52    Joy:        OH:: hOnestly;
53                I cannot stAnd the mAn;
54                it's just [(XXX XXX)]
```

Focusing on lines 41 and 43, and 44 and 46, it will be seen that the story recipient does not prosodically match or upgrade the storyteller's prior turn on these occasions. On the contrary: while Lesley uses exceptionally high pitches in her evaluative turns, Joyce shifts to low pitches in her responses. This is particularly clear in lines 44 and 46: see Figure 8.

Joyce's prosody here is diametrically opposed to Lesley's, both in terms of intensity and of pitch.[36] Yet her turn does not come off as lacking in affiliation. Rather, because it is a lexically explicit negative assessment of the antagonist that is congruent with the stance Lesley has displayed, Joyce is perceived to be endorsing this stance, although from a different perspective. All three of Joyce's congruent negative assessments (lines 46, 50, and 52–3) depart noticeably from the prosody Lesley is using in prior turns, yet as can be seen from the story trajectory, there is no question but that her story reception is perceived to be affiliative.[37]

Cases like that shown in Figure 8 provide a useful corrective to the description given thus far of affiliating versus nonaffiliating responses to displays of anger and indignation in conversational complaint stories. While congruent negative assessments have been seen to be verbally affiliative and to be *typically* done with prosodic matching or upgrading, it is not the case that their affiliative import depends *exclusively* on the latter. Instead, depending on the confluence of situational and contextual factors, congruent negative assessments can display verbal affiliation without prosodic matching or upgrading.[38] Yet when the means deployed in responding are verbally inexplicit, as in response cries and sound objects, the details of prosodic delivery appear to be crucial for determining presence versus absence of a story recipient's affiliation. Here the degree of empathy is displayed quite primordially through "crying out" with the other or not.

The affiliative import of prosodic matching or upgrading is short-lived. Without some verbal reinforcement it is likely to vanish as talk progresses. In this respect, like head nods, which are insufficient markers of affiliation at story completion, so

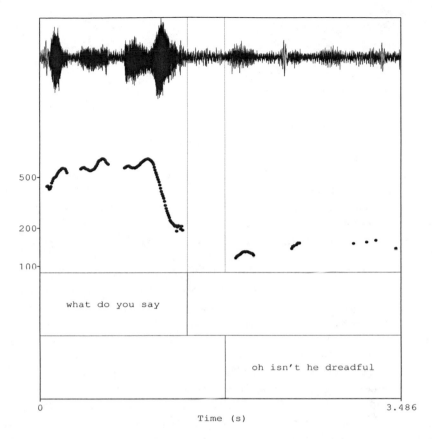

Figure 8
Wave form and pitch track for lines 44–6 in Extract 1

response cries and sound objects with prosodic matching and/or upgrading, although they may be effective in the moment, are less apt, without the reinforcement of words, to convey lasting affiliation as the storytelling episode unfolds.

CONCLUSION

This study began by examining verbal and vocal means for conveying affiliation in response to displays of anger and indignation in conversational complaint stories, and contrasted them with verbal and vocal means for displaying nonaffiliation. Initially there appeared to be a correspondence between verbal affiliation and prosodic matching or upgrading versus verbal nonaffiliation and prosodic downgrading. With response cries and sound objects, the contribution of prosodic formatting to the display of affiliation versus nonaffiliation was shown to be even more crucial. However, purely vocal affiliative displays are as a rule reinforced verbally in following turns, suggesting that they may be perceived as momentary and fleeting. Participants who wish to show affiliation and to go on record as showing affiliation will as a rule choose a combination of response cry and verbal reinforcement.

Finally, it was seen on at least one occasion that a verbal device for conveying affiliation, the congruent negative assessment, need not have matching or upgraded prosody at all to come off as affiliative. The reasons for this would repay closer study. For the moment suffice it to note that conversational complaint stories typically involve affects related to anger and indignation brought about by a third party's reprehensible behavior toward the storyteller. Prosodic matching, however, can only be expected to the extent that affects are "shared" by teller and recipient, and shareability depends ultimately on whether participants have the same "entitlement to experience" (Sacks 1992, vol 2, p. 242).[39]

In conclusion, this study has attempted to show how displays of affiliation are *achieved* in the reception of conversational complaint stories. These displays are not randomly placed but instead made relevant by the storyteller at precise moments in the storytelling episode. At such moments, tellers monitor closely how their story so far and its affective dimension are being received. Story recipients make carefully timed displays of affiliation (or not) through the deployment of a range of verbal, vocal, and embodied resources, whose affective import is not inherently given but derives from the way they are "fitted" (or not) to the local context. "Fittedness" takes on especially concrete dimensions in the case of the voice, where pitch, loudness, voice quality, and other prosodic and phonetic characteristics of the response can match or upgrade those of a prior turn or not. Voice in displaying affective stance is not a spontaneous expression of some inner state but rather a carefully deployed and manipulated resource, used in complex interaction with verbal and other non-verbal resources. All in all, reception in conversational complaint stories serves as a further instantiation of Sacks's "order at all points" (1992–1995, p. 484).

NOTES

1. The research has been carried out in conjunction with the project "Emotive involvement in conversational storytelling," funded by the Cluster of Excellence "Languages of Emotion" at the Free University in Berlin, Germany. See also Selting (2010a).
2. See also Holt (1996, 2000), Drew (1998) and Heritage (2011), who deal with the same story from slightly different perspectives.
3. This and all further transcripts are rendered in GAT 2 (Selting et al., 2011) in order to give a more systematic representation of prosody.
4. The use of "something," a prospective indexical (Goodwin, 1996), is cleverly chosen here to encourage Joyce to ask "what" (line 4), thereby making the story appear solicited rather than volunteered.
5. Following Heritage (2011, p. 161), an empathic response is "an affective response that stems from the apprehension or comprehension of another's emotional state or condition, and that is similar to what the other person is feeling or would be expected to feel" (Eisenberg & Fabes, 1990).
6. After a brief pause, Joyce subsequently recycles this turn to "oh isn't he drea:dful" (line 46).

7. Heritage's (2011) analysis of this episode spots a moment of divergence in the basis of Joyce's empathy when she assesses Mr. R. as a person on independent grounds rather than in terms of his behavior (Lesley's grounds). He suggests that "independently accessible aspects of a scene are often preferred by an empathizer, who wishes emphatic affiliation to transcend the particulars of a report, and to escape into independent agreement that is not merely responsive to the reports' details alone" (2011, p. 181).

8. The story is thus also remarkable in being a schoolbook example of oral narrative structure (see e.g., Labov, 1972). Not all conversational stories are as tightly structured; this is because, in Jefferson's words, they are "sequenced objects articulating with the particular context in which they are told" (1978, p. 219).

9. I am grateful to Barbara A. Fox for providing me with access to these data.

10. A vertical bar in the transcript line is used to mark the onset of relevant visible behavior. The description of the behavior follows an aligned vertical bar in the unnumbered line immediately below.

11. Tricia's "o::h" in line 35 is arguably a response to line 32 but it is noticeably delayed.

12. In "Verbally Ambivalent Responses and Prosody," below, I return to a more precise analysis of how these tokens are produced and what their affiliative import is.

13. Interestingly, she makes lack of alignment ("I didn't have your full attention") rather than lack of affiliation the grounds for complaint.

14. See also Ruusuvuori (2005), who conceptualizes empathy as a state of mind in which the empathizing person *understands* the other's experience.

15. As it later transpires, Nancy has also called Lesley up and asked *her* to help out. So at this point Lesley already knows that Joyce has said no.

16. The initial particles "well yes," due to their prosodic delivery (rapid articulation, no stress or accent, no rhythmic break), do not constitute a possible turn constructional unit or separate (agreeing) action of their own. For this reason, Lesley's "because"-clause is hearable as providing a reason for what Joyce has said, not for her own agreement.

17. Lesley's account is delivered with strongly affective prosody: high, sharp pitch peaks and syllable stretchings, which also make an affiliative *vocal* display of annoyance. For a discussion of prosodic means of displaying affiliation, see "Timing and Prosodic Matching," below.

18. Further empathic techniques discussed by Heritage (2011) (found not only in the reception of complaint stories) are parallel assessments ("I love it"), subjunctive assessments ("this sounds so good"), and observer responses ("I wish I could have seen her face").

19. The inbreath and micropause arguably embody an affective uptake of Dinah's hyperbolic climax.

20. See also Goodwin and Goodwin (1987), who argue that assessments which are produced concurrently with the assessable are more strongly affiliative than ones which are produced afterward, in next turn.

21. Prosodic matching is also considered a means for displaying empathy in mother–baby interactions, as described by Beebe, Rustin, Sorter, and Knoblauch (2003).

22. In an independent study of resources for declining empathic moments, Heritage (2011) calls this type of response an "ancillary question" and points out that it simultaneously enforces a change of topic.

23. This story is also discussed in Holt (1996) and Drew (1998).

24. Drew calls this kind of description "overdetermined" (1998, p. 318).

25. In these figures the weak production of Geri's "yeah"s is apparent in the reduced vertical extension of the wave form as compared with that of Shirley's prior "you know"s. Breathiness does not show up in these diagrams.

26. *Vocal* is used here in the sense of "made with the speech apparatus."
27. This list is not exhaustive and *excludes* the sounds made in laughing and crying. See also Ward (2006) for another list of nonlexical sounds encountered in English conversation.
28. *Sonorant* sounds are ones produced with a relatively free flow of air through the oral and/or nasal tract. They are typically voiced.
29. In addition, Lesley's turn may contain an element of potential criticism of Joyce for having suggested that Nancy call Lesley in the first place (personal communication, Paul Drew).
30. Or more precisely on the first consonant of the nonanonymized name. See Kohler and Niebuhr (2007) for a phonetic study of this phenomenon in German.
31. Its timing precludes its being heard as a concurrent assessment of line 34.
32. Another instance of a prosodically downgraded response cry can be found in the "oy" produced by Geri in line 147 of Extract 5c. It does not match the pitch peaks in Shirley's prior turn (lines 141–5) and is significantly softer and weaker in articulation. Not surprisingly, it is also treated by the storyteller as lacking in affiliation.
33. A further example of response cry plus lexical reinforcement can be found in the story segment preceding Extract 5: Geri responds quite empathically (but as it turns out prematurely) to a candidate climactic moment in Shirley's story by producing a click followed immediately by a more substantive, affect-laden remark supportive of the teller's (perceived) stance:

Shmucky kid (Frankel, Geri and Shirley)

```
20    Shi:    °hh so she cAme in and she starts asking me if I'd seen GAry.
21            gary KLEI:N;
22            (.)
23            °h I said YEAH he is here tonight;
24            °h she said <<h> well would you go FIND him please>=
25            ='n tell him to give me my TEN dollars that he owes me;

26            (.) °h    [hh                      ]
27    Ger:              [(((click)) WHAT do you] have to get [in on that] fO[r;]
```

34. This is projectably "oh for goodness sake:", see lines 43 and 50.
35. This is reminiscent of the convergence between troubles telling episodes and service encounters as described by Jefferson and Lee (1981).
36. In this sense it may be another form of prosodic orientation, called "nonmatching" by Szczepek Reed (2006, p. 57).
37. The asymmetry of pitch deployment here may relate to the fact that Joyce is evaluating an experience to which only Lesley has "entitlement" (see Couper-Kuhlen, forthcoming).
38. Initial observations suggest that this may happen especially when the recipient does not share entitlement to the experience but is presenting their (congruent) stance from an independent perspective (see Couper-Kuhlen, forthcoming).
39. See Heritage (2011), for a study of how asymmetric rights to experience make the display of empathy a delicate matter, and Couper-Kuhlen (forthcoming) for a discussion of how entitlement to experience affects the vocal dimensions of empathic recipient responses in storytelling.

CHAPTER 7

༄

Being Equivocal

Affective Responses Left Unspecified

AULI HAKULINEN AND MARJA-LEENA SORJONEN

INTRODUCTION

Expressions of affect, that is to say, resources for expressing one's emotional stance toward what one is talking about or what the coconversant has said or done in her previous turn, are used in all levels of the language used in spoken interaction. As Niko Besnier (1990, p. 421) has noted, "A multichannel phenomenon, affect floods linguistic form on many different levels of structure in many different ways" (see Ochs & Schieffelin, 1989, for examples of verbal resources from a range of languages; an extensive treatment of affect in the grammar of one language, see Hakulinen, Vilkuna, Korhonen, Koivisto, Heinonen, & Alho, 2004, pp. 1613–37). Certain parts of speech—evaluative adjectives, interjections and expletives as well as other intensifying expressions (e.g., adverbs)—have become specialized for affective use.

Some interjections are termed by Goffman (1981) as "response cries," referring to items such as *Oops!* or *Eek!*, which are used as self-directed remarks when one is alone, not engaged in interaction with others. Interjections are used, for example, when one slips on an icy road, witnesses a vase falling, or has forgotten one's keys at home. According to Goffman, response cries are conventionalized (ritualized) to the extent that they are also used in interaction with others, as a way of displaying one's attitude toward what the coparticipant has just said (e.g., *Ouch!* as a response to a plumber's telling what the bill will be; *Oh wow!* as a response to a telling about another's fate, Goffman, 1981, pp. 107–8).

Recent studies on the expression of affect and emotion in English have drawn attention to the affective load of response cries and their modifiability (see Goodwin & Goodwin, 1987, for an earlier formative study, also 1992). In his discussion of responding to reports of personal experience, Heritage (2011) states that the equivocal character of response cries enables them to be used to evoke and claim empathic affiliation with the coconversant more closely than, for example, by using "my side" assessments, which, while claiming affiliation, remain more distant from the other's experience. However, according to Heritage (ibid.), the affective stance is typically specified subsequently by the recipient. This resonates with the following observation by Sacks (1992, vol. 1, p. 495; Sacks uses the term "expletive" for the expression *Oh God*).

> "Oh God" expresses a pain, and "Christmas has gotten so damn painful" explains the pain that's been expressed. With the expletive, then, one is told to listen to the sentence that follows, by reference to what the expletive expresses; to hear what follows as an account of how come the expletive was produced.

Couper-Kuhlen (chapter 6) shows how the affiliative weight of response cries rests heavily on the prosodic matching or upgrading of the response compared to prior talk when responding to a complaint story. Like Heritage, she also points out the relevance of a subsequent reinforcement of the affect display with a more substantial and explicit utterance. In their study (2006) on surprise tokens—*wow, gosh, oh my God, ooh, phew*, and so on—Wilkinson and Kitzinger view them as interactionally organized performances, interactional achievements, rather than as involuntary emotional eruptions (see also Heath et al., in this volume, chapter 10).

The expression we will explore in this chapter, *voi että*, in many ways resembles Goffman's response cries, and it can also be seen as performing an affect similar to what Wilkinson and Kitzinger have observed. In other words, it lacks referential meaning but is not devoid of meaning: it has become conventionalized as an index of affect display. Whereas *voi että* is an expression that can be said both to oneself and to one's coparticipant in interaction, we will explore the latter usage only. This response consists of the interjection *voi* followed by *että*, used in other contexts as a subordinating connective ("that") introducing a complement clause ("she said **that** tomorrow she will". . .), or alternatively, as a particle in an utterance-initial position evoking another voice (see Laury & Seppänen 2008). We will discuss the import of *että* to the interpretation of the response on p. 148.

In many languages, interjections often combine with other elements to form more substantial response types. One of these is a construction for providing an affective response to the coparticipant's prior turn, consisting of [Interjection + Connective/Question word + Adjective], for example, "Oh how horrible" in English (Pomerantz, 1975, p. 35). In Finnish, examples of this phrasal construction are *voi ku kiva* ("*voi* how nice") and *voi kun hirveetä ~ tylsää* ("*voi* how awful ~ boring"), where *ku(n)*, translated here as "how," is a connective with meanings that are temporal, causal and conditional (Herlin, 1998). In the absence of more precise equivalents in English, the *voi* in the previous example could be translated as "oh." However, unlike the English *oh*, *voi* is not a general, epistemic change-of-state token but indexes affective stance.

Another format used in responses with affect is of the type [Interjection + Noun]: *voi luoja* "oh God." This construction type, as well as the previous one, characterizes as either negative or positive a state of affairs that has been mentioned in the preceding talk (in the prior turn or in the longer preceding sequence). The nouns used in these phrasal constructions are idiomatic and language-specific. In Finnish, the noun may characterize a given state of affairs, such as *voi ihme*, "oh miracle," *voi hurja*, "oh wild," *voi luoja*, "oh God," *voi paska*, "oh shit," *voi räkä*, "oh snot," *voi nenä*, "oh nose." These expressions treat the object of the evaluation as something unexpected, unfortunate, or disappointing. However, other less clear cases of this format are used in connection with such positive emotions as joy, happiness, and so on. In another set of cases, the noun is an endearment term and characterizes the recipient, for example, *voi nuppu*, literally "bud," *voi kulta*, "gold," *voi muru*, "morsel," conveying empathy toward the coparticipant.

A slightly different kind of construction, consisting of *voi* followed by a personal pronoun, can be used for expressing a stance toward the coparticipant, or toward any person(s) participating or otherwise involved: *voi sua*, "you" (singular), *voi teitä*, "you" (plural); *voi niitä*, *voi heitä*, "them," *voi meitä*, "us," *voi mua*, "me." The interjection functions here as the head of the phrase and the pronoun is in an object case form (partitive case). As the nominal element in these constructions is a pronoun and not an adjective or a noun, the affect or stance expressed is not made lexically explicit but is more dependent on the immediate context. Accordingly, *voi mua / meitä*, "oh me / us," may be heard as expressing self pity, literally "poor me / us," whereas *voi sua*, "oh you," can have a less specific, and in the last resort more context-bound, import toward what the coparticipant has just been doing or telling, how s/he has been treated, or how s/he has been behaving (childishly, too ambitiously, etc.).

In all these phrase-like expressions, the affective interjection *voi* acts as a head and the rest of the construction specifies the valence (*voi ihme*, "miracle"), or the object of the affect (*voi sua*, "you"). The response type that we will be focusing on, *voi että*, is the most "open" one of the response types initiated with the interjection *voi*. In this construction, there is no characterizing element; *voi että*, in addition to being used as a self-directed remark, merely voices recognition of the coparticipant's prior turn as one that has made an affective response relevant and that displays attunement to that affect, whatever it might be. As we pointed out above, *että* is basically used as a subordinating conjunction or as a turn-initial epistemic particle. What we would like to argue here is that the openness of *voi että* can be derived from its basic uses that project more to come. When nothing follows it, the coparticipant may, as it were, fill in the relevant affect that is left unspecified by the response itself. (For *voi että* initiating a longer, phrasal or clausal turn, see Extract 2, below.)

The kind of verbal action that *voi että* performs can be described in Finnish with the verb *päivitellä*. This verb is translated in the Finnish–English dictionary with the alternatives "wag one's tongue," "wonder at," "complain," or "lament" (Hurme, Malin,

& Syväoja, 1984, s.v. *päivitellä*). However, all these translations seem to us to have a more specific meaning—and for the most part a more negative one—than *päivitellä*; the act of *päivitellä* need not specify what kind of stance its speaker is conveying. The closest (American) English equivalent for the verb might be the "delocutive"[1] expression *OMGing* ("oh-my-god-ing"). In our data collection[2], *voi että* both forms a turn at talk by itself (Extract 1) and occurs turn-initially (Extract 2). We mainly focus on the former type. In addition, *voi että* can be either preceded by a particle or followed by an adverb within the same turn (see Extracts 9–11 below). (For a key to the glossing symbols, see the Appendix, p. see the appendix to this volume .)

Extract 1 [Kotus, Hair salon; H = hairdresser, C = client]

```
01          (16.0)    ((H is cutting C's hair. They are listening to news
                      broadcast about the escape of a Swedish murderer.))

02  H:      Ai    se    on    edelleen  karkuteillä  se,   (.)   Ruotsin,
            Oh    he    is    still     at large     the,  (.)   Sweden's,

03          (2.0)
04  C:   →  #Voi että#.
05          (4.0)

06  H:      Mutta  määhäl   luin    tänä    aamuna    ku - - - - - -
            But    I y-know  read    this    morning   that - - -
```

Extract 2 [Field notes]

(a)

Voi   että   sulla   on   hyvät   puheet
PRT   PRT   you-ADE   is   good   speeches
Voi että you do speak well

(b)

Voi   että   mitkä   maisemat.
PRT   PRT   what.PL   scenery-PL
Voi että what scenery.

In what follows, we will discuss some of the basic usages of this nonpredicating, open type of response cry when it is provided as a response to a telling (informing, announcement of good or bad news, etc.). We will show that *voi että* clusters in those contexts where there is some ambiguity and that it orients to that ambiguity. First, we will discuss cases where the ambiguity has a sequential nature (e.g., what the climax of the story is or what the main line of the story is). Second, we will show that this ambiguity may be due to the valence of the affect that is expressed by the main speaker (e.g., whether the news is good or bad). These two kinds of ambiguity are often intertwined. Finally, we will discuss the closing implicativeness that a *voi että* response may have, both in itself and in connection with certain adverbs.

RESPONDING TO SEQUENTIAL AMBIVALENCE

The lexically open and unspecified nature of a response with *voi että* leads to the question about the relevance of that kind of meaning display, the affordances it offers to its speaker. One way to determine that is to explore both the character of the preceding talk to which the recipient offers this kind of affect display, as well as the subsequent talk by the coparticipant. Let us take an example from a telling sequence. The ambiguity here pertains to what the main point (climax) of the telling is. In Extract 3, Anna's *voi että* in line 10 responds to Kati's report of an incident that happened to her brother: he dislocated his knee. That report is occasioned by a piece of news from the teller that her brother will start a new job (data not shown) and her subsequent evaluation of that as "quite good" (line 1), for which an explanatory elaboration is projected (*silleen niinku*, "in the way like") but not produced. Instead, Kati adds a parenthetical utterance, and it is in this utterance that she reports the incident that happened to her brother. This utterance is marked as being about something that the recipient does not have previous knowledge of (*sä et oo kuullukkaa*, "you haven't heard about that"). On the other hand, in line 3 with the adverb *tosiaan*, "indeed," Kati conveys that this is an incident she has been talking about earlier (cf. Hokkanen, 2008).

The report in lines 2–3 is offered as a nonaffective description in that it lacks lexical stance-taking elements or heightened prosody. It is produced with a slightly rising final contour that projects more talk to come (see Routarinne, 2003, p. 200; Ogden & Routarinne, 2005). On the other hand, the content of the utterance is treatable as a telling of bad news and as such, something that could be elaborated on. In this sequential context, the recipient faces a dilemma concerning how to respond. Here, Anna responds in ways that orient to the sequential place of the report as being ambivalent.

Extract 3 [SKL Sg 101:2 Knee]
```
01 Kati:   mut  mut  (0.8)  mut  se        on    ihan  hyvä  silleen niinku
           but  but         but  DEM.SG is       quite good  so     like
           but but (0.8) but it's quite good in the way like

02         sä    et   oo   kuullukaa    siitä       ku.hhh
           you   NEG-2be   hear-PPC-CLIDEM.SG-ELA   as
           you haven't heard about that when.hhh

03         tosiaan Sakella     meni tota  se<     (.) polvi sijoiltaan?
           really  name–ADE  went PRT  DEM.SG   knee dislocated
           Sakke indeed got uh his< (.) knee dislocated?

04 Anna:   Ai  [jaa.              ]
           oh  I [see.             ]
05 Kati:       [Tai  se     oli   ] (.) neljä päivää siellä (.) ni   sit  (.)
               [Or   DEM.SG was   ] (.) four  days  there  (.) and  then
```

06   <u>sen</u>häm   mä kirjotinki   et   se   on siel   Siilijjärvellä?,'
          DEM.SG-CLI I   wrote-1-CLI   that DEM.SG be there townNAME-ADE
          I did write about <u>it</u> that he's in Siilinjärvi?,'

07 Anna: *Mm, mm,*

08 Kati: .mhh Ni   tota   (.) n<u>e</u>ljä päivää ehti   olla
                 PRT PRT   four   days   have.time-PST   be
          .mhh So er (.) <u>fo</u>ur days he managed to stay ((there))

09   ni   sil   meni   polvi sijoiltaa?,
          PRT   DEM.SG-ADE go-PST   knee   dislocated
          and he got his knee dislocated?,

10 Anna: **V<u>o</u>:i että.**

11 Kati: Ni   (.) sit se   joutu   ootas   nyt eka siel Siilijjärvel
          PRT   then DEM.SG have.to.go-PST wait-IMP now first there townNAME
          so (.) then he had to go wait a sec f<u>i</u>rst in Siilinjärvi

12   terveyskeskukseen ja   sit Kuopion   (.)   yliopistolliseen
          health-center-ILL and   then cityNAME-GEN   university-ADJ-ILL
          to the health center and then to the central university

13   keskussairaalaan   ja   sitte.hh e Mikkelin (.)
          center-hospital-ILL and   then   cityNAME-GEN
          hospital in Kuopio and then.hh e to the central hospital

14   kes↑kussairaalaa   ja   sit se   lei↑kattiin   siellä.mhh
          center-hospital-ILL and then DEM.SG operate-PAS-PST there
          in Mikkeli and then he was ope↑rated there.mhh

15   ja   [sitte]
          and   [then]
16 Anna: [Siis]
                [So]
17   (.)
18 Kati: [ni,]

19 Anna: [>m<u>i</u>-] m<u>i</u>ten se   n<u>ii</u>m mones   paikkaa sit   niinku,
          how how DEM.SG so   many-INE place-PAR then like
          [>h<u>o</u>-] h<u>o</u>w come he ((was)) in s<u>o</u> many places then like,

The recipient first (line 4) responds to the telling of the incident in terms of its
news value with the news receipt *ai jaa*. Upon hearing *ai*, the teller continues. Then,
instead of elaborating on that incident and explicating her stance, the teller backs up
to provide additional background to the event, formulated as a reminder of shared
knowledge (*senhäm mä kirjotinki*, "I did write about it") (line 6), getting minimal
acknowledgments from the recipient that imply acceptance of the formulation of

common ground (line 7). The teller then incorporates that information into a fuller elaboration of the news (lines 8–9). This revised report on the incident contains a lexical element that frames the news as less than bad: in the description of the duration of the time the brother was in the civil service before injuring his knee, the choice of the verb *ehti* ("managed") portrays the incident ironically as quasi-intentional. The choice of the verb could also be interpreted as projecting bad news. The turn, however, is uttered with a final contour that is rising, continuation-implicative, projecting that some main news is yet to come.

The *voi että* response (line 10) receives the telling as something to which an affective response is in order, but it does not lexically specify that affect. In this way this response orients to the sequential context and is fitted to it. Furthermore, the *voi että* is produced with a falling final contour and a slight vowel stretch in the first word (marked with a colon), suggesting that the news is to be treated as potentially bad. Also, the turn is composed of *voi että* only, and not of, for instance, *voi kauheeta*, "oh how awful," which would explicitly express the recipient's stance toward the protagonist of the story. Instead, this response transfers the turn back to the teller and leaves the development of the talk to her.

In her following turn, the teller launches into a detailed narration of the subsequent events, which indicates that the incident with her brother's knee was not designed as the climax of the narration (line 11 on). The turn is also initiated by the particle *ni*, indicating a move to the main line of telling (see Vilkuna, 1997). In this way, the brother's dislocated knee is marked as being backgrounded in relation to the consequences of the incident, a long and winding trip from one hospital to another. What this example illustrates is that in a sequential context where the ambivalence lies in whether to respond to a piece of potentially negative news at a place where the main point of the telling is yet to come, the recipient expresses an affective treatment of that prior talk by using a *voi että* response. This leaves the kind of affect lexically unspecified, and to be inferred from the content of the prior talk. Being a minimal response, *voi että* also allows a continuation of the telling: It displays affect but does not derail the ongoing, incomplete telling as a more substantial response might. Considering that this is a "sympathy" context, that is, there has been a report of a misfortune experienced by someone close to the teller, *voi että* can be heard as implying sympathy.

In the preceding example, the recipient responded with *voi että* at a place where the prior speaker had left room for a response but where the sequential implication of the coparticipant's prior utterance was ambivalent. However, in the following extract, the character of the ambivalence of how to respond to the prior talk is more intricate, connecting with the main line of telling and its sideline elaboration. In this fragment, the recipient responds with *voi että* within a segment of highly affective troubles telling. Marja is telling Eeva about her tearful day, as it was her close colleague's last day at work. The summing up of the detailed events of that day evokes an empathic response from the recipient in line 28. Then, from line 33 on, Eeva proceeds to account for her extensive crying by describing how important that colleague is to her. This segment contains *voi että* responses in lines 40 and 51.

Extract 4 [SG S 21 A 3 Last day at work]
25 M: *tää   on   [ollu   kyllä]*
         this   is   be-PPC   surely
         this has [surely been]

26   [*.mthh*]

27 M: [*yh*[*tä   vol:laamista   helvetti   tää   ilta*].*mt*
         one-PAR   howling-PAR   hell   this   evening
         [ju[st a hell of a ho:wling this evening].tch

28 E: *h   [Voi:::   nu:ppu:::.]*
              PRT   bud
         h   [Oh:::   ho:ney:::.]

29 M: *s'   tuntuu   0   jotenki   n*[*ii   #öö#   tyhjälle   ]*
         DEM.SG   feel-SG3   0   somehow   so   empty-ALL
         it feels somehow   s[o uh empty   ]

30 M: *sen   pai:kka   sit   #taas jonku   ai   [kaa   täs   että]*
         DEM.SG-GEN place   then   again   some-GEN   time-PAR   here   PRT
         her pla:ce then #for awhile here so

31 E: [*Nii:*,   ]

32 M: *.hhhhhh.t   ku   sen   kans   on   sillee   o   aika*
                   since   DEM.SG-GEN   with   be-SG3   in.that.way   be-SG3   quite
         .hhhhhh.t °as one has been like quite

33   *paljo   0   ollu   tekemisis   noin   niinku hhhh   privaatisti*
         much   0   be-PPC   doing-PL-INE   PRT   like   private-ADV
         a lot in contact with her like hhhh in private life

34   *kan*[*s   (se   on   mut)*] *ottanu   semmoseks   oikee   #m#*
         also   DEM.SG   be   I-ACC   take-PPC   such-TRA   really
         as well x(she has taken me)x in fact sort of

35 E: [*Joo:*.   ]

36 M: *.hhh   <suojel-   suojeltavaksee   jotenki*
                   protect   protect-PAS-PC-TRA-POS3   somehow
         .hhh <pro-under her protection somehow

37   *et   ku,hh   et   ei   oo   toisella   äitii   nii*
         PRT   as   PRT   NEG.SG3   be   other-ADE   mother-PAR   PRT
         so as, hh one doesn't have a mother so

38   *hänem   pittää   kattoo   [perääv   vähä   ja,   .mh   ]*
         s/he-GEN   must   look   [after   a.little   and   ]
         she has to look after (("me")) a little and, .mh

39 E: [*.mt*   ]

40 E: → [***Voi:: e:ttä:,***]   ]

41 M: [*hirveesti   lohduttanu   mua   niinku täs   S-*   ]
           terrible-ADV comfort-PPC   I-PAR   PRT   here 1nameM
           [she has comforted me an awful lot like in this S-

42 M: *Sven   hom#mis   et*
           1nameM stuff-PL-INE PRT
           Sven business like

43   *vittuuks   sie   tuos   jätkäs   s(h)e   o(h) n(h)i(h)inku*
           cunt-PAR-Q-CLI you   that-INE bloke-INE DEM.SG   be   like
           what the fuck you ((see))in that jerk he i(h)s l(h)ike

44   *todella   .hh [h   [se   ei   o*
           really   DEM.SG   NEG   be
                      .hh [h   [he really isn't
                           [[

45 E: [*he he* [*he he*

46 M: *siun   arvonen   et   ky:l   sie   löyvät*
           you.SG-GEN worth   PRT   surely   you   nice-SG2
           worthy of you so you'll surely find

47   *mukavam#piiki   että#   (.) @↑iha just   semmone   tyyppi*
           nice-COM-PL-PAR-also PRT   right   just   such   type
           nicer ones so# (.) @↑just the kind of jerk

48   *joka   ei   niinku ei   pysty   tällasee*
           that   NEG   like   NEG   be.capable this.kind-ILL
           who isn't like isn't capable of forming this kind of

49   *#aikuisee   .mh   ihmissuhte(h)e(h)see*
           grown.up-ILL   human-relationship-ILL
           #mature.mh relati(h)onshi(h)p

50   *ja   ka(h)ikkee   .hee   .hee   .nff*
           and   a(h)ll that   .hee   .hee   .nff

51 E: → <***Vo***[***i:: että:,***>
                   [

52 M: [*Joo: ku-   £kuule   tää   oli   nii:n*]
            PRT   listen listen-IMP.SG2 this be-PST so   ]
           [Yeah: li- £listen this was so::   ]

53   *masentavaa   #ja molemmat ties   tän   etukäteen*
           depressing-PAR and both-PL   know-PST.SG3 this-GEN   beforehand
           depressing #and ((we)) both knew this beforehand

54	*et*	*täst*	*ei*	*tuu*	*p<u>u</u>lkkistakaa#,=*
	that	this-ELA	NEG	come	anything ((figurative))

that this is going nowhere#,=

The first *voi että* in line 40 is provided as a response to a telling, the gist of which is that the colleague has acted as a mother figure to the teller. The response occurs after a projection of a continuation (*ja*, "and," line 38), where there is a hitch in the speaker's talk.

The utterance to which *voi että* responds is marked as an explanation (*ku*, "as," line 37) for why the colleague had taken the teller under her protection. Marja's illustration of the nature of "protection" is presented as the reported speech of the colleague's words (lines 37–8). By virtue of the reference forms (*toisella*, "the other one," referring to the teller, Marja; *hänem*, "she," for the colleague) and of the present tense of the verb (*oo*, "have"), this utterance is an instance of free indirect speech. Moreover, the pronoun *toinen*, "the other one," which is an endearment word used particularly in addressing babies and pets, conveys the motherly affect expressed by the colleague. (For affect conveyed by reported speech, see e.g., Günthner, 1999.) The function of this reported speech is to specify of the importance of the colleague in the teller's life.

By virtue of its openness, the *voi että* response simultaneously addresses several aspects of the prior turn. As illustrated by the reported speech, this display of affect can be heard as recognizing the generic value of a person mothering a younger colleague. At the same time, it receives the telling as evidence of the kind of loss experienced by the teller and displays affiliation with her—in fact, Marja is not only losing her colleague but will be facing motherlessness once again. In other words, a response that leaves the affect and its object lexically unspecified allows multiple aspects of the prior talk to be addressed simultaneously.

Overlapping the *voi että* response, the teller (line 41) proceeds to offer a further illustration of the colleague's comforting, this time in relation to a disappointing boyfriend. On line 51, the recipient faces a dilemma of whether to respond locally, to the criticism of the boyfriend (through stereotypical descriptions of his failures: "he really isn't worthy of you," lines 43, 46; "who isn't capable of forming this kind of mature relationship," lines 48–9), or to continue expressing sympathy toward the teller who has lost her colleague, thereby orienting to the main line of the story. The choice of *voi että* is a way of counterbalancing these two lines of talk.

In the preceding examples, *voi että* responded to a co-participant's telling that was located within and as part of a larger activity and was not the climax (Extract 3) or the key action (Extract 4). But even when the telling of a piece of news recognizably forms the main action (Jefferson, 1981; Maynard, 2003), the placement and framing of this telling within a larger segment of talk may pose a dilemma to the recipient. Despite being located in a sequential place that lends itself to making a news announcement, the character of the news may not be self-evident. In this context, the recipient may use *voi että* as a response to the telling. Here, sequential ambiguity merges with the valence of the affect conveyed (see Maynard & Freese, in this volume, chapter 5).

In the following example from a telephone call, *voi että* (line 18) is given as a response to a telling that the call recipient Sanna has presented as the second item in her response to the caller's "how are you" question. This second item follows a telling about her puppy's sickness (cf. Extracts 9 and 10). Starting in line 11, Sanna reports a state of affairs containing information that is newsworthy and announceable: she is expecting a baby. The *voi että* that occurs here is the caller Kalle's third response within the activity. Before that, he responds to the telling twice with a display of ritualized disbelief (line 13, *sinä vai*, "you mean you"; line 15, *ei kai*, "you don't say").

Extract 5 [SKL Sg S14 A02 Baby]

```
01 K:   Joo     joo .. mhhh   Mut     se    oli    täpärällä         sitte.
        PRT     PRT .mhhh     But     it    was    a narrow escape then.

02 S:   ↑Nii:ih.  Mä   ajattelin      vaa    et    ku        ottaa
        PRT       I    think-PST-SG1  just   that  when   0  take-SG3
        ↑Yea:h. I just thought that when one takes

03      tollasen      sekarotusen      koiran      ni    (.)   £ne       on
        that.kind-GEN mixed.breed-GEN  dog-GEN     PRT         DEM.PL    be-SG3
        a mixed-breed dog like that (.) £so they are

04      nii   ter(h)veitä       hhehhh   ja    vas  [tustuskykysiä
        so    healthy-PL-PAR             and   resis[tance-capable-PL-PAR
        so hea(h)lthy hhehhh and resis[tant

05 K:                                         [Nii:.

06 K:   Nii  [tietenki joo]
        Yes  [of.course yes]

07 S:        [Et     mä en       sit   kysyny      et     on      sit
             PRT     I NEG-SG1   then  ask-PPC     PRT    be-SG3  then
             [So I didn't ask if there is right away

08      heti          kauhee    kuolemantauti     °että°    [.hh
        immediately   awful     death-GEN-illness  PRT      [.hh
        a terrible fatal illness °so°    [.hh

09 K:                                              [°Joo°.hh (.)
10.     mt Voi että °sent'n°

11 S:   No   ehkä     mä   voin.hh kertoo    teille        ennen     ku.hh
        PRT  maybe    I    can-SG1 tell      you.PL-ALL    before    when
        Well maybe I can.hh tell you before.hh

12      Hanna  ehtii       j- juoruilla    et     mä   odotan      lasta.
        1nameF have.time   gossip          that   I    expect-SG1  child-PAR
        Hanna has time to g- gossip that I am expecting a baby.
```

13 K: → *Sinä*   *vaih,*
           you.SG   or
           You mean you,

14 S: *Nii;*

15 K: → *E(h)i*   *kai,*
           NEG   maybe
           You do(h)n't say,

16 S: *Nii, mä eilen,*   *(.) kerroin*   *Hannalle.=Mä aatte'n et   Hanna*
           PRT I yesterday   tell-PST-SG1   1nameF-ALL I think-? that 1nameF
           Yes, I told Hanna yesterday.=I thought that Hanna

17   *varmaan jossain   vaihees*   [*.hhh °'t]te°*
           surely   some-INE phase-INE   then
           will certainly at some point [.hhh then
                                                    [   ]

18 K: →   [**Voi että,**]

19 S: *ilmottaa*   *teille,*
           announce   you.PL-ALL
           inform you,

20 K: *.mt Ihanaah,* *.hh tota, mitä*   *tota onks*   *se*   *ö- nyt*
           lovely-PAR   PRT what-PAR PRT be-SG3-Q DEM.SG PRT
           .mt Lovely,.hh uhm, what uhm is it er

21   *suunniteltuu vai .hh vai sillai*   *puoliks, .hh vai vai*
           planned   or   or   that.kind half-TRA   or   or
           planned or.hh or sort of half,.hh or or if one may

22   *miten, jos 0 saa   kysy[ä.*
           how   if 0 may-SG3 ask
           how (("is it")),if one may as[k.

23 S: [*ehhih   No   eiköhän   ne*
                                       [PRT   NEG.SG3-Q-CLI DEM.PL
                                       [ehhih Well don't they

24   *jotenki,*   *aina,*   *suunnittelemalla tuu*   *et[tä*
           somehow   always   planning-ADE   come   PRT
           somehow, always, come through planning[so

23 K: [*Nih*

A number of features in this segment attract attention. To begin with, the news is told straightaway in the topic and sequence-initial turn (lines 11–12), without preparing the recipient for it and its quality with, for example, a presequence (cf. Terasaki, 2004 [1976]). Second, the turn itself is formulated in a way that gives the impression that the teller is begrudgingly delivering the news, as if under duress: it starts with a clause that names the action as telling but hosts both the modal adverb *ehkä*, "maybe" and the modal verb *voin* "I can." Third, the *et*-clause ("that"-clause, line 12) postpones the news even further in the turn. At a place where the object of telling would be due next (after *kertoo teille*, "tell you.PL," line 11), the teller initiates a temporal clause instead (*ennen ku Hanna ehtii*, "before Hanna has time".). That clause sets the telling as if it were competing temporally with the telling of the same news by a mutual friend, Hanna, and this clause describes her potential action as her spreading gossiping (*juoruilla*), thereby implying a justification for Sanna's telling of the news at this point. It is only then that Sanna delivers the news. The ultimate reason for this telling may well be that a friend needs to learn important news firsthand, not from the gossip that is being spread by others. Nonetheless, making this state of affairs explicit places the news and its telling in a rather peculiar light.

Thus the roundabout way that the telling about the pregnancy is presented can pose a dilemma to the recipient. The tokens of ritual disbelief on lines 13 and 15 can also be interpreted as signifying genuine surprise. In any case, these tokens create a space for the teller to elaborate on her news, or to express its affective significance. However, the teller first merely provides a confirmation (line 14), and then, as a response to the second display of disbelief by the recipient, moves on to elaborate the framing instead of the news itself (lines 16–17). That elaboration implies that the current recipient (Kalle) is not among the primary recipients but suggests that Hanna is a link between Sanna and Kalle. At this point, the recipient responds with *voi että*.

The *voi että* response is produced when the teller has reached a recognition point in her elaboration (line 17) and where it becomes clear that the news would have been told to the recipient at some point. After two tokens of ritual disbelief, the recipient's expression of surprise or joy would have been in place. As Sacks (1992, Vol. 2, p. 572) has noted, an expression of appropriate emotion typically follows expressions of surprise. (See also Wilkinson & Kitzinger, 2006; Maynard & Freese, chapter 5) On the other hand, the recipient is facing a dilemma, as the teller herself has moved away from the (good) news and elaborated on the frame instead. The recipient then solves this dilemma by responding without explicit evaluation.

One could claim that, as *voi että* is being produced at a sequential place for an expression of affect but is equivocal about the appropriate valence of the affect, this equivocal response therefore aligns with the equivocal way the news was told. At the completion of the teller's utterance, the recipient (line 20) explicates his stance with the evaluative adjective *ihanaa*, which we have translated as "lovely" but which in its strength is slightly stronger than the English response *lovely*. Even this response is delivered in such a way, without any variation in pitch but with a flat, stylized prosody, that it still leaves open the affective valence of the telling. From the responsive adjective, the recipient proceeds to ask about the circumstances of the teller getting pregnant. This question further illustrates the difficulty that the recipient has in assessing the affective valence and this message could perhaps be interpreted as the pregnancy not being planned, but being a mishap instead. In this case *voi että* is used as a response to an utterance in which the teller merges the telling of the news to an evaluation of the way in which the news would be spread: both the status of the telling as a piece of news to be told by the teller to this recipient, as well as the affective valence of the news, were ambivalent.

The sequence we have discussed here can be analyzed within the larger context of the call. As can be seen at the beginning of the extract (lines 1–8), the telling about the pregnancy is not the teller's first piece of news, but the telling starts immediately following the end of the preceding topic about the teller's sick puppy (lines 7–8), with no link to the previous talk. Thus, also in this way, at a point where a move to close the telephone call (preclosing) would be possible (the reason for the call has already been dealt with, see note 4), the news about the pregnancy is placed as if it is of secondary importance when compared to the news about the sick puppy (see Sacks, 1992, Vol. 2, p. 88). Furthermore, earlier in the call, before Sanna launched into the topic of the sick puppy, when asked, she stated that nothing unusual had happened to her and her husband.[3]

In this section, we have discussed extracts in which the recipient of a narration or news announcement has faced a dilemma: the utterance to be responded to has been sequentially ambivalent. In these instances, the recipient resorted to the response cry *voi että*. In Extract 3, potentially bad news turned out not to be delivered as a story climax but as background to the main line of the story. In Extract 4, *voi että* twice addressed a sideline while the main storyline was continued, thereby not selecting the detail to be an object of further talk. Extract 5 provided an illustration of how difficulty may arise concerning the placement of a piece of news with respect to the telling about another piece of news because the recipient may not be able to decide on the news value and valence of the news. Each of these examples contained an ambiguity of affective valence that was intertwined with sequential ambiguity. In the next section, we will focus more explicitly on the ambiguity of valence.

AMBIGUITY OF VALENCE

So far we have discussed *voi että* as a response to the sequential implications of prior talk that has been somehow ambivalent. Even though the prior talk may not clearly express ambivalence, the recipient may use the unspecified and open character of *voi että* to treat the prior talk and its affective valence as equivocal. For instance, the recipient may not feel comfortable in sharing his or her stance with the teller. The next extract is an illustration of this. In this extract, Jaana is hosting a party of four, and during that event recounts to her guests the problems she has encountered with her siblings when they divided up inherited items. One of her siblings, Jaana's brother, was particularly greedy and tried to take anything he could get his hands on. This excerpt is from a telling about how the brother would not relinquish even the smallest of items. The response *voi että* then starts in overlap with the teller's assessment *Se o iha hassua* ("That is quite silly," line 30).

Extract 6 [SKL Sg 355, Crystals (47:47)]

12 Jaana: [*No   sitte   oli   semmosia   kr*i*stalleja*
             PRT   then   be-SG3   such-PL-PAR crystal-PL
             [Well then there were the kinds of crystals

13   *kato   ku   nois   amppeleis   roikkuu,*
             look-IMP PRT   those-INE   hanging.pot-PL-INE   hang-SG3
             you see that are tacked on the hanging flower pots

14   (0.2)

15 Mirja: *N[ii.*
             Y[es
              [

16 Jaana: [*Ku äiti   oli   jostai   ostanu   ja   k*e*ränny   niitä,   .hh*
             PRT mother be-PST some   buy-PPC and collect-PPC DEM.PL-PAR
                                   where-ELA
             ['Cos mother had bought and collected them somewhere,.hh

17   *No   L*ii*salla   on   semmonen amppeli   mistä*
             PRT   1nameF-ADE   be   such   flower.pot which-ELA
             Well Liisa has a hanging flower pot from which

18   *puuttuu   kai   <n*e*ljä.>*
             miss   perhaps   four
             <four.> pieces may be missing.

19   (1.0)

20 Jaana: *Ja   niitä   oli   siinä   p*a*rik*y*mmentä, ja   ne   rupes*
             and SG3.DEM-PAR be-PST around twenty   and DEM.PL start-PST
             And there were about tw$e$nty pieces, and they started to argue

21   *n*ii*stäki   sit   et   kumpiki   ne   ois   halunnu   .hh mä*
             DEM.PL-ELA-CLI then   that both.of.them DEM.PL   would want-PPC   I
             over those as well as both would have wanted them.hh I

22   *s'no   että @*o*nhan niitä   siinä että p*i*stäkää ne   p*ua*liks,@*
             say.PST   that   be-CLI   DEM.PL-PAR   there that divide   DEM.PL half-TRA
             I s'd well @there $a$re ((a lot)) of them there just div$i$de them,@

23   (0.2)

24 Jaana: *Nii se   *a*nto kuule   ↑n*e*ljä   Liisan*
             so   DEM.SG gave listen-IMP   four   Name-GEN
             So he g$a$ve just imagine ↑four in Liisa's

25   kät[tee   ja   tunki   loput]   t*a*skuunsa.
            hand-ILL and   jam-PST   rest   pocket-ILL-SG3.POS
            han[d and jammed the rest in his p*o*cket.
                        [   ]

26 Mirja: [mheh heh heh he,   ]

27   (0.8)   ((Jaana and Mirja are gazing at each other,
                             Mikko starts to move his gaze to Jaana))

28 Mikko: *Mut*
            But

29   [*eiks*   *toi*   *ny*   *jo*<   ]
            NEG-Q-CLI   that   PRT   already
            [isn't that   ]
            [   ]

30 Jaana: [↑*Se*   *o*   *iha*   *has*   ] [*sua*,   ↑
            [↑That   is   quite sil   ] [ly,   ↑
                                                  [

31 Mirja: →   [*<Voi et*[*tä*,*>*   ]
                                                          [

32 Mikko: [*Mut eiks toi oo nii*]*nku*
                                                but NEG-Q that be like
                                                [But isn't that for that

33   *m*uu*to*   *sit*   *niinku* *h*e*lpotus*   *ku*   *tommonen h*o*mma*
            otherwise then like   relief   PRT   that.kind business
            matter then like a relief when that kind of j*o*b

34   *on*   *niinku*   [*o*hi,   *eks*-
            is   like   past   NEG-Q
            is like [over, isn't-
                            [

35 Jaana: [*O*n,
                                is
                                [Yes.

36 Mirja: [*Nii*,   *i*hav   *v*a*rmasti*
                                PRT   quite   sure-ADV
                                [*Nii*,   absol*u*tely

When the teller reaches the climax of the story (lines 24–5), one of the recipients, Mirja, begins to laugh at a recognition point in the utterance. While laughing, she withdraws her gaze from the teller and turns her head aside, returning her gaze to the teller only after she stops laughing. At a place where the utterance and the telling have reached a possible completion, the recipients can express their stance toward the telling, for example by affiliating with the teller's criticism and disapproval. However, neither of them responds in this way, and a silence ensues.

The teller and the recipient Mirja, who are sitting side by side, exchange mutual gazes; the recipient Mikko, who is seated opposite the teller, then moves his head and gazes at her. Mikko then begins a contrast-implicative utterance (*mut*, "but," line 28). When she hears Mikko's utterance, the teller proceeds to pursue a response (cf. Pomerantz, 1984a) with an assessment that explicates her disapproving stance toward her brother's conduct that she has just been telling about. In overlap at a point of recognition in that assessment, Mirja utters the *voi että* response. By using this token, she expresses an affective stance but leaves the valence of the affect equivocal. In offering this type of open response, Mirja does not take a stance on his conduct, leaving the more explicit evaluation to Jaana, who is the primary experiencer of the event and the person who has firsthand knowledge of the protagonist in this narration.

In Extract 6, the recipient had a choice in assessing the incident she has just been told by joining the teller in expressing disapproval, but she got around it by using *voi että*. In this way, she neither commits herself to explicitly disapproving of Jaana's brother's behavior, nor does she produce an explicitly amused assessment (see line 26). But the situation may be the other way round, that is, there may be ambivalence in the valence inherent in the main speaker's talk. Both in telling news and in responding to it, the central aspects are the news value of the event or the state of affairs and its overall affective character, for example whether it is good news or bad news and explicitly in what way either good or bad (see Maynard & Freese, chapter 5). This type of ambivalent valence was present in several of the examples in the previous section. Let us now have a closer look at some of them.

In discussing Extract 5, we suggested that after two tokens of ritual disbelief, an expression of surprise or joy by the recipient would have been in place. Displays of surprise are here indeed followed by the affective response *voi että*. But the way the news announcement is delivered results in the valence of the news itself being ambivalent. Here the framework involves heading off possible gossip that may start to circulate. There is no token of joy or excitement in either Sanna's announcement (lines 11–12) or in the further elaboration following Kalle's expressions of surprise or disbelief. In short, the situation in this fragment differs from the previous one: The equivocalness or ambivalence is already present in the telling, that is, whether it is good news or bad news, and is subsequently reflected in the way the news is receipted: When *voi että*, the open type of response occurs, it does not make explicit the speaker's stance to the news.

In our analysis of Extract 4 above, we focused on the aspect of sequential ambiguity with respect to the two *voi että* responses, that of ambiguity between the main line and the sideline of the telling. But we also briefly remarked that *voi että* may simultaneously orient more locally to the ambivalence of the affective valence in the narration. The latter one of the two *voi että* responses in that fragment occurs within a segment which is told as a direct quote (starting in line 43). The spicy language in the first part of the quotation (*vittuuks*, "what the fuck"; *jätkäs*, "in that jerk") is received as laughable by the recipient (line 45; the teller herself also laughs in line 43). The teller then proceeds to present the colleague's criticism of the boyfriend and his failures, saying the last words of the utterance through laughter and ending it with a sniff (.*nff*, line 50). At this point, two conflicting affect displays have been made, laughter and crying. As a receipt of the entire quote, *voi että* (line 51) is a way of counterbalancing a compassionate stance toward the teller and an orientation to the amusing way that the situation is narrated. The quote also opens up a third possibility, that of assessing the unfaithful boyfriend with a more explicit response (e.g., "what a cheat"). (On direct quotes in amusing stories, cf. Holt, 2000a.) The affective character and empathy of this response is made more explicit by the prosodic means of vowel lengthening and by the prosodic peaks (indicated by underlining) that occur in both parts of the response.

In the following Extract 7, the ambiguity of affective valence relates to the issue of whether the diagnosis of the teller's sick puppy is good or bad. In this case, the recipient prefaces his *voi että* response with the particle *no* (line 39) and this adds an aspect of hesitancy to the response. This extract is from the same telephone call as Extract 5. As her first response to the caller Kalle's "how are you" question (data not shown), the recipient, Sanna, starts a long, detailed narration about the recent illness of her puppy. Throughout the detailed telling, Kalle has responded with acknowledgment tokens. He then inquires about the diagnosis (lines 29–30), marking the question as an inference (*sit*, "then," line 29) and implying an understanding that no specific diagnosis of the dog's ailment was offered by the vet. Kalle's question can be heard as an effort to direct the talk away from the details of what ails the puppy toward closing the topic. However, after a confirmation, the teller proceeds to elaborate on the kinds of tests that were made, and finally arrives at a possible closure of her answer and the topic by specifying the illness that the puppy had (line 38). At that point the recipient (line 39) produces the particle chain *no:. hh voi että*.

Extract 7 [Sg S14 A02 Sick puppy]

```
27 S: ='t      se        oli     kyllä   sit     ni    et    se        ripuloi
       PRT     DEM.SG    be-PST  sure    then    PRT   PRT   DEM.SG    poo-poo-PST
       =so it was really so that it dropped the diarrhea

28     tänne joka   paikkaan °'t   se       oli      kyl     semmosta°
       here  every  place-ILL that DEM.SG   be-PST   really  such-PAR
       all over here °so that's what it was like°

29 K: No    mut   ei        siit          selvinny    sit     et
       PRT   but   NEG.SG3   DEM.SG-ELA    clear-PPC   then    PRT
       Well but it did not become clear then
```

30   *mitä se oli.*
     what-PAR DEM.SG be-PST
     what it was.

31 S: *.hh   ↑Ei sil   selvinnny et sil   otettii*
     NEG.SG3 DEM.SG-ADE clear-PPC PRT DEM.SG-ADE take-PAS
                          -PST-4
     .hh ↑No it did not become clear so they did take from it

32   *kyl- sil   oli   tavallaan niinku .hh noit*
     really DEM.SG-ADE be-PST kind.of like   those-PAR
     in f-it had in a way kind of like.hh the

33   *penikkataudin oire-   esioireita.*
     distemper-GEN symptom predrome-PL-PAR
     sympto-predromes of distemper.

34 K: *Mm.*

35 S: *Et silt   otettiin   ne.   hh penikkatauti,*
     PRT DEM.SG-ABL take-PAS-PST-4 DEM.PL   distemper
     So they took the.hh distemper,

36   *(.) näytteet mut ne   oliki   negatiivisia   että*
       sample-PL but DEM.PL be-PST.SG3-CLI negative-PL-PAR PRT
     (.) samples but they were in fact negative so then

37   *sit se oli   vaa (0.6) t'llene*
     then DEM.SG be-PST just   kind.of
     it was just (0.6) kinda

38   *<paha hengitysteiden   ja   suolistoinfektio.>*
     bad respiratory-tract-PL-GEN and bowel-infection
     <bad respiratory tract and bowel infection.>

39 K: → *°No:° (.)   .hh voi °ettäh°.*
     PRT   **PRT** **PRT**

40 S: *°Et se on nyt [ollu-°*
     PRT DEM.SG be now be-PPC
     °So it has now [bee-°

41 K: [.mff .mt No onneks se selvis.
                 [.mff .tch Well luckily it escaped.

42 S: *.hh Nii, no onneks ↑se ↓selvis nii—*
        PRT PRT luckily DEM.SG escape-PST PRT
     .hh yes, well luckily ↑it ↓escaped yes (.) so—

The response in line 39 can be understood as a hesitation concerning the type of appropriate receipt of the report. This response is produced *sotto voce*, and the *voi että* is preceded by an elongated version of the particle *no*. *No*, which often indexes a change in or departure from the previous line of activity (Raevaara, 1989), is also deployed here as a means of stalling for time in making the decision about the right kind of affect display. The prior utterance of the teller is formulated as if it were carrying potentially negative news (*paha*, "bad," line 38). However, earlier on (line 33), a suggestion had been made of a more serious alternative diagnosis—that of distemper, a disease that is fatal. In this context, a diagnosis of a respiratory tract infection can be heard as less bad news (cf. also *vaa*, "just," line 37). The hesitation may well be connected to this ambivalence of the news value, and the choice of an equivocal response, *voi että*, is a solution when the speaker may not be well versed in assessing the relative seriousness of animal ailments. Nonetheless, the equivocal expression *voi että* is not sufficient to bring the topic to a close, which leads to the subsequent effort by the recipient, the optimistic idiom in line 41 (*No onneks se selvis*, "Well luckily it escaped"). We will return to the issue of close implicativeness in the following section.

In this section, we have argued that the recipient occasionally faces ambivalence in more senses than one: the talk that projects an affective response may give rise to sequential ambiguity, and this may be intertwined with the valence of the affect conveyed in the prior turn itself. As Extract 6 illustrates, this is not always the case. In this example, there was a possibility of a genuine choice as to the affective valence of the response, and the recipient did express an affective stance but left the valence of the affect equivocal: She neither committed herself to an explicit disapproval of the behavior of the protagonist in the story nor produced an explicitly amused assessment as a reaction to the way the protagonist was presented by the teller. On the other hand, our reconsideration of Extract 5 demonstrated how in the talk that was responded to, two types of affect were intertwined: In the overall frame of the telephone call, the news announcement was placed in a secondary position. In addition, the news itself was formulated in an equivocal fashion. In Extract 4, the response *voi että* oriented to an amusing formulation within a larger framework of a narration that rendered empathy relevant. Finally, Extract 7 revealed a dilemma faced by the recipient with regard to a diagnosis: *voi että* was equivocal with respect to the valence of the affect, instead of choosing between relief and compassion.

VOI ETTÄ AS CLOSE IMPLICATIVE

Let us return to the events described in Extract 5. Our discussion focused on the way the news about Sanna's pregnancy was delivered and the way in which the recipient formulated his receipt of that news. In the following instance, we analyze how the previous topic concerning the call recipient's sick puppy is brought to an end and what role the *voi että* plays as a response in achieving this.

Extract 8 takes up where Extract 7 left off: the sick puppy episode continued for quite a while, and the cause of the illness has already become clear. In the extract presented below, the telling is drawing to an end, with another mention of the puppy's recovery (line 44). Despite the recipient's effort to close the topic with an idiomatic expression (line 47), the topic is once more revived as the teller advances a hypothetical alternative concerning her own thoughts and conduct (line 48 onward). At a point where the teller has changed to *sotto voce* and projected a possible summing up (*että*, "so," line 54), the recipient, after an acknowledgment token (*joo*, line 55), responds with *voi että sent[ää]n*. The adverb *sentään*, in a final position, could be freely translated as "really" or "indeed," which adds to the affective weight of the response.

Extract 8 [SKL Sg S14 A02 Baby; part of Example 4]

44 S: *Ja   se   rupes   sit   paranee   ku   se   jo   viikon   söi*
        and DEM.SG began   then recover   when DEM.SG already week-GEN eat-PST
        And then it started to recover as it had even taken

45   *antibiootiaki   ilman   et   sil   oli   mitään,*
        antibiotic-PL-CLI without PRT DEM.SG-ADE be-PST   any-PAR
        antibiotics for a week without it having had any,

46   *(0.4)   .hh   vaikutust.*
                        effect-PAR
        (0.4)   .hh   effect.

47 K: *Joo   joo .   . mhhh   Mut   se   oli   täpärällä sitte.*
        PRT   PRT   .mhhh   But   it   was a narrow escape then.

48 S: *↑Nii:ih. Mä   ajattelin   vaa   et   ku   ottaa*
        PRT   I   think-PST-SG1 just that when 0 take-SG3
        ↑Yea:h. I just thought that when one takes

49   *tollasen   sekarotusen   koiran   ni   (.) £ne   on*
        that.kind-GEN mixed.breed-GEN dog-GEN PRT   DEM.PL be-SG3
        a mixed-breed dog like that (.) £so they are

50   *nii   ter(h)veitä   hhehhh   ja   vas [tustuskykysiä*
        so   healthy-PL-PAR   and resis [tance-capable-PL-PAR
        so hea(h)lthy hhehhh and resis[tant

51 K: [*Nii:.*

52 K: *Nii [tietenki joo]*
        Yes [of.course yes]

53 S: [*Et   mä   en   sit   kysyny   et   on   sit*
        PRT   I   NEG-SG1   then ask-PPC PRT   be-SG3 then
        [So I didn't ask right away if there is

54   *heti   kauhee   kuolemantauti   °että° [.hh*
            immediately awful death-GEN-sickness PRT
            a terrible fatal disease °so° [.hh

55 K: [°Joo°.hh (.)

56   →   *.mt Voi että °sent´n°=*

57 S: *=No ehkä   mä voin   .hh kertoo teille   ennen   ku   .hh*
            PRT   maybe   I   can-SG1   tell   you.PL-ALL before   when
            Well maybe I can.hh tell you before.hh

58   *Hanna ehtii   j- juoruilla et   mä   odotan   lasta.*
            NameF have.time-SG3   gossip   that I   expect-SG1 child-PAR
            Hanna has time to g-gossip that I am expecting a baby.

The response *voi että sentään* includes in its scope a segment longer than the preceding turn.

This is hearable as a response to the entire telling of the puppy's illness, and it implies that the recipient has nothing more to add. In so doing it suggests a closure of the topic. Thus, as his final response, the recipient offers one that affiliates with the affect-relevant character of the telling without specifying the type of the affect or the target of the display (the puppy, the teller). The understanding of the affective valence of the response is left to be inferred from the kind of telling this has been. This inference is based on the placement of the response, its placement within the turn, and subsequent to a *sotto voce* acknowledgment token *joo* (line 55). These cues guide the understanding of the response as targeting the entire telling. The teller aligns with the closure-implicative character of the response and proceeds to a telling about her pregnancy.

The following example is from the same conversation as the one above, and here the recipient, the producer of the *voi että sentään* response, proceeds to a new topic soon after his response (line 85). The participants are talking about Sanna's pregnancy.

Extract 9 [SG S14 A02 Baby]

79 K: - - - *millois   se   nyt on kuins   pitkällä   se   nyt   on,*
               when-CLI DEM.SG PRT be how-CLI long-ADE   DEM.SG now   is
               - - - when is it now how far is it now,

80 S: *No se,   heinäkuun yhestoist päivä on se   laskettu   aika,*
          well DEM.SG July-GEN   eleventh   day   be DEM.SG counted   time
          Well it, July eleventh is the estimated date,

81 K: *Kesävauva.hh*
          Summer baby.hh

82 S: *°Nii°*

83 K: → **Voi**   **että** **sentään**. .hh °onnea   kauheesti°
                                           luck-PAR awfully
        Voi   **että** **sentään**. .hh °many   congratulations °

84 S: °Kiitos°
           °Thanks°

85 K: Hassua   mä   just   aattelin   tota (.).hh   itseasias   sua
           funny-PAR I   just   think-PST-1   PRT   in.fact   you-PAR
           Funny I was just thinking uh (.).hh of you in fact

86   eile   illalla   mä aattelin   mitähän   kuuluu—
           yesterday evening-ADE I   think-PST-1 what-PAR-CLI is.heard
           last night I was thinking how you are doing—((talk about
           a movie follows))

The talk about Sanna's pregnancy has continued for quite some time already. At the beginning of the segment, Kalle inquires about the current stage of her pregnancy. After learning of the baby's due date and after receiving a confirmation of his turn that implies a positive stance toward the pregnancy (line 81), Kalle produces the *voi että sentään* response. Here, *voi että* expresses an affective stance toward the preceding talk, and *sentään* (literally, "after all," "at least") indexes that the scope of this response compasses the entire state of affairs with all its ramifications. From the *voi että* response, Kalle moves on to congratulate Sanna, thereby finalizing his stance to the affective valence of the news as good. Sanna receives his congratulations minimally, displaying that she has nothing more to add to the topic. After Sanna's response, Kalle moves on to a new topic. As in the previous example, the finally positioned *sentään* can be heard here to underline the relevance of closing the ongoing topic and activity.

Thus, subsequent to *voi että* within the same prosodic unit, the scope of the adverb *sentään* covers a longer stretch of talk, and as a result, conveys that the whole topic is ready for closure. However, at some sequential places, when *voi että* occurs alone, it may be heard as closing implicative. This is the case in Extract 6 above, in which the recipient of a telling about the greedy brother used *voi että* at a point where either a condemnation or an expression of amusement was due. But in fact, this segment occurs within the larger activity of talking about inheritance and the event of distributing it to the siblings, and that may have an impact on the recipients' responses. The brother's greed had been mentioned earlier, and at that point the recipients indicated their affiliation with the teller. Furthermore, the segment about the crystals occurs following another instance exemplifying the brother's conduct. The delay in responding after the climax of the telling (line 27), and the production of the *voi että* response (line 31) may convey that for the recipients, the topic of the brother's conduct has been exhausted and is ready to be closed. Moreover, the readiness to close the topical talk about the brother's conduct was also evident in the question posed by the other recipient (lines 32–4): He suggested that completing the distribution of their inheritance was a relief to the teller. In the following fragment from Extract 4, the second of the *voi että* responses leads to a change in the narration: in overlap with it, the main speaker returns to the main line of the story (line 52).

Extract 10 [= part of Example 4]

47	*m*u*kavam#piiki*		*että#*	*(.)*	*@*	*↑ih*a	*just*	*semmone*	*tyyppi*
	nice-COM-PL-PAR-also		PRT			right	just	such	type
	nicer ones so# (.) @↑just the kind of jerk								

48	*joka*	*ei*	*niinku*	*ei*	*pysty*	*tällasee*
	that	NEG	like	NEG	be.capable	this.kind-ILL
	who isn't like isn't capable of forming this kind of					

49	*#aikuisee*		*.mh*	*ihmissuhte(h)e(h)see*
	grown.up-ILL			human-relationship-ILL
	#mature.mh relati(h)onshi(h)p			

50	*ja*	*ka(h)ikkee*	*.hee*	*.hee*	*.nff*
	and	a(h)ll that	.hee	.hee	.nff

51 E: →	**<Vo**[**i:: että:,**
	[

52 M:	[*Joo:*	*ku-*	*£kuule*	*tää*	*oli*	*n*i*i:n*]
	PRT	listen	listen-IMP.SG2	this	be-PST	so
	[Yeah: li-£listen this was so::]					

53	*masentavaa*	*#ja*	*m*o*lemmat*	*ties*		*tän*	*etukäteen*
	depressing-PAR	and	both-PL	know-PST.SG3		this-GEN	beforehand
	depressing #and ((we)) both knew this beforehand						

In this section, we have suggested that the *voi että* response may also have closing implicative import. This becomes clearer when the response contains the adverb *sentään* in the same prosodic unit. In this case, *sentään* implies that it encompasses a longer stretch of prior talk than the immediate turn, thereby suggesting a closure of the larger activity.

Our data suggest that *voi että* as a response on its own, its minimality and unspecificity, may also be used as a closing-implicative device in contexts where an activity (e.g., complaining) continued for quite some time.

CONCLUSION

In this chapter, we have discussed the use of what we refer to as the open-type affective response *voi että* in different contexts. This response type was found to occur at places where the prior talk contained a display of affect in some way. However, the presentation of affect was treated as being ambivalent by the recipient. We have argued that by deploying a response type that expresses an affective stance but does not make the stance lexically explicit, the recipient orients to the ambivalence of the sequential implications and/or affective character of the prior talk. For example, had the recipient used an expression that included an evaluative adjective (*voi kauheeta*, "oh how awful"), she would have not only explicated her stance, but would also have potentially derailed the activity underway when it was not clear where the telling was leading. More locally, a more explicitly evaluative response would have pinpointed the character of the affect when the main speaker had not yet done this. These two kinds of ambivalence were often intertwined.

The equivocal nature of the response was not judged to be insufficient for the purposes of the main speaker in our data. Were it felt to be insufficient, the main speaker would have moved on to pursue a stronger or more explicit response from the coparticipant. Furthermore, the *voi että* speaker herself did not (Extract 5 excepted) subsequently reinforce, that is, explicate, her stance, unlike in the descriptions of the English response cries by Heritage (2011) and Couper-Kuhlen (chapter 6). That no explication of her stance by the *voi että* speaker was followed was related to the specific sequential and activity contexts in which *voi että* was used (sequential ambivalence and/or ambivalence of valence; exhaustion of the overall topic and activity).

Voi että is part of a larger paradigm of phrasal affective responses. We have argued that, due to its open character (that is, there being no lexical specification of the affect), it is often a convenient solution in affective situations where, in one way or another, its speaker faces sequential ambiguity and/or ambiguity of valence. In some instances, *voi että*, either by itself, or combined with the particle *sentään*, seems to be followed by a topic closure or at least seems to implicate such a closure.

The different examples of *voi että* responses seem to have in common that the speaker who utters them is, as it were, going through the motions, but not really engaging herself in an explicit evaluation or assessment of the affect as evidenced by the telling of the coparticipant.

DRAMATIC POTENTIAL OF THE EQUIVOCAL AFFECT DISPLAY

The equivocal affect display expressed by *voi että* is conventionalized and recognizable to the extent that its meaning potential is also made use of in literary dialogues. We will present one example here as an illustration. The dramatic potential of *voi että* is used to its full effect in a recent production[4] of Edmond Rostand's play *Cyrano de Bergerac*. The gist of the play is that two men are in love with the same young woman, Roxane. Cyrano has a long nose and is not particularly handsome, but he is a brilliant penman, whereas young Christian is beautiful but also "a man of few words." Cyrano has altruistically assisted his rival by composing masterly love letters to the young woman they both love. The dramatic peak of the play is reached when Roxane, visiting her newlywed spouse on the military front, confesses that she in fact loves "the soul" of Christian rather than his looks (scene 4. VIII). The segment that contains *voi että* is the following.

Extract 11 [Cyrano de Bergerac, Scene 4. VIII]

French	Finnish	English
ROXANE:		
Eh bien! toi-même enfin	Nyt olet vihdoin saanut	Ah! how you err!
l'emporte sur toi-même,	voiton kuvastasi,	'Tis now that I love best—love well!
Et ce n'est plus que pour	ja rakkauteni syy on	'Tis that Which is thy
ton âme que je t'aime!	yksin sielussasi[5]	true self, see!—that I adore!
CHRISTIAN (reculant):		(turning away)
Ah! Roxane!	**Voi että**	**Hush!**
- - -		
ROXANE:		
Et la beauté par quoi tout	Sua rumanakin	Ugly! I swear I'd love
d'abord tu me plus,	rakastaisin,	you still!
Maintenant j'y vois mieux et je	vannon sen.	
ne la vois plus!		
CHRISTIAN:		
Oh!	**Voi että**	**My God!**
. . .		

The Finnish translation *voi että* captures brilliantly the dilemma faced by Christian. He is still trying to conceal from Roxane the fact that the real author of the letters is Cyrano, not he himself; but he is nevertheless ecstatic to receive Roxane's declaration of love. By uttering *voi että*, he can be heard to express his happiness about Roxane's confession, but at the same time, he turns to the knowing audience, with whom he shares the disappointing secret of not possessing a "soul" worthy of Roxane's love. At his *voi että* response, the audience burst into loud, appreciative laughter. It seems to us that both the French original and the English translation lack this equivocalness, which is probably left to be expressed by means of prosody and gestures.

NOTES

We would like to thank Paul Drew for fruitful discussions on the topic, and Elizabeth Couper-Kuhlen, Markku Haakana, and especially Anssi Peräkylä for comments and insightful ideas on an earlier version of this chapter. We are grateful to Kathleen Moore for shaping up our English and improving the textual cohesion.
1. The term "delocutive" is used, for instance, in French linguistics to denote the verbs derived from expressions that describe a speech activity (from Latin *loquor*, "to speak").
2. *Voi että* occurs predominantly in everyday talk. Our database consists of approximately thirty-five interactions including both face-to-face conversations and telephone calls. In those data, we have encountered approximately twenty-four instances

of *voi että*. Most of our data come from conversations among friends and family members, but we have also included a number of videotaped institutional interactions, for example from a health center and from a hair salon. In addition, we have made extensive field notes. While not all speakers in our data use *voi että*, some use it very frequently. However, it is not possible to construct a profile of a typical user based on the data—the expression is used both by old and young, by women and men.

3. The overall context is even more intricate. At the outset, the caller Kalle has told Sanna the reason for the call, an invitation to a New Year's party. After that, when asked, he mentions a recent painful incident that occurred in his family. In response to that, Sanna reveals that she is aware of the situation and has even been talking the previous day about that particular incident with their mutual friend Hanna. Following that, Kalle asks Sanna how things are with her, whereupon she launches into the story about her sick puppy. In other words, the telling about the puppy follows talk about an awkward event in Kalle's family. In that type of sequential context, Sanna may have reasoned that telling the news about a happy event (pregnancy) might create too radical a change in the affective line of talking.

4. A literary translation of the play has been produced by Pekka Lintu (1993). In the staging of the play by Ryhmäteatteri ("Group Theatre") at Suomenlinna, Helsinki, during the summer of 2010, the text was considerably modified toward a spoken vernacular. It is in this version that the response *voi että* was deployed.

5. The original French text and the English translation are available on the internet at http://www.gutenberg.org.

CHAPTER 8

✿

Laughter in Conversation

The Case of "Fake" Laughter

MARKKU HAAKANA

INTRODUCTION

Conversation analysis is (in)famous for its insistence on a detailed transcription of talk-in-interaction, including features that are not verbal (e.g., breathing, laughing, pausing). The transcription system developed by Gail Jefferson (see e.g., Jefferson, 2004a) guides the transcribers, for example, to measure pauses by a tenth of a second and to write down audible inbreaths and outbreaths minutely. This focus on the fine interactional detail reflects the idea that interaction contains—at least potentially—"order at all points" (Sacks, 1984b, p. 22). Jefferson (1985; see also 2004b, 2010) made this point specifically about laughter; she showed how laughter should be transcribed in its specifics, rather than by merely marking its presence in the conversation. For instance, she started with a transcript which had laughter reported in parenthesis such as the following:

Extract 1 [Jefferson, 1985, p. 28, Extract 7]
Louise: ((through bubbling laughter)) Playing with
          his organ yeah I thought the same thing!

And then she transcribed the same turn in the following way:

Extract 2 [Jefferson, 1985, p. 29, Extract 8]
Louise: heh huh.<u>hh</u> PLAYN(h) W(h)IZ <u>O</u>(h)R'N
          ya:h I thought the same

The detailed transcript reveals that Louise first laughs through some laugh particles (*heh huh*), and then, within her turn, she laughs only during some specific lexical items ("playing with his organ") which form a reference to sexual activities. Jefferson's point was that if we do not transcribe laughter in detail, we may lose something in the analysis. In this specific case (and in others like it), she argued that the speaker specifically laughs through the obscene part of her talk, making it more difficult for her recipients to hear the obscenity. In other words, the speaker distorts the production and reception of this part of the utterance. This means that laughter does not just "flood out" uncontrollably, but rather is "put into the turn" in a methodical fashion. So laughter is seen as a device that the interactants use in systematic ways to perform different kinds of interactional actions.

Following the work of Jefferson, conversation analysts have learned to pay close attention to how laughter unfolds in interaction, and to transcribe it on a token-by-token basis[1], as the following two extracts show. Both extracts present instances of two speakers laughing together: Extract 3 is from Jefferson (1979) and Extract 4 is a short example from Finnish data (not translated here; see Extract 11, lines 1–3 later).

Extract 3 [Jefferson, 1979, Extract 3]
Ellen: He s'd well he said I am cheap he said,
        .hh about the big things. he says but not
        the liddle things, hhhHA [HA HA HA
Bill: [heh heh heh

Extract 4 [Fatty.telephone]
Vesa: Nii:.   Kato [nehän sanoo että<]   (.) pysäkillä
Simo: [°Ai jaa:.°   ]
Vesa: seisoessaan @No nysse tulee@.
Simo: Aa hah [hah hah haa .ha
Vesa: [eh heh heh .hhh iih

Such transcription of laughter is not without its challenges, however. Even though we tend to write down the sounds of laughter as tokens such as *heh* or *hah* (as in the previous extracts), the interactants do not—for the most part—laugh through such clearly distinguishable tokens. Laughter is a multimodal phenomenon, combining vocal, visual (e.g., smiling), and bodily (e.g., shaking of the torso) elements; the vocal elements of laughter are often described as "inarticulate" (on the production features of laughter, see Glenn, 2003, pp. 8–13). This means that tokens such as *heh* and *hah* are partly symbolic, presenting the type of sounds of which laughter consists. And we have come to associate these tokens with laughter, perhaps partly through the conventionalized written versions of laughter (e.g., in fiction, in text messages, in emails, etc.).[2]

However, sometimes the interactants in spoken conversation do indeed produce these tokens as articulated lexical items; they utter the tokens *heh* and *hah* as "words." This is the topic of the present chapter; I shall analyze the uses of these lexicalized laugh tokens as occasions of "fake" laughter in Finnish conversations. In the following, I shall first present some previous findings on fake laughter and then proceed to analyze the uses of it in my data.

FAKE LAUGHTER: PRELIMINARIES

"Fake laughter" can refer to two different phenomena. The first is when interactants produce laughter even though it is not spontaneous. Here, the speaker intends to do the expected response in a given interactional slot and consequently she "forces" herself to produce laughter that is meant to be understood as "real" and to sound spontaneous (cf. Mulkay, 1988, p. 118). The second phenomenon is when the interactants produce the sounds that are conventionally associated with laughter in a way that makes it clear that the laughter is not to be interpreted as being "real"; that is, the laughter is designed to be fake. This second type of "laughter" is the focus of this study. I shall refer to this phenomenon as "fake laughter," and occasionally also as "lexicalized laughter," since it involves using the laugh tokens (*heh, hah*, and others) as more or less articulated lexical elements. The distinction between fake and real laughter is by no means clearcut; rather, there is a continuum of different kinds of laughs. This study focuses on the clearest, most articulated cases of fake laughter in the data.[3] Nonetheless, even these cases sometimes include features of "real" laughter, as the examples in this chapter show.

In conversation and discourse analytical work, laughter in general has received quite a lot of attention. Several studies have analyzed the sequential realization of laughter sequences, how laughter is invited and responded to, and the functions of laughter in interaction (see e.g., Jefferson, 1979, 1984, 1985, 2004b, 2010; Jefferson, Sacks, & Schegloff, 1987; Glenn, 1989, 1991, 2003, 2010; Haakana, 1999, 2001, 2002, 2010; Holt, 2010; Adelswärd, 1989; Norrick, 1993). Fake laughter, however, has received much less attention. To my knowledge, there are no previous studies concentrating on fake laughter in interaction, but this type of laughter has been discussed briefly in some studies.

Bell (2009) analyzes responses to failed humor, and says that fake laughter and groans have been seen as "prototypical responses to failed humor" (Bell, 2009, pp. 1825–6). In her data, however, the responses to failed humor vary considerably, and fake laughter is not a very frequent response type.[4] Several studies analyzing humor and laughter mention fake laughter, albeit using different terminology: for instance, Chiaro (1992, p. 112) talks about "sarcastic laughter," Sacks (1974, p. 351) and Norrick (1993, pp. 8, 36) about "mirthless laughter," and Bell (2009) and Haakana (1999, pp. 9–10) use the term "fake laughter." Nevertheless, the description of the phenomenon in these studies is the same. Fake laughter is seen as a device that is used as a response to a "failed" joke. By producing fake laughter, the recipient of a joke can simultaneously show that s/he has understood the joke (and understood it to be a joke) but does not find the joke amusing; that is, fake laughter reflects a negative evaluation of the joke and a lack of the expected affect, amusement, or mirth. Typically it is seen that a joke renders laughter as being relevant as a next action, and by not laughing as a response, the recipient could be interpreted as not having understood the joke. If s/he wants to make it known that the reason for not laughing is the quality of the joke, fake laughter offers one option for accomplishing this (on others, see Bell, 2009). In short, fake laughter fills the slot for real laughter but displays a new, unexpected stance to the previous talk: what is offered as amusing is manifestly treated as not amusing.

To illustrate the phenomenon, I present an example from Jefferson (1979). She does not describe the quality of laughter in this extract, but it certainly appears to be fake laughter. Jefferson (1979, pp. 93–4) presents some cases in which not laughing as a response emerges as a conversational issue in its own right. The following is a case in point:

Extract 5 [Jefferson, 1979, Extract 26, p. 94]
Roger: Well it struck me funny.
         (1.0)
Al: HA, HA-HA-HA
Ken: hh
Roger: Thank you

After a joke, Roger comments on the lack of laughter in his turn that evaluates the joke as funny. In response, after a long pause, Al produces laugh tokens which seem like fake laughter: the tokens are transcribed as being loud (in capital letters) and there is no breathiness marked in the turn. The laugh tokens produce the expected response type, but by producing them in this fashion, Al communicates that the joke does not deserve a genuine response; Roger's "thank you" is then obviously ironic.

In the next sections, I analyze the uses of fake laughter in Finnish conversations. I shall show that the lexicalized laugh tokens have several types of usage in conversation. Some but not all occurrences of fake laughter deal with failed humor. Furthermore, even in the joking sequences, fake laughter is used in different ways. The analyses of the data show that fake laughter occurs in similar contexts to real laughter, and that it often co-occurs, in various ways, with real laughter. I start by considering cases in which fake laughter is utilized in joking sequences and then proceed to its uses in different kinds of interactionally delicate contexts.

The analysis is based on data from Finnish everyday conversations between friends. For this study, I listened to twenty hours of conversations: both telephone conversations (ten hours) and face-to-face interactions (ten hours). The data contained approximately thirty instances of fake laughter, most of them in the telephone conversations. This suggests that, according to the present data, fake laughter is not a very common phenomenon in interaction. Furthermore, the majority of the instances were produced by a couple of speakers and sets of speakers; interestingly, the use of lexicalized laughter in the data seems to be a device utilized by the younger speakers, especially by the young men. However, the present database is not large enough to make generalizations about the sociolinguistic distribution of the practice.

FAKE LAUGHTER AND EVALUATION OF HUMOROUS TALK

When an interactant produces a humorous turn-at-talk, the expected response is usually laughter. As the following examples from Jefferson (1979) illustrate, recipient laughter can be arrived at in different ways. One way is that the speaker can merely produce the laughable utterance and then the recipient(s) start(s) laughing:

Extract 6 [Jefferson, 1979, Extract 4, p. 81]
Mike: He says. I gotta git outta dih mood befo' I can git
          outta d [i   [h ca:::h
Gary: [A [h ha ha
Curt: [U-huh-huh

The producer of the laughable can also laugh at the end of the turn (or within the turn) and in doing so she invites the recipient to laugh. In Extract 7, Ellen laughs at the end her turn, and Bill subsequently joins in the laughter in overlap:

Extract 7 [Jefferson, 1979, Extract 3, p. 81]
Ellen: He s'd well he said I am cheap he said,
        .hh about the big things. he says but not
        the liddle things, hhhHA [HA HA HA
Bill: [heh heh heh

Sometimes the producer of the laughable can first wait for the recipient to laugh, and if that does not happen, laugh herself after a pause and invite the recipient to laugh. This occurs in Extract 8:

Extract 8 [Jefferson, 1979, Extract 2, p. 80]
Joyce: Cuz she wz off in the bushes with some buddy, tch!
        (0.7)
Joyce: ehh[hhhhhhh!
Sidney: [Oh(hh)h hah huh!

The fake laughter in my data occurs in similar interactional slots as the laughter in Jefferson's examples.[5] Let us begin by analyzing a case in which the recipient of the joking turns-at-talk produces fake laughter. In Extract 9, three speakers are on the telephone: Tiina is on one end, and Sini and Arto on the other. Sini and Arto have recently moved away from Helsinki where Tiina lives, and they are now in the middle of a major renovation of their new house. Just before the extract, Tiina asks whether the renovation takes up all of Sini's and Arto's time. In response, Sini reports that they have done other things as well, for instance, visited Helsinki, which Tiina treats as news. In lines 1–3, Sini elaborates by giving the details of the visits, and in line 11, Arto announces a personal bit of news, adding his report to Sini's list with the turn-initial particle *ja* ("and"). The sequence starting from Arto's news is of interest here; the fake laughter in focus occurs on line 15 and it is indicated in bold face (and is similarly indicated in other examples). (For a key to the glossing symbols used, see Appendix, pp. 290.)

Extract 9 [SG S08 Trio.telephone]
01 Sini: *no   me   oltiin   lauantaina   häi:ssä   ja< (0.4)*
              PRT   we   be-PAS-PST-4 Saturday-ESS wedding-INE and
              well we were on Saturday in a wedding and< (0.4)

02   *perjantaina   mä   olin   töi:ssä   ja   maanantainaki   mä*
                Friday-ESS   I   be-PST-1   work-INE and   Monday-ESS-CLI I
                on Friday I was at wo:rk and on Monday too I

03   *ol(h)in   t(h)öissä.*
                be-PST-1   work-INE
                w(h)as at w(h)ork

04   Tiina: ↑*aha* [*a.*
                ↑I see.

05   Arto: [*ja   mä   olin   maanantaina   rosiksessa.*
                 and   I   be-PST-1   Monday-ESS "court"(slang)-INE
                [And I was on Monday in court.

06   Arto?: *.nf*

07   Tiina: *rosiksessa.*
                court-INE
                in court.

08   Arto: *mm:,*=

09   Tiina: =*mitä   sä   siel   *[*teit.*]
                what   you   there   do-PST-2
                =what did you   do [there.]

10   Arto: [*.hh*] *mä olin   todistamassa?*
                                I   be-PST-1   witness-INF-INE
                    [.hh] I was a witness?

11   Tiina: *ai   sä   olit   to:distamas.   =sä   et   ollu*
                PRT   you   be-PST-2 witness-INF-INE you NEG-2 be-PPC
                oh you were a wi:tness.=you weren't the

12   *syytetty* [*nä.*
                accused-ESS
                  accus [ed.

13   Arto: [*e:n ollu.*
                 NEG-1 be-PPC
                 [no: I wasn't.

14   Tiina: *aha.*
                I see.

15   Arto:→ **ah hah hah**   [**hah**
16   Tiina:→   [**hy-hmyh**

```
17.        mhh   [hhhhhh  ]hh   °↑<vai  [sellas]ta,>
                                 PRT     such-PAR
           .mhh  [hhhhhh  ]hh  °↑<so    [that's it,]>

18  Arto:→       [°yh hyhm°]            [↑joo:.]
                 [°yh hyhm°]            [↑yeah:.]

19  Tiina:  no   onks    teil      ollu    kivaa      siellä?,
            PRT  be-Q    you.PL-ADE be-PPC  nice-PAR   there
            well have you had a good time there?,
```

Arto's fake laughter (line 15) is produced in response to Tiina's reactions to his news about having been in court. Tiina subsequently treats Arto's announcement as newsworthy in several ways: she topicalizes the report by repeating the key element of the turn (*rosiksessa*, "in court," line 7), minimally confirmed by Arto (line 8), and she then asks for the reason for Arto's court visit (line 9). On line 10, Arto reports that he was there as a witness. Tiina first repeats Arto's report and prefaces it with the particle *ai*, which indicates that she treats the issue as news (on *ai*, see Hakulinen et al., 2004, §1028). Subsequently, she presents another possible reason for being in court (being accused); this is constructed as a negatively framed declarative utterance that seeks Arto's confirmation, which he then provides (line 13). On line 14, Tiina further treats Arto's talk as new information, but this time, by using another milder response particle, *aha* (Hakulinen et al., §1049). Thus, in the evolving sequence, Tiina reacts to Arto's role as a witness as being something that is unexpected, as if some other court-related identity (as the accused) would be more likely. This is obviously meant to be a joke, and the joke has a teasing quality, as teasing often involves attributing a problematic or "deviant" category to the person being teased (Drew, 1987, p. 244).

During the sequence, Tiina does not laugh herself, nor does Arto, but he does produce lexicalized laugh tokens. On line 15, his turn consists of *hah* tokens, which are produced in an articulated manner, without breathiness or the spasmodic character that is typical of real laughter. Through this fake laughter, Arto shows that he has recognized Tiina's joking in the previous sequence but does not find the joke funny enough to actually laugh.[6] Tiina's response (line 16) also has a laughter-like quality: it resembles a short laugh but has an artificial character, and the same holds for Arto's *yh-hyhm* on line 18. Tiina briefly acknowledges Arto's fake laughter and also the "failure" of her attempted joke: for a brief moment, the participants are involved in shared fake laughter. What follows is a change of topic (cf. Holt, 2010, on shared laughter in topic termination). Through a clearly audible long inbreath and the utterance *vai sellasta* ("so that's it"), Tiina strongly signals the end of the present topic and subsequently initiates a new one by asking a question on another matter (line 19). It seems that Arto's fake laughter is not only heard as a sign of his nonappreciation of the joke, but also as a sign of his willingness to close the topic.

A joke also fails in the following extract. This time, however, it is the producer of the laughable who utilizes fake laughter. This extract comes from a telephone conversation between two male friends who (with another friend, Jukka) are leaving for a trip on the following day. During their call, they discuss packing and the schedule for their

departure. Before the extract, it has become clear that Reijo and Jukka should be at
Pekka's house around two o'clock in the afternoon. Pekka, however, cannot get out of
work before 3:30 P.M. Reijo considers the time issue to be a problem in several ways
(before the extract and during the whole phone call). On lines 3–5, Pekka suggests
how Reijo and Jukka can spend their time waiting.

Extract 10 [Sg94 1A1 Yawning.telephone]
01 Pekka: ((yawning:)) hhöh [hmm]
02 Reijo: [tota,]
                                  [uhm,]

03 Pekka: mä   sain: #yy# ison   kasan   lavoja   duunis(t) tota
           I   get-PST-1 big-GEN pile-GEN platform-PL-PAR   work ELA   PRT
           I   got: #uhm# a big pile of wood from the work uhm

04   noin ni eilen   et,h jos teill   jää   vapaata aikaa   ni
           PRT   PRT yesterday PRT if   you.PL-ADE   remain free-PAR time-PAR PRT
           yesterday so that,h if you have some free time

05   tehän   voitte   tossa alkaa pilkkomaan   niitä.
           you.PL-CLI   can-PL2 PRT   start chop-INF-ILL   DEM.PL-PAR
           you can y'know start chopping the wood.

06   (0.6)

07 Pekka:→ #hO:H HAH HAH# eh hmh hmh heh heh.hhh
08   (.)

09 Reijo: °joo.°
           °yeah.°

10   (1.0)

11 Reijo: olik   sul   muuta.
           be-PAST-Q   you-ADE else-PAR
           did you have anything else.

12   (0.9)

Pekka starts (line 3) by reporting that he has received a big pile of wood and then makes
a suggestion for the men: if they have to wait for him, they can spend the time chopping
the wood. Reijo does not respond to this suggestion in any way, and after a substantial
silence (line 6), Pekka takes the turn again. His turn consists of two kinds of laughter:
first, he produces fake laughter which is very loud (hOH HAH HAH), followed by laughter that sounds more "real." By using fake laughter, he indicates that the previous turn
was meant as a joke (cf. Jefferson's case in Extract 8) and deals with the lack of response
by Reijo, treating his turn as failed attempt at humor. The subsequent laughter, however, can be heard as still making laughter relevant as a response at this point.

Reijo does not join in the laughter at this point, either. He acknowledges Pekka's previous actions with the response token *joo* (line 9), which can be heard as closing-implicative (cf. Sorjonen, 2001, p. 282) and then provides the question *oliks sulla muuta* ("did you have anything else"). On the surface, the question is asking whether Reijo has anything more to say on the issue, but nevertheless, it implies that no further talk on the topic is needed. According to my observations, this type of question seems to be conventionalized as an ironic marker of nonappreciation of the coparticipants line of talk (e.g., joking). Pekka, however, chooses to continue by the joking and laughingly suggests the possibility of renovation work (not shown here); Reijo does not join the laughter, the topic dies and Reijo moves on to talk about packing-related issues. In Extract 10, the speakers display different stances to the talk by Pekka: Pekka himself treats his talk as laughable but Reijo does not. This difference perhaps reflects the disagreement concerning the departure time for the trip. As I mentioned, Reijo treats the fact that he has to wait for Reijo as being problematic, but Pekka does not: he can joke about it, and his "joke" has a somewhat teasing quality (cf. Extract 9).

In Extracts 9 and 10, fake laughter was utilized to show that a joke failed. In Extract 9, the recipient displayed a nonamused stance by using fake laughter, and in Extract 10, the producer of the laughable utilized it to deal with the lack of appropriate response. In the following extract, fake laughter also works to evaluate a joke, but the reason for its use is not the recipient's actions. Extract 11 differs from the previous ones in several aspects. As in Extract 10, it is the producer of the laughable who resorts to fake laughter, but here, it is produced immediately after the laughable, and so it does not seem to deal with the lack of response. Moreover, while the jokes in Extracts 9 and 10 were spontaneous and made up on the spot, the joke in Extract 11 is a standardized package that the speaker has not created: thus, in 11, the teller of the joke is just an animator of the joke, not the author of it (see Goffman, 1981; on standardized and situational humor, see e.g., Mulkay 1988, p. 56).

Extract 11 is from a call between two male friends living in Helsinki. Before this extract, Simo has told that he is soon going to visit the city of Tampere. The mention of that city activates a joking mode: Vesa starts producing humorous material that plays on the stereotypes associated with Tampere (such as how people speak and what they eat). He ends up telling two "packaged" jokes. Both jokes have the same format ("do you know what X is in Tampere dialect") and play with the dialectal forms of some Finnish words (the jokes are impossible to translate[7]). On lines 1 and 3, Vesa produces the punchline of the first joke. In response, Simo laughs on line 4 and Vesa joins in the laughter (line 5) and then proceeds to another joke during the same turn:

Extract 11 [Sg S08 Fatty.telephone]

```
01   Vesa:   nii:.   kato   [nehän         sanoo  että<]  (.)  pysäkillä
             PRT     PRT    DEM.PL-CLI     say    that         bus.stop-ADE
             yes:.   see    [they say y'know<] (.) when standing

02   Simo:                  [°ai jaa:.°      ]
                            [°oh I see.°     ]
```

03   Vesa: *seisoessaan   @no   nysse   tulee@.*
             stand-INF-INE PRT   now + it come-SG3
             at a bus stop @no nysse tulee@.   ((not translated))

04   Simo: *aa hah*   [*hah hah haa .ha*   [.*ih   .ih   .ih*

05   Vesa: [*eh   heh   heh   .hhh   iih   £ja* [*tiet   sä   mikä   on*
                                                         and   know-2 you   what   is
                        [*eh   heh   heh   .hhh   iih   £and do you   know what   a*

06   [*kuljettaja£   tampereeksi,*
             driver   tampere dialect-TRA
             [driver is £in Tampere dialect,

07   Simo: [.*ih hhhh*
08   (0.2)
09   Simo: #*n:::noh*#?

10   Vesa: *myy:rä.=.hh   @onks   sulla   myyrä   lippuja@* ((not translated))
             sell/mole   be-Q   you-ADE   sell/mole   ticket-PL-PAR

11   →   **Ah**[**h AH** (.) **HAHh**
12   Simo: [.*hh hh*

13   Simo: °*ih hih hih* [.*hhh* #*eee.*#.   ]

14   Vesa: [*hauskoja   vits(h)ej(h)ä*] *£vai£,*=
                        funny-PL-PAR   joke-PL-PAR   or
                        [funny jok(h)e(h)s   ] £or what£,=

15   Simo: =#*£sä   oot   ol*[*lu   Tameree*|*lla.£*#
             you be-2   be-PC cityNAME-ADE
             =#£you have b[een   in   Tampere.£#

16   Vesa: [*hi   *[*£niin o(h)onk(h)i*
                                         PRT   be-1-CLI
                        [*hi   *[*£yes I h(h)av(h)e*

The joke in lines 5–6 takes the structure of a question ("what is . . ."), which is framed with another question ("do you know"). In response, Simo produces the response token *no* (line 9), which functions as a go-ahead response (Sorjonen, 2001, pp. 211–16). The pause (line 8) and the response token indicate that Simo does not know the answer and this makes it relevant for Vesa to continue with the joke. Vesa then (line 10) produces the punchline of the joke by first providing the answer (*myyrä*) and then an utterance that puts the word in context. As soon as he finishes this utterance, Vesa produces strong fake laughter (line 11) which is delivered through *ah hah* tokens. This fake laughter is produced at a point when the recipient has not had a chance to respond to the joke. Consequently, the fake laughter does not deal with the lack of response. Indeed, Simo's response is laughter (line 13) through which he displays his understanding and appreciation of the joke. Vesa's fake laughter is therefore voluntarily offered as an evaluation of the joke. He shows that even though he is delivering the joke (and a similar one before), he does not necessarily find it (or them) especially funny. Through the fake laughter he communicates that he does not take full responsibility for the quality of the joke. His subsequent turn, *hauskoja vitsejä vai* ("funny jokes or what"), is ironic, assessing the quality of the whole joking sequence that has just taken place.

The examples in this section have shown that fake laughter can be used in joking sequences in several ways: it can be used by the recipient of a candidate laughable (Extract 9) or by the producer of the laughable (Extracts 10 and 11). Fake laughter can be used as a device to deal with the failure of a joke, both by recipient and teller, but it can also be used as an evaluation of the joking materials by the teller when nothing seems to be wrong with the flow of the joking sequence. The fake laughter in these extracts took various forms but what they have in common is that they all include tokens that feature *ha(h)*-type sounds. In the following section, we shall turn to other uses of lexicalized laughter, as well as to other laugh tokens.

FAKE LAUGHTER AND DELICATE TALK

Not all laughter in interaction is connected to humor, jokes, and amusement. Laughter is used to display various kinds of affective stances, and consequently, not all laughter by a speaker is designed as an invitation to the recipient(s) to join in. For example, Jefferson (1984) demonstrates that troubles tellers recurrently use laughter when announcing a trouble but the recipients are not invited to share the laughter; rather, the troubles teller displays "troubles resistance" with the laughter and the recipient needs to take the trouble seriously and display "troubles receptiveness." Haakana (1999, 2001) shows that patients use laughter during medical interaction to deal with the various kinds of interactional problems: they recurrently laugh, for instance, in the turns that portray their lifestyle choices in a bad light or problematize the advice and instructions given by the doctor. This kind of laughter does not get reciprocated by the doctors. Kurhila (2008) and Laakso (1997, pp. 92–4) report that non-native speakers and speakers with aphasia use laughter in signaling troubles in speech production. Furthermore, Adelswärd (1989) argues that unilateral (nonreciprocated) laughter is used to frame the talk in different kinds of problematic interactional contexts (e.g., in self-praise, stating ignorance, misunderstanding, and embarrassment), and Norrick (1993, pp. 39–40) observes that laughter can used to signal embarrassment and nervousness.[8]

Fake laughter can also be used to signal various affective stances. In the data, the fake laughter often occurs in different kinds of problematic and delicate interactional slots, which are again contexts in which real laughter could and does occur. In these contexts, the lexicalized laughter does not orient to amusement or lack of it. However, I do not intend to suggest that there is a clearcut division between (fake) laughter that is oriented to "amusement" (or lack of it) and to "delicate talk." For instance, delicate actions and topics are certainly often produced in a humorous tone. Nevertheless, in the cases of this section, something other than joking occurs, even though the cases sometimes have jocular aspects as well. The following extract provides an example. In Extract 12, two young men are on the phone. Timo is about to go to Niko's place to pick up Niko and his girlfriend. In line 1, Niko reports that they are ready to leave "whenever," which is contested a short time later by his girlfriend, whose voice can be heard in the background (line 5). She corrects Niko's statement by modifying "whenever" to "not right away." In lines 6–7, Niko produces a turn that ends in fake laughter:

Extract 12 [Sg122 A6 Woman.telephone]

```
01  Niko:   okei,   me  ollaan  valmiina   lähtöön       millon vaan,
            PRT     we  be-PAS  ready-ESS  departure-ILL when   just
            okay, we are ready to go whenever,

02  Timo:   ((in English)) all right,
03  Niko:   >ni tota<
            >so uhm<

04          (.)

05  X:      ((from the background)) °tai  no   ei   nyt   ihan  heti°°
                                     or   PRT  NEG  now   quite immediately
                                     °well not quite right away°

06  Niko:   >nii no  joo< nyt  ei    oo<  kauheesti  #vaatteita
            PRT PRT PRT  now  NEG   be   terribly    cloth-PL-PAR
            >yes well yeah< now there isn't< #much clothes

07  →       päällä ja  noin mut#  heh  [heh he  ]
            on     and so   but
            on     and so   but#  heh  [heh he  ]

08  Timo:                            [↑ai  jaa ]  sitä vaan  paneksitaa
                                      PRT  PRT    PRT  just  fuck-PAS
                                      [↑oh I see you're just fucking

09          siellä,
            there,

10  Niko:   e:i   me  m:itään   n:aksita  e vaan katotaan    Herkulestah
            NEG   we  anything  fuck(slang) just watch-PAS  Hercules-PAR
            n:o we're no:t fucking at all we're just watching Hercules
```

The laugh tokens in Niko's turn (line 7) do not seem to be evaluating (failed) humor. Rather, the turn can be understood as including several delicate aspects: in his turn, Niko has to modify his previous estimate about "being ready" and he does this because of his girlfriend. Furthermore, he reports not having too much on (as a reason for not being ready immediately), which could be heard as a reference to his (or their) "being nude" and therefore is also open to sexual implications.[9] And indeed, Timo immediately produces a sexual interpretation of Niko's turn (Timo's turn in 8–9). In other words, the use of the laugh tokens seems to mark the turn as being rather delicate (on laughter in talk about sex and other "taboo" topics, see Jefferson, 1985; Jefferson, Sacks, & Schegloff, 1987). However, by producing laughter not as real laugh tokens, but rather as lexicalized fake laughter, Niko does not really display his being "embarrassed," or some other such affect, but makes the affect display from a distance, showing what kind of display could be relevant in that kind of context. Furthermore, despite the potentially delicate nature of the talk, the speaker is perhaps designing it to be taken up as a potential source for a sexually oriented interpretation and even joking—as the recipient then interprets it (lines 8–9). Even though Niko at first denies the sexual implications (line 10), the talk continues with sexually loaded innuendos (not shown here).

Let us now turn to a more detailed analysis of two examples of fake laughter in delicate contexts: Extract 13 is a request sequence, and Extracts 14 and 15 are part of a complex invitation sequence. In both cases, the speakers use the *heh* tokens as part of the delivery of their actions. What is interesting here is that there seems to be a division of labor between the different tokens: as we saw earlier, *hah* (and *hoh*) tokens were used in joking contexts, whereas the *heh* tokens seem to be more specialized for dealing with delicate talk.

Extract 13 is from a telephone call between Sini and Pekka, and before this extract, Pekka starts a sequence by asking whether Sini knows a certain person (a musician) who is connected to the school where Sini studies. This question turns out to be part of a request sequence, and it aims to determine whether Sini knows the musician well enough to introduce him to Pekka. The presequence continues at length, as Pekka asks three times in various ways how well Sini knows the person. Before this extract, Sini has already asked why Pekka is asking these questions, but he has not yet answered. Sini produces a turn which further seeks the rationale of the previous inquiries: her *mitä* ("what") (line 1) produced with laughter shows that she finds Pekka's inquiries both puzzling and amusing.

Extract 13 [Sg124 A1 Donhuono.telephone]
```
01  Sini:    m(h)i̲(h)t(h)ä. h
             wh(h)at(h). h

02  Pekka:   eiku   se      on se,  (.)  Don Huo̲:nojen    ki̲taris[ti.]
             PRT    DEM.SG  be DEM.SG   bandNAME-GEN    guitarist
             no, 'cause he's the (.) Don Hu̲onot guitarist.

03  Sini:                                             [ni̲]in on.
                                                       [yes he is.

04  (0.3)

05  Pekka:   <va̲u:h>  (.) mä >a̲attelin   vaa  ku   tää,<   k´   mä  luin<.h
             wow          I   think-PST-1 just PRT this  PRT  I   read-PST-1
             <wo̲:wh> (.) I <just thought that since this< I was reading<
```

06   *Hesaria*   *ja*   [*.h tääl*] *oli*
            newspaperNAME-PAR and   here be-PST
            .h Hesari   and [.h here] was

07 Sini: [.nss   ]

08 Pekka: *just   tää   <että> opiskellu   taide ja*
            exactly this   that   study-PPC art   and
            just like <that> has studied in a school of arts and

09   *>viestintäoppilaitoksessa<   .hhmth   taivutettu bändin*
            communication-school-INE   bend-PPC band-GEN
            >communication<.hhmth has been utilized for the

10   *hyötykäyttöön >ku se   on ohjannu<   sen   niitten (0.2)*
            utility-use-ILL PRT DEM.SG be direct-PPC DEM.SG-GEN DEM.PL-GEN
            band's use >since he's directed< that n(h)ew (0.2)

11   *u(h)uen   videon.*
            new-GEN   video-GEN
            video of theirs.

12 Sini: *joo.*
            yes.

13 Pekka: *.hhh ja >tota<   mä aattelin   heti   soittaa sulle   ja kysyy*
            and PRT   I   think-PST-1   immediately call-INF you-ALL and ask
            .hhh and >uhm< I   thought   immediately to call   you and ask

14   *että, #n# että, (.) >että sä   vois[it] varmaa e:sitellä*
            that   that   that   you   could-2 surely introduce
            that #n# that, (.) >that you could maybe introduce

15 Sini: [*joo,*]

16 Pekka: *mut   sille   mut [(sit)   ]*
            I-ACC DEM.SG-ALL but   then
            me to   him but   [(then)   ]

17 Sini: [*heh eh heh   .nss*]

18 Pekka: → [**heh heh**   ]

19 Sini: [*a(h)i j(h)a(h)a,*] *he he*
            [o(h) I(s)he(h),] he he

20 Pekka: → **heh   heh**

21 Sini: *.nsss eikä   ku (.) siis se   oli   (- - -)*
            NEG-CLI PRT   PRT DEM.SG be-PST
            .nsss no because   (.) I mean it was (- - -)

In response to Sini's question Pekka starts his explanation by reporting that the person he has asked about is a guitarist in a band (line 2) and the subsequent interjection *vau:h* ("wow") indexes his great appreciation of that person. He then reports that while reading a newspaper, he discovered that the guitarist had studied in the same school as Sini and had been producing a video for a band there (lines 5–11). Finally, on line 13 he comes to the actual reason for his call: he was planning to ask Sini to introduce him to the musician (presumably to have him help with his own music-related plans). On line 16, the particle *mut* ("but") can be heard as projecting a continuation that is in contrast with Pekka's intended request: judging from the presequence (not shown), it seems that Sini does not know the musician well enough to arrange the introduction. Sini responds to Pekka's plan by laughing (line 17) and with the response token *ai jaa* (still with laughter) which indicates a change of state; she realizes at this point what Pekka was after.

Pekka does not join Sini's laughter, but instead, he produces fake laughter on two occasions: he uses two *heh* tokens on lines 18 and 20. These tokens do not sound responsive to Sini's laughter, but rather, they seem to be postcompletion stance markers (cf. Schegloff, 1996b, p. 92) on Pekka's own turn. The reason for Pekka's phone call is potentially delicate: requests in general are seen as being interactionally tricky (or even dispreferred) actions (see e.g., Schegloff, 2007, pp. 82–6), and here the request can be interpreted as being opportunistic, as Pekka would like to take advantage of both his friend (in making the introduction) and probably also of the musician. Furthermore, Sini has already indicated (before the extract) that she does not really know the musician. Using fake laughter, Pekka displays that he is aware that his actions could be understood as problematic. However, again, as the laughter is fake, the affect display is made from a distance, he is indicating the kind of affect display that would be typical of and expected in this kind of situation rather than actually indexing the affect in question.[10] Here the fake laughter is a device that makes the delivery of the action easier and at the same time keeps the request potentially actual. Starting at line 21, Sini goes on to again state that she does not know the musician very well, but the issue of that introduction is not treated in explicit terms.

In the following extract, fake laughter is used in another delicate activity context, in responding to an invitation. Simo has called Vesa to invite him to a housewarming party. The invitation sequence is complex and occurs in sequences throughout the phone call. When Simo first offers the invitation, Vesa merely acknowledges it minimally and changes the topic. This is already a sign of a dispreferred response type (see e.g., Schegloff, 2007, pp. 58–81). Vesa then returns to the invitation and reports some problems in accepting it and even in responding to the invitation. In Extract 14, Vesa promises to let Simo know if he can attend the party. However, Vesa reports that he has things to do that make it difficult for him to even say when he can tell Simo whether he can come to the party. In the middle of his report, Vesa produces very clearly articulated laugh tokens, *heh heh* (line 5).

Extract 14 [Sg S08 Fatty.telephone]

```
01   Vesa:   nii     nii:.    .mt    [niin  mä  lähen  joo:    kyl   me  ]
             PRT     PRT             PRT    I   go-1   PRT     PRT   we
             so so:.          .mt    [so I'm going    yes:    we    will ]
```

```
02   Simo:              [ILMOTtele        siitä.          ]
                        let know-IMP2     SG3-ELA
                        [LET me know      about it.       ]


03   Vesa:   soitellaan siit        hyvissä      ajoin     mä o-   mun    pitää
             call-PAS DEM.SG-ELA good-PL-INE  time-INS  I     be? I-GEN must
             call about it in good time I a- I have to now

04           nyt mu- mul    menee kato me- mä meen  ens   viikon=
             now   I-ADE go    PRT  we? I   go-1  next  week-GEN
             I- I'll be you see we- I'll go next week

05  →        =l(h)oppuna taas  heh heh  tonne.hh faijan       joku
             end-ESS     again            there   father-GEN  some
             e(h)nd again heh heh there.hh my father's some

06           tä:ti vai mikä se       nyt olikaa     jota     faija on nähny
             aunt or what DEM.SG now be-PST-CLI that-PAR father be see-PPC
             au:nt or what was it now that father has seen

07           joskus      pienenä    ni.hhh se      otti     vitoset eli
             sometime small-ESS PRT  DEM.SG take-PST five-PL in.other.words
             some time when he was young so.hhh she "took the fives"

08           kuoli  ni (.)   mä (.) perjantaist sunnuntaihin
             die-PST PRT   I          Friday-ELA Sunday-ILL
             died in other words so (.) I (.) from Friday to Sunday

09           meen Lieksaan?,      (—)
             go-1 placeNAME-ILL
             I'll be in Lieksa?,
```

In lines 1 and 3, Vesa promises to let Simo know in good time if they can come to the party and moves immediately to report something that he has to do; by reporting the issue here, he implies that it is an obstacle in replying to the invitation. In his turn, Vesa states that he is attending the funeral of his father's aunt, and Vesa's fake laughter occurs in the middle of this report (line 5). His fake laughter is produced as a parenthetical element in the turn, occurring at a point when Vesa has reported the time (next weekend) of the future trip. He laughs within the word *viikonloppuna* ("weekend"), and the lexicalized laugh tokens are positioned after the adverb *taas* ("again"). Here, the adverb marks this funeral trip as one in a series of activities that he plans to do in the near future. Simultaneously, that trip is one more matter that stands in the way of Vesa accepting the invitation or even responding to it. To understand this one-in-a-series character, we need to examine a previous stage of the same conversation. Earlier, when Vesa first starts responding to the invitation, he lists several commitments that he might have to honor on the day of Simo's party. Vesa also utilizes laughter at this point. Before Extract 15, Vesa has already mentioned something that he might be doing on the day of that party (going to another city, Jyväskylä), and in line 1, Simo continues responding to that report. In line 6, Vesa moves on to the following possible obligation:

Extract 15 [Sg S08 Fatty.telephone]

```
01   Simo:   [ai:  siel    tapahtuu  sellasta,[h
              PRT  there  happen    such-PAR
              [oh: there are things like that happening there,

02   Vesa:                              [joo:   .hh
                                        [yeah  .hh

03           >tota< (.)  tai   si-e:  ei::#v#  se<       se
             PRT         or           NEG    DEM.SG  DEM.SG
             >uhm< (.) or th-n: no::#v# it<  it

04           luultavasti   ei:     tota,mh  [h  #ei:#   ]  toteudu  #y#  tää
             probably     NEG  PRT                NEG         realise         this
             probably won't uhm,       mh[h #won't# ]  happen #y# this

05   Simo:                                   [hhh         ]

06   Vesa:   keikka  mut  s(h)itt(h)e  on  t(h)oi:nen   mahol'suus
             gig       but   then         be  another    possibility
             thing but th(h)e(h)n there's a(h)nother possibility

07           et      mä  meen  Vaasaan.
             that   I    go-1  cityNAME-ILL
             that I'll go to Vaasa.

08   →       [heh  heh.hh]h[h  £et   se        on  sa]ma   mei:ninki
                              that  DEM.SG be   same      "idea"
             [heh  heh.hh]h[h  £so it's the same idea.

09   Simo:   [aha        ]  [oho                     ]
             [I see       ]  [Oh                      ]

10   Vesa:   [mut   ]
             [but   ]

11   Simo:   [mieshän]    on  ruvennu  matkai[lee.  ]
             man-CLI      be  start-PPC  travel-INF-ILL
             [the man has started travelling.          ]

12   Vesa:                              [joo:: ]  [mut tot-   ]
                                        [yeah:]  [but uhm  ]

13   Simo:                                          [£mi-  mites]
                                                              how
                                                    [£ho-  what]
```

14   *tää   #tällane   o.#*
         this this.kind be
         is this about.

When Vesa proceeds to tell of something else he might be doing, he uses laughter that occurs within the talk on those items indicating the transition to another issue (*sitte*, "then," *toinen*, "another," line 6). After naming the city, Vaasa, he produces two laugh tokens which are intriguingly between real and fake laughter; the tokens themselves sound quite articulated but at the end of them, a breathy sound occurs that is on the verge of real laughter.

In both Extracts 14 and 15, Vesa uses laughter, real and fake, in listing the things that stand (potentially) in the way of accepting the invitation or of responding to it. His use of laughter treats these reports (and the number of them) as potentially delicate: he is engaged in a dispreferred activity (not accepting an invitation by giving numerous accounts), and the list of his other commitments could be heard as problematic in the sense that they could also be understood as excuses. I do not mean to suggest that Vesa is making up the trips up in order to avoid going to Simo's party, but by using laughter he indicates his recognition of how his talk might be heard. In Extract 15, we can see that Simo treats Vesa's trips as being something quite unexpected, since he topicalizes Vesa's travel plans as news (lines 11 and 13–14), and his turn can be heard having an ironic keying (e.g., in his choice of the reference term *mies*, "man"). The difference between the extracts is that in 15, which occurs first in the conversation, Vesa's laughter is (partly) "real" laughter, whereas in 14, the laughter is clearly articulated. This perhaps reflects the speaker's growing awareness of the potentially problematic nature of his actions: in Extract 14, he more clearly indicates his understanding of how his accounts might sound excessive to the recipient.

The extracts in this section have shown that not all occurrences of fake laughter deal with jokes and failed humor. On the contrary, fake laughter is used in different kinds of contexts, to display different kinds of affective stances. The present data show that fake laughter is often used in slots where something interactionally tricky or delicate is taking place. Through the laugh tokens, the interactants can indicate that they recognize the delicate nature of the action at hand. By not laughing, but rather by producing laugh tokens in a lexicalized manner, they both display what kind of affect could be relevant at that point and also distance themselves somewhat from that affect. Contextually, this distancing can have various kinds of interpretation; like real laughter, fake laughter is a highly contextual and complex phenomenon, performing different functions in different contexts as well as simultaneously in each specific context.

CONCLUDING DISCUSSION

In this chapter I have analyzed the occasions of fake laughter that are realized through articulating such laugh-related sounds as *hah* and *heh*. Even though this kind of fake laughter does not seem to be very frequent in conversation (at least according to the present database), it does seem to be an orderly, recognizable phenomenon. As conversation analytical studies on laughter have shown, laughter is a highly conventional interactional device. The interactants use laughter in systematic ways in interaction, thus displaying their cultural knowledge of where laughter "belongs" in conversation. Interactants seem to know that certain types of actions invite laughter as a response and know that speakers have different ways of inviting them to laugh; on the other hand, speakers also know that not all types of laughter serve as signs of jokes and amusement, but that laughter is used for other purposes as well, such as to signal and to relieve interactional unease in different kinds of contexts. As I have shown, fake laughter occurs in those interactional contexts in which real laughter is utilized and expected; thus, the speakers display their knowledge of the contexts of laughter. Furthermore, the interactants use fake laughter in several kinds of contexts in which different functions of laughter are salient (such as responding to a joke versus delicate talk). In this way, they display their recognition of the various functions of laughter, and the kinds of affect indexed with it. And they even seem to make this difference relevant by choosing different laugh tokens for different contexts: my data suggest that *ha* (and *hoh*) tokens are used in joking contexts and *heh* tokens are more typical of delicate interactional environments.[11]

In using laugh tokens in an articulated way, the speakers display their knowledge of typical interactional practices. However, by producing the laughter as fake, they distance themselves from conventional practices, and this is used to accomplish several kinds of function. In the joking contexts, fake laughter is used to evaluate the humor and its success in the sequences. As I have shown, fake laughter can be used in responding to a joke, marking it as a failure, but the producer of the joke can also utilize fake laughter to evaluate her or his own joking materials; this is sometimes responsive to a lack of uptake of the joke, but not always. In the joking contexts, the fake laughter is used in various ways to deal with a (possible) lack of amusement, which is the affect display that is typical of these sequences. In the cases of delicate talk, fake laughter also builds a distanced relationship to the affective stance indexed with (real) laughter: the interactants indicate their awareness of the relevance for an affect display in the context, but do not display that affect, at least not fully. Rather, they show the possibility and conventionality of such an affect display in the context. This distancing can be used to accomplish different kinds of tasks in different contexts; as real laughter, the fake versions of it are employed for a vast variety of functions.

The practice of doing the affect display from a distance, as fake, seems to be typical of conversations between speakers who know each other very well; all the speakers in the conversations using fake laughter seem to be very good friends. In this kind of intimate conversation, some of the "norms" of conversation can be relaxed and the interactants can act in ways that they (probably) would not choose to do when interacting with people they do not know so well.[12] On the occasions studied in this chapter, it does not seem to be important to commit to the affect displayed by laughter, but it does seem to be important to show that the speakers recognize the relevance of affect display in the specific contexts.

The study of fake laughter opens interesting paths for further research. For instance, the lexicalization of laughter illustrates one way that a language may develop new lexical items, interjections: affective vocalizations can develop into interjection-like items. The line between nonlexical vocalizations and interjections is fuzzy; for instance, the

Iso suomen kielioppi (Comprehensive grammar of Finnish; Hakulinen, Vilkuna, Korhonen, Koivisto, Heinonen, & Alho, 2004) states that "interjections are in between verbal and nonverbal vocalizations" and "if the vocalization has a conventionalized phonological form, it can be seen as an interjection" (§1709). From the point of view of Finnish, tokens such as *heh (heh)* nicely fit the set of interjections which already includes items such as *huh*, *höh*, and *hyh*. In the present data, it seems that the combination *heh heh* is the most conventionalized one: it often occurs as a clearly articulated item, can be placed in the midst of the syntactic structure of the turn (see Extract 14), and can even be used as a part of a verbal construction, filling a slot typically occupied by a noun phrase (data not shown). Furthermore, it seems that the written forms of laughter, and other vocalizations (e.g., found on the internet), could support the lexicalization of these items in spoken interaction as well. In short, these lexicalization processes and paths deserve further study.

Furthermore, there surely are other "fake" affect displays, such as fake smiling and other facial expressions, and fake versions of other affective vocalizations (e.g., crying). However these kinds of affect displays are to my knowledge largely unresearched (see however Sandlund, 2004, pp. 260–67 on some such displays in academic seminars). I hope to have shown in this chapter that the analysis of the "fake" versions of affect displays can help our understanding of affect displays in general, their conventionality in interaction, and the interacts' own knowledge concerning when affect is relevant in interaction and how it is conventionally displayed.

NOTES

1. The same approach has been applied to some other affective vocal phenomena, namely crying (Hepburn, 2004; Hepburn & Potter, 2007, this volume, chapter 9) and cries of pain (Heath, 1989).
2. The tokens *heh* and *hah* (and others such as *hih* and *häh*) are even present in dictionaries. For instance, the *Kielitoimiston sanakirja* (New dictionary of modern Finnish, 2006) includes entries for *hah* and *heh*. They are described as interjections used in "describing laughter," for instance: *heh heh heh, olipas se hassua!*, ("heh heh heh, that was funny!").
3. These are instances that the original transcribers of the materials have usually described as being "fake" laughter in the transcripts.
4. The study by Bell (2009) is not based on audio- or videotaped interactions. Students were asked to insert a joke that "would be likely to fail" in their interactions and to write down the interactions.
5. In some cases, it is more accurate to say that the fake laughter occurs *around* the same contexts as real laughter, as it can be somewhat delayed from the laughter slot.
6. Of course, it is difficult to say why Arto does not find the "joke" funny. However, the joke does have a kind of self-evident quality; there are only so many court-related identities that a layperson can have, and implying the more problematic one seems like an easy option. Furthermore, by choosing this line of acting, Tiina selects away from some other sequential trajectories, e.g., asking about the details of the court case (which, on the other hand, Arto may be unwilling or unable to provide).
7. These jokes used to circulate in Finnish culture and they play with the dialectal forms of the words. The joke on lines 5–10 contains the dialectal verb form *myyrä* (in stan-

dard Finnish, *myydä*), which is the joke: the word *myyrä* in standard Finnish means "a mole." Thus, in the utterance *onks sulla myyrä lippuja*, "do you have tickets to sell," the infinitive verb form *myyrä* ("to sell") is reanalyzed as a noun referring to the bus driver.

8. It is quite typical of conversation analytical studies that the instances of laughter (or other affect displays) are not linked to specific affects such as "embarrassment" (cf. e.g., Couper-Kuhlen, 2009). Rather, the studies talk about the actions that laughter is used to perform or the keyings that laughter brings to the actions it is attached to (e.g., invites laughter, responds to laughter, shows troubles-resistance). I too shy away from affect ascriptions such as "embarrassed laughter" or "nervous laughter" that are often used both in lay parlance and in studies of laughter.

9. The utterance *nyt ei oo kauheesti vaatteita päällä* does not include an explicit person reference (roughly translated as "now there isn't much clothes on") and leaves it open as to who is not (fully) dressed, only Niko or both Niko and his girlfriend.

10. I have discovered instances of similar types of requests (i.e., asking for a favor) produced with real laughter. In these cases, the one who laughs uses laughter to mark the request as a delicate, interactionally challenging action. In Extract 13, Pekka produces a distanced version of this kind of laughter. However, due to space restrictions, a detailed comparison of these types of cases cannot be included in this chapter.

11. In the present database, almost all occurrences of fake laughter consist of the tokens *hah* (sometimes in connection with *hoh*) and *heh*. I have not found examples of the token *hih* used in a similar way; this is interesting, since in the written forms of interaction (at least in the present-day Finnish interactions, such as in Facebook or chat rooms), *hih* is widely used. I do have one example of a lexicalized *häh häh* used in spoken interaction. In dictionaries, *häh* is is described as "evil" or "mean" laughter (*Nykysuomen sanakirja*, s.v. *häh*). And indeed, this fits quite well the use of the *häh* tokens in my data and this further suggest that the speakers indeed perceive a difference between the laugh tokens.

12. Previous research has demonstrated that for instance teasing (Drew, 1987) and other-correction (Haakana & Kurhila, 2009) are actions that occur especially in interactions between speakers who are close.

CHAPTER 9

∽

Crying and Crying Responses

ALEXA HEPBURN AND JONATHAN POTTER

While psychological approaches to emotion start with experience or physiology, conversation analysis (often abbreviated to CA) starts with emotion as a public and communicable object. Thus with crying, the initial focus is not on how it feels and how it is related to grief or loss but on how crying appears in human conduct and the elements that make it recognizable. How crying unfolds in interaction, and how it is responded to, becomes the focus for study. Analysis in this chapter will therefore highlight the profoundly public nature of such matters, how they can be recognized and normatively organized.

To begin with, we will (a) briefly review the existing literature on crying; (b) discuss the complex features of the conduct that is collected together under the vernacular category crying; and (c) address the delicate interactional challenges involved in recognizing and responding to crying. The chapter will draw on an extensive program of work on interaction in the UK National Society for the Prevention of Cruelty to Children (NSPCC) child-protection helpline (Hepburn, 2004; Hepburn & Potter, 2007, 2010) as well as other materials where crying is publically available for study.

TRADITIONAL CRYING RESEARCH

Tom Lutz (2001) has produced an excellent overview of sociological, psychological, historical, and anthropological work on crying. He considers, for example, the representation of crying in paintings and literature and the social significance that is thereby revealed. Research exploring crying as it appears in talk-in-interaction is curiously absent. As Lutz notes, up to now most research on crying has been conducted from an individual psychological perspective. Hepburn (2004) surveyed several strands of work. One strand focused on the causes of crying in infancy and the effects of such crying on attachment (e.g., Barr, Hopkins, & Green, 2000). Most research has

used an instrument known as the Crying Patterns Questionnaire, developed by St. James-Roberts (1988), with no attempt to represent the nature or interactional organization of crying. Another strand of work has focused on adult crying. This work has typically used the Adult Crying Inventory (Vingerhoets & Becht, 1996). This is used, for example, to provide an overall score of the propensity to cry that can be related to cultural, national or gender variables (e.g., Peter, Vingerhoets, & Van Heck, 2001).

More recently, as is common across the social and behavioral sciences, there has been an interest in linking crying to evolutionary and neurological structures. For example, Sander and Scheich (2005) suggest that the auditory cortex, amygdala in the left hemisphere, and insula in the right hemisphere are particularly associated with the perception of both crying and laughing; indeed, they suggest that the right insula is a key structure involved with emotional self-awareness. Newman (2007) suggests crying is a universal mammalian trait associated with shared brain structures (the "cry circuit"). Elsewhere thematic analysis of open-ended interviews has been used to elicit peoples' experiences of, for example, crying babies in a neonatal ward (Kurth et al., 2010).

What these varied studies have in common is that they treat crying as a unitary phenomenon (although with possible scalar properties) and they focus on an individual's experience or perception of crying, accessed by questionnaire, interview, or brain scans. No interaction is enabled between participants, and perception rather than interaction is seen as fundamental and the primary route to cognitive processing.

Crying in interaction

Prior to the current program of work, studies considering crying have been sparse. Manzo, Heath, and Blonder (1998) interviewed stroke patients and found crying in half of their interviews. They used this as a basis for considering crying as a feature of social interaction, but their work did not attempt the tricky task of representing crying; rather they showed the value of seeing emotions as socially constructed. They strongly emphasized the way crying is interactionally occasioned, although they did not go far beyond this general claim. In the other study Whalen and Zimmerman (1998) studied "hysteria" in 9-1-1 calls. Their study is striking for their attempt to capture some features of the caller's distress rather than simply naming it. However, their main analytic focus was not on features of the caller's distress but on the way the call-takers used the term "hysteria" in electronic records to account for the absence of information that is required for a complete form. Nevertheless, like Edwards (1997) they argue for treating "emotion" (in this case, "hysteria") in interactional terms. As they put it:

> rather than look "inward" at the internal states of the individual vehicle of expression, or "outward" to social institutions or culture, the study of the social construction of emotion is anchored in the interactional matrix in which the expression occurs: its form, its placement, its response and the organizational and interactional origins of its accountability (Whalen & Zimmerman, 1998, p. 158).

Our recent work on crying has been able to use Jefferson's (1985) work on laughing as a guide for developing a program of research. Prior to Jefferson's work, merely reporting that laughter had occurred was often treated as sufficient for research purposes. Jefferson's paper showed how a detailed transcription of the sounds that make up laughter could reveal previously unnoticed interactional properties, including a delicate coordination of elements of laughter with ongoing activities. Further research by Jefferson and others followed this through to highlight the involvement of laughter with different interactional tasks (for a summary of this work, see Glenn, 2003). This provided a template for considering crying.

Jefferson (1984b) noted that if we assume that laughter, like crying, is an uncontrolled bodily function—a "flooding out" that is therefore not part of the ongoing vocal interaction—we will be tempted to merely note that it occurred, rather than transcribe it in detail. This has happened in the majority of research in the area of crying. Jefferson took an example where laughter was originally presented in a transcript as "bubbling through" the talk, and showed that with a more detailed transcript the laughter was only present in that part of the talk that involved "the saying of an obscenity" (1985, p. 30) (see also Haakana, in this volume, chapter 8). A more developed transcript is therefore vital to any understanding of the variety of interactional features of laughter in different contexts. We will now consider what can be revealed by a more careful exploration of some of the interactional elements of crying.

Features of crying

Some of the basic features of the transcription of crying are detailed below, using an example from the live transmission of the British reality television program *Pop Idol*, where aspiring musicians are having their singing performance evaluated by a panel of experts who give direct and often quite scathing feedback. This has the particular advantage that it can be reproduced as a web resource without the ethical issues that rule out other more sensitive materials.[1] Video material also allows some inspection of nonvocal aspects of the interaction. This extract comes after the contestant returns to join others who have been watching his performance and the judges' highly critical comments on his singing. Ant and Dec are the hosts, Cont is the contestant who has just performed.

Extract 1 [Pop Idol Crying 2005]
```
01   Cont:    [((mouthing, shakes head,    [smiling))
02   Dec:                                  [((puts hand on
03   Dec:     [  Cont's shoulder))    ]
04   Cont:    [((thumb wiping eye))  ]
05   Cont:    [°.snih°]
06   Dec:     [Y'er  ['t.  ]
07   Ant:     [       [°↓a'r]ight.°]
08            (0.3)
09   Cont:    ↑↑Yeah,
```

```
10              [    (1.2)                                        ]
11              [  ((thumb stays on eye, looking down))    ]
12    Cont:     °.hh° (.)    .SHHIH
13    Ant:      Take ye time there don't worry.
14              (0.4)
15    Cont:     I'  [ve ↑never  ]    ↑had that e- in my life
16    Dec:          [don' worry.]
17    Ant:          [(a'↓right.) ]
18    Cont:     performin.=I've gone on sta:ge ((touches eye))
19              (.) bin character ((touches nose)) ~all that
20              sorta stuff an~ (.)
21    Dec:      Mm.
22    Cont:     A've- it's ~↑weir:d °↑it's ↑↑weird an°~
23              [ ((camera pans to other Cont wiping her eye)) ]
24              [                 (0.7)                        ]
25    Dec:      An you've worked har:d fer this haven't you.
26              Up- up to this point    [ah mean] you knaw: ye've
27    Cont:                             [Hhh.h  ]
28              (0.4)
29    Cont:     ~THAt wasn' #ma best.#~ That wus the one
30              thing ah ~wanted to #do,~ (.)
31    Cont:     [ ((touches eyes, faces camera] hand down))
32    Cont:     [ .h[h h]HHh (0.2) HHHh    ]
33    Cont:     ~If you'n understan this ad 'ome,~
34              (0.6)
35    Cont:     ~Er:m~ (0.3) I- I wanted to sa:y (.) a c'd (.)
36              >~cum out an say a couldna done any better,~<
37              [~↑↑budda coulda↑↑ ↑↑↑done~]
```

We will consider features of crying roughly in the order that they appear in the extract(s), first noting how they will appear in transcript.

Silence is represented with timed pauses, and one of the features of crying is often extensive silence where it would not be normatively expected—extended pauses, missing uptake, and unfilled places in adjacency pairs. Under certain interactional conditions (especially phone calls where there are no visible indications) silence can be treated by recipients as suggestive that the speaker is seriously upset. Note, for example line 10 where the recipient might have been expected to offer more, but does not; the "take your time" from the presenter on 13 orients precisely to the failure to speak in a relevant slot.

Sniffs come with varying degrees of volume and stretch, represented as inhalation, with the addition of various voiced vowels and consonants, caused by nasal or "wet" sounds: for example, Extract 1, lines 5 and 12, "°.snih" and ".SHHIH." One role

for sniffing can be to signal the incipience of the crier's next turn, which can give it a floor-holding role in the interaction that is similar to a hearable inbreath (Hepburn, 2004), for example, see Extract 2 below, line 6. It can also be a hearable display (combined in Extract 1 with silence) that the speaker would speak if they were not so upset, or that a bout of more disruptive sobbing has not completely passed.

Elevated pitch occurs when the speaker is continuing through a crying episode, probably caused by muscle constriction in the throat and vocal chords. In Extract 1, the speaker struggles with delivery of the description of his problems with singing, becoming increasingly high pitched on line 15 and lines 22 and 37. This extreme pitch shift (marked with upward arrows), typically accompanies talk that begins to break down into sobbing. Here the speaker's upset inflects a description where a reason for being upset is offered.

Tremulous or wobbly delivery is represented by enclosing the talk in tildes (~) (e.g., Extract 1, lines 19–20, 30, and 34). This can be less disruptive than sniffs, sobs, or high-pitched delivery, as speakers can continue speaking in a tremulous manner for extended periods. As with many of the elements of upset, tremulous delivery alone can be treated by recipients as a sign of emotional or psychological distress (Hepburn, 2004).

Aspiration during words has been represented by one or more *h*s. As with laughter, parentheses (*h*) are used to represent plosive breathing; outside of parentheses the *h* represents a more "breathy" sound. It is different from sobbing in that the aspiration occurs during or directly before or after speech.

Like tremulous voicing and high pitch, aspiration is a feature of speakers' attempts to talk through a crying episode. This can be seen in Extract 2, below, in line 8. Aspiration of this kind, like tremulous delivery, can be the first cue to recipients that there is upset of some kind. This kind of aspiration may sound very similar to laughter (a difficulty also found with sobs). In line with the policy of trying to have the transcript embody the least analytic presupposition, the aspiration is not marked as crying as opposed to laughing. One reason for this is that the difference between the two is generally obvious from the context in which it occurs, and where it isn't obvious, this difference may be a problem for participants.

Sobbing is represented with normal in- and outbreaths, often but not always including "voiced vowels," which can be elevated in pitch. When they are sharply inhaled, exhaled, or spasm-like this is represented by enclosing them in reversed angled brackets (>huh huh<) which borrows from Jefferson's use of them as an indication of a faster pace. Sobbing is probably the most familiar and recognizable feature of crying, and is usually the most disruptive to ongoing interaction. However, in the corpus of adult crying that we have worked with, full-scale bouts of sobbing are rare. Extract 2 provides an example (e.g., lines 1, 3, and 4).

Further problems with delivery are evidenced by *mouthed* (Example 1, line 1) or *whispered* talk, enclosed between double degree symbols (°°). Both may result in talk that can be very difficult to hear, and may arise due to physiological changes in the muscles around the vocal chords. In the following extract from the NSPCC child-protection helpline, where sobbing is already in progress, we can see whispered talk in line 8. (CPO stands for child protection officer.)

Extract 2 [JK Distraught dad 29.4.01]

```
01   Cal:    >.Hhih.hhihhh<
02   CPO:    D'you want- d'y'wann'ave  [a break for a    ] moment.=
03   Cal:                              [Hhuhh >.hihh<]
04           =>hhuhh hhuhh<
05           (0.6)
06   Cal:    .shih
07           (0.3)
08   Cal:    °°khhay°°
09           (1.8)
10   Cal:    .shih >hhuh hhuh[h]<
```

Additional features of voice quality may be part of recognizable upset, such as creaky delivery (represented by #) or staccato delivery (represented with the itera-tion of a "cut off" symbol (e.g., "it-is-cut-off-"). Activities such as swallowing and throat-clearing may also accompany upset.

Visual features of upset may include trembling face and/or hands; tears; touching eyes or face; looking down or hiding one's face, or turning away; combined with more characteristic facial features of screwed-up eyes; downturned mouth with eyebrows drooping down from the middle of the face; flushed appearance, especially around the eyes and nose.

Examination of *interactional features* suggests that crying rarely switches on in full form; rather, various signs of possible distress can accumulate, sometimes with con-siderable subtlety. These may appear as an inflection of one or more elements of crying into the ongoing interaction without disrupting it, at least initially. Crying can also involve sequences of talk that break away from ongoing activities and are instead occupied with the crying itself, such as apologies from the crying party, soothing, reassuring, sympathetic, empathetic, and diagnostic moves from the crying recipient (e.g., Extract 1, lines 2, 3, 7, 8, 13; Extract 2, line 2). The crying recipient can continue to orient to the ongoing talk, or can orient to the disruption of the talk (in an institu-tional setting like the NSPCC: "take your times" are common (Hepburn, 2004; Hep-burn & Potter, 2007, and see Example 1, line 14) or they can respond more directly to the upset evidenced by the speaker (e.g., Extract 3, line 17, below). Our corpus of crying calls is at present not sufficient to allow distinctions between these and fur-ther options in collecting and analyzing uptake to crying, as we continue to further explore some of the interactional dimensions of upset in the rest of this chapter.

RESPONSES TO CRYING IN MUNDANE AND INSTITUTIONAL SETTINGS

This section will apply our understanding of features of crying and actions of crying recipients, developed in earlier research on child-protection helpline data (e.g., Hep-burn & Potter, 2007, 2010), to a call between two middle-aged sisters living in Aus-tralia. In doing so, we consider the relevance of recent discussions about empathy and epistemic access (e.g., Heritage, 2011) and discuss the value of analytic distinctions between empathy and sympathy (Hepburn & Potter, 2007). As we work through this section we should note that there is a tension between decomposing "crying" into a range of different elements and discussing "responses to crying," suggesting that crying can be considered as a unitary phenomenon. In what follows we will use "crying responses" as a catch-all for activities coordinated in relation to specific features, or collections of features, of crying, as described above.

Crying and sympathy

In earlier work, we suggested a distinction between empathic and sympathetic turns, reserving the term empathy for "on the record" claims of, or displays of, understanding of the other's perspective (Hepburn & Potter, 2007). By contrast, we suggested that sympathy tokens need not be propositional; they do not explicitly specify the nature or cause of what is being addressed sympathetically, nor formulate the speaker's understanding of the emotional state of the party who is evidencing distress. Rather, as noted by Hepburn (2004), they are mainly identified by the prosodic delivery of the turn—usually stretched, sometimes with elevated or rising–falling pitch and/or creaky delivery, sometimes explicitly involving some kind of token such as "oh" or "aw," sometimes with softened volume and increased "breathiness" or aspiration. Although they can mirror prosodic elements of crying, sympathetic turns are hearably specific to the action of sympathizing or soothing. We discuss the appearance and import of sympathetic turns in our extended analysis of the example below.

In the following call, Jill is phoning her sister Kerry; the initial business for Jill is to thank Kerry for a lunch invitation but decline it, the account for refusal being work commitments. Kerry asks her about a weekend trip and Jill reports having fun, but notes the absence of various parties who might have been expected to spend time with her. Jill's listing of why others could not attend, combined with her somewhat abrupt delivery, leads Kerry to identify possible trouble, as we see in line 1.

Extract 3 [TS 0.58]
```
01   Kerry:   You a' [ri:ght? ]
02   Jill:          [That's a ]beoud it. Hh
03            (.)
04   Jil:     Aoh yeh?
05            (0.2)
06   Jil:     >Spose ↑so<
07            (.)
08   Ker:     Tch Yeah?
09            (0.3)
10   Ker:     °↓Yeh.
11            (1.2)
12   Ker:     Bit of a loose end?=Did you have a lot've
13            time ↑off?=or:
```

```
14              (2.0)
15    Jil:      ~↑N::u:h.
16              (1.4)
17    Ker:      #O::aw::,=a'y'hev'n a hard ti:me,
18              (1.0)
19    Jil:      ~Mm::,
20              (.)
```

Kerry's enquiry on line 1 gets two fairly minimal, delayed, and equivocal responses from Jill on lines 4 and 6 (note that line 2 is a somewhat delayed conclusion to her summary narrative of her weekend). In line 8 Kerry pursues elaboration on Jill's answer, and in its absence on line 9, offers a quiet "yeh," with downward intonation, that sounds like it is closing off this pursuit. This may be part of what Hepburn and Potter (2010) have suggested is a general attentiveness by crying recipients that they avoid initiating actions with which the crying party will have difficulty. This also suggests that Kerry is already hearing trouble, despite the absence of any actual elements of upset (apart from slightly extended transitions and lack of elaboration of talk from Jill). In her next attempt, rather than seeking elaboration of how Jill is feeling, Kerry offers for confirmation a candidate gloss on Jill's emotional state ("Bit of a loose end?"[2], line 12). As a contracted "yes / no interrogative"[3] (hereafter YNI; see Raymond, 2003) this makes more of the conversational running than "yeah?" and immediately offers a possible reason for that feeling—Jill has had "a lot've time off" also offered as a YNI for confirmation. Jill's delayed response in line 15 ("~↑N::u:h.") displays upset— her negative answer is delivered with elevated pitch, and is clipped,[4] tremulous, and stretched, and is followed by silence where elaboration might have been expected. Although a "type conforming" response (Raymond, 2003) "no" rejects the assumptions in Kerry's question. It is useful to note here that crying or upset is not delivered as an action as such, or as a turn with propositional content, but rather as something that inflects or leaks into the talk, even interfering with its progressivity.

The delivery and delay are then treated by Kerry as diagnostic of upset,[5] and her extended sympathy token combines a "change of state" token, "oh" (Heritage, 1984b), with a "sympathy" token, "aw," which, as Hepburn (2004) noted, tends to be conveyed largely in features of the delivery of the response—here creaky and stretched, with gently rising intonation. This type of token, combined with varying calibrations of sympathetic prosody, can be especially useful in institutional environments, for example in our helpline calls, where maintaining appropriate institutional neutrality, especially where the caller is still offering important information, can be more important than more "on the record" empathizing with the caller's difficulties. Extract 4 below offers an example of this from our child-protection helpline interaction:

Extract 4 [HC Boy in Attic]
```
01    Caller:   ~I'M ON mahh~.h((ihh (0.2) ~I(h)'m des((perate((
02              ah really am~ ((((hhu[hh((   .hh]
03    CPO:                       [Mm::,    ]
```

```
04   Call:   ~Somebody doesn't do something soon ah'm gonna
05           e-~ (0.2) >.h((ihh< (0.5) ~>↑AH dunno waddam
06           gonna do.=I'll die anyway.<~ °a-↑a-° >i[hhuhh<]
07   CPO:                                          [↑M: m ]::,=.hh
08   Call:   .H↑↑uih (.) °shih°
09           (0.4)
10   Call:   °°h↑↑i:  [h°°]
11   CPO:            [So] maybe life is very very  f[rightening.]
12   Call:                                         [~'E doesn't]
13           take- the- the p'lice
```

Here the caller is reporting her worries about the house she lives in, and the lack of support from the police in reporting a crime. As she builds to the summary of the report, she shows increasing signs of upset, culminating in her turn on lines 1–6. On lines 3 and 7 the CPO's continuers, "Mm," are increasingly strongly inflected with "sympathetic" gently rising and falling contours. These turns acknowledge the feelings of the caller and validate her upset, while on line 11 the CPO starts to gently build a course of action that runs counter to the caller's formulation of the police as the problem, allowing a return to helpline business. A more elaborate (and less common) version of sympathy in our helpline interaction can be seen in the call below:

Extract 5 [NSPCC AD Grandson black eye]

```
01   Caller:  An she won't ~answer my phone or anythin' and
02            I'm jh's s(h)↑o whorri[ed th't some'ing c'd]
03   CPO:                           [°O h:      m y     °]
04            ↑hhappen  [↑to ↑↑'im >.HH<] h
05   CPO:               [   °g o: s h:   ]
06   CPO:     #Oh: go:s[h#]
07   Call:             [°.S]hih°
08            (0.5)
09   CPO:     .HHhh
10            (0.5)
11   Call:    °.Shih°=
12   CPO:     =I mean is your relationship with her normally-
13            is it (.) e-normally okay,=or is it normally
14            a bit (.) rocky anywa:y.
```

The child protection officer's response ("oh my gosh" lines 3, 5) to an emotionally delivered problem presentation by the caller is in the form of a combined news receipt and marker of surprise, which also acknowledges that something untoward has been described. The CPO's turn is stretched, quieter than normal (perhaps in acknowledgment that it is persisting in overlap across the caller's turn), and repeated with creaky delivery on line 6.

This type of sympathetically inflected turn acknowledges the feelings of the other, without topicalizing them or going on the record with propositional content. It therefore allows CPOs to acknowledge and validate the upset without explicitly aligning with the caller's project in the call—here the caller is complaining about her daughter-in-law. As we see in lines 12–14, not topicalizing the upset allows a speedy return to helpline business. Responses such as the CPO's "#Oh: go:sh#," that break out of the more standard institutional pattern, are less common on the helpline. Yet, as Hepburn (2004) showed, failure to attend to a caller's distress can lead to interactional trouble. We consider the role of "empathic" responses in the following section.

Crying and empathy

In our understanding, empathy involves "on the record" claims of, or displays of, understanding of the other's perspective (Hepburn & Potter, 2007). Unlike sympathy tokens, displays of empathy are propositional.

We rejoin Extract 3 with some overlap, having left Kerry's turn after the sympathetic token "#O::aw::" on line 17. The sympathy token is followed by a display of empathy.

Extract 6 [TS 1:09]

```
12   Ker:    Bit of a loose end?=Did you have a lot've
13           time ↑off?=or:
14           (2.0)
15   Jil:    ~↑N::u:h.
16           (1.4)
17   Ker:    #O::aw::,=a'y'hev'n a hard ti:me,
18           (1.0)
19   Jil:    ~Mm::,
20           (.)
21   Ker:    #Aoh:: ↑Jill:_
22           (0.2)
23   Ker:    .Hhlh ((inbreath through tongue/teeth))
24           (0.2)
25   Ker:    ↑Poor old gir:l, hh
26           (0.8)
27   Ker:    °Oh dee:ya, hh
28           (0.4)
29   Ker:    .shh
30   Jil:    .tdh[h h h]
```

Kerry latches a further polar question onto her sympathy token, presenting a more propositional display of Jill's current state ("having a hard time") for confirmation. The effect is to move the sequence away from where it started—whether Jill has been at a "loose end"—into a new sequence occupied with dealing more explicitly with the nature and cause of Jill's upset.

We can see the value of Kerry's move to yes / no interrogative turns in this context, in that the interrogative frame builds Jill as having the primary right to her own experiences, but at the same time constrains the terms of a response (Raymond, 2003). This type of constraint may be useful for a recipient having difficulty in producing a response; it could be as small as one word—yes or no. The idiomatic constructions—"at a loose end" and "having a hard time"—are fitted to building a normalized and generalized version of events that would perhaps be comforting, in the sense that it makes the upset more understandable[6]. All of this contributes to providing an empathic reaction to Jill's upset without requiring her to elaborate on that upset, other than projecting agreement.

Jill's turn on 19 is fitted to both the action and format of Kerry's YNI, which projects agreement. In addition to confirming that she is indeed having a hard time, the delivery of Jill's turn displays her emotional state. "Mm" can be a minimal form of confirmation that doesn't involve much in the way of oral or vocal effort, and is therefore useful for a speaker having difficulties with both. By stretching and emphasizing the turn, Jill may be compensating for not producing a more elaborate response, as well as providing a clear display through the extended tremulous delivery, that she is upset. From line 21 onward, Kerry's contributions take again a sympathetic rather than empathic form. In line 21 she issues a sympathy token ("#Aoh::") and an address term which seems to orient to Jill's vulnerability. On lines 25 and 27 Kerry offers two further idiomatic formulations of sympathy ("↑Poor old gir:l," and "°Oh dee:ya,"). All of these turns share some of the general features of "sympathy" discussed above—elevated pitch, increased breathiness, stretched and creaky delivery. This set of turns also illustrates another feature that we found in helpline crying sequences; the noncrying party, in this case Kerry, keeps the interaction moving by producing and sometimes recycling a series of turns. Each is spaced to give a more extended transition space for the crying party to contribute, but the delay is not so long as to leave them with responsibility for an uncomfortably long silence if they do not. A similar series of turns can be seen on lines 8–18 of Extract 3.

Crying in mundane and institutional environments

This chapter begins to extend our studies of crying in interaction from institutional materials to more mundane settings. Although we can't do a systematic comparison with one call, we can start to speculate on possible differences, while also indicating directions for future study.

One interesting point of comparison relates to the types of questions that are formulated. As we've noted up to now in our mundane example, yes / no interrogatives are an important resource for recipients of upset. Elsewhere (Hepburn & Potter, 2010) we have noted that a particular form of YNI, a "turn medial" tag question, is a common feature of responses to upset in helpline interaction. By "turn medial tag question" we mean an utterance containing some kind of declarative statement which is tag formatted, typically a negative interrogative is tagged on at the end.

Having issued a tag question, sometimes speakers can continue by adding more, as in line 5 of Extract 7 below, where a caller has been disclosing abuse he suffered as a child:

Extract 7 [JX male survivor]

```
01   Caller:   >°°↑Ghhd- al- like↑°°< (0.2) °°↑↑i°° (1.4)
02             °°↑↑bleedin ↑↑k:id°°
03             (1.9)
04   Call:     °°Ghho' I'm a°° °↑↑grow:n man↑↑°
05             (1.7)
06   Call:     K.HHhh   Hh[h]
07   CPO:                  [Th]ere's:: a bit of the child in ↑all
08             of us an- (0.7) an  [that's the h(h)urt chi(h)ld ]
09   Call:                         [ .Hhhh      Hhhh       ]
10   CPO:      there is↑un' it. with you at the moment.
11   Call:     °.Hhhhh° >hh< >h< >h<
12             (3.5)
13   CPO:      ↑Don't worry, °th- i-° take your ti:me.
14             (1.4)
```

In our helpline corpus, turn medial tag questions are recurrent both in advice and crying sequences, while being relatively rare elsewhere. We suggested that such formatting manages the problem of providing a formulation of the other person's state or business, where they may not yet have offered such a thing. This is done by treating the recipient as being in a position to confirm the adequacy of the formulation, while either filling the transition space or continuing after it. In Extract 7 above, the CPO's tag formatted turn responds to the caller's prior self-deprecating turn (lines 1–4), that he is acting like a "bleedin kid" by getting so upset. The turn generalizes and normalizes the caller's actions ("there's a bit of the child in all of us") and tag formats precisely the part of her turn that claims the most understanding of the caller's state—"that's the hurt child there." This combined with their turn medial position, which gives these tag questions a weakened response requirement (Hepburn & Potter, 2010) means that they are an ideal interrogative in an environment where the recipient may not respond but that lack of response should not appear too problematic.

A typical example of a turn medial tag question can be found in Extract 1, lines 22–3, reproduced here:

Extract 9 [from Extract 1: Pop Idol]

```
22   Cont:     A've- it's ~↑weir:d °↑it's ↑↑weird an°~
23             [ ((camera pans to other Cont wiping her eye)) ]
24             [ (0.7)                                        ]
25   Dec:      An you've worked har:d fer this haven't you.
26             Up- up to this point [ah mean] you knaw: ye've
```

Here the presenter, Dec, offers a description that emphasizes that the crying contestant has worked hard; that is, he has done the all the right things to get to where he is. Dec thereby displays empathic insight into the crying contestant's situation, which also provides reassurance by countering the suggestion that the problem causing distress is caused by the contestant's own neglect of practice and preparation. As we've suggested, this type of affirming description of the crying party's business is a common feature of declarative components of tag questions in crying sequences. It's interesting to note that this practice is not peculiar to institutional environments:

Extract 10 [TS 1:27]

```
45   Ker:   .TCH=°Haw:h dear.°
46   Jil:   °>Huh huh huh hu[h<°]
47   Ker                 [  I ]t's frustrating
48   Ker:   [isn'it.    ]=too [:. Because noth]ing happens:.
49   Jil:   [°huh huh°]      [M m::::.         ]
50          (.)
51   Jil:   °U- Yea:h.
52   Ker:   .Shh (0.2) uHHHhh an ye just kinda left in
53          limbo.=really,=aren't you.
54   Jil:   u- ~Y::↑ep
55          (0.3)
```

Kerry's two tag questions in lines 47–8 and 52–3 present a formulation of Jill's emotional condition for agreement—in a state of frustration, left in limbo. We have described explicitly propositional constructions of the recipient's emotional state such as these as empathic (as opposed to sympathetic) responses to upset (Hepburn & Potter, 2007). They therefore issue a turn that can be agreed or disagreed with, in a way that sympathetic responses don't.

One key difference between the NSPCC examples and our mundane crying example is that Kerry is adopting a more personal stance toward Jill—addressing her by first name in Extract 6 line 21, and using an idiomatic term of endearment on line 25—"↑Poor old gir:l,". Note that "old girl" is listed in various internet dictionaries of slang as an affectionate Australian idiom for a woman, wife, or mother. It is suggestive of a close relationality that would be inappropriate on the helpline. This phrase is notable as it both acknowledges Jill's upset, and claims entitlement to tell her about her "poor" condition. In doing so it also warrants the accountability of the upset; it shows that Kerry can see that Jill is not needlessly crying, but is a victim of circumstances.

Another key difference is in the lack of turns in this mundane material that license the disruption to ongoing business—the "take your times" common in our helpline corpus. Instead, accounting for crying appears in a more subtle form, in the declarative structures of tag questions presented for agreement. All of these features suggest that adult crying, and perhaps especially the disruption it causes to the progressivity of sequences, may be accountable, and that displaying sympathy and/or empathy can involve the recipient doing the accounting for the interactionally disabled crier.

SUMMARY AND CONCLUSIONS

This chapter has reviewed a range of features of crying, and argued for the value of detailed transcription of both crying and the various responses to crying. Careful transcription allows us to understand crying as a collection of loosely associated and sometimes escalating practices, and opens it up, like laughter, for more specific interactional analysis. The complex interactional nature of crying then starts to become evident. Our analyses across a range of projects suggest that crying is something that typically inflects talk, sometimes interferes with, dramatizes, or underscores talk, and sometimes replaces talk, rather than appearing as an action or set of actions in its own right. This makes its uptake particularly complex—it involves orientating to something that is displayed or to the manner of its delivery, rather than to an action, claim, or proposition. The manner in which crying appears in adults, and the sense of it as something to be accounted for, especially in institutional environments, can also make it seem that the crier is unwilling for their state to become part of public discourse—and this can create tricky problems in responding.

We have started to document the delicate interactional challenges involved in recognizing and responding to crying. We focused in particular on a call between two sisters, which enabled a number of comparisons with our helpline data. This has involved close attention to (a) the participants, for example, their prior relationship, what access they have to the ongoing events in one another's life; and (b) the type of data and whether there is some ongoing institutional task being performed, such as a game show, a helpline call, two sisters or two friends talking.

One obvious point of comparison is with actions that orient to the crying as disruptive of progressivity. For example we found that turns such as "it's alright" and "take your time" are common in our child-protection helpline data, and also in the television game show data. However no such turns were found in the call between the two sisters. This suggests their role as actions that license the disruption of interaction, which makes them of particular use in institutional talk, where the empathic responder is engaged in some kind of institutional role, which is disrupted by the upset party. Such issues related to institutional specificity are very important but await further studies to develop them fully.

By contrast, some responsive actions were recurrent in both types of data, notably sympathy tokens, continuers, or news receipts with sympathetic inflection. These are often followed by actions that orient to the upset as normal in the circumstances, and responses that license the crier's upset as having an appropriate cause, such as "having a difficult or hard time." These types of responses therefore seem to cut across other issues such as how well the interlocutors know one another, and relate instead to the intensity of the emotional experience.

We also sought to engage with and extend findings from existing literature. Manzo, Heath, and Blonder (1998) have argued that understanding how emotion is "socially constructed" may be a useful starting place to allow insights into how patients may be "pathologized" in clinical encounters. This study has implications for the development of this line of research by starting to detail normative responses to crying in everyday interaction, and therefore what may be "missing" in clinical or other institutional contexts.

Recently, Heritage (2011) has discussed empathy in ways that are partially over-lapping and partially divergent from our understanding of empathy. For Heritage, the (empathizing) recipient's access to interlocutor's experience is a key issue. He suggests that it is important to distinguish between the different levels of access the (would-be empathic) recipient has to whatever events, sensations, or activities are under way, as this will be reflected in their entitlement to offer their own comments or evaluations. On this view, crying could be something that raises the "problem of experience," as the more intense the emotion, the greater the moral obligation to respond empathically and yet also the more difficult this will be, given that "the experiencer has primary, sole and definitive epistemic access" to it (2011, p. 160).

There are a number of differences between our findings and Heritage's more recent paper. Our previous work examining issues of empathy and sympathy in responses to crying has been based solely on helpline interaction, which adds a layer of complexity to the kinds of issues of epistemics and access that Heritage discusses; child-protection officers are nearly always speaking to a caller whom they have never talked to before. Another difference from the type of data examined by Heritage is that callers are not simply making empathic turns relevant by recalling emotional experiences, rather by displaying upset during interaction, a speaker gives fairly immediate and direct access to how they feel.

In line with Heritage's (2011) recent work on empathic responses, we paid particular attention to the sense in which prosodic inflection can show attentiveness to the upset party's emotional state, and thereby display some kind of empathy. Where responses to crying in helpline interaction are concerned, we have found it useful to distinguish between sympathetic and empathic responses. We offered an analysis of Extract 6, in which the CPO acknowledges upset through the use of sympathetic tokens ("my gosh") but subsequently moves the topic on without providing the propositional content that would have made her response to the caller's upset more "empathic." Clearly, this discussion is partly semantic—however, distinguishing between these two terms allows something to be marked that also seems to be marked interactionally. In particular, because propositional examples go "on the record" in the way that the less propositional ones do not, they require more attention to epistemic matters, and can start a course of action occupied with topicalizing the upset itself, rather than resuming ongoing projects.

As Heritage (2011) would predict, strong emotions may present the recipient with a profound intersubjective dilemma. On the one hand, strongly expressed emotions place increased response demands on the recipient; on the other hand, they are typically harder to access. We could argue that in some ways the reverse is true with crying, where recipients have a fairly unequivocal display of the crying party's emotional state, though perhaps not its causes. As our analysis suggests, even among people who know one another well, like Kerry and Jill, descriptions of troubles can be precisely calibrated to mark out causal factors and what is currently at issue, for example whether issues of blame or accountability have become more acute. As both Buttny (1983) and Edwards (1997, 1999) have noted, formulations of emotional states are precisely calibrated to support particular actions. This calibration is likely to be hard to achieve on behalf of another speaker. It follows that, in a normative sense at least, speakers have primary rights to describe their own emotional states, and so doing it for them will be marked in various ways to show this, such as through interrogative formatting.

Our findings also show the value of using a more procedural definition of empathy, building on earlier research (Hepburn & Potter, 2007, 2010; see also Ruusuvuori, 2005). We have suggested that empathic actions are typically formed from two key elements: (a) a formulation of the crying party's business or emotional state (poor thing, frustrated, hurt); and (b) some kind of epistemic marking of the contingency or source of that formulation, for example by using yes / no interrogatives, constructions such as "I guess," or by tag formatting. In this way, the crying recipient can claim some access to this type of experience while deferring to the rights of the upset party to define the nature of their troubles.

The study of crying as an interactional phenomenon has only just started. One of the consequences of decomposing "crying" as a simple vernacular category into a range of different phenomena is that it allows a much more fine-grained interactional understanding of the way "upset" and "distress" can emerge and be consequential in interaction. Our discussion above is indicative of some of the relevant analytic avenues that are opened up, but many questions are dependent on the collection of further materials, in particular more mundane materials and ones from different settings (within and outwith established relationships, in the context of "bullying" or criticism, and so on). Of particular interest is interaction where there is no outright sobbing and disruption to the progressivity of talk, and yet there are elements such as croaky or tremulous voice, increased delay, and so on. Moreover, there are a range of institutional issues to be addressed, such as the way crying is managed in "therapeutic" environments and environments of heightened conflict, such as hostile cross-examinations and relationship disputes. There are also important developmental issues, in particular questions of how crying emerges and is managed in families with young people and infants (see Wootton, this volume, chapter 3), and whether interaction in such environments can be seen as laying down a template that is consequential for what comes later.

ACKNOWLEDGMENTS

We would like to thank to Dr. Jess Harris, University of Queensland, and Dr. Marian May, School of Business, University of New South Wales, for useful input, and to Gail Jefferson for earlier help in developing original transcripts of crying. We would also like to thank Anssi Peräkylä and Marja-Leena Sorjonen for very useful, detailed, and insightful editorial comments

NOTES

1. See http://www.lboro.ac.uk/departments/ss/centres/darg/Hepburn_1.htm2.
2. That is, feeling unsettled or that things are incomplete.

3. "Bit of a loose end" is a contraction of the idiomatic "are you at a bit of a loose end" where the interrogative syntax is replaced by interrogative intonational contour. It nevertheless projects a yes or no response, although like many polar questions, a simple yes or no response would seem insufficient.
4. "Clipped" refers to a formulation of "no" that avoids the "oh" sound, leaving the speaker with "uh," which can sometimes be more elaborately clipped by a "p," as in "nup." Such responses often seem to display the redundancy of the eliciting turn.
5. As Hepburn (2004) noted, in the right situation the mere presence of one or two elements of crying can be treated as indicative of upset.
6. Hepburn and Potter (2007) found a similar pattern of idiomatic constructions with yes and no interrogatives in responses to upset in their helpline data.

CHAPTER 10

ᴄᐵᴐ

Revealing Surprise

The Local Ecology and the Transposition of Action

CHRISTIAN HEATH, DIRK VOM LEHN,
JASON CLEVERLY, AND PAUL LUFF

Attention, if sudden and close, graduates into surprise; and this into astonishment; and this into stupefied amazement. The latter frame of mind is closely akin to terror. Attention is shown by the eyebrows being raised; and as this state increases into surprise, they are raised to a much greater extent with the eyes and the mouth widely open. The raising of the eyebrows is necessary in order that the eyes should be opened quickly and widely; and this movement produces transverse wrinkles across the forehead. The degree to which the eyes and mouth are opened corresponds with the degree of surprise felt [. . .] One of the commonest sounds is a deep 'Oh'; and this would naturally follow as explained by Helmholtz from the mouth being moderately opened and the lips protruded.

Darwin, 1872/2007, pp. 281, 288

In brief, our subject externalises a presumed inward state and acts so as to make discernable the special circumstances which presumably produced it.

Goffman, 1981, p. 89

The longstanding debate concerning the expression of emotions, whether they are universal or culturally specific, a debate that emerged at least from the publication of Darwin's (1872/2007) treatise, continues to pervade studies of emotion and, as Fridja (1986) shows, underpins distinctive bodies of research. The debate rests, in part, on the highly variable expression of emotion and is fuelled by methodological debates that call into doubt evidence for a universal connection between psychological or even physiological states and their behavioral manifestation (see for example Ekman, 1999). The debate however has tended to draw attention away from an important aspect of emotion, in particular the ways in which expression is occasioned by, and sensitive to, the circumstances in which emotions arise. Surprise is particularly interesting in this regard, since it is commonly understood as a response to something unexpected, even untoward, arising within the local ecology (Darwin, 1872/2007). In contrast with a number of the other emotions, surprise has received relatively little attention, and still less research that has explored the ways in which surprise is interactionally constituted with regard to an object or event within the environment.

There are a number of important exceptions that touch on these issues. First and foremost, Goffman (1981) directs attention to the socially organized production of "response cries," including those that display surprise, and considers the ways in which they externalize "a presumed inward state [. . .] so as to make discernable the special circumstances which presumably produced it" (p. 89). And while not concerned with the ways in which the immediate physical environment provokes surprise, Wilkinson and Kitzinger (2006), in their analysis of "reaction tokens" in conversation, demonstrate the ways in which the expression and organization of surprise are systematically tailored with regard to the sequential import of spoken "source turns" within conversation. In a rather different vein, Goodwin & Goodwin (2000) touch on the ways in which an unexpected event within the environment is rendered visible and responded to with surprise, and Katz (1996), in an insightful ethnography of a funhouse, explores the ways in which participants configure each other's humorous response to distorting mirrors.

These studies point to the ways in which surprise is embodied in two senses; on the one hand it is occasioned by, and organized with regard to, the emerging interaction, and on the other, its expression entails both bodily conduct such as a characteristic facial expression as well as talk. Like Darwin's (1872/2007) original treatise, Katz (1996) and Goodwin & Goodwin (2000) also consider the way in which an emotion can be provoked by an object or event that arises within the ecology and can serve to engender a particular course of action or interaction. In this chapter, we wish to build on these initiatives to consider the ways in which surprise is both embodied within interaction and embedded within a feature of the ecology; the emotion reflexively constituting and being constituted by a particular object or event.

Our own interest in surprise derives in part from our studies of conduct and interaction in museums and galleries. These studies are primarily concerned with re-thinking response or reception theory and in particular exploring the ways in which engagement with works of art, craft, and the like, arise in and through interaction; interaction between those who may be together as well as those who just happen to be in the same space (vom Lehn, Heath & Hindmarsh; Heath & vom Lehn). There is a longstanding tradition that believes that museums and galleries should serve to occasion surprise and astonishment and it is not only certain forms of contemporary art that have been designed to provoke emotion. Indeed, Shearman's (1992) splendid discussion of the work of Donatello reveals the ways in which works of art in the early Renaissance were increasingly designed to engender an animated, emotional response. Moreover, it is worthwhile bearing in mind that "Stendhal's syndrome" remains a diagnostic category in Italy; a syndrome that was first used to describe the symptoms of shock and awe that overcame people, especially young ladies from England, in the nineteenth century when they first encountered the beauties of Florence.

Unfortunately, it is relatively rare to find examples of heightened emotional response in museums and galleries, but surprise does happen and when it happens, it arises within interaction, interaction that occasions the momentary emotional sense and significance of particular objects and events.

OCCASIONING SURPRISE

While the photographs of surprise found in Darwin's (1872/2007) important treatise on the emotions in man and animals, pictures drawn from Duchenne, and more recent images found for example in Ekman and Friesen's (1975) works often appear a little melodramatic, it is not unusual to find animated expressions of surprise, even of astonishment, in the most seemingly innocuous situations. Consider for example Figures A and B related to Extract 1 in, which Jo reveals her surprise at an object that unexpectedly arises as she looks at a large painting of a tranquil Renaissance scene on display at a contemporary art and craft event in London.

A   B

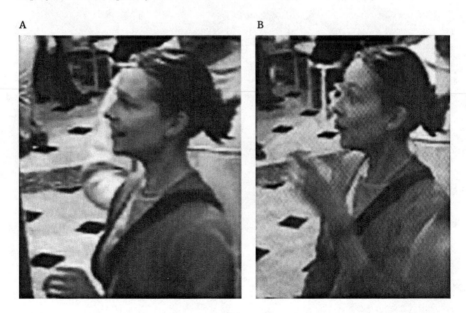

Ooh:::↑ooh,

Figures A and B related to Extract 1

Jo's response reveals many of the characteristics of surprise described by Darwin (1872/2007) and others (for example Ekman & Friesen, 1975, and Fridja, 1986). It involves a marked change in facial expression and bodily comportment. It includes the sudden and exaggerated raising of eyebrows, the transverse wrinkling of the forehead, and the rounded, open mouth—immediately covered by the hand. Her dramatic facial expression is accompanied by a sudden bodily movement away from the object of surprise and a cry of "Ooh:::–ooh,."

The painting is part of an art installation named *Deus Oculi*, designed by Jason Cleverly. It consists of three elements; a large landscape painting in an early Renaissance style and, on either side, two apparently painted hand-held mirrors. In the centre of each of the faux mirrors is a concealed camera. In the scene of the painting are the busts of two figures with life-size faces. Each face also consists of a door that can be opened to reveal a screen. When someone looks into the mirror their face appears on the screen and they become part of the landscape replacing one of the figures. The conceit then is to place the spectator within the work of art to provoke curiosity, intrigue, and surprise. In Extract 1, Jo approaches the installation soon after Beatrice and her partner, and Beatrice attempts to explain what it does. She soon abandons the attempt and rather than describe its operation enables Jo to experience the piece for herself. We join the action as Beatrice attempts to explain how the installation works.

Extract 1 *Deus Oculi*

B:	If you look through there you're on (here).
	<u>Look</u> (.) if you: (.) get get (.) Come here,
J:	Mmmm
B:	If you stay there
J:	O.kay
B:	Look. Watch watch
	(0.3)
J: →	Ooh:::↑ooh,
	(1.2)
J:	How c[an] (that) be (happening)
B:	[Yeah isn't it great (.) it's <u>visual</u>
	<u>art</u> (.) you see (.) it's all sort of
J:	(how wonderful)
J:	(Does that mean) doors spyhole things ( )
B:	yeah it's fan:tastic isn't it brilliant

With "Come here" and "If you stay there" Beatrice repositions Jo so that she stands directly in front of the picture and looks at the small screen that lies behind the open door of the face. Voicing the instruction "Look. Watch watch," Beatrice walks toward the mirror and peers directly into the camera; appearing in the landscape. As Beatrice appears in the picture, Jo issues her surprise (Figures C, D, and E related to Extract 1).

C   D   E

↑   ↑   ↑
Look   Watch watch   Ooh::: ↑ooh,

Figures C, D, and E related to Extract 1

Jo's surprise is occasioned by the action(s) of Beatrice. On abandoning an explanation and demonstrating its operation, Beatrice creates an opportunity for Jo to see and experience for herself the installation's operation and the surprise it creates. To enable Jo to see and encounter the image, Beatrice reconfigures how Jo is oriented to the scene and provides the resources to enable Jo to anticipate the unexpected. Jo's surprise is produced on cue, with regard to the action(s) of Beatrice, and serves to engender discussion concerning the wonder and operation of the installation. Surprise therefore arises with regard to action(s) of the coparticipant, actions that not only serve to reconfigure Jo's bodily and visual orientation, but enable her to anticipate that something unexpected may occur within the immediate environment. In demonstrating rather than describing the installation, Beatrice occasions a first-hand experience of the phenomenon; an experience that serves to engender, warrant, and produce surprise.

Jo's surprise is not simply on cue, but established, and elicited, by virtue of Beatrice's actions. The actions through which Beatrice configures Jo's bodily and visual orientation, serve to project the relevance of Jo responding to the object with surprise. Surprise is a sequentially appropriate response to the coparticipant's actions. Jo has the responsibility to react, and react with some surprise to the object that has been revealed. In other words, irrespective of whether Jo is indeed awestruck by discovering Beatrice's image in the painting, it is incumbent upon her to react to the event (consider Wilkinson & Kitzinger, 2006). This is not to say that the emotion is disingenuous but rather that in this case, surprise is a sequentially and situationally appropriate response, not simply to the event, but to the ways in which the event is rendered visible and the obligations that arise and rest therein.

Jo's (display of) surprise operates retroactively and proactively. It is contingently designed to address various features of the emerging interactional circumstances and the physical environment in which it arises. The surprise is timed to co-occur with Beatrice's full facial image appearing on the screen, even though the image progressively emerges. In this way can be seen as dramatically responsive to the event and in particular the ways in which she has been encouraged to discover and experience the "surprisable." Her orientation toward the image in the picture, and one suspects the vocalization "ooh:::–ooh," is sustained until Beatrice begins to move away from the camera, thereby progressively removing the image that engendered the surprise. Immediately Beatrice begins to withdraw and Jo turns toward Beatrice. She does not however abandon her expression of surprise but rather preserves her raised eyebrows and open mouth as she enquires "how can (that) be (happening)," a sense therefore that the display of emotion is sustained and visually presented to Beatrice who would have heard but not seen Jo's dramatic response. Moreover, by preserving her visible expression of surprise, Jo not only serves to warrant her subsequent queries, but also provides an animated display and appreciation of the event that Beatrice kindly created. Jo's dramatic outburst is responsive to the action(s) of Beatrice, not simply in producing the "surprisable," and configuring Jo's orientation so that it could be seen and experienced, but in establishing a sequential environment in which it is appropriate for Jo to be surprised, and surprised at a particular moment. In turn, her surprise and its per-severance serve to engender further exchange concerning the character of the installation and its remarkable operation.

It is worthwhile raising a further issue that bears upon the organization of sur-prise. As Ekman and Friesen (1975/2003) suggest, unlike other emotions surprise may not stand alone, but is frequently coupled with an associated emotion. Depend-ing on the object or event, and the ways in which it has been presented or configured, surprise may be accompanied and or followed by disgust, sadness, joy, pleasure, and the like (for a related discussion on blending of emotions, see Turner & Stets, 2005). The way in which surprise is prefigured, as in this case for example, may serve to project the associated emotion that might accompany the surprise. In the case at hand, for instance, as Jo raises her eyebrows and opens her mouth at the onset of her surprise, the mouth is upturned on either side, so when a little later as her fingers open to reveal her "surprised mouth" (Figures F and G related to Extract 1) she is smiling, a smile that is preserved throughout her subsequent query. From the outset there is an expression of pleasure, of good humor, even laughter, that arises by virtue of the ways in which Jo is encouraged to experience the installation's operation. In the very ways in which the expression is designed and evolves, by virtue of the ways in which the mouth and the eyes are opened and the eyebrows raised, Jo displays and produces the form of surprise and emotion that is sequentially appropriate and in-stantiated on this occasion.

F

Figure F related to Extract 1

G

Figure G related to Extract 1

Jo's surprise therefore, her natural emotional response to the face that appears within the picture, is designed with regard to the interactional circumstances in which it arises. Its onset for example co-occurs with the full image of the face appearing in the picture and the emerging smile that accompanies the onset of the surprise suggests the character of the response that will arise. Her outcry, vocalization, is modulated to resonate with the distance and gathering of the relevant participants, Beatrice and her partner, but does not draw the attention of others within the same space. Even the hand that covers the mouth reveals a certain decorum from the outset of the emotional expression while serving to underscore the drama of the response. The expression of surprise, like that of other emotions such as pain (see for example Heath, 1989), is contingently shaped, formed, within the course of its articulation with regard to the presence and conduct of others. So in the case at hand, for example, Jo would appear to cease the vocalization of surprise just at the moment that Beatrice turns from the camera and thereby removes the image, and yet she preserves aspects of her facial display—including wide open eyes, raised and wrinkled eyebrows— enabling Beatrice to see for herself Jo's surprise. The shape of Jo's emotional response therefore serves to both dramatically appreciate Beatrice's demonstration and encourage further discussion and inquiry. The quality of the moment's contingent and emergent expression therefore is of some interactional significance. In other words, it is not simply that we find that the seeming minutiae of emotional expression are socially organized with respect to the form of behavioral response that people use to show surprise, but they are timed and designed with regard to the sequential and interactional import of the action(s) that encourage and engender its production.

SURPRISE AND "NOTICEABLE" PRESENCE

It is not unusual for people to discover for themselves an object or event within the environment that they find surprising and to attempt to "share" their experience with those they are with. Unlike the example discussed in the previous section, the encounter with, and experience of, the object or event is not deliberately created through the action(s) of the coparticipant, but rather arises independently; the surprisable serving to warrant encouraging others to notice, even experience, the incongruent or curious feature that has been drawn to their attention.

It is worthwhile considering the following fragment. Vanessa and Simon are slowly walking through the area that contains *Deus Oculi*, looking at the various pieces.

Extract 2 *Deus Oculi*

V:	→	<u>Ooh:look</u> (.) you just popped up <u>the(h)re</u>:(hh)
		(0.7)
V:		heh
		(0.4)
V:		You jus:(t) heh (.)°hh
		(0.2)
V:		°heh
S:		There's an eye::,
		(1.2)
V:		Ye<u>rs</u>: there's eye (here) hah
		(0.5)
S:		Let me see you,

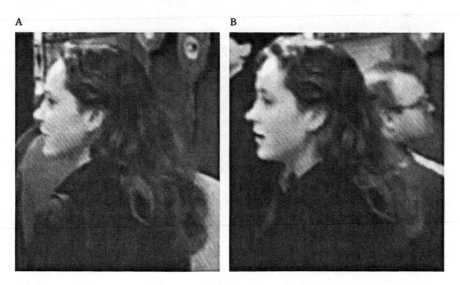

Ooh: look

Figures A and B related to Extract 2

Vanessa's surprise consists of "Ooh:look," coupled with the eyebrows being momentarily raised and the eyes opened wide. Her facial expression stands in marked contrast to her casual inspection of the objects on the wall. The surprise token "ooh:" is coupled with the instruction "look" with a smile emerging on her face. The surprise is occasioned by her partner, Simon, happening to peer into the camera, and momentarily appearing in the portrait of the figure in the painting.

Vanessa's surprise serves to render a feature of the ecology accountable and "noticeable." It encourages, indeed instructs, the coparticipant to temporarily abandon the activity in which he is engaged, inspecting one of the objects on the wall, and turn immediately to discover the source of the surprise. The outcry "Ooh: look," coupled with the facial expression of surprise and its visible orientation, serve to render an object or event not simply worthy of attention, but legitimately something that should be looked at, here and now. In a sense, therefore, in contrast with the way in which an action in talk may be "noticeably absent" (Sacks, 1992, vol. 1, pp. 35–6), that is sequentially relevant and yet, for instance, withheld by a coparticipant, in this case a feature of the ecology is rendered "noticeably present." It is noticeable and accountable by virtue of its incongruity within the local scene of objects and events. It serves to legitimize surprise and the demands it places on the coparticipant. In this way it is rendered relevant, and sequentially relevant, encouraging if not obliging the coparticipant to abandon, if only temporarily, the activity in which he is engaged to discover and look at the object or event that occasions surprise. Surprise may warrant another's looking, but the legitimacy of its claim is accountable with regard to the character and significance of the surprisable and its standing with regard to the demands of any current activity.

Darwin (1872/2007) suggests that the wide-open eyes and raised eyebrows characteristic of the expression of surprise provide the resources to enable the subject to scrutinize a potential threat. This may well be the case. They may also have a communicative function. Coupled with the alignment of the face, the eyes and eyebrows provide a resource to enable others to scrutinize the immediate environment and detect the "surprisable." They exaggerate the visual orientation of the surprised, assisting others in the discrimination of the environment. As Vanessa begins to utter the word "look," Simon, begins to withdraw from the mirror and to turn and look at the object or event that has engendered the surprise (see Figures C, D, and E related to Extract 2). Toward the completion of the word "look," Vanessa begins a gesture, raising her right hand she points at the screen, providing additional resources through which he can discover the object, the "noticeable." Accompanying the gesture from its outset is an utterance, or at least the beginning of an utterance that provides a sense of what he is looking for "you just popped up the(h)re:(hh)."

Unfortunately, as Simon begins to move away from the mirror, his image progressively disappears from the screen, and so, the very surprisable that occasions and legitimizes Vanessa's surprise is no longer visible.

Vanessa's utterance "you just popped up the(h)re:(hh)" and the accompanying gesture are interesting in this regard. As Simon begins to move away from the mirror in response to Vanessa's surprise and to look at the image toward the end of the word "look," she produces an utterance that is sensitive to the transitory character of the surprisable, not for instance "you're here," or "you've popped up here," but rather "you just popped up there."

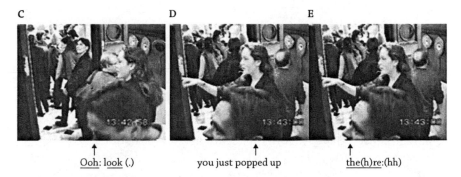

C   D   E

Ooh: look (.)   you just popped up   the(h)re:(hh)

Figures C, D, and E related to Extract 2

The action transforms, as the changing scene emerges; the import of "look" and the accompanying gesture recast, is no longer concerned with Simon seeing the surprisable for himself, but rather with explaining, accounting for the surprise. Indeed the laughter that infuses the word "the(h)re:(hh)" coupled with her momentary glance toward the camera and "puzzled" expression reveals how the scene has transformed as he begins to look for the surprisable.

Surprise serves to transform the ways in which people momentarily orient to the immediate environment. It encourages, even demands, that a coparticipant look at the object or event in question and provides the resources, in the very ways it is produced, to enable the coparticipant to discriminate the environment to discover the surprisable. In this regard, the expression of surprise also gives a sense of the associated emotion or demeanor that might be associated with the object or event, that for example it is matter of curiosity, perhaps humor, or undoubtedly in other circumstances, horror or disgust. In the case at hand, for example, as Simon begins to withdraw from the mirror in response to the initial "Ooh: look," he appears to adopt a slight smile as if in expectation of the character of object or event that has drawn Vanessa's attention. The production of surprise and the accompanying instruction serve to establish the sequential and interactional relevance of looking at and discovering the object or event and the form of emotion that might be associated with the surprisable; the surprised providing the resources for the other to determine the location and character of the object or event that will be discovered. In this way surprise generates a particular form of sequential relevance, an immediate demand upon the other, the recipient, to temporarily abandon an activity which they are engaged in to look at, detect, and determine the surprise, to see for themselves just what it is that served to provoke the emotional response; the response thereby retrospectively warranted by virtue of the coparticipant discovering the object or event that engendered the response and legitimized its "intrinsic" interactional and sequential demands.

There is therefore a matter of legitimacy that accompanies surprise and the emotional reaction that it entails. There are rights and responsibilities associated with surprise and conventions concerning what constitutes legitimate surprise and its appropriate situational expression. In a way, perhaps not unlike the constraints on, and rights to, emotional response to the personal experience and tragedies of others, so cogently discussed by Sacks (1992, vol. 1, pp. 242–8) in his analysis of stories and storytelling, surprise and our expression of surprise are subject to constraint and obligation that can serve to call in question the measure or even legitimacy of the emotion. In part this constraint derives not simply from conventions that may underlie and inform emotional functioning and expression, they may indeed be culturally and situationally specific, but rather from the ways in which they are legitimized within the circumstances at hand, the activities in which people are engaged and the emerging interaction. That is, the expression of the emotion surprise, encourages, and on occasions demands, others to undertake a particular course of action, even if that action involves no more than temporarily abandoning some current concern to attend to the surprisable. Objects and events are legitimately noticeable in part by virtue of how they stand with regard to, and how they are consequential for, the activity in which people are engaged; an activity that they, if only momentarily, to attend the surprisable.

In consequence, what we find surprising and how surprise is expressed may have as much to do with the sequential and interactional import of the expression of surprise and its implications for any current activity as it has with the measure of the object or event that underpins, legitimizes, or even causes the emotional reaction.

TAKING THE MEASURE OF SURPRISE

Surprise reveals a particular standpoint toward an object or event; a standpoint that does not involve, for example, giving a particular opinion or interpretation of an object or event, but revealing one's subjective, emotional reaction. Surprise encourages a coparticipant both to look at the object or event and experience it in a particular way—to find it worthy of note, surprising, and align at least with the associated emotion, be it awe, humor, disgust, horror, or whatever. In Extract 2., the transitory character of the object undermines Vanessa's ability to have Simon see and be surprised and amused by his image appearing in the painting, though a little later she is able to demonstrate what happened. He shows some surprise and much amusement. In some cases however a person's surprise may fail to engender the sequentially appropriate response.

A

Figure A related to Extract 3

Consider the following extract drawn from the exhibition *Body Worlds*. The exhibition consists of a collection of plastinated corpses, body sections, and body parts sometimes set in various animated poses. In the following fragment, two women, Karen and Susan, arrive in the vicinity of a display case containing a series of bottled human embryos and fetuses at various stages of development. Before looking at the embryos, Karen remarks "D'you know this: (.) doesn't bother me"; continuing a matter that was being discussed earlier—how some of the exhibits on display disturb even cause revulsion. Susan looks at the first of the embryos. As Karen begins to turn round to look at the exhibits, Susan raises her eyebrows, looks more closely, crying out "°Oh:(h): loo(h)::k."

Extract 3 *Body Worlds*

K: D'you know this: (.) doesn't bother me
          (0.2)
S: → (°thh) °Oh:(h): loo(h)::k↑
          (4.2)
S: → °Wo(h)w::(hh)::
          (2.2)
K: It's that little thin:g: that makes you feel so sick
          (0.8)
S: Wow:::
          (0.2)
S: It's °fascinating

B   C

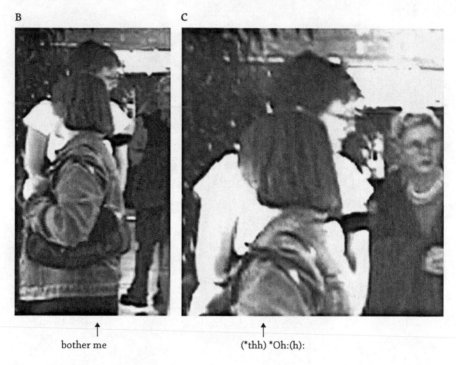

↑   ↑

bother me   (*thh) *Oh:(h):

Figures B and C related to Extract 3

Susan's outcry, "(°thh) °Oh:(h): loo(h)::k," and its accompanying bodily movement, not only encourages Karen to look at the smallest fetus, but evokes a sense of
surprise and wonder. The quiet breathlessness of the utterance—as if her breath has
been taken away in awe of the object—coupled with Susan's open mouth, wide-open
eyes, and raised eyebrows, encourages Karen to look at the tiny embryo and share her
wonder.

During the 4.2 second silence, Karen turns and looks at the embryo, but produces
neither vocal nor visible reaction. She shows no surprise, nor wonder. After a few
moments, Karen turns and looks briefly at the other embryos, and then begins to
withdraw from the display case. Karen responds to an aspect of the sequential import
of Susan's exclamation and surprise, she turns and immediately looks at the smallest
of the embryos but fails to align with the emotion; she produces neither surprise nor
wonder at the sight of the embryo.

Susan does not abandon her dramatic response to the embryo, nor her attempt to
have Karen appreciate its significance. As Karen turns and looks at the other embryos and fetuses, Susan follows the realignment of her orientation, turning slowly
and looking progressively at the various exhibits. In turning, Susan preserves her
open mouth, wide-open eyes, and raised brows, displaying her continuing wonder at
the successive curiosities. In contrast, Karen produces no visible or vocal reaction to
the exhibits.

D E F

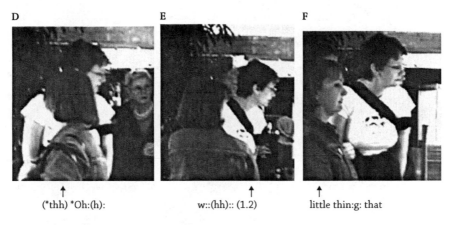

(*thh) °Oh:(h):   w::(hh):: (1.2)   little thin:g: that

Figures D, E, and F related to Extract 3

Having quickly glanced at the all of the exhibits, Karen begins to turn away from the display case, in preparation to move on to a different part of the exhibition. Susan makes a further, and final, attempt to have Karen display at least some appreciation of these remarkable objects. She reproduces her initial response with "Wo(h)w::(hh)::," a quiet, breathless, almost overwhelming reaction to the embryos. Her reinvoked emotional response arises just as Karen begins to back away from the cabinet and serves as an attempt to encourage some appreciation of the extraordinary objects on display (see Figures D, E, and F related to Extract 3). Sadly it fails. Susan abandons her expression of awe, lowering her eyebrows, and closing her mouth. At that moment, her friend produces "it's that little thin:g: that makes you feel so sick"; a comment that suggests a very different emotional reaction to the embryos, more of disgust than wonder. Karen's reaction, coupled with her backing away from the cabinet, unsurprisingly serves to discourage any further attempt by Susan to have her appreciate, still less be awestruck, by the embryos.

In passing it is worthwhile considering the following extract (see Figures A and B related to Extract 4). A couple walk along the glass case and look at the embryos. The woman, Sheila, arrives at the first fetus, a tiny human being, eight weeks old, with the limbs noticeably beginning to develop while her partner, Bruce, reads the label below in the cabinet. As Sheila turns to and inspects the fetus she produces a highly animated reaction—"°hhh(G)Oh: my Go:d, oh my God, oh my Go:rd," and vibrating her whole body, backs away, looking wide-eyed at the exhibit.

Extract 4 *Body Worlds*

S: → °hhh(G)Oh: my Go:d, oh my God, oh my Go:rd
      (3.2)
S: → °hhhyou used to be that size
B: Mmhmm
      (3.4)
S: → hhh tha(h):t is:, un:believ:able
S: Look at the difference from that to tha:t

A   B

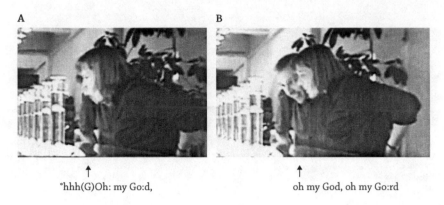

↑   ↑
°hhh(G)Oh: my Go:d,   oh my God, oh my Go:rd

Figures A and B related to Extract 4

Sheila's outburst and her accompanying visible conduct encourage Bruce to turn from the label and look at the fetus; her bodily movement encouraging his coorientation to the particular exhibit. He turns smiling to the embryo; his gaze arriving toward the end of the first "God." With "Go:rd," she begins to move toward the embryo to take a closer look. Bruce neither comments on, nor follows Sheila's example by looking more closely at the exhibit, but rather retreats, walking around his partner to inspect the fetuses further along the cabinet.

As he reappears on her other side, Sheila attempts to encourage Bruce to appreciate the significance of the exhibit that has excited her emotions, pointing toward the particular embryo and remarking on its size. He once again looks at the exhibit, but provides minimal appreciation—simply nodding his head and producing "Mmhmm." A moment later, as he begins to turn toward the other side of the cabinet, one suspects in preparation to move on from the exhibit, Sheila reproduces her awe and wonder of the fetuses, articulating a breathless "hhh tha(h):t is:, un:believ:able," her mouth and eyes wide-open, an outcry that not only reinvokes the emotion but also through its articulation verbalizes the grounds for astonishment.

In both Extracts 2 and 3 we find one participant encouraging another to look at an object within the immediate environment. The ways in which the object is drawn to the attention of the other, however, not only serve to encourage an inspection of the relevant object, and provide the relevant resources to enable its discovery, but implicate the character of the object and the ways in which it might be responded to. It is not simply that something is revealed in the world, but it is rendered visible, and legitimately demands the attention, by virtue of its distinctiveness, indeed its ability to provoke surprise. In other words, surprise and the attitude embedded within that surprise, in these cases awe and wonder, encourage the coparticipant to see and experience the object in a particular way, not necessarily to show surprise but to align with the emotion that accompanies that surprise. In both these cases, while the coparticipant does indeed immediately turn and look at the surprisable, they fail to align with the associated emotion, and we find the surprised making successive attempts to secure some appreciation of the object in question (on pursuits of emotional reciprocity, consider Peräkylä and Ruusuvuori, in this volume, chapter 4). It is not simply that the coparticipant fails to find the object surprising, but rather perhaps that in failing to align with the associated emotion, the legitimacy of the original emotion reaction is undermined.

We have remarked upon the idea that surprise is not infrequently linked to a secondary or associated emotion, be it joy, disgust, humor, fear, and the like. It is interesting to note that in these instances we can begin to see how participants may orient to the secondary or, better, the associated emotion in the ways in which they respond or even fail to respond. We have noted for example how the very design of surprise or our response to another's surprise may embody humor or pleasure in the same way that one suspects that fear or disgust may be entailed the emerging expression of surprise. In both these cases, we also begin to see how the reaction to another's surprise addresses the obligation to inspect the object that is been rendered visible and relevant while failing to align with the secondary emotion, perhaps in both cases awe and wonder. And in both extracts, we find the surprised attempting to secure the appropriate alignment toward the emotion that is associated with the initial surprise. At least in Extract 4, the surprised secures a smile and minimal acknowledgment, whereas in Extract 3, a rather different secondary emotion is invoked, namely disgust.

THE COLLABORATIVE DISCOVERY OF AND REACTION TO A SURPRISABLE

"Recipient design" is involved (to use Harvey Sacks's term) and so quickly applied as to suggest that continuous monitoring of the situation is being sustained, enabling just the adjustment to take place when the moment requiring it comes.
$$\text{—Goffman, 1981, p. 98}$$

From at least Darwin (1872/2007) onward there has been an interest in whether there is significant variation in the ways in which people, and people of different cultures, express emotion. Less attention has been paid, to draw on Goffman's (1981) distinction, to the situational and situated characteristics, and the ways in which in which different people, within particular circumstances, respond to a particular object or event that serves to engender, for example in our case, surprise. Of particular significance in this regard may not necessarily be the qualities of the stimulus, nor the psychological dispositions or cultural characteristics of the actors, but rather the presence and conduct of others and the ways in which an object or event is noticed, revealed, and appreciated.

It is worthwhile briefly considering a relatively complex extract in which five or six people come to discover and experience the surprisable—a person's image momentarily appearing in the *Deus Oculi* portrait. Tim and Mary look at a series of mirrors hanging on the wall directly opposite the landscape, while a group of four—two couples, Joan and Al, and Doug and Sandra—enter the scene and begin, in turn, to walk past the picture (Figure A related to Extract 5).

A

Doug — — Tim

Sandra — — Mary

Joan — — Al

Figure A related to Extract 5

We join the action as Joan asks Al, who is in the lead, where he is going. As he passes the landscape, Al looks into the far mirror and Doug, who is drawing up the rear, notices Al's image appear in the painting. He cries out "Oh look (0.2) look look." The response of Mary and Tim arises concurrently with Doug's reaction and explanation.

Extract 5 *Deus Oculi*

J:		Where are you going now?		
		(0.2)		
Al:		Dun' know		
		(4.2)		
Al:		[looks into mirror]		
D:	→	Oh look (0.2) look look	M:	(Oh) no:::::
		(.)	M:	°hhhh Go::d
D:		When he is over there	T:	°Wow
		and the camera is over he:re	M:	It's ma:h:d
Al:		Yeh		
		(.)		
(J):		(°argh [::::::)		
Al:		[Then (Doug) (0.2) look (0.2) at this camera		
		(0.2)		
J:		I didn't see that		
D:		Now you know look I(f). if you look		

As Doug reveals his surprise, Mary, who with Tim has just turned around and is now looking toward the picture, expresses her own surprise with "(Oh) no::::: °hhhh Go::d." Together the two distinct responses appear something like the following (Figures B, C, and D related to Extract 5). We have added the dashes simply to show how the overlap is structured in relation to the distinct contributions.

B   C   D

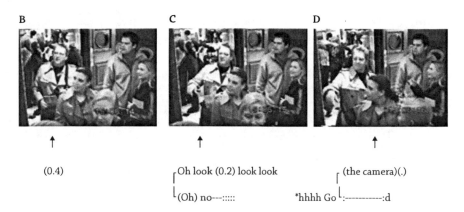

    ↑   ↑   ↑

(0.4)   ⌈Oh look (0.2) look look   ⌈ (the camera)(.)

                     ⌊(Oh) no---:::::   °hhhh Go ⌊:-----------:d

Figures B, C, and D related to Extract 5

Despite both expressing surprise at the same event, the sudden appearance of Al in the portrait, the two reactions are very different. Doug's initial response, "Oh look," and his subsequent instructions, "look look," are primarily concerned with having his friends turn and discover the surprisable. Indeed, as Doug produces °oh look" he simultaneously begins a gesture that points toward the image. Sandra begins to orient toward the image, but Joan walks on regardless. Doug repeats his demand, producing "look look," and recycles his gesture as Joan and Al begin to turn toward the portrait, pointing at the screen. Al's image disappears as he backs away from the camera, so by the time the others look at the picture there is no longer a surprisable and Doug is left to explain what happens, "when he is over there . . .," rather than his friends experience for themselves.

In contrast, Mary's surprise is very different. Her initial surprise is expressed through "(Oh) no:::::" coupled with her hunching her shoulders and raising her eyebrows. She also turns from the image toward Al, realizing that it is he who has suddenly appeared in the painting (see Figure B). While her actions dramatically reveal her own surprise, they are not concerned with revealing the object of that surprise to Tim, or any other person for that matter. From the outset, the expression of her surprise is sensitive to the presence and orientation of Tim. It presupposes that he too has noticed the image in the picture and she does not attempt establish his orientation toward the event. Tim turns with Mary to momentarily look at Al, and then with her, turns back to look at the image (see Figure D). She produces "°hhhh Go::d," Tim, "°Wow"; the two concurrent exclamations commenting on the puzzling link between the mirror and the picture rather than simply the surprise of finding Al in the picture. And whereas Doug attempts to explain what has happened to his friends, Mary, knowing that Tim has seen and experienced the event for himself, comments on the apparent operation of the installation with "it's ma:h:d."

It is interesting to note that while the actions and interaction of Mary and Tim, and Doug, Sandra, and their friends, appear to emerge independently within distinct interactional environments, it may be the case that their discovery and response to the surprisable is, at least at certain moments, interrelated. First, it will be recalled, that as Doug, Sandra, and their friends enter the scene, Tim and Mary are looking at the objects on the opposite wall. As Al initially looks at the picture he opens the face window in the landscape before moving on; this action, the manipulation of the installation, appears to encourage Tim and then Mary to turn and look at what is happening. In consequence they are both oriented toward the installation when Al appears. Second, it is interesting to note that while the vocalization of the initial surprise by Doug and Mary co-occur, immediately in response to Al appearing in the picture, there appears to be a distinct separation of the subsequent talk that largely avoids overlap or incursiveness between the two conversations—despite the curiosity and excitement of the occasion. Third, it may be the case that Mary's comment "it's ma:h:d" is sensitive to, even occasioned by, her overhearing Doug's attempt to explain to Sandra and his friends how the installation appears to operate, her exclamation arising as Doug attempts to explain the operation of the installation.

The expressions of surprise by Doug and Mary therefore have very different interactional significance and sequential import. Whereas the one is concerned with encouraging others to see and discover an object of surprise, the other provides an immediate environment for the other's reaction to and appreciation of the object. And whereas the one serves to stall at least initially Sandra's progress through the space and have her turn toward the screen, the other encourages both an appreciation of the object and mutual exploration of its constituent components; an exploration that leads a little later to Tim and Mary trying out the installation for themselves. The two concurrent expressions of surprise would appear, right from their outset, to be prospectively oriented in this way, not simply responsive to something curious that has arisen within the environment. With "Oh" of "Oh look" Doug glances momentarily from the picture toward his friends and back to the picture and begins his pointing gesture toward the screen; the surprise shaped from its onset to encourage his friends to look at and see what he has seen while simultaneously providing the resources to enable its detection within the environment. Whereas Mary's "(Oh) no::::" displays surprise and creates an opportunity for, perhaps even obliges, her partner to reveal his reaction, it does not encourage or demand that the other turn and look at the object. Indeed, almost from its outset, Mary's surprise appears to be sensitive to Tim's orientation toward the same scene and his independent access to the event, encouraging exploration and comment on the installation rather than revealing the surprisable.

DISCUSSION: SURPRISE AND THE IMMEDIATE ENVIRONMENT

There is a longstanding recognition in the social sciences that the local environment plays an important part in the structure and organization of social interaction. How the environment features in the emerging production of social action has received less attention and we have little understanding of the ways in which actions and events are rendered intelligible and consequential by virtue of their reflexive interdependence with occasioned aspects of the ecology. Surprise is interesting in this regard. As Darwin (1872/2007) and others suggest, it is not uncommon to find surprise inextricably embedded within particular features of the environment, its production and intelligibility dependent upon the object or event that occasions, even engenders, the emotion (see also this volume, chapter 2).

While an object or event that arises within the immediate environment may occasion or engender surprise, its expression is dependent upon a social and interactional organization that informs its production and intelligibility. We find for example that the very ways in which surprise is articulated, through vocalization, facial expression, and bodily comportment, are sensitive to the presence and conduct of others, primarily but not only those whom you are with, and are designed to encourage, if not demand, the coparticipant to discover and look at the surprisable. Surprise and the expression of surprise therefore are not simply a response to an untoward or unexpected object or event, a reaction, but rather, in the very ways in which it is gauged and articulated, interactionally consequential; it implicates particular forms of action from a coparticipant, action that should occur in immediate juxtaposition with the surprise. What that action is, that is how a coparticipant should properly respond, is accomplished in and through the ways in which surprise is produced and its reflexive independence with the surprisable. For instance, the very ways in which surprise is designed provides the resources for a coparticipant to be able to determine the location and object of surprise within a highly complex and even transitory environment; the expression serving to display the emotion, implicate action, and provide the resources to enable that action to be produced. Surprise then can form a pivotal action, working retroactively to cast or recast an object or event as surprisable, while proactively implicating sequentially relevant action(s) from a coparticipant, its production serving to create a particular form of coparticipation distinct from some concurrent activity.

The expression or articulation of surprise, however fleeting, serves to reflexively establish an object or event as surprising and thereby claim a legitimate demand on the attention of the other(s). The expression of surprise therefore is not only oriented toward its sequential import for the conduct of others, but also subject to moral and situated standards or conventions that bear upon the measure of surprise. We are entitled to be surprised in certain circumstances, but our surprise, and our expression of surprise, is constrained by what can be seen as situationally, even personally, appropriate; the emotion has to be warranted with regard to the character of the object or event or question, its relevance to the individual, the circumstances, the activity at hand, and the like. It is interesting to note for example that in Extract 4, in re-expressing her awe ("hhh tha(h):t is:, un:believ:able") in the light of her partner's minimal response, Sheila grasps her heavily pregnant stomach. Surprise does not necessarily demand that the coparticipant be surprised or express a similar emotional response, but it encourages if not demands, that a coparticipant turn and look at the object or event in question and establishes the relevance of the other's response to the surprisable. In this regard, it is interesting to note how the surprised may not simply be sensitive to how the other responds, but in various ways attempt to reproduce their own emotional response to encourage at least an appreciative reaction from the coparticipant. In one sense therefore, surprise can render the surprised vulnerable to the reaction of the other and whether the other is willing to treat the object or event as worthy of surprise.

In this regard, it is worth reflecting on the character of surprise and the ways in which surprise does not necessarily stand alone but rather can prefigure or fore-shadow a second emotion such as humor, fear, disgust, sadness, and the like. Though the expression of the associated emotion may immediately follow surprise, it can, and one suspects frequently does, infuse the articulation of surprise, so that the others are aware, as surprise is being is articulated, of the associated emotion it foreshadows. Surprise therefore may not simply demand that the other turns to discover and see, if not experience for themselves, the object or event in question, but implicates a particular form of experience and response from the coparticipant. So for example a coparticipant, by virtue of the ways in which surprise is expressed, can be encouraged to find the object or event as humorous, even awesome or astonishing, and yet of course can withhold alignment to the implicated emotion, or can even, as we have seen, imply a very different emotional response.

In this chapter we have touched on two forms of surprise that have rather distinct sequential characteristics. In the first, surprise is occasioned by the coparticipant configuring the bodily and visual orientation of the other to enable an unexpected object or event to be seen. Surprise is responsive to the actions of the other and a sequentially appropriate reaction to the object. Indeed it might even be suggested that it is incumbent on the other to show surprise in response to the surprisable. The second form of surprise is rather different. Independently of the actions of a coparticipant, an object or event that arises within the immediate environment occasions surprise and in articulating surprise an individual encourages the coparticipant to discover for themselves the surprisable. In these cases, while it is incumbent upon the coparticipant to look at and see for themselves the object or event in question it is rare to find, at least in our data, the initial reaction immediately followed by the coparticipant displaying surprise. In other words, despite the coparticipant being encouraged to see and experience the object or event for themselves, untainted by description or characterization of what to expect, the initial emotion is rarely responded to by a similar emotion reaction—despite the object or event, in some cases, being seen and experienced for the first time. In other words, while surprise may encourage another to look at, even appreciate, an object or event, it rarely occasions surprise, though it does encourage a coparticipant to align to the object or event in particular way—to adopt a certain standpoint or attitude in tune with the "secondary" emotion.

The interactional organization of surprise in the materials discussed here stands in contrast to the conventional ways in which we consider sequential character of practical action. An individual may occasion surprise and engender the appropriate response from a coparticipant, but the response, or reaction, is not to the other, as it might be for example in a telephone conversation, but rather to the object or event that has been brought to their attention within the local milieu. Similarly, a surprise may occasion a coparticipant to react, but the reaction, the response, is not directed toward the other, even though it is interactionally relevant for the other, but rather to an occasioned feature of the immediate environment. In expressing surprise, or occasioning another to be surprised, an individual transposes action to an object or event, and in this way encourages a coparticipant to respond that object or event as if it is independent of the actions though which it was brought to their attention. Surprise creates a sequential environment, through which a coparticipant is encouraged to discover and react to an object or event within the immediate scene, the coparticipant embedding interactional significance and implicativeness within the local milieu. In this way, objects and events, even inanimate objects, are entailed with action relevance, engendering a particular way of seeing and responding that is situationally and interactionally produced. The sense and intelligibility of the participant's actions, including their surprise and their response to the surprise of others, are accomplished by virtue of the occasioned interdependence of action and a feature of the immediate environment.

It is hardly surprising that there has been a longstanding interest, from Darwin (1872/2007) onward, in the relationship between nonverbal behavior and emotion; as Ekman (1982) and others powerfully demonstrate, the face is one, if not the, principal vehicle through which the emotions are expressed. In turn, studies of emotional expression have traditionally reflected the methodological commitments of research into nonverbal behavior, research that distinguished between different channels or modes of communication and analytically treated the visible as distinguishable from the verbal. In this respect, despite reservations concerning the terminology, the growing interest in "multimodal communication" is to be welcomed in particular for its widespread commitment to the analysis of embodied action and interaction. Notwithstanding these initiatives, however, and despite some important exceptions, the ways in which action is produced with regard to, and made intelligible by virtue of, occasioned features of the local ecology remain neglected. This is perhaps particularly curious with regard to the organization of the emotions, since as Darwin (1872/2007) and others point out, it is not unusual for objects and events within the local environment to provoke some of our stronger emotions. Even so, how those emotions are expressed and managed may be as much to do with the presence and conduct of others, both those that we are with and others who just happen to be, as Goffman (1981, p. 3) suggests, "within perceptual range of the event," as it does with character and severity of the surprisable.

ACKNOWLEDGMENTS

We would like to thank all those, visitors, artists, and curators, who kindly gave us permission to videorecord their conduct and interaction in museums, galleries, and exhibitions. We would like to thank members of the Work, Interaction and Technology research centre at King's College, London, including Jon Hindmarsh, Menisha Patel, Helena Webb, and Lewis Hyland, who contributed to our understanding of the materials discussed in this paper, and Robin Meisner for her insights and encouragement. Anssi Peräkylä and Marja-Leena Sorjonen deserve particular mention for their extensive comments on an earlier draft of this essay. The research of which this chapter forms part was funded by the AHRC project "Enhancing interpretation: new techniques and technologies for the arts and decorative arts" (Reference No. B/RG/AN10805/APN17441).

CHAPTER 11

༄

Responding to Emotion in Cognitive Psychotherapy

LIISA VOUTILAINEN

The different types of psychotherapy are based on different conceptions of what helps the patients in the therapy. At least the traditions of cognitive therapy and psychoanalysis seem to share two basic lines of thought: one that emphasizes changes in the patient's knowledge about him- or herself as a key to change, and another that emphasizes the therapeutic relationship in which new experiences of emotional expression and response can take place. Psychoanalysis and cognitive therapy conceptualize these orientations differently, but the basic tension between the "investigative" and "experiential" emphases are evident within both traditions (see e.g., Greenson, 1967; Beck, 1976; Stern, 2004; Warner, 1997; Greenberg, 2004). However, in the actual practice of psychotherapies, these two aspects of therapeutic work are probably profoundly integrated. This assumption is indeed supported by the data that will be discussed in the present study.

This chapter offers descriptions of the ways in which a psychotherapist responds to her patient's disclosures of a negative emotional experience in cognitive psychotherapy[1]. I will analyze the different kinds of responses that function as empathic and the role they play in the therapist's more investigative projects of interpreting the patient's experience or in challenging her dysfunctional beliefs. In other words, I will describe some ways in which the therapist *combines* the two orientations of therapeutic work: emotional responsiveness and actions that direct the talk toward more investigative work with the patient's experiences. To further elucidate the relation between empathy and investigative work, I will also show a case of misalignment between the participants where the patient recurrently moves to an expression of a negative emotional experience (anxiety) whereas the therapist strongly pursues a more investigative line of action.

The data consist of fifty-seven audio recorded sessions in cognitive therapy with a constructivist emphasis. The therapy integrates the means of traditional cognitive

therapy (such as questioning dysfunctional cognitions and beliefs) and "constructivist" elements such as focusing on personal meanings and their history (see
Guidano, 1991; Toskala & Hartikainen, 2005). The fifty-seven sessions were recorded
during the two-year long therapy of a single patient (one session per week) and focus
on the last eighteen months of that therapy. That is, the patient and the therapist
remain the same in all the examples. The practices that are reported here come from
data collections that include approximately fifty cases of a patient's disclosure and a
therapist's initial response to it.

In the disclosures, the patient describes how she feels about someone or something,
or what someone or something is like. In many cases, these two kinds of actions—
describing an affective experience and evaluating an object or state of affairs—
intertwine in the patient's talk. In broad terms, these disclosures can be considered
to be emotional: in them the patient describes the way she feels with regard to
important people or events in her life and how she relates to them. The descriptions also involve lexical and prosodic expressiveness.

The therapist's responses to these disclosures have similarities with affiliating responses to troubles tellings (Jefferson, 1988; Ruusuvuori, 2007) and complaints
(Drew, 1998; Drew & Walker, 2009): the therapist takes up the affective stance that
the patient has expressed or implied and indicates that she treats it as real and valid.
In other words, the therapist expresses the relevance of the emotional content in the
patient's previous turn. By presenting a claim of affiliation or by displaying that she
is able to understand how the patient must feel, the therapist shows understanding,
compassion, or agreement with the emotional aspects of the patient's talk (Ruusuvuori, 2007, pp. 598–600). In terms of clinical work, this kind of affiliation can be
referred to as empathy or as validation of the patient's emotion (Greenberg & Elliot,
1997; Bachelor, 1988; Linehan, 1997). I will use the terms affiliation, empathy, and
validation interchangeably in this chapter.

Below I will describe how these affiliating, empathic responses are combined with,
or build grounds for, the therapist's actions that suggest a more investigative work
with the experience in question. I will begin with the responses in one turn in which
the therapist combines empathic response and a slight shift of perspective toward a
psychotherapeutic interpretation of the experience.

EMPATHY AND INTERPRETATION

The patient's disclosures of problematic emotional experiences in my data typically
involve two kinds of elements: those that refer to the patient's emotional experience
and those that refer to "outer reality" (past or anticipated events and actions of other
people). The therapist's responses may focus on either of these aspects. In the
responses that are discussed in this section, the therapist focuses on the patient's
inner, subjective experience rather than on the outer reality.

In the responses that refer to the patient's inner experience, the therapist typically interprets[2] the patient's experience: she points to something that she hears that
is implicit in the patient's experience in a way that slightly challenges the patient's

description of it (cf. Vehviläinen, 2003; Peräkylä, 2004; Antaki, 2008; Bercelli, Rossano, & Viaro, 2008; Rae, 2008). These interpretations invite self-reflection from the patient, and they direct the talk toward the "investigative" direction of psychotherapeutic work: the therapist invites the patient to think about her experience in a new kind of way.

However, the interpretations in my data always go hand in hand with empathy (see Voutilainen, Peräkylä, & Ruusuvuori, 2010a). In this section, I will focus on one way in which the therapist combines empathy and interpretation: on responses that display empathy but also to some extent interpret the patient's experience in the very same turn at talk. I will also show how these "slight interpretations" can create the basis for more overt interpretations.

The first extract below is a case in which the therapist, in this case in a very subtle way, adds an interpretative element to her initial, empathic response to the patient's description of her experience. Before the segment, the patient has talked about her experience of being an outsider in her childhood family. The therapist has suggested that the patient may have felt being left out when her sister was born. The patient has not taken up this suggestion as such, but talked about how she remembers that she felt pity for herself because her parents did not notice her feeling bad. The patient started her turn with *Nii kyllä mä sitä muistan ainaki kironneeni tai surkutelleeni*, "Yeah I do remember having at least cursed or felt pity for myself for that" (not shown), which partly aligns with the therapist's suggestion but retains an agnostic stance toward it. The patient did not indicate more precisely whether she was referring to the time when her sister was born or to a more general childhood experience. The extract shows the end of this description. Although the patient is heard to talk about her own experience, she designs the beginning of the description by using utterance types that do not contain an element referring to the experiencer (up to line 8).

Extract 1

```
01   P:   (0.5)   et        kun   ei    tosiaan   huomata.
                  that       as    not   really    notice-PAS
                  (0.5) that 'coz one is not really noticed

02        (0.9)

03   T:   Mm-↓hm.

04        (2.9)

05        Vaik          oli   niin   kauheen   paha   olo.
          although      was   so     awfully   bad    feeling
          Although ((I)) felt so awfully bad.

06        (.)

07   T:   .mt Nii.

08        (3.4)
```

09   P: *Et   kysy£thään   (.)   kysytään   vaan   että   .hhhhh£   (0.5)   miks   mä*
          PRT   ask-PAS   ask-PAS   just   that   why   I
          So ((I'm)) £asked (.) just asked.hhhhh £(0.5) why I

10   *en   voi   olla   normaali   tai   niinku   muutki   että.*
          not   can   be   normal   or   like   others   PRT
          can't be normal or like others so.

11   (0.4)

12   T: *Mmmm.*

13   (.)

14   P: mhhhhhhhhhh.

15   (2.5)

16→ T: *Et   sä   isit   tarvinnu   sillon   enemmän*
          so   you   would   have   needed   then   more
          So in that time you would have needed more

17→   *huomioo ja*
          attention and

18   (.)

19   P: *Nii.*
          Yes.

20   (.)

21   T: *Ehkä   se   on   ollu   just   se   tilanne   sillon   ku   Mari*
          maybe   it   is   been   just   the   situation   then   when   NAME
          Maybe it has been just the situation when Mari

22   *on syntyny   (.)   myös   (.)   samaa   aikaa.*
          born   also   same   time
          was born (.) too (.) in the same time period.

23   (1.5)

24   P: *Nii   (.)   en   muista   mu-#(3.3)   mutta   voi   hyvinki   olla.*
          Yeah   (.)I   don't   remember   bu-#(3.3)   but   it   can   well   be   so.

25   (15.3)

In lines 1, 5, and 9–10, the patient describes her problematic childhood experience: how she felt pity for herself as her parents did not notice her feeling bad but
merely asked her why she could not be normal and like others. The utterances have

affective elements: intensifiers *niin kauheen*, "so awfully" (line 5), *vaan*, "just" (line 9), and the passive verb forms *ei huomata*, "is not noticed" (line 1), and *kysytään*, "(I'm) asked" (line 9), which can be heard as emphasizing the experience of being dismissed and misunderstood. The therapist responds minimally in lines 3, 7, and 12, leaving space for the patient to continue. These responses display acknowledgment and, most strongly by the *Nii* in line 7 (which responds to the patient's description of her past emotion), also indicate affiliation (see Sorjonen, 2001, pp. 131–154).

In the focus turn in lines 16–17, the therapist formulates the patient's description by saying *Et sä oisit tarvinnu sillon enemmän huomioo ja*, "So in that time you would have needed more attention and." This formulation, rephrasing the gist of the patient's problematic experience, functions as an empathic reflection and as a recognition of the patient's experience of being dismissed and disappointed.

On the other hand, however, through the temporal expression *sillon*, "that time," and the verb choice *tarvinnu*, "needed," the therapist slightly takes distance from the emotional experience as such (being dismissed by and disappointed at the parents) and points to the patient's state of mind (the state of need) at a specific period of time. So, albeit in a very subtle way, the therapist's turn also interprets the patient's experience, shifting the perspective.

This interpretative element becomes more salient in the therapist's subsequent turn in lines 21–2, where she, after the patient's confirmation (where the patient confirms that she accepts as valid what the therapist said), continues *Ehkä se on ollu just se tilanne sillon ku Mari on syntyny*, "Maybe it has been just the situation when Mari was born." This utterance renews the therapist's earlier suggestion that the patient may have felt left out when her sister was born.[3] In line 22, the therapist adds *myös (.) samaa aikaa*, "too (.) in the same time period," and in so doing, somewhat qualifies her suggestion about the direct connection between the birth of the patient's sister and her experience of being dismissed and disappointed.

However, the therapist's action here in lines 21–2 is a more overt interpretation than her previous utterance in lines 16–17: the therapist now explicitly makes the connection between the time period when the patient's sister was born and her feelings of being an outsider and unnoticed in the family. At this point, the therapist's prior turn (lines 16–17), which was initially an empathic response, serves as part of this more overt interpretation: the lexical choices *tarvinnu*, "needed," and *sillon*, "that time," in line 16 are retrospectively attributed to the meaning of needing more attention in that specific time when there was a new baby in the family (cf. Vehviläinen, 2003, and Peräkylä, 2004, on preparing for interpretation in psychoanalysis).

The therapist's first substantial response to the patient's description in lines 16–17 served a dual task: to empathically recognize the patient's experience of being dismissed and disappointed, and to interpret that experience by placing it into a specific context.

The next example is another case in which the therapist combines empathy and interpretation in her initial response. In this segment, the interpretative element in the initial response is stronger than in the previous example. This extract occurs a few minutes later in the same discussion. Before the segment, the patient has stated how it is evident that her younger sister really is her father's favorite child. The extract begins in the middle of the patient's description of her father's relation to her sister.

Extract 2

01   P: *se on oikeen (1.3) lellitty ja #e:# ei varmaan*
          She is really (1.3) spoiled and #e:# surely not

02   *niinku (1.9) tai isä pitää sitä varmasti ihan*
          like (1.9) or father surely will see her just as if

03   *pikku (.) vauvana niinku (.) #vielä#.hhhhhh*
          she was (.) a little baby like (.) #still#.hhhhhh

04   *kymmenen vuoden päästäki £hheh.hhhhhhh£*
          after ten years £hheh.hhhhhhh£

05   (1.2)

06   *m-mmm että (.) kyllä se niinku (2.3) tai ei*
          mm-mm so (.) she ((is)) like (2.3) or not

07   ↓*lellitty mut siis sillä lailla ei se niinku*
          spoiled but I mean in such a way she's not like

08   *(2.0) mut semmonen.hhhhhhhhhh (.) että isän*
          (2.0) but such.hhhhhhhhh (.) I mean the apple of

09   *silmäterä.*
          my father's eye.

10   (.)

11   T: *Mm-hm.*

12   (3.6)

13 → T: *Niin   no   aikamoinen   menetys   sulle.*
          PRT   PRT   quite   loss   you+to
          Well quite a loss to you.

14   (.)

15   P: *Mmm-m.*

16   (.)

17   T: *Sääki   oisit   halunnu olla isän   silmäterä.*
          you+also   would.have   wanted   be   father's eye-pupil
          You would have also wanted to be the apple of your father's eye

18   (.)

19   P: *Nii hhh.*
          Yeah hhh.

20   (0.4)

21   T: *Tai jonku silmäterä (.) m[mmmm.*
            Or an apple of somebody's eye (.) [mmmmm.

22   P: [*Nii.*
                                              [Yeah.

23   (3.9)

24   P: *.hff Ja totta ↑kai ↑tai ↑VIELÄKIN ↓haluais ↓olla*
            .hff And of course or STILL one would want to be

In lines 1–4 and 6–9 the patient describes how her father pays special attention to her little sister. The description has an affective tenor: the patient uses the intensifiers *oikeen*, "really," and *varmaan*, "surely" (line 1), and an exaggerated construction *pikkuvauvana niinku vielä kymmenen vuoden pääsläki* "as a little baby still after ten years," (line 4) which convey a sneering stance toward her father's treatment of her sister.

During the focus turn (line 13 after the patient's repair from *lellitty* "spoiled" to *isän silmäterä*, "apple of my father's eye," in lines 7–9), the therapist responds with *niin no aikamoinen menetys sulle*, "well quite a loss to you." This names and describes the quality of the patient's negative emotional experience and thus claims empathic recognition of the experience. The experience is presented in an upgraded way (her choice of the word *menetys*, "loss," refers to the patient's experience as a rather severe one, and she further intensifies it with *aikamoinen*, "quite"). The turn design resonates with the expressive elements in the patient's description, resembling a second assessment (Pomeranz, 1984c).

While displaying empathy, the therapist nonetheless makes a perspective shift that involves interpretation: she implies that in describing her father's relation to her sister, the patient is actually talking about her own painful experience. The particle chain *Nii no* (translated as "well") in the beginning of the turn implies that this turn slightly changes the line of action. The therapist explicates an experience that has not been referred to by the patient and empathizes with that experience. In this sense, the interpretative perspective shift is stronger in this case than in the response that was shown in the previous extract.

The patient nevertheless minimally acknowledges and confirms the therapist's suggestion (line 15), though she does not elaborate on the issue. In lines 17 and 21, the therapist explicates the interpretative contents of her previous turn, stating what the "loss" contains: the patient would have liked to have had the same kind of attention (be the "apple of father's eye too," or "the apple of somebody's eye"). These expansions, more overtly than the initial response, which did not contain any finite verb and thus did not set a time frame of the experience, also shift the focus from the present (from the patient's father's current relation to her little sister) to the past, to the patient's childhood experience. In this way the therapist's practice is similar to what was shown in the first extract: the initial response established the basis for a more overt interpretation.

What is important here is that in both cases, the therapist's subsequent interpretations that followed her first response to the patient would have been already sequentially possible and relevant where the initial response was produced (lines 21–2 in the place of 16–17 in Extract 1; line 17 in the place of line 13 in Extract 2). They however would have sounded more challenging in that sequential position and they would have missed the empathic elements. The less overt interpretations also gave the patient the opportunity to unpack the interpretations herself, or to resist them. The patient did not use this opportunity in these examples. However, the patient's response to the therapist's less overt interpretation was different in these two examples: while in Extract 1 the patient confirmed the interpretation (line 19, *nii*), in Extract 2 the response was less committal (line 15, *mmm-m*).

EMPATHY AND QUESTIONING BELIEFS

I will next turn to another type of therapist's empathic response to the patient's disclosure: turns that express a complaint toward a third party. Using an example that is divided into two data extracts, I will illustrate how these responses serve a central therapeutic task: questioning the patient's dysfunctional beliefs. In other words, these cases also demonstrate that the therapist's empathy is interwoven with a more investigative line of action.

The therapist's responses that are discussed in this section display similarities with the responses that were discussed in the previous section in that they show empathic recognition of the patient's emotional experience. However, they also involve something else: they make a statement about the state of affairs in "outer reality." More specifically, they comment critically on the conduct of a person with whom the patient has had a problematic experience. In this respect, these responses are similar to responses that express affiliation with a complaint (e.g., Drew & Walker, 2009; Ruusuvuori & Lindfors, 2009). In Extract 3 I will show a case of such a response. I will then analyze another extract from the same session in which the therapist uses this response as a resource for challenging the patient's thinking.

In Extract 3 below, the participants talk about the patient's recent conflict with her partner. Her partner had been away from home at night without telling her where he was. Before this extract, there have been several occasions in which the therapist and the patient have mutually formulated how the partner's behavior was reprehensible and how it did not meet the standards of proper conduct in a relationship. In other words, the therapist has already affiliated with the patient's complaint about the partner before the instance shown below (on the escalation of a complaint, cf. Drew & Walker, 2009). The extract follows one such turn by the therapist.

Extract 3

01   P: [*Nii (.) et* ↑*kyllä (.) kyllä*
                 [Yeah (.) so ↑indeed (.) indeed

02   *mun niinku (.).hfffff (.) hi-#hi-#hieman #nnn#*
         I like (.).hfffff (.) was li-#li-#little #erm#

03   *.hhhhhh lievästi sanottuna pahalta tuntu (0.3)*
         .hhhhhh to put it mildly it felt bad (0.3)

04   *[ja tuntuu se että.*
         [and it still feels that way.

05→ T: *[.mt (.)   mun   mielestä   ihan   oikeutetusti   ja   mun*
                    my   mind   quite   justly   and   my
         [.tch (.) I think quite justly and I

06→   *mielest   toi   on   ↑huonoo   °koh[teluu°.*
        mind   that   is   bad   treatment
        I think that is ↑ mistrea   [°tment°.

07 P: [*Nii (2.0) ↑mut ↑että ↑ku*
                              [Yeah (2.0) ↑but ↑I ↑mean

In lines 2–3 the patient describes the feeling she had (*pahalta tuntu,* "felt bad") about her partner's conduct and qualifies it with *lievästi sanottuna,* "to put it mildly," that often implies the opposite (i.e., that it felt really bad). With *et kyllä,* "so indeed" (line 1), the patient indicates that this is an upshot of the previous talk: her partner's bad conduct made her feel bad and continues to do so (line 4). In her response in lines 5–6, which overlaps with the patient's turn, the therapist agrees with the stance by stating *mun mielestä ihan oikeutetusti ja mun mielest toi on huonoo kohtelu,* "I think quite justly and I think that is ↑mistrea°tment°." The therapist marks her stance as her own opinion (*mun mielestä,* "I think / to my mind," in lines 5 and 6). By indicating her stance, she indicates that she not only recognizes the patient's inner, subjective experience of being mistreated but also comments on the partner's conduct from her (the therapist's) own perspective. By this kind of "personal statement" the therapist shares the patient's critique toward her partner: she displays that the criticism is justified not only in terms of the patient's experience, but also in terms of social norms. In short, this turn resembles an affiliation with complaints in everyday talk (Drew & Walker, 2009).

Like Extracts 1 and 2, where the therapist combined empathy with interpretation, the type of response shown in Extract 3 is also connected to more investigative work. The next extract reveals how the therapist, later in this same session, connects this empathic response to an action that challenges the patient's reactions. In this case, the mutually expressed critique of the patient's partner serves as grounds for the therapist's argument that questions the patient's belief about being faulty. The extract begins in the middle of the therapist's initiative action that points to the patient's dysfunctional reaction to the conduct of her partner.

Extract 4

01   .*hhhh että sää tuota:*   *hhhh*   *(0.7)*   *tuo*   *kuulostaa*   *tosi*
       .hhh that you e:rm   hhh   (0.7)   that   sounds   really

02   ↑*pahalta* [*et sä*
       ↑bad   [that you

03   P: [*Mmmm hhhhhhh.*

04→ T: *mietit*   *et*   *sä*   *tapat*   *itses*   *ja.hhhhhhh*
       think / thought   that   you   kill   yourself   and
       think / thought that you will kill yourself and.hhhhhhh

05→   *ku*   *oikeestihan*   *se*   *menee*   *niin*   *et*   *(.)*   *Ville*
       as   actually-CLI   it   goes   so   that   NAME
       as actually y'know it goes so that (.) Ville

06→   *kohtelee*   *sua*   ↑*huonosti*   *(.)*   *ja*   *sä*   *päätät*   *tappaa*   *itsesi*
       treats   you   badly   and   you decide   kill   yourself
       ↑mistreats you (.) and you decide to kill yourself

07→   .*hhhh.=*

08   P: =£*Mhhh£.*

09   (1.2)

10   P: *Nii:.*

11   (.)

12   T: *Sen*   *takia*   *et*   *Ville*   *käyttäytyy*   *huonosti*   *(.)*
       because   that   NAME   behaves   badly
       For the reason that Ville is behaving badly (.)

13   *Ville*   *on*   *ääliö.*
       Ville   is   an idiot

14   (.)

15   P: *Nii:.*

16   (1.8)

17   T: *Ei*   [*eihän*   *se*   *nyt*   *kuulosta*   *kovin*   [*hyvältä*
       NEG   NEG-CLI   it   PRT   sound   very   good
       ((It)) doesn't [it doesn't sound very   [good does it

18   P: [£*hhhh (0.3).hhhh no ehh.hh*   [*no ei: (.)*
              [£hhhh (0.3).hhhh well nohh.hh   [well no: (.)

The therapist points out (lines 4–6) how the patient has had suicidal impulses when her partner has mistreated her. The factual state of affairs—the partner has mistreated the patient—has been collaboratively agreed on earlier in the session (Extract 3 contained one of these instances). The therapist therefore uses the mutually expressed complaint about patient's partner's actions both as a resource of and as grounds for challenging the patient's dysfunctional trait (converting the experience of being mistreated into considering suicide). This kind of strategy is recurrent in the data (see Voutilainen, Peräkylä, & Ruusuvuori, 2010b). In terms of therapeutic work, here the therapist challenges the patient's belief that concerns seeing oneself as at fault for mistreatment by others, which has been an issue that they have worked on throughout the therapy process. This practice can be seen as not only questioning the rationality of the patient's feelings of faultiness, but also through agreeing with the complaint by the patient of her partner, as validating her healthy reactions: feelings of anger toward the mistreating partner.

In Extracts 1–4 I demonstrated two basic ways in which the therapist combines empathy and investigative work with the patient's emotional experiences. Extracts 1 and 2 involved a practice which focuses on the patient's inner experience and its history, whereas Extracts 3 and 4 illustrated a practice in which the therapist pointed out her opinion about things in the "outer world" to question the patient's dysfunctional belief. In both of these practices, the therapist's first substantial response to the patient's description both displayed empathy, and served to direct the therapeutic work toward a more investigative orientation.

A DEVIANT CASE: MISALIGNING FRAMES

What was described above is the way in which the therapist in my data typically responds to her patient: the first substantial response to the patient's emotional description is an empathic response. In other words, the therapist does not suggest alternative perspectives without first conveying an understanding and validation of the patient's experience in question (cf. Jefferson, 1988). However, the data contain a deviant session in which the therapist is more challenging and displays less recognition of the patient's experience. The patient, in turn, recurrently returns to the expression of her experience. There is an emerging misalignment (see Stivers, 2008) between the participants, which the therapist later in the session topicalizes and which then is discussed and mitigated during the session (see Voutilainen, Peräkylä, & Ruusuvuori, 2010c).

I will next show extracts that illustrate the therapist's unusual "merely investigative" way to respond to the patient's disclosures (and the patient's resistance to that investigative mode) in this session; and how this misalignment is consequential for the interaction. By looking more closely at this "deviant case," I aim to show that both the frame of emotional expression and response, and the frame of investigative therapeutic work that I have discussed in this paper, were inherent but potentially misaligning frames in the psychotherapeutic process in question.

Extract 5 shows the therapist responding to the patient's emotional experience in a detached way, without displaying affiliation. In the session from which the following extracts were taken, the participants talk about the patient's general feeling of anxiety, a professional failure that is (partly) related to that anxiety, and later in the session they also discuss the patient's expectations about the therapist's reactions to her professional failure.

The extract below begins from a point where the therapist topicalizes the patient's anxiety. Before the therapist's turn, the patient ends an account about facilities in her workplace and how she does not have to worry about them at the moment.

Extract 5

```
01   P:   silleen  tarvi(h) (1.2) tarvi sitte ressata että,
          like no need(h) (1.2) need then to worry about it so,

02        (5.7)

03   P:   .hhhh hmmm

04        (4.1)

05   T:   .hfff Ja   nyt   kröh kröhöm
          .hff  And now krh  krhhm ((clears throat))

06        (0.5) ja sä jotenki tätä niinku pohdit et miks nyt
          (0.5) and you are somehow like pondering that why I am

07        oon sitte niin ahdistunu ja jännittyny        [.hhh
          then feeling so anxious and nervous now       [.hhh

08   P:                                                 [Nii,
                                                        [Yeah,

09        (0.9)

10   P:   ↑Nii (0.8) #joteki on niinku viime aikoina aina#
          ↑Yeah (0.8) #somehow I have these days felt#

11        .hhh #mh# hhh ollu kauheen (0.3) ahdistunu olo (.)
          .hhh #mh# hhh felt terribly (0.3) anxious (.)

12        #jatkuvasti ja semmonen huono olo# (1.4)
          #constantly and had like a bad feeling# (1.4)

13        niiku fyysisesti ja psyykkisesti he.hhh (2.0)
          like physically and mentally he.hhh (2.0)

14        hirveen väsyny ja,
          awfully tired and,
```

15   (4.0)

16→T: *Mut   onk-   #tarkottaaks   s-#   (0.7)   #mth#   ahdistus   siis*
        but   is-Q   mean-Q   DEM.SG?   anxiety   PRT
        But is-#does it mean # (0.7) #mth# anxiety then

17→   *et   enemmän   ahdistunu   ku   masentunu   vai   et   sekä   että*
        that   more   anxious   than   depressed   or   that   both   and
        that more anxious than depressed or both and

18→   *sekä   masentunu   että   ahdistunu   [.hhh*
        both   depressed   and   anxious   [.hhh

19   P: [*.hhh hfff No varmaan*
                                                     [.hhh hfff Well I guess

20   *enemmän a̲hdistunu,*
        more a̲nxious,

21   (1.2)

22   T: *#Mut   sä   oot   akasemmin   ollu   enemmän   masentunu*
          but   you   have   earlier   been   more   anxious
          #But earlier you have been more like depressed

23   [niinkö#,
        [is that right#,

24   P: [*Nii*
          [Yeah

25   *(0.7) nii (.) no se̲kä että,*
        (0.7) yeah (.) well b̲oth and,

26   (0.3)

27   T: *Mh,*

28   P: *hff*

29   (2.8)

30   P: *Mut semmonen #niiku#.hhh #mmm# a̲hdistus semmonen*
          But that #kind of#.hhh #mmm# a̲nxiety that kind

31   *(0.4) mh (0.3) #semmonen pu̲ristava tunne*
        of (0.4) mh (0.3) #that kind of pre̲ssing feeling or

32   *tai semmonen niinku#,*
        that kind of#,

33   T: ↑#M::h#,

34   (1.0)

35   P: #t*u*skanen olo#,
           #ag*o*nized feeling#,

In lines 5–7 the therapist, rather than focusing on the patient's experience, refers to the patient's cognitive action of wondering about the reasons for her anxiety and nervousness (the patient herself has not brought up the "why" question but it can be heard as implicit in her disclosures on her unusual nervousness). The therapist's utterance invites the patient to distance herself from her experience and to scrutinize it.

In her response, the patient nonetheless does not take up this kind of reflection. Instead, she first provides a confirmation (line 8) and then (lines 10–13) describes what her experience is like, using several intensifiers (*kauheen*, "terribly," *jatkuvasti*, "constantly," *hirveen*, "awfully"). The patient thus offers her utterance as an expression of a problematic emotional experience. In so doing, she invites an affiliating, empathic response from the therapist (cf. Extracts 1–3 above). The therapist's response (lines 15–17), however, does not display affiliation, but poses a question concerning the quality and quantity of the patient's anxiety. The therapist formulates her question as one about the meaning of the patient's words, indicating that she is not able to recognize fully the experience the patient has described (cf. Extracts 1–3). The question is marked as a departure from the preceding topical line of talk with *mut*, "but," and with that question the therapist directs the patient away from the "expressive mode" toward a diagnostic examination of her affect (cf. orientation to professional action versus troubles telling in Jefferson & Lee, 1992; Ruusuvuori, 2007). As a result, the therapist maintains her project of detailing the anxiety in a detached way that she introduced in lines 5–7.

The subsequent turns reveal how the participants further maintain their misaligning positions. After the patient's answer in lines 19–20, the therapist asks a follow-up question (lines 22–3) that retains her diagnostic line of action. In the expansion of her response (lines 30–32, 35), the patient returns to describing the anxiety, thereby not taking up the detached position that the therapist offers her. It is important to add that in the following turn, not shown in the extract, the therapist then shows empathic recognition of the patient's experience.

Through the beginning part of this session, the misalignment between the frames of action of the participants continues: the patient recurrently returns to expression of anxiety, whereas the therapist pursues investigation of its reasons. This leads to a culmination in the misalignment, shown in the next extract from a later stage of the discussion. After yet another expressive disclosure by the patient, the therapist calls into question the patient's experience. Prior to the extract, the patient has stated that she would prefer just to close the curtains and sleep. In the beginning of the extract, the therapist asks whether this would really alleviate the patient's problem.

Extract 6

01   T: [*#Onks täs nyt semmonen#* (.) *#kyseessä et siihen oikeesti*
                [#Is this now# (.) #the kind of thing that it really

02   *could be helped by it#* (.)*.hhh*
              a̲u̲ttais se# (.).hhh

03   P: *Nii mh he.hh (.) #emmä tiiä#* (1.5) *#mmh#* (4.5)
            Nii mh he.hh (.) #I don't know# (1.5) #mmh# (4.5)

04   *tuskin se nyt (0.9) #mitään ra̲tkasis tai#,*
            probably it wouldn't (0.9) #solve anything or#,

05   (12.0)

06   P: *#Emmä tiiä ku: kotona on jotenki niin#.hh*
            #I don't know 'co:z at home it is somehow so#.hh

07   £tu̲rvallinen   #ja#   (0.5) #hyvä   olla#£#semmonen että ei#
            £sa̲fe   #and#   (0.5)£#go̲od   to be#£#like that not#

08   *(2.0)   #mmm (0.7) #ei   tota# (1.5) #jos ei   tarvii*
            (2.0)   #mmm (0.7) #not like# (1.5) #if you don't have to

09   *mihinkään mennä ei jännitä mitään*
            go anywhere you are not nervous about anything you

10   *ni ei oo pahoinvointia#*
            don't feel sick#

11   *(.) #ainakaan niin usein tai#.hff (0.3) #mmh#,*
            (.) #at least not so often#.hff (0.3) #mmh#,

12   (.)

13→ T: #Eli   sul   on   oikeesti   on   sit   kotona   jos sä   panisit
            PRT   you have for.real   have then home.at if you would.put
            #So you for real feel then at home if you drew

14→   verhot   kiinni   ni   sulla oikeesti   olis   siellä#.hhh
            curtains closed PRT you for.real would.have there
            the curtains you would for real #.hhh feel#.hhh

15→   >#hyvä olo#<   [hhh
            >good there#   [hhh

16   P: [*No e̲::i välttämättä jos on<* (.)
                      [Well n̲o::t necessarily if I have< (.)

The patient answers with the particle *Nii*, laughter particles, and *emmä tiiä*, "I don't know" (line 3), and by stating that it (staying home) probably would not solve anything (line 4). The patient conveys her understanding of the therapist's point and somewhat minimally accepts it. However, following a pause of 12 seconds (line 5), the patient then engages in accounting for her preference to stay at home (lines 6–11). That account has an affective tone: she utters the expression *turvallinen ja hyvä olla*, "safe and good to be," in a smiley, soft voice, and leaves the experiencer unmentioned in the utterance, which all can be heard as inviting a recognition of the experience. In her response (lines 13–15), the therapist nevertheless reformulates the patient's words in a way that, instead of expressing empathic recognition, calls into question the patient's description of her experience (conveying skepticism through the adverb *oikeesti*, "for real," in lines 13 and 14). The therapist thus strongly directs the patient to rethink her experience. In contrast to Extracts 1–3 above—and in contrast to this therapy in general—the therapist's response to the patient's disclosure is therefore overtly challenging and does not involve affiliating elements.

In her subsequent turn, the patient produces the action that the therapist made relevant (re-estimates her experience). Through the timing of her turn, she now seems to orient to the paradoxical presuppositions in the therapist's turn: the question made a structural preference for the confirmation of the statement about feeling good at home but, on the other hand, the therapist displayed skepticism toward this claim. The patient's response is marked as dispreferred by the particle *no* ("well") and the lengthening of the negation word *e::i* but it is not delayed, but rather it is delivered somewhat rapidly after the therapist's turn (see Pomerantz, 1984b). This rapid response is hearable as tense and orienting to an argument, an orientation that the patient then maintains as she continues to describe a situation where she indeed feels good at home (not shown in the extract).

I will present next an extract from later in this session in which the participants discuss their problems in their interaction. They do not refer to these problems as misalignment between the "emotional" and "investigative" frames as I have above, but they link them to the patient's unwillingness to talk about her recent professional failure and her possible concern about the therapist's being disappointed in her. However, it can be argued (see Voutilainen, Peräkylä, & Ruusuvuori, 2010c) that the misalignment of frames is how these issues occur in the interaction before they are brought under discussion.

Before this extract, the participants had talked about how the patient had felt that other people pressure her and are disappointed in her, owing to a failure in her professional life. The therapist has asked whether the patient feels that the therapist also thinks that way about the patient. The patient admitted that she does think that the therapist could be disappointed. In response to this, the therapist explained that she is not disappointed but can empathize with the patient if she herself is disappointed. After some talk about other people's expectations, the therapist again topicalizes the patient's attribution of disappointment in her and links it to what had happened between them earlier in the session:

Extract 7

01   T: *.hfff Niin mä jotenki vaan aattelin*
           .hfff Yeah I was just thinking

02   *että tota::   h hff 5.7).hfff (.) #mth et mä ajattelin*
           that e:rm::h hff (5.7).hff (.) #mth so I was thinking

03   *just tätä mm me̲idän välist suhdetta ja sit sitä et*
           exactly about this mm relationship between u̲s and then

04   *että ku m# (.) ku mul mul oli hiukka semmonen .hhh*
           that as m# (.) as I   had a   bit such.hhh

05   *#tu̲-#(.)tu̲nne itelläni et   sä: e::t# et niiku sä et*
           #fe̲-#(.)fe̲eling myself that you: do:n't# that you like

06   *oikeesti ois halunnu @£pu̲hu: mun kans k(h)oko*
           would not have really liked to @£ta:lk about this

07   *[jutusta£@,*
           who(h)le thing with me [at all,

08   P: *[#Nii nii no nii ehkä olikin niin emmä*
           [#Yeah yeah well yes maybe it was so I did

09   *sitä# [(0.7) #analysoinu   et#,*
           not# [(0.7) #analyze   it that#,

10   T: *[.hhh*

11   P: *mi̲ks mä en halu: mut oli semmonen*
           why I don't wa:nt but ((I)) had that kind of

           #olo   että ei#,
           feeling that NEG.SG3
           #feeling that I don't,

13   T: *Mm,*

14   P: *@halu:@,*
           @want to@,

15   (1.5)

16   T: *Mm,*

17   P: *[#M::h#,*

18   T: *[#Ja mä mm# (.) #emmäkää sitä*
           [#And I just# (.) #I did not think about it in the

19   *ensiks ajatellu   [mä vaan#,*
        first place either [I just#,

20 P: [*Mm,*

21 T: *#mietin et kuulostaa siltä että#.hh   [hh*
        #thought that it sounds like that#.hh [hh

22 P: [*#£Mm£# hff*

23 T: *että sä: oot nyt jotenki   £vastaha[koisella*
        that yo:u are now somewhat £in   a [reluctant

24 P: [*Mm,*

25 T: *tuulella ja£*
        mood and£,

26 P: *he he he he   [he.hh*

27 T: [*#ja sä oot ollu joskus erilainenki ja*
                       [#and you have sometimes been different and

28   *mm# (.) #tai must on tuntunu erilaiselta [ni#,*
        mm# (.) #or I have felt different [so#,

29 P: [*Mm,*

30   (1.2)

31 T: *#mth ni voisko se sit liittyy jotenki*
        #mth so could that then somehow link to

32   [*tohon asiaan#,*
        [that issue#,

33 P: [*Nii kyllä varmaan joo,*

        [Yeah I guess so,

Here the therapist explicates that there were difficulties in the interaction between the participants earlier in the session and suggests that these problems were linked to the patient's belief that the therapist is disappointed in her (which is referred to as "that issue" in line 32). The patient confirms that suggestion (line 33). The therapist points out in lines 21, 23, 25, and 27–8 that she arrived at this interpretation because she noticed that the patient "is somehow in a reluctant mood" and she has felt different with the patient at other times. The patient aligns with the therapist's description of that interaction (lines 22, 24, 26, and 29), and following this extract the participants continue to talk about the patient's thoughts and feelings about the therapist's reactions and how she feels that others (including the therapist) do not understand the extent of her anxiety. The patient also discloses that the therapist said something in the previous session that the patient perceived as evidence that the therapist did not understand the patients' anxiety.

In this extract, the participants explicate that there was something problematic in the interaction in the phase of the session from which the Extracts 5 and 6 were taken. On the surface of interaction this occurred when there was a misalignment of lines of action: the patient resisted the therapist's investigative line of action, whereas the therapist did not display the affiliation that the patient was inviting. Extract 7 shows how this misalignment was consequential: the participants ended up explicating the reasons for it. They therefore treated this kind of misalignment as being deviant. Nevertheless, in the latter part of the session, this misalignment became a resource of therapeutic work as the participants reflected upon it and went on to discuss issues such as patient's attribution of disappointment to the therapist and the patient's experience of not being understood by the therapist (see Voutilainen, Peräkylä, & Ruusuvuori, 2010c).

I have shown above how the therapist of the data combines empathy and investigative work with her patient's experience in different ways. To summarize, usually the therapist's first substantial response is empathic, and the more investigative interventions may either be delivered simultaneously, or follow later. The extracts from the "deviant" session however showed a case in which the patient's "emotional" frame and the therapist's "investigative" frame clashed so that misalignment between the participants emerged. I will next discuss the "emotional" (empathic) and "investigative" (interpreting or challenging) aspects in the therapist's actions in relation to both conversation-analytic concepts and to the aims of cognitive-constructivist therapy.

THERAPEUTIC MODIFICATIONS OF EVERYDAY PRACTICES

In their discussion on the convergence of troubles telling and service encounter, Jefferson and Lee (1992, p. 535) suggested that in the everyday activity of troubles telling, the focal object is the teller and his or her experiences, while in a service encounter the focal object is the problem and its proprieties. In the case of psychotherapy, these aspects might be seen as being fundamentally interwoven, since psychotherapies by and large aim at changing the patients' relation to their experiences (see Peräkylä, Antaki, Vehviläinen, & Leudar, 2008, p. 16). In very general terms, psychotherapy involves discussing problems that are the patient's experiences. Psychotherapy therefore is an institutional context in which the patient's emotional experience (at least in the sense of the topic of talk) cannot be treated as irrelevant or as a minor issue (cf. Jefferson & Lee, 1992; Ruusuvuori, 2007).

In a sense the therapist's empathic, affiliating actions can be seen as taking the position of a troubles (or a complaint) recipient. Likewise the actions of interpreting and challenging beliefs can be seen as orienting toward problem-solving, but in psychotherapy the important difference is that the interpretation and challenging do not result in solutions as such, but new understandings regarding the problem. The order of these actions, that is, that affiliation precedes more investigative work, resembles Jefferson's (1988; Jefferson & Lee, 1992, p. 531) template of the troubles-telling sequence in which the "work up" of the trouble (e.g., advice or diagnostic considerations) occurs only after an orientation to the experience. However, unlike the troubles-telling sequence, the therapist's "work up" is not closing-implicative, but it sets in motion further work on the problem: the therapist invites the patient to reflect on her experience in relation to her therapist's suggestions.

It is important to note, however, that the therapist's affiliation is not only affiliation in the sense of everyday talk, but it also serves the interpreting and challenging of beliefs. First of all, it has an intrinsic institutional purpose, as empathy is regarded as a condition for successful psychotherapy (Rogers, 1957; Bohart & Greenberg, 1997). Moreover, as was shown above, the therapist's affiliating turns establish the basis for interpreting or challenging actions. This means that within the context of psychotherapy, the everyday practices of troubles telling are modified for institutional purposes.

The misalignment in Extracts 5 and 6, in turn, can be seen as a misalignment between the activities of troubles telling and the therapeutic work on the problem: the patient invites the therapist to take the position of troubles recipient whereas the therapist orients to the investigative line of action. The mismatch between the frames of the teller and her experiences and the problem and its proprieties (Jefferson & Lee, 1992) now arises, especially in Extract 5. Nevertheless, that this kind of continuing mismatch is possible suggests that these two frames—troubles telling and working on the problem—are both inherent parts of (at least this particular) psychotherapy.

PROFESSIONAL THEORIES IN PRACTICE

The distinction made above is between the therapist's responses that focus on the patient's inner experience and those that focus on the "outer world." In the "experience oriented" responses, the therapist displayed empathic recognition of the patient's experience, and in the same turn, interpreted that experience, for example by suggesting links to the patient's childhood experiences. The response in Extract 3 showed the therapist focusing on the "outer world" by agreeing with, and therefore validating, the patient's criticism toward a third party. This was later linked to challenging the patient's dysfunctional beliefs.

In terms of the professional literature of cognitive therapies, the therapist's work described above might be seen as involving an integration of different professional theories (Peräkylä & Vehviläinen, 2003). The practices of validating criticism and questioning beliefs are perhaps closest to traditional cognitive therapy, which examines a patient's irrational thinking and tests the correctness of those beliefs (in relation to factual evidence, i.e., the "outer world") (Beck, 1976; see also Linehan, 1997, pp. 370–74). The extracts where the therapist combines empathy with interpretation, in turn, might be linked to cognitive–constructivist therapy, which works with personal meaning organizations, that is, with the historical construction of the patient's inner experience (Guidano, 1991). Furthermore, the therapist's ways to respond, first empathically and so in a way to "stay" in the emotional experience before distancing from it, resonate with emotion-focused therapy (Greenberg, 2004), which suggests "accessing" emotional experiences that are seen as primary and adaptive, such as anger as a reaction to mistreatment or sadness as a reaction to loss. The therapist's work in the deviant session (Extracts 5–7) connects to the literature on working with ruptures in therapeutic alliance through metacommunication (Safran, Muran, Wallner Samstag, & Stevens, 2001): the therapist topicalized the problems in the interaction and so turned the misalignment between the participants into a resource for therapeutic work. In her actual practice the therapist thus seems to use flexibly—and at the same time, in conversation analytic terms, orderly—elements from different psychotherapeutic theories, which in the literature sometimes seem to be contradictory.

NOTES

1. I would like to express my gratitude to Anssi Peräkylä and Johanna Ruusuvuori who have worked with me on the data and on the questions that I discuss in this paper.
2. By the term "interpretation," I refer to an institution-specific action, to a psychotherapeutic interpretation, not to interpreting in the more general sense.
3. The verb tense (*on ollu*, "has been") in the therapist's turn can be heard to imply that the patient does not remember directly these time periods. In this way, the turn is delivered more as an interpretation than as a question.

CHAPTER 12

⌘

Knowledge, Empathy, and Emotion in a Medical Encounter

JOHN HERITAGE AND ANNA LINDSTRÖM

INTRODUCTION

In his *Lectures on conversation*, Sacks suggests that fundamental differences exist between entitlement to knowledge and entitlement to experience. A person can be entitled to knowledge by virtue of being given it:

> That is to say, if I tell you something that you come to think is so, you are entitled to have it. And you take it that the stock of knowledge that you have is something that you can get wherever you get it, and it is yours to keep. (Sacks, 1992, vol. 2, p. 244)

In contrast, Sacks observes, "the stock of experiences is an altogether differently constructed thing." Sacks illustrates the distinction using a phone call in which the caller describes a horrifying car crash that she witnessed, and he asks:

> What happens to stories like this one once they are told? Do stories like this become the property of the recipient as they are the property of the teller? That is, the teller owns rights to tell this story, and they give their credentials for their rights to tell the story by offering such things as that they saw it, and that they suffered by it. Now the question is, does the recipient of a story come to own it in the way that the teller has owned it; that is, can the recipient tell it to another, or feel for it as the teller can feel for those events? (Sacks, 1992, vol. 2, p. 243).

Merely to pose the question in this way is to recognize fundamental differences in the ways that knowledge and experience are recognized and treated in social interaction and beyond. While knowledge is generally treated as something that can be shared, and hence as an object of transmission, comparison and evaluation, experience is treated as singular, particularized, and, at the limit, ineffable. It is this characteristic that can create difficulties for recipients of reported experiences (Heritage, 2011). For the latter may encounter these reports in terms of an obligation to affirm the nature of the teller's experience and its meaning, and to affiliate with the experiencer, yet they may lack the experiences and associated epistemic rights with which to fashion emotionally congruent stances.

The difficulties involved in affiliation may be compounded when the experience under description is a "trouble" (Jefferson, 1988) involving a stigmatized psychological state like depression (Lamoureaux, 2010), or that may be felt to be associated with unnatural or morally contaminated feelings, each of which may add an additional layer of difficulty in the achievement of recipient empathy. A further obstacle to the achievement of empathic connection may arise from the institutional context of an interaction. Jefferson has described two alternative stances toward troubles telling. In the first the recipient aligns to the troubles teller as a "troubles recipient," permitting the teller to invite and receive affiliation concerning the problematic state of affairs (Jefferson, 1988). In the second, the recipient responds as a "service supplier," offering possible remedies for the troublesome state of affairs, but not emotional affiliation (Jefferson & Lee, 1981). When troubles about emotions are told to medical providers, such as a primary-care physicians or community nurses, the latter are professionally mandated to offer remedies (in the form of medication or psychotherapeutic referral), but not affiliation with the problem (Ruusuvuori, 2005, 2007).

Finally, the disclosure of emotional troubles is structured within a normatively formatted troubles-telling sequence. A prominent feature of such sequences is the management of exit from them into ordinary topics. Standard methods of exit from them involve optimistic projections about the future (Jefferson, 1984a, 1988). The latter, however, may be understood as merely pro forma, and resisted by the troubles teller, yielding a series of "rounds" or "pulses" about troubles telling over the course of an interaction which may further strain the capacities of the recipient for empathic affiliation (Jefferson, 1984a).

In this chapter, we explore some aspects of this dilemma through a series of interchanges between a primiparous British mother and a community nurse, conducted over a series of weekly home visits. During these visits the mother confesses to difficulties in bonding with her newborn daughter, and the nurse makes a number of attempts to reassure her that she will soon form an appropriate emotional connection with her child. Across these sequences of interaction, the mother's disclosure of anxiety and depression, together with "unnatural" feelings about her baby, is addressed by the community nurse in ways that are both professional and empathic and constrained within the normative structures of troubles telling.

BACKGROUND

As a part of the United Kingdom health services, community nurses (known as "health visitors"; HV below) are members of primary healthcare teams with a special focus on the promotion of health and the prevention of illness. Historically, their work is mainly centered on mothers with young children. In this context, their task is to establish a positive and enabling relationship with the mothers in their care, and to advise and support them on a wide range of issues connected with child and maternal health and wellbeing. Much of this work is done through home visits that health visitors conduct on a universal basis. Ideally, these visits are frequent early on in the life of the newborn, attenuating in frequency over time. Advice-giving is a prominent feature of the early visits, especially with primiparous women who may not have a reservoir of previous childcare experience to draw on (Heritage & Sefi, 1992).

The data on which this chapter is based are drawn from a substantial corpus of self-administered audiotape recordings by health visitors in a large industrial city in central England.[1] The health visitors recorded the first six of their weekly visits to a range of mothers evenly divided between first time mothers, and mothers who had previously had one or more children. In all some seventy-five visits were recorded. This chapter is based on a longitudinal analysis of all six visits involving a pairing of single mother and health visitor (for earlier work where the same data are addressed, see Heritage & Lindström, 1998). To provide a context for our analysis of this and other practices we will first briefly characterize the entire series of visits between this mother and her health visitor.

Like most of the first visits in the larger database from which this series of visits was drawn, the first visit was mostly occupied with bureaucratic tasks such as obtaining the vital statistics of the baby, registering the baby for immunizations, and explaining the schedule of health checkups for the baby (Heritage & Sefi, 1992). The health visitor physically examined the baby during this visit, and gave some advice on basic babycare. She also asked the mother about her birth experience, and advised her on post-partum care. The proper care of baby and mother was also the main topic of the second visit. The mother is slightly more forthcoming in this visit than she was in the first. In this visit the mother volunteers for the first time that she does not yet have strong feelings for her baby. Between the second and third visits the baby got a chest infection, and the mother had mastitis. The proper care for these medical problems occupied a great deal of the third visit.

The fourth visit provides the focus for our analysis because it is here that the mother's difficulty in bonding with her baby is most explicitly dealt with. Initially the interactants discuss the baby's current sleeping and feeding schedule. The mother acknowledges that the baby's erratic daytime schedule is taking a toll on her, and this leads to more extended talk about the emotional difficulties of mothering. The mother is still expressing concern that her baby does not properly settle between feeds during the fifth visit. This visit is much shorter than the others as the mother is on her way out when the health visitor arrives. The baby's feeding is also extensively discussed during the sixth visit. After briefly examining the baby, the health visitor recommends medication for colic. Future concerns, such as day care are also discussed during this visit.

The ensuing analysis has been divided into three episodes. As we move from episode one to episode three the mother's depiction of her relationship with her baby becomes increasingly serious. In the first episode (taken from the second of the six visits), she presents her problem within a natural developmental idiom and downplays its importance. In the second and third episodes (from the fourth visit), she increasingly abandons this idiom, and expresses more anxiety about her situation. The health visitor's responses match this development, and she tends to respond in increasingly experiential terms as the mother moves from the natural to the moral realm.

A BONDING PROBLEM: EPISODE 1

The following sequence is the first time the mother discloses that she is not yet connecting with her baby. She offers this information in response to a query by the health visitor (line 1). This query is done in the midst of a number of mothering activities—changing and nursing the baby—and it is uttered with a raised voice over the baby's crying. While the question opens up a space in which the mother can raise difficulties and concerns, the question itself is designed for an affirmative response and is optimized for a favorable sociomedical outcome (Heritage, 2010). The mother's response however is significantly delayed and qualified (line 2), and adumbrates significant reservations about her transition into motherhood (lines 6, 7, and 10):

Extract 1 [Episode #1 [3A2:27]]

```
01    HV:   >Do you think you've settled very quickly into motherhood,<
02    M:    Uhm (1.2) ye::s I suppose so (I mean).
03          . . .
04          ((7 lines of data omitted in which Mother tends to the baby.))
05          . . .
06    M:    I still feel I've got to sort of really grow to:, (1.5) ehm pt .h
07          feel that she is my ow:n and rea::lly
08          (1.2)
09    HV:   Mm:,
10    M:    love her lots
11          (.)
12    M:    I mean I like he:r and I think she's wonderful'n (0.6) but
13          I don't feel "ohhh look at m[y ba:by"
14    HV:                               [No,
15    M:    .h It doesn't really worry me cause I know it'll come with
16          ti:me.=
17    HV:   =It does [yes.
18    M:             [But ehm-
19    HV:   Yeah. .h Well when I first had mi:ne I couldn't stand the sight
20          of him?
21    M:    °Heh heh heh,
22    HV:   (.hh W'l-) 'e wasn't exactly pretty looking he had .h some
23          forceps marks all over his [head,
```

24	M:	[Oh lo[rd ((wavering voice))
25	HV:	[(It was all) sort of a weird
26		shape you kn[ow,
27	M:	[Yes
28	HV:	Huh huh huh huh [huh .hh
29	M:	[pt
30	HV:	ehm But pt e [hm it's something as you sa:y that does come,
31	M:	[The:re ( ) ((to baby))
32	M:	Yeah,
33	HV:	And it's eh it's when they start responding to you when
34		they a[re
35	M:	[That's right.
36	HV:	ehm they're looking forward to you they're looking out
37		for you and you find then that you know you can feel
38		quite wa quite wa[rm towards them,
39	M:	[°Yes
40	HV:	.hh but I think the first weeks ((clears throat)) pt they
41		take a lot out of you and and nothing is,
42	M:	Nothing is- that that's right there's no feedback

Although the mother's disclosure is in response to the HV's question, she is none-theless the one who introduces the emotionally and morally sensitive issue of maternal bonding. She introduces this issue in a natural and normalizing idiom. In stating that "I've got to sort of really grow to:, (1.5) pt.h feel that she is my own" (lines 6–7) she depicts the desired feeling as one that naturally will come with time. As part of this portrayal, the mother hesitates at line 8 before com-pleting the turn that suggests that she is not experiencing fully loving feelings for her child. Having stated that she still has to learn to love her baby "lots," the mother then revises her stance at line 12, but then contrasts her moderate feel-ings with a position that is depicted and vocally animated (via an "exaggerated" softness and breathiness in the delivery) as excessive infatuation ("I don't feel 'ohhh look at my ba:by'"). This line is perhaps the peak moment of disclosure in this episode.

Subsequently, the mother begins to exit this disclosure sequence via an optimistic projection (Jefferson, 1988) in lines 15–16, that once again emphasizes a natural developmental trajectory into bonding. It is this projection that the HV takes up and reinforces (line 17). Her response first *confirms* the mother's position with a partial repeat (Schegloff, 1996a; Raymond, 2003; Stivers, 2005; Heritage & Raymond, 2005, forthcoming), prior to an agreement token ("Yes"). She then grounds this confirma-tion by describing similar feelings that she had toward her own child (lines 19–20, 22–3, and 25–6). In thus acknowledging a parallel experience (Heritage, 2011), the HV normalizes the mother's feelings and then initiates an exit from the sequence by explicitly agreeing with the mother's earlier optimistic projection (explicitly reinvoking and reusing the mother's own earlier remarks at line 30). Subsequently she moves to a less empathic and a more generalized perspective (indicated with "they" in "it's when they start responding to you . . .") in describing the behaviors associated with bonding, and then moving to a more external and professional style of generalization ("I think the first weeks ((clears throat)) pt they take a lot out of you," to further normalize the mother's experience. Within this segment, she implicitly lowers the mother's expectations by using the description "quite warm" (line 38), rather than "love" or "affection," to describe the onset of maternal feelings. The sequence ends with explicit agreement from the mother in line 42 and an effort at collaborative completion of the HV's unfinished utterance.

The predominant tone of this segment is naturalizing and developmental. The extent of the HV's attempt to parallel the mother's experience is relatively minimal and does not quite match the mother's experience. There are two key differences between the mother's and the HV's tellings. First, while the mother emphasizes her lack of emotional closeness with her baby, the HV stresses her dislike of her baby's physical appearance. Second, the HV provides an external reason for her dislike (the forceps marks). Such an account is not available to the mother. Thus, though she initially abandons her "professional" stance in dealing with the mother's anxieties, the HV's response is not fully aligned to the mother's. An extended exit to this sequence was initiated by the mother's return to an optimistic projection (line 15-16), and the HV's subsequent support for that position within, first, an experiential and, subsequently, a professional frame of reference.

As earlier noted, the mother and baby fell ill between the health visitor's second and third visits. The treatment of the illness occupied most of the third visit. We will therefore now turn to the fourth visit, where the mother's feelings toward her baby are once again addressed.

A BONDING PROBLEM: EPISODE 2

Relatively early in the fourth visit, after the health visitor has heard about some feeding problems with the baby, she reassures the mother that the situation will improve. The next episode (Extract 2) emerges from this sequence, and is best understood as arising from the mother's weak agreement (line 4) that she has come through the first six weeks very successfully ("with flying colors"). The HV initially pursues response with an incremental tag question (line 5) and, when the mother does not immediately respond, she probes with "do you feel as though you have or j'st." Unlike the query in line 5 this probe, especially the turn-ending "or j'st" is built for the possibility of disagreement (Lindström, 1995, 1997). In questioning the mother about her feelings, the HV preserves the validity of her own evaluation in lines 1–3 (she does not address whether the mother has "come through with flying colors" or not, but rather whether she *feels* as though she has). In contrast with the previous episode, the mother does not present her problem in terms of a lack of feelings that will come. Instead she indicates that her experience of motherhood has not met

her expectations, while simultaneously acknowledging that these expectations might
be too high (lines 8 and 10–14).

Extract 2 [Episode 2, Part 1 [3A4:4]]

```
01    HV:    Ah: .hh and- you know the next six weeks you'll find things so
02           much easier .hh and you've come through this first six weeks
03           with flying colors may I sa:y huh [huh huh
04    M:                                      [Yea:h,
05    HV:    Haven't you.
06           (.)
07    HV:    Do you feel as though you have or j'st-
08    M:     Not really- I don't know perhaps I expect too much of myself.
09    HV:    Ah
10    M:     And perhaps I expect too much of Phoebe as well I you know I
11           expect her to be a perfect baby and every time she does something
12           that's (0.5) <not brilliant> I (.) think that this is the start
13           of bad things to come you know and I really worry about that and
14           get all uptight °and°,
15    HV:    .hhh Well there's no such thing as the perfect mother
16           and there's no such thing as the perfect [baby.
17    M:                                              [babie:s
18    HV:    .hh And we're all different, (0.2) .hh but you really have done
19           very well this first six weeks it's your first baby, .hhh=
20    M:     =°M[m°
21    HV:       [And you've coped exceedingly well I mean how can I .hh
22           impress on you [just how well you've coped, .hh and I wouldn't
23    M:                    [°Mm°
24    HV:    be saying that if I thought otherwise.
25    M:     Mm:
26    HV:    You have coped very very well.
```

The HV's response in lines 15–16, which asserts that there are no perfect babies or
mothers, agrees with the mother's criticism of her own perfectionism, and is thus hearably reassuring in intent. She then goes on to reassure the mother in very explicit
terms, using a series of upgraded evaluations: "you've coped exceedingly well I mean
how can I .hh impress on you just how well you've coped, .hh and I wouldn't be saying
that if I thought otherwise. You have coped very very well." In the ensuing segment
(not included on our transcript) the HV suggests some medical and social reasons why
this mother has had a more difficult time than most. She then reverts back to the idea
that the mother sets herself too high standards and claims that this is "a common
failing of nurses." The mother is a nurse, and the HV's claim is hearably designed to
establish a link between the experiences of the two women. The mother agrees with
this observation.

Extract 3 shows the remainder of this sequence. In this segment the HV gives an extended description of her own outlook as a "know it all" and perfectionist new mother (lines 1, 5, 7, 9–10, 12, 14–16). She then restates her prior generalization that this is a professional shortcoming of nurses (lines 18–19) and ends the sequence by directly addressing mother's earlier observations in the previous segment about expecting too much (lines 8 and 10): "You have got to sort of .hh not- not °worry so much°. Just try try and take things a little bit e:hm easier .hh let things flow over your head a bit."

Extract 3 [Episode 2, Part 2]

```
1    HV:   Nobody was worse than me I may [say.
2    M:                                    [Heh heh heh
3    HV:   Huh huh huh huh .hhh
4    M:    Mm
5    HV:   I was a typical case of somebody who knew everything,
6          (.)
7    HV:   Didn't I [heh heh heh .hh
8    M:             [Heh heh heh
9    HV:   And now I realise th't, .hh I have to learn every
10         da(h)y [hhh .hhgh And take days as it comes and not ehm .hh
11   M:            [Mm
12   HV:   (0.4) but it took me years to- to get to that frame of mi:nd
13   M:    M[m hm
14   HV:     [where I could .hh say well you know I don't think I handled
15         that very well and just accept it you know just eh shrug your
16         shoulders to a certain extent.
17         (2.4)
18   HV:   But having said that I think that ehm pt nurses are on
19         the (ball) like that.=In the long run you see you just
20         .hhh you ehm you do achieve a lot because you have these
21         high [ideals.
22   M:         [Mm
23   HV:   .hh But if the ideals .hh are really (0.5) >getting on top of
24         you< then of course you won't achieve so much.
25   M:    Mm=
26   HV:   =You have got to sort of .hh not- not °worry so much°.
27   M:    (°Mm°)
28   HV:   Just try try and take things a little bit e:hm easier
29         .hh let things flow over your head a bit.
30         (0.8)
31   M:    Yea:h.
32         (0.5)
```

33	HV:	Are you feeling depressed at all?
34	M:	Oh ye:s I feel dr(h)e(h)adful I feel rea:lly sort'v
35	HV:	Have you been (.) [weeping
36	M:	[low
37	M:	Oh y(h)es heh [(every night)
38	HV:	[Every <u>da:y</u>?
39	M:	Yes (.) usuall(h)y.

As in Extract 1, the HV works hard to establish a parallel experience with the mother, and to ground its origins in shared professionalism. As part of this process the HV resists the mother's earlier attempt to place part of the blame for her situation on her baby's behavior (see Extract 2, lines 11–14). She had earlier rebutted this suggestion with the observation that there's no such thing as a perfect baby (Extract 2, line 16) and preempted the mother's self-blame with the earlier "there's no such thing as a perfect mother" (Extract 2, line 15). She now proceeds to take up the possibility that the mother may be making excessive demands on herself, by constructing a parallel with her own experience as a nurse and a mother, culminating in the advice that the mother should learn to "let things flow over your head a bit" (line 29). In contrast to Extract 1, the mother is notably unresponsive, acknowledging the HV's remarks with the briefest of continuers at lines 4, 11, 13, 22, 25, and 27 (Gardner, 1997). The HV's final recommendation at lines 28–9 is met at first with silence and, subsequently, by a notably pallid form of acceptance (Heritage & Sefi, 1992). It is at this point that the HV asks the mother if she is depressed, attracting a response that treats it as self-evident that she is (Heritage 2002), that is infused with troubles resistant laughter (Jefferson 1984).

A BONDING PROBLEM: EPISODE 3

The next episode, which takes place later in the fourth visit, is the most complex we will be dealing with. We have therefore divided it into four segments that we will discuss separately. The episode shows a progression toward much greater self-disclosure by the health visitor, and a highly empathic attempt to construct her experience in parallel with the mother's. It is during this episode that the health visitor starts to address the possibility that the mother is constructing her feelings as "unnatural" and morally suspect.

The first of the following four segments begins at the conclusion of the discussion of the mother's depression. The mother has accounted for her feelings in terms of the baby's excessively demanding behavior during the day. The HV moves to exit this sequence with the suggestion that during the next period either the baby will become less demanding or the mother will be able to better cope with the baby regardless of its behavior. Line 1 is a summary recycle of this suggestion that pursues acceptance. After a pro forma agreement (line 2), the mother initiates a significantly more serious depiction of the state of her emotional bond with her child. In lines 4–5, the mother states she feels "cheated," and then assesses her experience of motherhood against what she invokes as the norm: "oh I'm not enjoying this at all and I should be:." When the HV does not immediately respond to this assessment, the mother upgrades her position by describing a situation in which another woman showed very strong feelings ("going all gushy," line 12) toward her baby. This woman is not introduced as a "normal" person but as "someone who is <u>desperate</u> to have a baby." Nonetheless, the mother treats this woman's expressed feelings as a contrastive "benchmark" (Smith, 1978) against which to evaluate her own: "And I think well <u>I</u> should be like this I should be feeling th't".

Extract 4 [Episode 3, Part 1 [3A4:9]]

```
01    HV:  And (e-) you know eh one or other will ha [ppen
02    M:                                              [Yeah
03          (1.8)
04    M:   I just feel really (s- I dunno) cheated I feel "oh
05          I'm not enjoying this at all and I should be:."
06          (.)/(.hh)
07    M:   And when I take her to see people and .hh there's
08          one friend of mine who is desperate to have a baby,
09    HV:  Mm
10    M:   She's got one already but she's (.) quite infertile
11          (0.5) and she picks up Phoeb- "Oh isn't she
12          beauti[ful" and () you see her going all gushy
13    HV:        [Yes well she is
14    HV:  Y[es
15    M:    [And I think well I should be like this I should be
16          feeling th't .hh "oh isn't she wonderful-" I mean I-
17          there's sometimes I look at her and I think she's
18          pretty [(good   ) you kno:w, but none of this
19    HV:         [Mm
20    M:   real sort of (.) "oh: I can't bear to not look at
21          her for five minutes" you know,
22          (0.6)
23    M:   Ehm (0.2) I don't know I feel really (0.6) as if: (.)
24          >I'm not her mother at all< (and) as if (.) somebody
25          else is going to come along knock on the door and say
26          "right I'll take her home now thank you."
27          (1.0)
28    M:   And (0.8) I suppose it'll come later but I jus-,
```

The mother then progressively describes her own relationship to her baby in increasingly distanced terms, moving from "sometimes I look at her and I think she's pretty good" (lines 17–18) to "I feel really (0.6) as if: (.) >I'm not her mother at all< (and) as if (.) somebody else is going to come along knock on the door and say 'right I'll take her home now thank you.'" (lines 23–6) This evocation of a concrete, but imaginary, process by which someone will come to retrieve the baby constitutes a very strong acknowledgment of estrangement. Faced with no immediate uptake to this depiction, the mother offers a most minimal, and "trailed off" optimistic projection: "I suppose it'll come later but I jus-."

The sequence continues as follows, the health visitor directly responding to the mother's telling:

Extract 5 [Episode 3, Part 2]

```
01   HV:   .hh Well it- it- can I assure you that I felt just like
02         that with my first one.=A[nd it does come later.
03   M:                            [Yeah
04   HV:   .hhh But it's (.) easy to say "yes it will come later."
05   M:    That's r [ight,
06   HV:            [I think (e-) falling in love with your baby
07         is sometimes instantaneous.
08   M:    [Mm:
09   HV:   [.hh And sometimes takes a long time .hh and I think
10         when you've had a difficult (.hh) labor that it
11         takes longer be[cause
12   M:                   [Yeah
13   HV:   You know y- physically and mentally you're exhausted
14         when the baby is there .hh and really I used to (0.2) wake
15         up °and think "that dratted baby is crying (ag(h)ain. hh)"°
16   M:    Yeah.
17   HV:   'n I'd think "oh::" (0.2) scream and go ma:d.
18   M:    Mm.
19   HV:   And um pt.h it was: (.) he was well over six weeks before
20         I felt any- you know [.hh
21   M:                         [Yeah
22   HV:   WELL GRADUALLY .hh (as 'e-) the more he smiled at me
23         you kn[ow the more I felt "oh well [s- perhaps he's not
24   M:          [Yeah                         ['s ri:ght
25   HV:   s(h)o b(h)a(h)d a(h)ft(h)e(h)r a(h) [ll huh huh huh .hh
26   M:                                        [That's right.
```

The initial component of the HV's self-interrupted turn-beginning could be heard to be going toward the subsequently realized "it does come later" (line 2). However, that eventuality would have risked being understood as "mere agreement." The revised beginning avoids this outcome and provides an independent basis for this agreement, and one moreover that is grounded in her own experience. With this shift, the HV moves from a "professional" to a "personal" basis on which to address the mother's concerns. That this shift is a kind of "afterthought" is also perhaps evidenced by her later, retrospective comment that it is "easy to say 'yes it will come later'" (line 4).

After glossing her own experience in lines 1–2, the HV offers some more professionally oriented generalizations about maternal bonding (lines 6–7 and 9). Like the advice she offered in the first segment (Extract 4), these generalizations are constructed within a developmental and naturalistic idiom. After suggesting the birth experience as a general factor impacting maternal bonding (lines 9–11, 13–14), the HV then shifts back to her own experience (line 14), returning to a claim she made in the second visit (see Extract 1, lines 19ff.) that she had not initially bonded with her child. This allows her to reassert on the basis of her own personal experience as a mother what she had earlier asserted merely as a professional generalization in the first of these problem segments (cf. Extract 1, lines 33ff.): that the baby's increasing responsiveness evokes maternal bonding.

In comparison with the first episode, this time there is a better match between the mother's telling and the HV's empathic parallel description. In the previous episode, the HV only briefly invoked her bonding problems, and seemed to explain them away in terms of the baby's appearance. In this episode, by contrast, the HV comes close to depicting her own situation as having been more serious than the mother's. In stating that it took well *over* six weeks before she bonded with her child, the HV renders the mother's disposition toward her six-week-old baby as less out of the ordinary. The mother responds to the HV's account by agreeing (lines 24 and 26) with the generalization that is implied. It is noticeable, in this account, that the HV's representation of her gradually dawning affection for her child ("oh well he's not so bad after all," line 25) is managed (via a litotes formulation [Bergmann, 1992]) as a movement from a negative to a less negative (or grudgingly positive) stance, and it is lightened by laughter which the mother, strikingly, does not join.

The third part of the episode under examination (Extract 6), in which the mother begins by disavowing any danger to the baby arising from her emotional state (lines 1 and 3–4), is shown below. The mother's initial and volunteered disclaimer strongly suggests that caregivers (and mothers in particular) continuously orient to an underlying normative dimension inherent in these interactions. The HV responds by first acknowledging the mother's statements (lines 2 and 5), and then significantly upgrades her response by complimenting the mother on the care of the baby: "she is beautifully cared for" (line 7). The mother then de-escalates the seriousness of her disclaimer by returning to her feelings "I just haven't got that (.) gushing loving feeling yet,". The term "gushing" invokes an earlier use of the term (Extract 4, line 12) where it was used to depict excessive feeling from a woman who was "desperate to have a baby." Here, the reuse of the term "gushing," with its connotations of excess, contributes to the sense of de-escalation, while the completion of the turn with the word "yet," and with its invocation of a possible change to come, may represent a first effort at sequence closure. The HV's response, with its explicit "(Well I think again . . .") reinvocation of the six-week period as one of adjustment, addresses both the mother's effort at closure and modulates into an optimistic projection that is tempered by a slight expansion of the time period in which bonding can expectably take place (lines 10–11):

Extract 6 [Episode 3, Part 3]

```
01   M:    I mean I'd never do anything awful to [her 'cause
02   HV:                                         [Mm
03   M:    I- I mean I care for her and look after her
04         and make sure she's clean a [nd (      )
05   HV:                                [Yes
06   M:    (      )

07   HV:   Well you do she is beautifully cared for .hh
08   M:    But I'd uh (1.5) I just haven't got that (.) gushing
09         loving feeling yet,
10   HV:   Well I think again in the next six weeks .hh you
11         will .hh eh start to get it.
12   M:    Mm
13   HV:   Um (1.0) but it may be slow to come (0.4) and I
14         think you have got to be patient [with yourself.
15   M:                                      [Mm
16   HV:   .hh I know that it is- I used to think well I've
17         handled a lot of children and and you have as well?
18   M:    Mm
19   HV:   And so ehm why I am I you know being s- sort of
20         apathetic about my own (0.4) but in fact ehm.h I
21         love him very dea:rly now that he is thirtyone hhhh
22         HUH HUH HUH HUH HUH HUH HUH
23   M:    £Promise it doesn't t(h)ak(h)e that long.£
24   HV:   HUH HUH .hh Oh no [it doesn't no .hh
25   M:                      [(Heh heh heh .hh)
26   HV:   No I w- you know between six weeks and three months
27         pt .hh I think the baby develops so much intellectually
28         you know they .hh they eh responding to you more and
29         more every day and (0.4) that process of falling in
30         love with the baby and the baby falling in love with
31         you.
32   M:    Mm
33   HV:   Through eye-to-eye contact and chatting her up a[nd
34   M:                                                    [°Mm°
35   HV:   Ehm nursing her and cuddling her (0.4) comes gradually,
```

Subsequently, the HV again shifts to her own experience as a mother (lines 16–17 and 19–22). Explicitly underscoring the similarity between her own and the mother's experience as health professionals (lines 16–17), the HV portrays her uncertainty about her own "apathy" about her child (lines 20–21). She then continues by jokingly implying that it took over thirty years before she developed real affection for her child. The mother responds to this by pleading in a "smile voice" that the HV "promise that it doesn't not take that long" (line 23). The HV's ensuing laughter (line 24) turn suggests that she appreciates the humor implicit in the mother's turn. At the same time, she shifts from a joking to a serious response by telling the mother when and how she can expect her maternal feelings to evolve (lines 26 onward). This last bit of advice is positioned from a more objective and professional stance, and can also be heard as an embedded instruction on how the mother ought to interact with her baby.

In the next and final part of Episode 3 (Extract 7), the health visitor overtly offers the most direct of her reciprocations of the mother's emotional experiences, and explicitly highlights the feelings of unnnaturalness and moral anxiety that are associated with difficulties in maternal bonding. The HV begins by upgrading her previous identification with the mother's feelings by relaying that she felt cold to her own child by comparison with other children she worked with professionally (lines 1–3). This observation reciprocates the mother's earlier assertion that she doesn't feel as if she is her baby's real mother (Extract 4, lines 23–4). The mother begins with a minimal acknowledgment (Gardner, 1997) of the HV's disclosure (line 4). Subsequently, she explicitly agrees with the HV (line 7), using an expression of confirmation ("that's right") to indicate that the experience the HV describes is a shared one. The mother goes on to express her appreciation of the HV's telling as "reassuring" (line 9)—a metacommunicative observation which incipiently undermines the mutuality of the sharing experience which the HV is undertaking, in favor of a more professionally oriented task focus. After a short silence, both women address this: the mother with a short laugh (line 11), the HV by renewing and upgrading an assertion of the genuineness of her experience (line 12).

This sets the stage for the final escalation of the HV's account (lines 13 onward) in which she describes a friend's negative reaction to her disclosure of similar feelings that the mother has disclosed to her. This sequence culminates in the acknowledgment by both women that these feelings are widely, if erroneously, regarded as unnatural and inappropriate.

Extract 7 [Episode 3, Part 4]

```
01   HV:   pt .hh But I can remember (0.8) sitting on the bed
02         cuddling him and thinking (0.8) "we:ll you know I got
03         more out of cuddling somebody else's baby sometimes,"
04   M:    Mm:
05   HV:   Mm?
06         (0.3)
07   M:    That's right.
08   HV:   Yeah?
09   M:    Oh that's alright.<That's reassuring.
10         (0.5)
11   M:    [heh heh heh
12   HV:   [No I- I mean I really did feel that .hhh and I remember
```

```
13            telling it eh- saying to somebody that I felt like this
14            and of course this was years ago when you didn't
15            discuss such th[ings you know,
16    M:                    [No that's right.
17    HV:   .hhh And this person being absolutely horrified and
18            telling me I was an unnatural mother,
19    ?:    pt
20            (0.2)
21    M:    And that made you feel even worse,
22    HV:   Oh yeah that rea:lly got me(h) hhhh w(h)ound up I c(h)an
23            t(h)ell you,
24            (0.5)
25    M:    No[:
26    HV:      [I was careful not to say it to anybody else for
27            yea:rs after that.
28            (0.8)
29    HV:   Yeah .hh but I think now it:'s all acknowledged and out
30            in the open and it is so (.hh) no:rmal to be like this
31            especially when you had ehm pt a rough time.
```

The HV begins this sequence by starting to describe how she told someone else about her feelings. At lines 14–15, she interrupts the narrative with a scene-setting generalization about the period and its social conventions, and then resumes with a general description of the friend's reaction as "absolutely horrified" and, in indirect reported speech, the explicit statement that she was an "unnatural mother" (lines 17–18). Through this narrative, the HV brings a profound level of moral (self-)condemnation to the conversational surface. And this is strongly responded to by the mother with a turn whose design is an incremental continuation to the HV's turn, and whose content ("And that made you feel even worse," line 21) is powerfully empathic in anticipating the HV's report of her reaction to the "horrified" response. The HV consolidates the mother's response with a report of a psychological reaction (being "wound up") that strongly echoes aspects of the mother's concerns, while setting them in a context of historical retrospect. This sets the scene for an exit to the sequence, which the HV accomplishes by a renewed normalization of the mother's experience, and a relativization to the historical past of the reactions she reported. Overall, this sequence involves maximal affiliation between the concerns and experiences of the two women (Jefferson, 1988).

The HV's parallel account, then, is done fully in the interests of normalizing the mother's experiences. The "horrified" external condemnation of the HV—who has passed on to a fully loving relationship with her son—is used as a resource to bond with, and reassure, a currently uncertain mother in a similar circumstance. The reported reaction that she was "an unnatural mother" is available, now contexted as an ignorant reaction from the historical past, as a resource to contrast with the HV's personal and experiential certainty that this mother's situation is not "unnatural" or even unusual. And the HV drives the moral point home further with a final coda in which she renews her earlier invocation of the period to relativize this reaction, and to normalize the mother's experience and reduce her feelings of emotional abnormality and isolation by invoking the contemporary standards in which these feelings are understood to be normal and "it:'s all acknowledged and out in the open."

DISCUSSION

In the data presented in this study, the topics of emotion and empathy emerge at several different levels. At the most basic, the mother is experiencing symptoms of depression which include dissatisfaction with her newborn, and with feelings about the inappropriateness of her reactions to her child. She describes these feelings through contrasts with how other women observably react to babies including her own, and through her description of puzzling experiences of distance in which she experiences her baby as someone else's. Just beneath the surface of these accounts is the idea that these feelings are "unnatural" when constituted within the framework of "feeling rules" (Hochschild, 1979, 1983) about how mother's should relate to and experience their babies, and commonsense knowledge which treats these feelings as fundamentally natural. The mother's conception of the inappropriateness of these feelings leads her at one point to disavow any possibility that she would "do anything awful" to her child (Extract 6, line 1). It is evident that she experiences these feelings as peculiar and difficult to interpret, and as isolating her from the common run of mothers.

At the interactional level, the mother's approach to the disclosure of her feelings about her child is complex and circuitous (Lamoureaux, 2010). At first during the second visit (Extract 1), her lack of bonding is simply presented as something that is emergent and "will come with time." Two or three weeks later, during the fourth visit, it is expressed by a withholding of assent to the health visitor's praise of how well she has coped, and to the subsequent advice that she should take things a "little bit easier" (Extract 3). Finally, her depression is acknowledged outright only when the health visitor, prompted by these withholdings and the mother's generally flat affect, asks explicitly whether she depressed (Extract 3).

If the mother's feelings are presented in terms of an experience of social and emotional isolation, many of the ordinary responses to her concerns will likely prove less than helpful. Both sympathetic responses (Jefferson, 1988), on the one hand, and optimistic reassurance based on generalizations about how things "generally work out" are likely to founder on the singularity and ineffability of the mother's situation. For the mother's feelings of singularity and isolation may render these expressions as little more than pro forma responses designed to pave the way toward the closure of an uncomfortable topic (Jefferson, 1988). Only in a context where the mother can feel that her experience is somehow shared, and therefore understood, can these expressions achieve a positive outcome.

The health visitor attempts to build empathic union with the mother across a number of the sequences that have been presented here. In Extract 1, when the mother presented herself as not fully loving her baby, the health visitor offered the parallel that "Well when I first had mi:ne I couldn't stand the sight of him?," thus beginning an effort to show an understanding of the mother's feelings. However she rapidly abandons this attempt in favor of describing the circumstances in which the mother–baby bond starts to form. In Extracts 2 and 3 she builds a connection with the mother as a fellow nurse, and counsels her against the perfectionism associated with the profession. In Extracts 5 and 6 she renews her claim to have had similar feelings of distance and alienation with her first baby. However it is only in Extract 7, when she reports describing these feelings to a third party who reacted with horror, that it becomes clear that she not only has experienced the same difficulties in bonding with her baby as the mother, but also that she has experienced the social and emotional isolation that those feelings are presently engendering in the mother. It is perhaps this double empathic union that allows the mother to feel that her circumstances have truly been understood and which lays the groundwork for the health visitor to establish a contrast between her past experience and the contemporary world in which these feelings are acknowledged as normal.

Thus, across the sequences in which the health visitor seeks to reassure and advise the mother about her situation, there is a stark contrast between those passages in which the health visitor offers generalized statements about the future course of the mother–child bond, and those in which she offers empathic parallels between the mother's situation and her own experience of similar concerns after the birth of her son. While the mother responds to the former in minimal fashion and without warmth, she responds to the latter in a full-hearted manner that registers their implications and suggests that she finds them supportive. In a context where the health visitor can function either as a "baby expert" or a "befriender" (Sefi, 1988), it is clear that the health visitor has earned the mother's confidence in the second of these roles, and that the mother benefits from the health visitor's empathic deployment of parallel experiences.

The problem of emotional bonding raised by the mother is a well-studied problem in medicine and psychology and, as we have seen, the health visitor initially tries to address it in terms of broad generalizations. After a certain point however, the health visitor is brought to empathically address the "phenomenology" of the mother's experience: her dramatic uncertainty about her feelings and her inability to project how they will alter. It is at this point that the health visitor invokes her own experience as a mother, rather than medical knowledge in general, as a resource with which to chart the likely future of this mother's relationship with her baby. As the process of sharing experience takes hold, the technical aspects of "baby expertise" that previously informed the women's interaction falls away, and the empathic understanding of the feelings associated with mothering assume a greater prominence. The mutual acknowledgment of shared difficulties in bonding with their babies and of the moral stigma associated with this problem may well have served to make this mother feel less isolated in her predicament, and more able to face the next phase in her relationship with her child. She was, we believe, reassured.

NOTE

1. Audiorecording was selected both because it was a straightforward technique for data collection to be used by the health visitors themselves and because video equipment and the additional persons who would be required to operate it would have constituted an intrusive distraction in a delicate setting. The audio record, however, has significant drawbacks. It is impossible to determine the spatial arrangement of the parties to the interaction and, on many occasions, the possibly important nonvocal activities of the parties. The significance of certain of aspects of the audio record is rendered equivocal by these lacunae. In developing our observations, we have avoided data manifesting these difficulties.

CHAPTER 13

༜

Epilogue

What Does the Study of Interaction Offer to
Emotion Research?

ANSSI PERÄKYLÄ

In this final chapter of the volume, we will elaborate on some of the results presented in the other chapters, in the light of some basic tenets of psychological, sociological, and evolutionary research on emotion. In general terms, we argue that the studies presented in this volume offer a new interactional perspective to many key phenomena of previous research on emotion.

WHAT DID WE FIND OUT IN THIS VOLUME?

Before specifying the new interactional perspective that the contributions to this volume offer to emotion research, we will try to sum up some of the key results of these contributions by reference to the questions that this volume set out to examine. Only some features of the rich contributions can be highlighted here.

Question 1: *How are emotional stances expressed and displayed verbally and nonverbally in social interaction?*

The collection demonstrates the need for taking into account the holistic character of expressing emotional stance. While all contributions to this volume enrich our understanding of the verbal and nonverbal means of conveying emotion in social interaction, the chapters dealing with prosody perhaps stand out as particularly rich and original. These chapters show specific prosodic patterns conveying emotion in particular social actions such as refusals (Goodwin and her colleagues, chapter 2), delivery of good or bad news (Maynard and Freese, chapter 5) or complaint stories (Couper-Kuhlen, chapter 6), as well as in relation to crying (Hepburn and Potter, chapter 9) and (fake) laughter (Haakana, chapter 8). Several chapters also show ways in which the prosodic displays of different speakers in action sequences are coordinated (through matching or upgrading), to create scenes of affiliation or empathy—or the lack of them. Regarding nonvocal means of emotional expression, some context-specific uses of facial expressions (Peräkylä and Ruusuvuori, chapter 4; Heath and his colleagues, chapter 10; Goodwin and her colleagues, chapter 2) were explored; these studies show how classical "basic emotion" expressions (see below), as well as more complex expressions, are put in interactional use. The relative alignment of bodies of participants in interaction, conveying stance toward the other or toward a proposed course of action, were examined by Goodwin and her colleagues. As for verbal means of expression of emotion, contributions to our understanding of response cries (cf. Goffman, 1978) deserve specific mentioning: we learned about the ways in which response cries in response to storytelling can convey affiliation, but need subsequent "verbal reinforcement" to fully accomplish it (Couper-Kuhlen, chapter 6), and about the uses of a particular type of response cry capable of conveying ambiguous emotional stance (Hakulinen and Sorjonen, chapter 7).

Question 2: *How does the expression of emotional stance contribute to the organization of action sequences?*
The contributions to the collection show that rather than being a contingent feature of interaction that occasionally occurs along with otherwise nonemotional actions, emotion is pervasively present in social action, oriented to and managed by the participants. The observations presented in many contributions are tied to particular actions and/or activities. The chapters do not address expressions of emotion "in general," but they show how displays of emotion emerge as integral parts of the organization of particular social actions. The actions involve for example responses to requests (Wootton, chapter 3) and directives (Goodwin and her colleagues, chapter 2) in adult–child interaction, as well as telling of stories or news (Couper-Kuhlen, chapter 6; Maynard and Freese, chapter 5; Peräkylä and Ruusuvuori, chapter 4) in interactions between adults. In some cases, we might suggest that emotion displays contribute to the very formation and recognition of the particular actions (cf. Schegloff, 2007, pp. 7–12), rather than being a contingent element in them: for example, a complaint story is hardly conceivable without emotion displays. The relation between emotion and action is articulated in a somewhat different way in contributions by Hepburn and Potter (chapter 9), and Heath and his colleagues (chapter 10): in these two chapters, a distinct display of emotion (crying or display of surprise) in itself constitutes a first action which makes relevant a particular second action by the coparticipant: a display of sympathy or empathy in response to crying, or attending to the surprisable object in response to a display of surprise. In these cases, arguably, the display of emotion is not only a constitutive *part* of an action, but rather, it is itself the action that makes a response relevant.

Question 3: *How is emotion regulated and managed in institutional encounters?*
The collection enhances understanding of variation in the institutional regulation of emotion in modern society. It shows institutionally facilitated as well as restricted ways of expressing and responding to emotion and elucidates the participants' asymmetric

obligations and rights in this. The contributions take up four specific institutional settings: helpline calls (Hepburn and Potter, chapter 9), art gallery (Heath and his colleagues, chapter 10), psychotherapy (Voutilainen, chapter 11), and health visiting with mothers of newborn babies (Heritage and Lindström, chapter 12). The institutional ramifications for the management of emotion in these settings are rather different: while in helpline calls, management of the caller's distress (manifested for example through crying) is a major task of the call-takers; in psychotherapy, professional empathizing with the client's emotion is counterbalanced by professional responses that seek to interpret and even challenge the client's emotional experience. Arguably, the objects in the art gallery are designed and displayed to afford emotional responses such as the ones described in chapter 10 by Heath and his colleagues. Finally, in the case of health visiting analyzed by Heritage and Lindström (chapter 12), the fact that the client felt that she did not have appropriate emotions became a key issue that the professional sought to deal with, eventually through reciprocal self-disclosures. There is still a way to go before microinteractional research can reach generalizations regarding the management of emotion in institutional settings, comparable to the generalizations that have been reached for example in comparative research on turn-taking or task orientation in institutional settings (see Drew & Heritage, 1992b; Heritage & Clayman, 2010; for a more general sociological view on emotions in organizations, see Sieben & Wettegren, 2010). In pursuing that direction, comparisons between the shape and the interactional management of specific emotional displays in institutional and noninstitutional settings will possibly prove to be of great importance—an avenue of analysis started in chapter 9 by Hepburn and Potter.

Question 4: *How does research on emotion contribute to existing theories regarding language and social interaction?*

All contributions to this collection demonstrate that rather than being a secondary function of language, affective and emotional meaning is central for understanding the use of language in social interaction. The chapters show that emotion is constructed and interpreted by reference to specific sequential positions in interaction, through the concomitant use of different kinds of resources. The importance of the sequential organization of action in interpreting the affectivity and affiliative character of verbal language is shown for example in the examination of an affectively "open" response type (Hakulinen and Sorjonen, chapter 7) and of the impact of a subsequent verbal reinforcement on the affiliative strength of response cries and sound objects (Couper-Kuhlen, chapter 6). The need to take into account the vocal displays of affect and affiliation in investigating verbal displays is shown in several chapters of the volume (Goodwin and her colleagues, chapter 2; Maynard and Freese, chapter 5; Couper-Kuhlen, chapter 6). In chapter 6 on affiliative and nonaffiliative responses to complaint stories, Couper-Kuhlen shows that while these two types of responses are typically fitted or nonfitted both verbally and prosodically to the teller's prior talk, the picture is not so simple: in the case of verbally ambivalent response the role of prosody is central, while some verbal responses come off as affiliative without prosodic matching or upgrading of the teller's talk typical for affiliative responses. Findings of this type lay the ground for the investigation of the relation between verbal and vocal displays of emotion. Another kind of fine line between verbal and vocal resources is brought up by Haakana in chapter 8, on "fake" laughter, also called by the author "lexicalized laughter," to indicate that the laugh tokens are articulated more or less as lexical elements. A central relevance of analyzing nonvocal conduct, for the expression of emotion and for understanding the affective import of verbal expressions in face-to-face encounters, is shown in the chapters of the volume from the point of body posture, facial expressions, and gaze (Goodwin and colleagues, chapter 2; Heath and colleagues, chapter 10; Peräkylä and Ruusuvuori, chapter 4; Wootton, chapter 3).

Each chapter in its own way contributes to a better understanding and a more focused exploration of emotion in conversation analysis and other lines of interactionally oriented research: these studies make visible various facets of the participants' perhaps ubiquitous orientation to each other's emotional state in social encounters. To understand the importance of this orientation, Tomasello's (2008) recent outline of the three basic "communicative motives" in humans is helpful. Based on developmental and evolutionary research, Tomasello suggests that human communication is driven by motivations of *requesting*, *informing*, and *sharing*. Much of classical and current microinteractional research has dealt with actions falling under the first two motives: "requesting" motivation encompassing all ways in which interactants make each other do something, and "informing" motivation encompassing ways in which they tell each other things about the world and themselves, and in so doing, orient to each other's epistemic positions and statuses. Sharing, for Tomasello, involves "I want you to feel something so that we can *share attitudes / feelings together*" (2008, p. 87, italics in original). The studies presented in this volume have demonstrated the viability of the realm of phenomena pertaining to this third communicative motivation as a topic for research on language and social interaction.

Now that we have highlighted some of the research results presented in this collection, it is time to turn to the discussion on the wider implications of these results.

IMPLICATIONS FOR RESEARCH ON EMOTION IN INDIVIDUALS

This book offers a selection of state-of-the-art studies specifying ways in which humans in interaction display emotions, how they understand and respond to each other's emotional displays, and how these displays arise from, and contribute to, the actions that they are involved in. To contextualize the results of these studies, we will outline some key features of the study of emotion in psychology, sociology, and evolutionary theory, where emotion has become a major research field during the past two decades. However, we do not have any unified social-psychological theory of emotion. What we do have instead are various, partially overlapping and partially conflicting, conceptualizations of emotional phenomena. In what follows, we will outline some of these conceptualizations, foregrounding those for which the studies of this book have implications. We will start from psychological theories dealing with emotions in individuals.

A rather widely accepted psychological view considers emotions as consisting of two dimensions: valence and arousal (Larsen & Diener, 1992). "Valence" refers to the basic quality of the emotion, that is, whether it is positive or negative (pleasant or unpleasant). "Arousal," on the other hand, refers to the intensity of the emotion on a scale between strong and weak. Positive and negative emotions can involve either a strong or weak arousal component. However, valence and arousal are not unrelated: extremely positive or extremely negative emotions tend to be intensive as well. In cognitive neuroscience and related research, the valence and arousal components of emotion have been shown to be organized differently in the human body: valence is related for example to the lateralization of the brain (see Harmon-Jones, 2003), while arousal is associated with the activation of the autonomous nervous system.

The breaking-down of emotions into components of valence and arousal arises from the investigation of individual experience and psychophysiology. Therefore, one might think that the distinction is not relevant in the study of social interaction. However, phenomena related to valence and arousal come up in the study of emotion in interaction: chapters in this volume show that in displaying and negotiating their emotional stances, participants to interaction orient to both the valence and the intensity of their displays. Thus, Maynard and Freese show in chapter 5 that it is an interactional task of the teller and the recipient of the news to establish, in real time, the valence of the events-in-the-world that they report as *good* or *bad*. This involves, as they put it, "collaborative, concerted action and interaction." As explicated in their chapter, the prosodic features of the delivery and the response are among key resources in this coconstruction. In interaction, valence of emotion can also be left unspecified—but as Hakulinen and Sorjonen show in chapter 7, this equivocality is in itself an interactional achievement. They examine a particular response cry in Finnish, *voi että*, which is apt for dealing with ambiguity of emotional valence.

Arousal—the intensity of emotion displays—is also oriented to by the participants. Chapters 4 and 6, by Peräkylä and Ruusuvuori, and by Couper-Kuhlen, among others, show cases where the intensity of the emotional display by a recipient of a story or announcement is treated as insufficient, as indexed by the efforts of the first speaker to elicit a stronger response from the recipient. In these cases, the participants are interactionally alive to the question of the (sufficiency of the) intensity of the display. In sum, studies in this volume suggest that participants in interaction monitor the valence of each other's emotional displays and the degree of arousal involved in them. Perhaps in most cases, this monitoring secures a relative attunement in emotional displays.

Alongside the conceptualization of the dimensions of emotion, another rather widely accepted (but not uncontested) distinction in psychological emotion research is the one between *basic emotions* and other emotional phenomena. Basic emotions are thought be recognizable across cultures. They consist of rather short-lived experiences, and they involve distinct physiological and experiential features, as well as specific facial expression. Basic emotions include joy, sorrow, fear, anger, surprise, and disgust (Matsumoto & Ekman, 2009). Basic emotions are thought to be evolutionarily continuous and grounded on "fundamental and universal adaptive mechanisms based on affect programmes" (Scherer, 2009). Other emotional phenomena—variously referred to as "secondary," "tertiary," or "social" emotions—involve more complex emotions, which may be blends of the basic emotions, and which are often anchored to culture-specific norms and rules. Social emotions, for example, are said to include shame, embarrasment, jealousy, admiration, guilt, gratitude, *schadenfreude*, and pity (Hareli & Parkinson, 2009).

Judging from the existing interaction research on emotions, including the chapters of this volume, pure forms of basic emotions are not very often found in naturally occurring interaction. Instead, what we encounter are blended and complex expressions. The chapters in this collection conceptualize their target emotions in rather various ways—reflecting the variability and complexity of naturally occurring emotional phenomena. Coming perhaps closest to basic emotions are the contributions by Goodwin and her colleagues (chapter 2), and Heath and his colleagues (chapter 10). The opening section of the former deals with displays of disgust, while the latter focuses on surprise as interactionally occasioned event. Both chapters show clearly the similarities between the facial expression they examine and the paradigmatic facial expressions of disgust and surprise, respectively, explicated by Darwin (1872/1998) and Ekman and Friesen (1975/2003). However, the authors also point out their difference from the "basic emotion" concept. Heath and colleagues emphasize that the expression of surprise in their data does not take place on its own, but intertwines with other emotions (such as awe and enjoyment). Goodwin and colleagues, on the other hand, approach the display of disgust not as an expression of the inner state of the individual (an avenue taken in the basic-emotions line of research), but as a multimodal practice that locates its target in the local geography of the interaction, and encompasses not only face but posture, prosody, and lexis as well. As for the rest of the chapters in this volume, they deal with complex emotional expressions (such as distressed behavior analyzed by Wootton, fake laughter analyzed by Haakana, or indignation analyzed by Couper-Kuhlen) and/or specific ineractional ramifications that accompany displays of various emotions. These expressions involve seemingly endless variation and mixture of emotion. The collection suggests that in everyday encounters the participants do most of their emotion work with these variable and blended emotions.

In everyday parlance, emotion is often used more or less as a synonym for *feeling*. Emotion is then understood as a subjective experience, something that the subject is aware of. Psychological conceptualization goes, however, beyond mere subjective awareness of feeling. Emotion is also understood to involve other facets, including *physiological*, *cognitive*, and *expressive* processes, as well as *action tendencies* (Scherer, 1996, p. 284). Much of the psychological theorizing on emotions has involved debate on the relations between these facets. We will review each facet, showing linkages to the contributions of the current collection—starting with the facets that are most directly linked to social interaction.

Expression is the facet of emotion that the contributions of this collection are most intimately linked to. The expressive aspects of emotion are understood as involving facial, vocal or other practices which embody, and/or convey to the environment, the emotional state of the subject. Charles Darwin's *The expression of emotion in man and animals* (1872/1998) is a classic of the field, suggesting among other things that some key emotions are associated with biologically rooted, universal facial expression in humans, and that these expressions have evolutionary precedents in other species. The most influential follower of this line of research is Paul Ekman, whose studies have offered empirical evidence for the universality of the facial expressions of joy, sadness, anger, astonishment, and fear, and who has also suggested that the facial expression of emotion is regulated by culture-specific display rules (Ekman & Friesen, 1969). The vocal expression of emotion is of no less importance. Psychological research on vocal expression of emotion has during the past decades specified the acoustic patterns that subjects in experimental settings associate with different emotions, and showed differences in the accuracy of acoustically based emotion recognition (e.g., showing that sadness and anger are recognized more accurately than disgust and joy) (see Scherer, 2003; Goudbeek & Scherer, 2009).

In most psychological research, expressive behaviors are understood as readouts of the subject's underlying emotional state. However, Darwin was the first to bring to attention the other side of the coin, by pointing out that the expressions are also in the service of social interaction. Expression of anger, for example, regulates social interaction, and it may be more beneficial for the animal or human subject to display readiness to fight through anger expression than to get engaged in fight itself, as the fight may have grave physical and social consequences (see Chevalier-Skolnikoff, 1973/2003, p. 28). Such interaction-centered understanding of facial expression has been further developed by Fridlund (1994), whose "behavioral ecology view" suggests that facial displays are social signals, communicating behavioral intentions or social motives, and that they do not necessarily have linkages to underlying psychosomatic affective states. Another articulation of the relation between expression and underlying affective state has been proposed in the so-called "facial feedback hypothesis," according to which emotion expression (particularly face) can enhance or create feeling states as well as physiological responses associated with emotion (see Kappas, 2008). If we intentionally smile—even if we hold a pencil in our mouth in a traverse position which forces a kind of smiling expression to our face—we get happier.

This collection is very much about the social organization of expression of emotion: the vocal (see, for example, the chapters by Couper-Kuhlen, Goodwin and colleagues, Hepburn and Potter, Maynard and Freese, and Haakana) and facial expressions (see for example, the chapters by Goodwin and colleagues, Heath and colleagues, and Peräkylä and Ruusuvuori), as well as body postures (Goodwin and colleagues). Alongside these modalities of emotion expression, the chapters of this collection also examine the rich grammatical (lexicosyntactic) resources that participants to interaction use in displaying their emotions (see especially the chapters by Couper-Kuhlen, and Hakulinen and Sorjonen)—something that most psychological theories of emotion only touch upon or do not deal with at all. In all contributions, the vocal or visual emotion displays are examined in the context of the unfolding of the verbal content of the utterances in question. The contributions suggest, therefore, that in everyday interactions, display and recognition of emotion are the result of the simultaneous use of various resources of expression which, as Goodwin and her colleagues (chapter 2) put it, "mutually elaborate each other." In investigating emotional expressions as communicative moves (see also Bavelas & Chovil, 2000) that arise from and contribute to the moment-by-moment unfolding of interactive situations, the contributions in the volume resonate with the interaction-centered understanding of expressions, put forward (in the context of facial expressions) by Fridlund (1994). The contributions enrich this line of research by explicating the communicative uses of emotional expressions in the matrix of the sequential organization of actions and activities, be they news deliveries, complaint stories, parental directives, and so on.

Even though this collection focuses on expression, the findings of the chapters speak also to other facets of emotion. One of them involves action tendencies. In the psychology of emotions, action tendencies refer to the human (or animal) disposition to act when in an emotional state. Motivation for action is a key component of emotion (Frijda, 2004). A typical action tendency is to fight when angry, and to run away when afraid. According to appraisal theorists (see below), the action tendency arises from an evaluation of the situation that the subject is in: it involves physiological and psychological preparedness to execute a particular action as a way to cope with the situation (see Zhu & Thagard, 2002). The studies in this collection elucidate the association between emotion and action from a particular point of view. Rather than discussing tendencies to act that would be inherently associated with particular emotions or emotional appraisals, the contributions to this collection show interactionally constructed trajectories of action, in the production of which emotion plays a central part. Just to give one example, Maynard and Freese (chapter 5) show how the delivery and reception of news involve emotion displays through prosody and lexical choice (word selection). Thus, the contributions to this collection do not approach action as a tendency that arises from the emotion. Instead, they approach action and emotion as inherently intertwined, showing trajectories of action the production of which at least customarily, if not necessarily, involves an interplay of emotion displays by the participants of the action.

The cognitive aspects of emotion involve what is commonly called "appraisal." Appraisal theories (Ellsworth & Scherer, 2003; Scherer, 2004) suggest that we evaluate our environment in terms of the significance of its objects and events for our goals, concerns, or wellbeing. Objects or events that have positive or negative consequences for us arouse (positive or negative) emotional responses in us (physiological responses as well as subjective feelings). Food or a caring partner incites positive emotions, whereas a threatening mob in a dark street incites fear. The central methodology used in the studies in this volume, conversation analysis, is not geared to describe cognitive processes, and the place of cognition in understanding interaction is indeed subject to debate (see e.g., Potter, 2006; Levinson, 2006a). The contributions to this volume do, however, speak also to the conceptualizations of emotion that foreground the appraisal processes. This is done perhaps most saliently by Wootton (chapter 3), who in his chapter shows how a child of two to three years produces strongly distressed emotional responses in situations where her parents breach the child's expectations or understandings regarding an upcoming course of joint actions—expectations that the participants established a moment before in their interaction. The findings of Wootton suggest a specification of the general tenets of appraisal theory: he showed that the child he was studying evaluated her immediate interactional environment, not only in terms of its affordances to her individual goals and concerns (for example by getting distressed in response to parental rejections of requests), but also in terms of the match between the actual courses of action and the locally established expectations. In a rather different way, the findings of Peräkylä and Ruusuvuori (chapter 4) are also linked to appraisal processes. They show how the evaluation of conversational objects brought about through tellings proceeds moment by moment, the tellers sometimes revising the initial evaluation through their facial expressions after the completion of the tellings.

Not all the facets of emotion described in psychological literature are directly addressed by the studies in this volume. These include the physiological aspects of emotion and the subjective experience of emotion. Over a hundred years ago, William James and Carl Lange pointed out the importance of physiology of emotion (see Dalgleish, 2009). They maintained that psychophysiological reactions in the body that are associated with emotion—such as cardiovascular activity, blood flow, respiration, temperature, muscle tension—are not the consequence of subjective emotional experience, but instead, these physiological events are direct responses to perception of an arousing stimulus in the environment (such as a meeting a bear in a forest, see James, 1884) and therefore precede the subjective experience of the emotion. While the physiology of emotion remains a topic of intensive experimental research (see e.g., Bradley & Lang, 2007), in the collection at hand, physiological aspects of emotion are not directly addressed. Observational methods based on video and audio recording (used by all authors of the collection) give access to the public display of emotion, not the physiological processes. This does not mean, however, that the phenomena described in these studies are completely separate from the physiological aspects of emotion. Earlier research shows that vocal and facial expression of emotion is linked to physiological processes in the body: not only in the sense that physiological changes result in changes in expression (see e.g., Scherer, 1989), but also the other way round: that changes in expression may result in physiological changes in the body (see e.g., Kappas, 2008). This suggests that there is a linkage between the phenomena explored in this volume—the organization of the interactional expression of emotion—and psychophysiological processes, but their explication must be left to future studies. (For an effort in this direction, see Peräkylä, Voutilainen, Henttonen, Ravaja, & Sams, 2010).

Another facet of emotion not directly addressed in the studies presented in this volume involves the subjective experience of emotion. Since James and Lange, the place of subjective experience in emotion has been contested. Much of the current psychology of emotions plays down rather than emphasizes the importance of experience in emotions. To a large extent processes related to emotions are automated and nonconscious. Experimental research has repeatedly shown that the evaluation of the objects and events in our environment, as well as the corresponding physiological changes and even actions, initially take place outside our consciousness (Zajonc, 1980; Nummenmaa, 2010, pp. 39–55). Despite its potentially great subjective significance, the experience of emotion can thus be considered a secondary stage in the emotion process. This de-emphasis of conscious experience in emotion research resonates with some of the theoretical tenets of conversation analysis, which is the methodology informing the studies of this collection: this method has traditionally emphasized the nonconscious or automated character of the choices of action that participants in interaction are involved in (see e.g., Sacks, 1992, vol. 1, p. 11), remaining "agnostic" regarding the actors' possible underlying experiences (Heritage, 1984a). Accordingly, the analytical focus of the studies presented is on the fine social organization of emotion displays, not on the accompanying experiences. However, the thoroughly interactional character of the phenomena examined in this collection adds another twist to the question of subjective experience in emotion. Throughout the contributions to this volume, the ways in which the interactants relate to *each other's* emotional states are in focus. So, in the studies of this volume, we are not addressing individual subjects' experiences of their *own* emotions, but rather, the subjects' possible experiences of the *other's* emotion. All contributions to this volume document interactions in which the visual, vocal, and verbal actions of the participants show their orientation to the other's emotional state, as indicated in this other's expressions. We cannot say whether, or to what extent, these orientations involve reading the subjective emotional experience of the other, but we can safely say that they involve reading of the other's actions as involving emotion.[1] Therefore, the question of significance of the experience of emotion becomes rearticulated in the context of intersubjectivity—but further answers must await future studies.

During the recent decade or two, much psychological research has revolved around the regulation of emotion (see e.g., Gross, 2007; Vandekerckhove, von Scheve, Ismer, Jung, & Kronast, 2008). In psychology, regulation of emotions is conceived as an individual competence, and as "the process by which individuals influence which emotions they have, when they have them, and how they experience and express these emotions" (Gross, 1998, p. 275). According to Gross and Thompson (2007, pp. 10–16) emotion regulation strategies involve the selection and modification of the situation that might arouse emotion, deployment of attention in a given situation, changes in the ways in which the situation is appraised, and modulation of the physiological, experiential, or behavioral response to the situation. The capacity of emotion regulation evolves through the maturation process of the individual (e.g., Thompson & Meyer, 2007).

The chapters in this collection offer a distinct perspective to regulation of emotion. Rather than considering the regulation as an individual capacity or as a process within an individual, the papers in this collection show naturally occurring interactive processes in which participants, in and through their interaction, create and regulate (and sometimes fail to regulate) each other's emotions. For example, Heath and his colleagues (chapter 10) show instances in which visitors to art galleries and museums direct their covisitors' attention to emotionally relevant objects and thus, sometimes successfully and sometimes less so, create situations where surprise or other emotional reaction is relevant. Likewise, Couper-Kuhlen (chapter 6) shows processes in which storytellers elicit (and again, sometimes fail to elicit) affiliative responses from their recipients. In their contribution (chapter 4), Peräkylä and Ruusuvuori suggest that there exists a parallel between individual regulation of emotion and the processes of interactional regulation: the former being anchored in the latter, both developmentally and as a real-time process.

IMPLICATIONS FOR RESEARCH ON EMOTIONS AS SOCIAL PROCESSES

Above, we have contextualized the contributions of this volume to existing research on emotion as a process within individuals. Emotion is, however, equally a social process; and the social, rather than individual, aspects of emotion are indeed closer to this volume. In what follows, some facets of social psychology and the sociology of emotions will be explored, again in order to contextualize the contribution of this volume.

At its ontogenetic beginning, early in individual life, social interaction is suffused by emotion.[2] During the first year of life, before acquiring language, an infant's vocalizations and other expressions serve as powerful means in conveying emotion: think of a crying baby or of a smiling and laughing infant. In their responses to infants' expressions, caretakers orient to the emotion import of these expressions. For example, by matching or mirroring the prosodic features of the infant's expressions, as well as her facial expressions and movements, the caretakers are understood to recognize and regulate the infant's emotional states (see Stern, 1985; Papoušek & Papoušek, 1989; Fonagy, Gergely, Jurist, & Target, 2002, pp. 154–9). Thus, arguably, early in human life, social interaction is there for the regulation of emotion. The continuities and discontinuities between emotional interaction in early interaction and in adulthood wait to be specified (Kahri, in preparation). Among the contributions to this volume, matching of expressions in adult interaction is addressed explicitly in chapter 6 by Couper-Kuhlen, who shows prosodic matching between the delivery and the empathic reception of complaint stories—a practice originating in the preverbal interactions between infants and caretakers. Contributions by Wootton (chapter 3), and Goodwin and her colleagues (chapter 2), offer two glimpses from emotional interaction at different junctures along the developmental path. Wootton shows distressed interactions between a two- to three-year-old child and her parents, and Goodwin and others show emotional responses to parents' directives in children aged four to ten.

Emotional contagion is a social process involving the human tendency to catch the emotions that others are experiencing. Already in the eighteenth century, philosopher Adam Smith suggested that mimicking the other's expressive behavior is a key mediator of emotional contagion. The contemporary view sees emotional contagion as "the tendency to automatically mimic and synchronise expressions, vocalisations, postures and movements with those of another person's and, consequently, to converge emotionally" (Hatfield, Cacioppo, & Rapson, 1993a, p. 96). There is a rich tradition of experimental research tracing aspects of this mimicry in facial expressions, prosody, and body movements (Hatfield, Cacioppo, & Rapson, 1993b). Recently, the neural basis of emotional contagion has been explored, especially in studies on mirror-neuron systems (Iacoboni, 2008). The theory of emotional contagion suggests that behavioral mimicry affects the emotional experience of the person who is mimicking the other (Hatfield, Cacioppo, & Rapson, 1993a, pp. 97–8), and thereby the subjects end up sharing an emotion. The evolutionary origins of emotional contagion are thought to be in the benefits that rapid adoption of others' emotions brings to an individual for example in situations of sudden danger, such as a predator attack (see e.g., Nummenmaa, 2010, p. 145). Emotional contagion is also a key mechanism in group formation: being part of group often involves sharing the emotions of the other group members (Collins, 2004; Sy Sy, Côté, & Saavedra, 2005).

Processes parallel to emotional contagion are dealt with in several contributions to this volume. Perhaps most directly, contagious processes were observed by

Couper-Kuhlen, and Maynard and Freese, in their respective studies on complaint stories and news deliveries: the recipients of stories of news tend to adopt key features of the vocal expressive behaviors of the tellers, and in consequence, a shared emotion is achieved. Importantly, however, the emotional contagion observed in these studies was regulated by the sequential organization of interaction: the recipients of complaint stories and news deliveries produced their emotional responses largely at the completion of the news delivery or narrative, rather than immediately after the tellers' emotional displays. The studies in this volume also show instances of limits to straightforward emotional contagion. Perhaps expectedly, the negative emotional displays of children studied by Wootton, and Goodwin and her colleagues are not directly reciprocated by their parents, but dealt with and regulated by responses that are emotional but do not involve direct sharing of the child's emotion. Heath and his colleagues offer an intriguing case that specifies a process of contagion, in their study on the organization of surprise at unexpected features in the environment. First, they show that the vocal, facial, and postural expression of surprise is "sensitive to the presence and conduct of others," "designed to encourage . . . the coparticipant to discover . . . the surprisable" (p. 231). What they examine, thus, is not an individual emotion that is then caught by a coparticipant, but it is an emotion that from the outset is designed to be attended to by the others present. On the other hand, Heath and his colleagues show that, in the case of surprise, what the other party actually catches is not quite the same emotion that the first party has displayed: the recipient typically does not reproduce the surprise but turns his or her attention to the surprisable, and in so doing legitimates the first party's surprise, and possibly shares the "secondary" emotion, such as amusement, accompanying the surprise. Thus, the studies presented in this volume suggest that the process of emotional contagion in naturally occurring interaction can be much more complex than a straightforward spreading of a given emotion from one subject to another.

What Arlie Hochschild (1979, 1983) calls "emotion work" is an aspect of social processes pertaining to emotion. Emotion work involves the individuals making their emotions comply with the norms and expectations ("feeling rules") of their society, by evoking, shaping, or suppressing their feelings (Hochschild, 1979, p. 561). Individuals control not only their emotional expressions, but also their physiological state (e.g., by trying to calm themselves down through breathing exercises), as well as the very experience of emotion. Different social positions (class, profession) entail different feeling rules and corresponding emotion work; Hochschild's work on the emotion work of flight attendants, evoking positive emotions (Hochschild 1983), is particularly illustrative.

In a way, all contributions to this volume illustrate practices of emotion work. As Maynard and Freese point out (chapter 5), their study explicates the moment-by-moment interactional processes, the end result of which is an emotional display that complies with the feeling rules relevant to the situation. The same also applies to other studies in the volume. When it comes to the forms of emotion work that are tied to particular social positions, chapters 11 and 12, by Voutilainen, and Heritage and Lindström, are of particular importance, as they show practices by two types of professional (psychotherapist and health visitor) that work with their clients' emotional experience. Emotional labor in these cases involves different forms of empathy. Heritage and Lindström's chapter also brings to the foreground the normative aspects of emotional labor, as they present a case study of professional–client interaction in which the client's primary problem is her lack of maternal feelings, which she considers "unnatural." By showing the interactional practices involved in emotion work in everyday or professional settings, the studies of this volume also offer a specification of the concept of emotion work: they illustrate that feeling rules of society do not influence individuals directly but rather in and through the interactional practices through which the emotional displays are shaped moment by moment.

Social constructionism is a multifaceted methodological and theoretical approach to the study of social and psychological phenomena (see e.g., Berger & Luckmann, 1966; Potter & Wetherell, 1987), with important implications for the study of emotions (see Sandlund, 2004, pp. 65–70). There are many variants of constructionism; for the study of emotion, discursive psychology (Edwards, 2005; Potter, 2006) is of particular importance. A central tenet in social constructionist (or discursive psychological) investigation of emotion is to call into question the distinction between the inner experience and the outer expression. Constructionists point out that in lay thinking, as well as in much psychological and sociological theorizing, emotions are understood as primarily inner processes which have consequences for outer expressions. In contrast, constructionist theorizing of emotions considers them as thoroughly public phenomena: something that is constructed, and oriented to, in interaction (Potter, 2006, p. 132). Emotions are done, they are public actions (Gergen, 1999). Moreover, references to emotions are a powerful resource in accounting for actions, and they are also accounted for in discourse (Coulter, 1989; Edwards, 1997); it is the task of social scientists to explicate these accounting practices. Whether emotions as constructions have something to do with the inner experiences of psychophysiological processes or not is something about which constructionist researchers remain (at best) agnostic.

The chapters of this volume resonate with and differently contribute to the constructionist study of emotion. Maynard and Freese explicate their indebtedness to constructionist thinking. Their chapter lays out practices through which emotions are done though public actions in social interaction. In a particular way, Haakana's chapter on "fake laughter" addresses the constructionist critique regarding the distinction between inner and the outer aspects of emotion. Fake laughter involves sounds that are conventionally associated with laughter, produced "in a way that makes it clear that the laughter is not to be interpreted as being 'real'" (p. 176). As Haakana shows, through fake laughter, speakers show that an emotion display would be relevant at that point in interaction (for example, after a joke or in a delicate situation), but they distance themselves from that very emotion. One might say that fake laughter is a practice in which interactants make use of the lay distinction between "inner experience" and "outer expression": they produce a display of emotion that is observably not indicative of the inner state usually associated to similar kinds of displays.

It may very well be that the interactants in chapters other than Haakana's treated each other's expressions in the "lay" way, as expressions of an inner emotional state. In other words, they possibly treated each other's lexical choices, prosody, facial expressions, and the like as indicative of an "inner" emotion. Regardless of whether or not we as researchers share that distinction, the evidence put forward in the chapters of this volume demonstrates that these displays were methodologically produced, employing intersubjectively valid means of expression, occurring in circumscribed sequential locations, and having definite sequential consequences.

While the constructionist view methodologically brackets the inner dimension of emotion and focuses solely on the public displays, there are other conceptual formulations that seek to integrate the inner and the outer in ways that still allow for the thoroughly social and methodic character of emotion displays. As Peräkylä and Ruusuvuori suggest in chapter 4, one such avenue arises from recent infant–caretaker interaction research, where researchers have suggested that there is an intimate connection between what they call "self-regulation of emotion" and the interaction regulation (Beebe & Lachmann, 2002, p. 22). According to this view, the same behaviors that entail interactional emotion displays, also serve for self-regulation, and for that reason, interactional regulation and self-regulation comprise a system. Another conceptual formulation comes from a quite different direction and seeks to eradicate the distinction between the outer and the inner. Such a position is explicated in the phenomenological philosophy. The radically intersubjectivist philosophy of Merleau-Ponty (1964a, 1964b; Zahavi, 2011) suggests that our emotions exist in our face and in our gestures, and are "not hidden behind them" (Zahavi, 2011, p. 4). This does not mean to deny the reality of the subjective experience of emotions, but to maintain that experience and expression are one, and that the experience is accessible to the other in the expression (and not through inferences based on the expression). A comparable position was taken by American pragmatist philosophers as discussed in chapter 5 by Maynard and Freese (see also Emirbayer & Maynard, 2011): pragmatists such as Dewey and James sought to "avoid the bifurcation of internal and external or mind and body and instead to convey the seamlessness of affective experience and the displays by which it is realized for coparticipants" (p. 110).

To sum up, the chapters in this volume explicate processes of doing or constructing emotions, and thereby contribute to the constructionist research program on emotions. Yet on the other hand, some of the chapters seek to find new, we might say "postconstructionist," ways of conceptualizing the experiential and expressive, or inner and outer, aspects of emotion. This reconceptualization is in its infancy and calls for future work.

IMPLICATIONS FOR RESEARCH ON EMOTIONS AND EVOLUTIONARY PROCESSES

The evolutionary perspective seeks to describe and categorize emotions in terms of the evolutionary processes that brought them into existence. The evolutionary understanding of emotion was recently encapsulated by Nesse (2009a, p. 160): "Emotions are specialized states, shaped in natural selection, that adjust many aspects of an individual in ways that increase the ability to succeed in situations that have posed consistent adaptive challenges over evolutionary time." Thus, emotions are there because the physiological changes, expressions, action tendencies, and other aspects of particular emotions have been helpful in dealing with particular recurrent situations that our ancestors have faced. Or, in Nesse's words, "[e]motions exist because they offered advantages in situations that recurrently influenced survival and reproduction over evolutionary time" (Nesse 2009a, p. 160).

Turner (2000; see also Turner & Stets, 2005, pp. 261–83) has suggested a particular sociological reading of what some of the demands of recurrent situations might have been in the evolutionary time when the emotional dispositions of humans were formed. The point of departure for Turner's argument is an empirically grounded assumption that the emotional repertoire of humans is more varied than that of other animals: apart from the evolutionarily continuous basic emotions, humans are disposed to a wide variety of blended and complex emotions which they learn through socialization. Turner suggests that the inclination to these varied emotions has enhanced social bonds between individuals. Thus, for example, guilt and shame enhance self-monitoring and corrective behaviors in individuals and thereby link them to the social group, while gratitude and pride enhance bonding in a positive way. The expansion of the emotional repertoire in our ancestors went hand in hand with the evolution of the ability to attune to and read the other's emotional responses (cf. Enfield & Levinson, 2006), which also, according to Turner, enabled the individual's capacity to "develop stronger, more nuanced, and more flexible bonds of social solidarity" (Turner & Stets, 2005, p. 270).

The contributions to this volume focus on the interactional "mechanisms" of emotions, rather than trying to explain how these mechanisms came into being in evolution, or how they serve the fitness of individuals (cf. Tinbergen, 1963; Nesse, 2009b). Focusing on mechanisms (rather than on their origins) is indeed the standard methodological choice in conversation analysis, interactional linguistics, and related fields on which the studies of this collection are based (see however the recent work by Enfield and Levinson, 2006). The current studies are not, however, irrelevant regarding evolutionary perspectives on emotion. They specify the phenomena (or in Tinbergen's [1963] terms, the mechanisms) the evolutionary origins of which need to be explained.

The discussion in this chapter has sought to explicate some of the ways in which the contributions to this volume have specified the existing understanding of interactional mechanisms of emotion. Thus, the contributions have described naturally occurring emotions that are not primarily preprogrammed individual responses to environmental changes beyond the control of the responding individual—such as is the classic situation described by William James (1884) of a human subject unexpectedly meeting a bear in a forest. These contributions have shown emotions as socially constructed phenomena occurring in the sequential time of human social action and interaction, involving expressions that are responsive to the expressions of cointeractants and designed for these cointeractants to perceive and to respond to.

The contributions have cast light on a number of emotional mechanisms in human social interaction, such as the elicitation of emotional response in the other, the attunement of one's emotional expression to that of the other, and the timing of one's expressions in the context of the sequential progression of interaction. Furthermore, the contributions have explicated mechanisms pertaining to the coordinated use of multimodal resources in the production of emotion displays, to the regulation and display of the actor's commitment to his or her emotional expression, and to the construction and display of appraisal of social situations that justify emotional responses.

It is a challenge for future research to specify to what degree these mechanisms are universal or culturally variable (cf. Wierzbicka ,1999), how they evolve in individual development, and to consider them in an evolutionary context. In doing so, one has to bear in mind what Nesse (2009a, p. 160) points out: not every aspect of emotional state or expression is useful in Darwinian terms. It may very well be that the subtle mechanisms of emotion expression and regulation examined in this volume are, in evolutionary terms, "epiphenomenal," that is, secondary phenomena occurring in parallel to, or derivative from, "core" emotional processes which only are functional in evolutionary terms. The "evolutionary core" of emotion might then involve, for example, individual responses to unexpected encounters with threatening, disgusting, or satisfying objects. However, it is reasonable to think that social encounters (as well as encounters between humans and bears) are among the recurrent situations in which emotions offer advantages for survival and reproduction. Therefore, the subtle other-oriented expressions, responses, and perceptions explicated in this volume may be crucial for cooperation and bonding, and therefore also, they may be among the mechanisms that have been useful for survival and reproduction in evolutionary time.

NOTES

1. Applying freely the concepts introduced by Tulving (1984), it is important to make a distinction between what might be called "autobiographical" emotional experience— the emotionally relevant memories and knowledge about past and current events that a participant of interaction may be referring to in talk—and what might be called "procedural" emotional experience, that is, momentary emotional stance embodied in the person's expressions. The recipient's access to the former is restricted in various ways (see especially Heritage, 2011) whereas the latter is much more directly observable to the recipient. The distinction becomes particularly clear in the contribution by Hepburn and Potter (chapter 9): while the recipient of crying might not know exactly why the cointeractant is crying (autobiographical emotional experience), he or she can directly observe that the cointeractant is in an emotional state (procedural emotional experience).
2. I wish to thank Mikko Kahri for invaluable help with the literature on infant–caretaker interaction.

TRANSCRIPTION CONVENTIONS

Unless otherwise indicated, in the examples of the chapters the transcription conventions used in conversation analytic research, developed by Gail Jefferson, are used.

Aspects of speech delivery

.	Falling intonation contour
,	Level intonation contour
?	Rising intonation contour
?,	Slightly rising intonation contour
↑	Rise in pitch
↓	Fall in pitch
_	Emphasis is indicated by underlining (e.g. c<u>a</u>t).
::	Lengthening of the preceding sound
<	At end of a word: the word is finished abruptly but not as a clear cut-off
su-	Word cut off
< >	Enclosed text spoken more slowly than the surrounding talk.
> <	Enclosed text spoken faster than the surrounding talk.
°°	Enclosed text said more quietly than the surrounding talk
£	Smile voice
~	Wobbly voice
#	Creaky voice
@	Animated voice
h *or* hhh	An audible aspiration
.h or .hhh	An audible inhalation.
.yeah	In front of a word: the word is said with inbreath.
(h)	Within a word indicates aspiration, often laughter

Temporal and sequential relationships

[	Utterances starting simultaneously.
]	Point where overlapping talk stops
(.)	Micropause: 0.2 seconds or less
(0.5)	Silences timed in seconds
=	No silence between two adjacent utterances

Other markings

( )	Item in doubt
(-)	Word in doubt
(())	Comment by the transcriber.

Chapter 6 uses the transcription conventions from GAT 2 (Selting et al., 2011).

In- and outbreaths

	Duration
°h / h°	approx. 0.2–0.5 sec.
°hh / hh°	approx. 0.5–0.8 sec.
°hhh / hhh°	approx. 0.8–1.0 sec.

Other segmental conventions, changes in voice quality and articulation

and_uh	Cliticizations within units
?	Cut-off by glottal closure
hm_hm, ye_es, no_o	Bi-syllabic tokens
<<creaky>>	Glottalized
<<:-)> so>	Smile voice

Other markings

(xxx), (xxx xxx)	One or more unintelligible syllables
(may i say/let us say)	Possible alternatives
<<coughing>>	With indication of scope
<<surprised>>	Interpretive comment, with indication of scope

Accentuation and pitch change

SYLlable	Focus accent
sYllable	Secondary accent
!SYL!lable	Extra strong accent
;	Falling to mid pitch
–	Level pitch
↑↑	Larger pitch upstep
<<h>>	Higher pitch register
<<l>>	Lower pitch register
^SO	Rising–falling pitch

Loudness und tempo change, with scope

<<pp>>	Pianissimo, very soft
<<p>>	Piano, soft
<<f>>	Forte, loud
<<ff>>	Fortissimo, very loud
<<all>>	Allegro, fast
<<acc>>	Accelerando, becoming faster

MULTILINEAR TRANSCRIPTION

Some of the chapters in this book deal with a language other than English. The examples in these chapters present one or two lines of glossing in the examples, so that at each numbered line, two or three lines of text are presented. The first line, presented in italics, provides the original talk. In two-line presentations, the second line is an idiomatic English gloss. In the three-line presentations, the second line is a word-by-word translation, possibly combined with grammatical gloss indicated by abbreviations; the third line provides an idiomatic gloss.

ABBREVIATIONS USED IN GLOSSING

The morphemes have been separated from each other with a dash (-).
   Case endings are referred to by the following abbreviations:

Abbreviation case approximate meaning

ACC	Accusative	object
ADE	Adessive	"at, on" (owner of something)
ALL	Allative	"to"
ELA	Elative	"out of"
ESS	Essive	"as"
GEN	Genitive	possession
ILL	Illative	"into"
INE	Inessive	"in"
INS	Instructive	(various)
PAR	Partitive	partitiveness
TRA	Translative	"to," "becoming," "into"

Other grammatical abbreviations

ADJ	adjective
ADV	adverb
CLI	clitic
COM	comparative
DEM	demonstrative
IMP	imperative
INF	infinitive
NEG	negation
PAS	passive
PL	plural
POS	possessive suffix
PC	participle
PPC	past participle
PRT	particle
PST	past tense
Q	interrogative
SG	singular
0	zero subject or object
1	1st person
2	2nd person
3	3rd person
4	passive person ending
1nameF	1st name, female
1nameM	1st name, male
NAME	name (e.g., place name)

REFERENCES

Adelswärd, V. (1989). Laughter and dialogue: The social significance of laughter in institutional dialogue. *Nordic Journal of Linguistics, 12,* 107–136.

American Psychiatric Association (1994). *Diagnostic and statistical manual of mental disorders* (4th ed.). Washington, DC: American Psychiatric Association.

Antaki, C. (2008). Formulations in psychotherapy. In A. Peräkylä, C. Antaki, S. Vehviläinen, & I. Leudar (Eds.), *Conversation analysis and psychotherapy* (pp. 26–42). Cambridge: Cambridge University Press.

Aronsson, K., & Cekaite, A. (2011). Activity contracts and directives in everyday family politics. *Discourse and Society, 22*(2), 1–18.

Auer, P., Couper-Kuhlen, E., & Müller, F. (1999). *Language in time: The rhythm and tempo of spoken interaction.* Oxford: Oxford University Press.

Bachelor, A. (1988). How clients perceive therapist empathy: A content analysis of "received empathy". *Psychotherapy: Theory, Research and Practice, 25,* 227–40.

Bamberg, M. (1997). Emotion talk(s): The role of perspective in the construction of emotions. In R. Dirven & S. Niemeier (Eds.), *Language and the emotions* (pp. 209–25). Amsterdam: Benjamins.

Barr, R. G., Hopkins, B., & Green, J. A. (Eds.) (2000). *Crying as a sign, symptom, and a signal: Clinical, emotional and developmental aspects of infant and toddler crying.* London: Mackeith Press.

Barth-Weingarten, D., Reber, E., & Selting, M. (Eds.) (2010). *Prosody in interaction.* Amsterdam: Benjamins.

Bateson, G. (1972). *Steps to an ecology of mind.* New York: Ballantine.

Bavelas, J., & Chovil, N. (2000). Visible acts of meaning: An integrated message model of language in face-to-face dialogue. *Journal of Language and Social Psychology, 19*(2), 163–94.

Beck, A. T. (1976). *Cognitive therapy and the emotional disorders.* New York: International Universities Press.

Becker, H. S. (1953). Becoming a marihuana user. *American Journal of Sociology, 59*(3), 235–42.

Beebe, B., & Lachmann, F. M. (2002). *Infant research and adult treatment: Co-constructing interactions.* Hillsdale, NJ: Analytic Press.

Beebe, B., Rustin, J., Sorter, D., & Knoblauch, S. (2003). An expanded view of intersubjectivity in infancy and its application to psychoanalysis. *Psychoanalytic Dialogues, 13*(6), 805–41.

Bell, N. D. (2009). Responses to failed humor. *Journal of Pragmatics, 41,* 1825–36.

Bercelli, F., Rossano, F., & Viaro, M. (2008). Clients' responses to therapists' re-interpretations. In A. Peräkylä, C. Antaki, S. Vehviläinen, & I. Leudar (Eds.), *Conversation analysis and psychotherapy* (pp. 43–62). Cambridge: Cambridge University Press.

Berger, P. L., & Luckmann, T. (1966). *The social construction of reality: A treatise in the sociology of knowledge.* Garden City, NY: Anchor Books.

Bergmann, J. (1992). Veiled morality: notes on discretion in psychiatry. In P. Drew & J. Heritage (Eds.), *Talk at work: Interaction in institutional settings* (pp. 137–62). Cambridge: Cambridge University Press.

Besnier, N. (1990). Language and affect. *Annual Review of Anthropology, 19,* 419–51.

Birdwhistell, R. L. (1970). *Kinesics and context: Essays on body motion communication.* New York: Ballentine Books.

Bishop, D. (1998). Development of the children's communication checklist (CCC): a method for assessing qualitative aspects of communicative impairment in children. *Journal of Child Psychology and Psychiatry, 39,* 879–92.

Bloch, C. (2008). Moods and emotional cultures: a study of flow and stress in everyday life. In M. Vandekerckhove, C. von Scheve, S. Ismer, S. Jung, & S. Kronast (Eds.), *Regulating emotions: Culture, social necessity, and biological inheritance* (pp. 312–33). Oxford: Blackwell.

Blum-Kulka, S. (1997). *Dinner talk: Cultural patterns of sociability and socialization in family discourse.* Mahwah, NJ: Lawrence Erlbaum.

Bohart, A. C., & Greenberg, L. (1997). Empathy and psychotherapy: An introductory overview. In A. C. Bohart & L. Greenberg (Eds.), *Empathy reconsidered: New directions in psychotherapy* (pp. 3–32). Washington, DC: APA Press.

Bolinger, D. (1989). *Intonation and its uses.* Stanford: Stanford University Press.

Bourdieu, P. (1977). *Outline of a theory of practice.* (R. Nice, Trans.), Cambridge: Cambridge University Press.

Bousfield, D. (2008). *Impoliteness in interaction.* Amsterdam: Benjamins.

Bradley, M. M., & Lang, P. J. (2007). Emotion and motivation. In J. T. Cacioppo, L. G. Tassinary & G. G. Berntson (Eds.), *Handbook of Psychophysiology* (3rd ed., pp. 581–607). Cambridge: Cambridge University Press.

Bruner, J. (1983). *Child's talk: Learning to use language.* Oxford: Oxford University Press.

Buttny, R. (1993). *Social accountability in communication.* London: Sage.

Button, G., & Casey, N. (1984). Generating topic: The use of topic initial elicitors. In J. M. Atkinson & J. Heritage (Eds.), *Structures of social action: Studies in conversation analysis* (pp. 167–90). Cambridge: Cambridge University Press.

Button, G., & Casey, N. (1985). Topic nomination and topic pursuit. *Human Studies, 8,* 3–55.

Caffi, C., & Janney, R. W. (1994). Toward a pragmatics of emotive communication. *Journal of Pragmatics, 22,* 325–73.

Cahill, S. E., & Eggleston, R. (1994). Managing emotions in public: The case of wheelchair users. *Social Psychology Quarterly, 57,* 300–312.

Carpendale, J., & Lewis, C. (2006). *How children develop social understanding.* Oxford: Blackwell.

Cekaite, A. (2010). Shepherding the child: Embodied directive sequences in parent–child interactions. *Text and Talk, 30*(1), 1–25.

Chevalier-Skolnikoff, S. (2003). Facial expression of emotion in non-human primates. In P. Ekman (Ed.), *Darwin and facial expression* (2nd ed., pp. 11–89). New York: Academic Press. (Original work published 1973)

Chiaro, D. (1992). *The language of jokes: Analysing verbal play.* New York: Routledge.

Chovil, N. (1991). Discourse-oriented facial displays in conversation. *Research on Language and Social Interaction, 25,* 163–94.

Clayman, S. E. (1992). Footing in the achievement of neutrality: The case of news interview discourse. In P. Drew & J. Heritage (Eds.), *Talk at work: Interaction in institutional settings* (pp. 163–98). Cambridge: Cambridge University Press.

Clayman, S., & Heritage, J. (2002). *The news interview. Journalists and public figures on the air*. Cambridge: Cambridge University Press.

Coates, J. (2007). Talk in play frame: More on laughter and intimacy. *Journal of Pragmatics, 39*, 29–49.

Cole, P., Barrett, K. C., & Zahn-Waxler, C. (1992). Emotion displays in two-year-olds during mishaps. *Child Development, 63*, 314–24.

Collins, R. (2004). *Interaction ritual chains*. Princeton: Princeton University Press.

Coulter, J. (1986). Affect and social context. In R. Harré (Ed.), *The social construction of emotions*. New York: Blackwell.

Coulter, J. (1989). *Mind in action*. Cambridge: Polity Press.

Couper-Kuhlen, E. (1986). *An introduction to English prosody*. London: Arnold.

Couper-Kuhlen, E. (1999). Coherent voicing: On prosody in conversational reported speech. In W. Bublitz & U. Lenk (Eds.), *Coherence in spoken and written discourse: How to create it and how to describe it* (pp. 11–32). Amsterdam: Benjamins.

Couper-Kuhlen, E. (2009). A sequential approach to affect: The case of "disappointment". In M. Haakana, M. Laakso, & J. Lindström (Eds.), *Talk in interaction. Comparative perspectives* (pp. 94–123). Helsinki: Finnish Literature Society.

Couper-Kuhlen, E. (2011). When turns start with *because*: An exercise in interactional syntax. In A. Meurman-Solin & U. Lenker (Eds.), *Connectives in synchrony and diachrony in European languages*, Studies in variation, contacts and change in English, 8. Helsinki: VARIENG. Retrieved from http://www.helsinki.fi/varieng/journal/volumes/08/couper-kuhlen/ (November 2011).

Couper-Kuhlen, E. (forthcoming). On doing empathy with the voice. Paper presented at the workshop on Affect and Interaction, Max Planck Institute, Nijmegen, December 2010.

Couper-Kuhlen, E., & Ford, C. E. (Eds.) (2004). *Sound patterns in interaction*. Philadelphia: John Benjamins.

Couper-Kuhlen, E., & Selting, M. (Eds.) (1996). *Prosody in conversation: Interactional studies*. Cambridge: Cambridge University Press.

Coupland, N., Coupland, J., & Giles, H. (1991). *Language, society and the elderly*. Oxford: Blackwell.

Craven, A., & Potter, J. (2010). Directives: Entitlement and contingency in action. *Discourse Processes, 12*(4), 419–42.

Curl, T., & Drew, P. (2008). Contingency and action: A comparison of two forms of requesting. *Research on Language and Social Interaction, 41*(2), 129–53.

Dalgleish, T. (2009). James–Lange theory. In D. Sander & K. R. Scherer (Eds.), *The Oxford companion to emotion and the affective sciences* (p. 229). Oxford: Oxford University Press.

Damasio, A. R. (1994). *Descartes' error: Emotion, reason and the human brain*. New York: Putnam.

Damasio, A. R. (1999). *The feeling of what happens: Body and emotion in the making of consciousness*. New York, San Diego, London: Harcourt Brace.

Darwin, C. (1998). *The expression of the emotions in man and animals* (Introduction, afterword, and commentaries by Paul Ekman). Oxford: Oxford University Press. (Original work published 1872)

Darwin, C. (2007). *The expression of the emotions in man and animals*. Chicago: Filiquarian Publishing.) (Original work published 1872)

Dickson, K., Walker, H., & Fogel, A. (1997). The relationship between smile type and play type during parent–infant play. *Developmental Psychology, 33*, 925–33.

Drew, P. (1987). Po-faced receipts of teases. *Linguistics, 25*, 219–53.

Drew, P. (1998). Complaints about transgressions and misconduct. *Research on Language and Social Interaction, 31*(3 & 4), 295–325.

Drew, P., & Heritage, J. (Eds.) (1992a). *Talk at work: Interaction in institutional settings* Cambridge: Cambridge University Press.

Drew, P., & Heritage, J. (1992b). Analyzing talk at work: An introduction. In P. Drew & J. Heritage (Eds.), *Talk at work: Interaction in institutional settings* (pp. 3–65). Cambridge: Cambridge University Press.

Drew, P., & Holt, E. (1998). Figures of speech: Figurative expressions and the management of topic transition in conversation. *Language in Society, 27*, 495–522.

Drew, P., & Sorjonen, M.-L. (2011). Dialogue in institutional interactions. In T. van Dijk (Ed.), *Discourse studies* (pp. 191–216). London: Sage.

Drew, P., & Walker, T. (2009). Going too far: Complaining, escalating and disaffiliation. *Journal of Pragmatics, 41*(12), 2400–14.

Du Bois, J. W. (2007). The stance triangle. In R. Englebretson (Ed.), *Stancetaking in Discourse: Subjectivity, evaluation, interaction* (pp. 139–82). Amsterdam: Benjamins.

Dunn, J. (1988). *The beginnings of social understanding*. Oxford: Blackwell.

Edwards, D. (1997). *Discourse and cognition*. London and Beverly Hills, CA: Sage.

Edwards, D. (1999). Emotion discourse. *Culture & Psychology, 5*(3), 271–91.

Edwards, D. (2005). Discursive psychology. In K. L. Fitch & R. E. Sanders (Eds.), *Handbook of language and social interaction* (pp. 257–73). New York: Erlbaum.

Edwards, D., & Potter, J. (1992). *Discursive psychology*. London: Sage.

Eisenberg, N., & Fabes, R. A. (1990). Empathy: Conceptualization, measurement, and relation to prosocial behavior. *Motivation and Emotion, 14*, 131–49.

Ekman, P. (1982). Methods for measuring facial action. In K. R. Scherer & P. Ekman (Eds.) *Handbook of methods in nonverbal behavior research* (pp. 45–135). Cambridge: Cambridge University Press.

Ekman, P. (1993). Facial expression and emotion. *American Psychologist, 48*, 384–92.

Ekman, P. (1999). Facial expressions. In T. Dalgleish & M. Power (Eds.), *Handbook of cognition and emotion*. New York: Wiley.

Ekman, P. (2003). *Emotions revealed*. New York: Henry Holt.

Ekman, P. (Ed.) (2006). *Darwin and facial expression: A century of research in review*. Cambridge MA, Los Altos, CA: Malor Books.

Ekman, P. (2009). Introduction to the third edition. In C. Darwin, *The expression of the emotions in man and animals* (Introduction, afterword, and commentaries by Paul Ekman) (3rd ed., pp. xxi–xxxvi). Oxford: Oxford University Press.

Ekman, P., & Friesen, W. (1969). The repertoire of nonverbal behavior: Categories, origins, usage, and coding. *Semiotica, 1*(1), 49–98.

Ekman, P., & Friesen, W. (2003). *Unmasking the face: A guide to recognising emotions from facial expression* (2nd ed.). Cambridge, MA: Malor. (Original work published 1975)

Elert, C.-C. (1964). *Phonologic studies of quantity in Swedish*. Stockholm: Almqvist and Wiksell.

Ellsworth, P. C., & Scherer, K. R. (2003). Appraisal process in emotion. In R. J. Davidson, K. R. Scherer, & H. H. Goldsmith (Eds.), *Handbook of affective sciences* (pp. 572–95). Oxford: Oxford University Press.

Emirbayer, M., & Maynard, D. W. (2011). Pragmatism and Ethnomethodology. *Qualitative Sociology, 34*, 221–61.

Enfield, N., & Levinson, S. (2006). Introduction: Human sociality as a new interdisciplinary field. In N. Enfield & S. Levinson (Eds.), *Roots of human socialtiy: Culture, cognition and interaction* (pp. 1–38). Oxford: Berg.

Englebretson, R. (Ed.) (2007a). Stancetaking in discourse: An introduction. In R. Englebretson (Ed.), *Stancetaking in Discourse: Subjectivity, evaluation, interaction* (pp. 1–25). Amsterdam: Benjamins.

Englebretson, R. (Ed.) (2007b). *Stancetaking in Discourse: Subjectivity, Evaluation, Interaction*. Amsterdam: Benjamins.

Ervin-Tripp, S., & Gordon, D. (1984). The development of requests. In R. Scheifelbusch (Ed.), *Communicative competence: Assessment and intervention* (pp. 298–321). Baltimore: University Park Press.

Ervin-Tripp, S., O'Connor, M. C., & Rosenberg, J. (1984). Language and power in the family. In C. Kramarae, M. Schulz, & W. O'Barr (Eds.), *Language and power* (pp. 116–35). Los Angeles: Sage.

Fineman, S. (Ed.) (2000). *Emotion in organizations*. London: Sage.

Fogel, A. (1993). *Developing through relationships*. Hemel Hempstead, UK: Harvester Wheatsheaf.

Fonagy, P., Gergely, G., Jurist, E. L., & Target, M. (2002). *Affect regulation, mentalization and the development of the self*. New York: Other Press.

Freese, J. (1997). Politeness and the introduction of positive information about self. Annual meetings of the Midwest Sociological Association, Des Moines, IA.

Freese, J., & Maynard, D. W. (1998). Prosodic features of bad news and good news in conversation. *Language in Society*, 27, 195–219.

French, P., & Local, J. (1983). Turn-competitive incomings. *Journal of Pragmatics*, 7, 17–38.

Frijda, N. (1986). *The emotions*. Cambridge: Cambridge University Press.

Frijda, N. (2004). Emotions and action. In A. S. R. Manstead, N. Frijda, & A. Fisher (Eds.), *Feelings and emotions: The Amsterdam symposium* (pp. 158–73). Cambridge: Cambridge University Press.

Fridlund, A. J. (1994). *Human facial expression: An evolutionary view*. San Diego, CA: Academic Press.

Fridlund, A. J. (1997). The new ethology of human facial expressions. In J. A. Russell & J. Fernandez-Dols (Eds.), *The psychology of facial expression* (pp. 103–29). Cambridge: Cambridge University Press.

Garcia, A. (1991). Dispute resolution without disputing. How the interactional organisation of mediation hearings minimises argumentative talk. *American Sociological Review*, 56(6), 818–35.

Gardner, R. (1997). The conversation object *mm*: A weak and variable acknowledging token." *Research on Language and Social Interaction*, 30(2), 131–56.

Garfinkel, H. (1967). *Studies in ethnomethodology*. Englewood Cliffs, NJ: Prentice-Hall.

Gergen, K. (1999). *An invitation to social construction*. London: Sage.

Gill, V. T. (1998). Doing attributions in medical interaction: Patients' explanations for illness and doctors' responses. *Social Psychology Quarterly*, 61(4), 342–60.

Glenn, P. J. (1989). Initiating shared laughter in multi-party conversations. *Western Journal of speech Communication*, 53, 127–49.

Glenn, P. J. (1991). Current speaker initiation of two-party shared laughter. *Research on Language and Social Interaction*, 25, 139–62.

Glenn, P. J. (2003). *Laughter in interaction*. Cambridge: Cambridge University Press.

Glenn, P. J. (2010). Interviewer laughs: Shared laughter and asymmetries in employment interviews. *Journal of Pragmatics*, 42, 1485–98.

Goffman, E. (1959). *The presentation of self in everyday life*. New York: Doubleday Anchor.

Goffman, E. (1961). *Encounters: Two studies in the sociology of interaction*. Indianapolis: Bobbs-Merrill.

Goffman, E. (1963). *Behavior in public places: Notes on the social organization of gatherings*. New York: Free Press.

Goffman, E. (1967). *Interaction ritual: Essays in face to face behavior*. Garden City, NY: Doubleday.

Goffman, E. (1978). Response cries. *Language*, 54, 787–815.

Goffman, E. (1981). *Forms of talk.* Philadelphia and Oxford: University of Pennsylvania Press and Blackwell.

Goldberg, J. A. (1978). Amplitude shift: A mechanism for the affiliation of utterances in conversational interaction. In J. N. Schenkein (Ed.), *Studies in the organization of conversational interaction* (pp. 199–218). New York: Academic Press.

Goodwin, C. (1981). *Conversational organization: Interaction between speakers and hearers.* New York: Academic Press.

Goodwin, C. (1986). Gesture as a resource for the organization of mutual orientation. *Semiotica, 62*(1/2), 29–49.

Goodwin, C. (1996). Transparent vision. In E. Ochs, E. A. Schegloff, & S. A. Thompson (Eds.), *Interaction and grammar* (pp. 370–404). Cambridge: Cambridge University Press.

Goodwin, C. (2000). Action and embodiment within situated human interaction. *Journal of Pragmatics, 32,* 1489–522.

Goodwin, C. (2006). Human sociality as mutual orientation in a rich interactive environment: Multimodal utterances and pointing in aphasia. In N. Enfield & S. C. Levinson (Eds.), *Roots of human sociality* (pp. 96–125). London: Berg Press.

Goodwin, C. (2007). Participation, stance and affect in the organization of activities. *Discourse and Society, 18*(1), 53–73.

Goodwin, C. (2010). Constructing meaning through prosody in aphasia. In D. Barth-Weingarten, E. Reber, & M. Selting (Eds.), *Prosody in interaction* (pp. 373–94). Amsterdam: Benjamins.

Goodwin, C. (2011). Contextures of action. In J. Streeck, C. Goodwin, & C. D. LeBaron (Eds.), *Embodied interaction: Language and body in the material world* (pp. 182–93). Cambridge: Cambridge University Press.

Goodwin, C. (forthcoming). Semiotic agency within a framework of cooperative semiosis. In J. Streeck, C. LeBaron, & C. Goodwin (Eds.), *Multimodality in human interaction.* Cambridge: Cambridge University Press.

Goodwin, C., & Goodwin, M. H. (1987). Concurrent operations on talk: Notes on the interactive organization of assessments. *IPrA Papers in Pragmatics, 1*(1), 1–54.

Goodwin, C., & Goodwin, M. H. (1992). Assessments and the construction of context. In A. Duranti & C. Goodwin (Eds.), *Rethinking context* (pp. 147–89). Cambridge: Cambridge University Press.

Goodwin, C., & Goodwin, M. H. (2000). Emotion within situated activity. In A. Duranti (Ed.), *Linguistic anthropology: a reader* (pp. 239–57). Malden, MA: Blackwell.

Goodwin, M. H. (1980). Processes of mutual monitoring implicated in the production of description sequences. *Sociological Inquiry, 50*(3–4), 303–17.

Goodwin, M. H. (1990). Byplay: Participant structure and framing of collaborative collusion. *Réseaux, 8*(2), 155–80.

Goodwin, M. H. (1990b). *He-said-she-said: Talk as social organization among black children.* Bloomington: Indiana University Press.

Goodwin, M. H. (2006a). Participation, affect, and trajectory in family directive/response sequences. *Text and Talk, 26*(4/5), 513–42.

Goodwin, M. H. (2006b). *The hidden life of girls: Games of stance, status, and exclusion.* Oxford: Blackwell.

Goodwin, M. H. (2007). Occasioned knowledge exploration in family interaction. *Discourse and Society, 18*(1), 93–110.

Goodwin, M. H., & Goodwin, C. (2000). Emotion within situated activity. In N. Budwig, I. Uzgiris, & J. Wertsch (Eds.), *Communication: an arena of development* (pp. 33–53). Stamford, CT: Ablex. (Also published in A. Duranti (Ed.), *Linguistic anthropology: A reader* [pp. 239–57]. New York: Wiley-Blackwell, 2000.)

Goodwin, M. H., & Goodwin, C. (2004). Participation. In A. Duranti (Ed.), *A companion to linguistic anthropology* (pp. 222–44). Oxford: Basil Blackwell.

Goudbeek, M., & Scherer, K. R. (2009). Vocal expression of emotion. In D. Sander & K. R. Scherer (Eds.), *The Oxford companion to emotion and the affective sciences* (pp. 404–6). New York: Oxford University Press.

Greenberg, L. S. (2004). Emotion-focused therapy. *Clinical Psychology and Psychotherapy*, *11*, 3–16.

Greenberg, L., & Elliot, R. (1997). Varieties of empathic responding. In A. C. Bohart & L. Greenberg (Eds.), *Empathy reconsidered: New directions in psychotherapy* (pp. 167–87). Washington, DC: APA Press.

Greenson, R. (1967). *The technique and practice of psychoanalysis*. New York: International Universities Press.

Gross, J. J. (Ed.) (1998). The emerging field of emotion regulation: an integrative review. *Review of General Psychology*, *2*, 271–99.

Gross, J. J. (2007). *Handbook of emotion regulation*. New York: Guilford Press.

Gross, J. J., & Thompson, R. A. (2007). Emotion regulation: conceptual foundations. In J. J. Gross (Ed.), *Handbook of emotion regulation* (pp. 3–26). New York: Guilford Press.

Guidano, V. (1991). *The self in process*. New York: Guilford Press.

Gumperz, J. J. (1977). Sociocultural knowledge in conversational inference. In M. Saville-Troike (Ed.), *Linguistics and anthropology*, Georgetown University Round Table on Languages and Linguistics (pp. 191–212). Washington, DC: Georgetown University Press.

Gumperz, J. J. (1982). *Discourse strategies*. Cambridge: Cambridge University Press.

Gumperz, J. J. (1992). Contextualization revisited. In P. Auer & A. Di Luzio (Eds.), *The contextualization of language* (pp. 39–53). Amsterdam: Benjamins.

Günthner, S. (1996). The prosodic contextualization of moral work: An analysis of reproaches in "why"-formats. In E. Couper-Kuhlen & M. Selting (Eds.), *Prosody in conversation: Interactional studies* (pp. 271–302). Cambridge and New York: Cambridge University Press.

Günthner, S. (1997a). Complaint stories: Constructing emotional reciprocity among women. In H. Kotthoff & R. Wodak (Eds.), *Communicating gender in context* (pp. 179–218). Amsterdam: Benjamins.

Günthner, S. (1997b). The contextualization of affect in reported dialogues. In R. Dirven & S. Niemeier (Eds.), *Language and the emotions* (pp. 247–75). Amsterdam: Benjamins.

Günthner, S. (1999). Polyphony and the "layering of voices" in reported dialogues: An analysis of the use of prosodic devices in everyday reported speech. *Journal of Pragmatics*, *31*, 685–708.

Haakana, M. (1999). Laughing matters: A conversation analytical study of laughter in doctor–patient interaction. (Unpublished doctoral dissertation). University of Helsinki, Finland.

Haakana, M. (2001). Laughter as a patient's resource: Dealing with delicate aspects of medical interaction. *Text*, *21*, 187–219.

Haakana, M. (2002). Laughter in medical interaction: From quantification to analysis, and back. *Journal of Sociolinguistics*, *6*, 207–35.

Haakana, M. (2007). Reported thought in complaint stories. In E. Holt & R. Clift, *Reporting talk. Reported speech in interaction* (pp. 150–78). Cambridge: Cambridge Unversity Press.

Haakana, M. (2010). Laughter and smiling: notes on co-occurrences. *Journal of Pragmatics*, *42*, 1499–1512.

Haakana, M., & Kurhila, S. (2009). Other-correction in everyday conversation: Some comparative aspects. In M. Haakana, M. Laakso, & J. Lindström (Eds.), *Talk in interaction: Comparative dimensions* (pp. 152–79). Helsinki: Finnish Literature Society.

Hakulinen, A., & Selting, M. (Eds.) (2005). *Syntax and lexis in conversation: Studies on the use of linguistic resources in talk-in-interaction*. Amsterdam: Benjamins.

Hakulinen, A., & Sorjonen, M.-L. (2009). Designing utterances for action: Verb repeat responses to assessments. In M. Haakana, M. Laakso, & J. Lindström (Eds.), *Talk in interaction: Comparative dimensions* (pp. 124–51). Helsinki: Finnish Literature Society.

Hakulinen, A., Vilkuna, M., Korhonen, R., Koivisto, V., Heinonen, T. R., & Alho, I. (2004). *Iso suomen kielioppi* [Comprehensive grammar of Finnish]. Helsinki: Finnish Literature Society. Retrieved from http://kaino.kotus.fi/visk/etusivu.php.

Hareli S., & Parkinson, B. (2009). Social emotions. In D. Sander & K. R. Scherer (Eds.), *The Oxford companion to emotion and the affective sciences* (pp. 374–5). Oxford: Oxford University Press.

Harkins, J., & Wierzbicka, A. (Eds.) (2001). *Emotions in cross-linguistic perspective*. Berlin: Mouton de Gruyter.

Harmon-Jones, E. (2003). Clarifying the emotive functions of asymmetrical frontal cortical activity. *Psychophysiology, 40*, 838–48.

Harré, R. (Ed.) (1986). *The social construction of emotions*. New York: Blackwell.

Harré, R., & Parrott, W. G. (Eds.) (1996). *The emotions: Social, cultural, and biological dimensions*. London: Sage.

Hatfield, E., Cacioppo, J. T., & Rapson, R. L. (1993a). Emotional contagion. *Current Directions in Psychological Science, 2*, 96–9.

Hatfield, E., Cacioppo, J. T., & Rapson, R. L. (1993b). *Emotional contagion*. New York: Cambridge University Press.

Heath, C. (1986). *Body movement and speech in medical interaction*. Cambridge: Cambridge University Press

Heath, C. (1988). Embarrassment and interactional organization. In P. Drew & T. Wootton (Eds.), *Erving Goffman: An interdisciplinary appreciation* (pp. 136–160). Cambridge: Polity Press.

Heath, C. (1989). Pain talk: The expression of suffering in the medical consultation. *Social Psychological Quarterly, 52*(2), 113–25.

Heath, C., & vom Lehn, D. (2004). Configuring reception: (Dis-)regarding the "spectator" in museums and galleries. *Theory, Culture & Society, 21*, 43–65.

Heinemann, T. (2006). "Will you or can't you?": displaying entitlement in interrogative requests. *Journal of Pragmatics, 38*, 1081–1104.

Heinemann, T., & Traverso, V. (Eds.) (2008). Complaining in interaction [Special issue]. *Journal of Pragmatics, 41*(12).

Heisterkamp, B. L. (2006). Conversational displays of mediator neutrality in a court-based program. *Journal of Pragmatics, 38*(12), 2051–64.

Hepburn, A. (2004). Crying: notes on description, transcription and interaction. *Research on Language and Social Interaction, 37*, 251–90.

Hepburn, A., & Potter, J. (2007). Crying receipts: Time, empathy, and institutional practice. *Research on Language and Social Interaction, 40*(1), 89–116.

Hepburn, A., & Potter, J. (2010). Interrogating tears: Some uses of "tag questions" in a child protection helpline. In A. F. Freed & S. Ehrlich (Eds.), *Why do you ask? The function of questions in institutional discourse* (pp. 69–86). Oxford: Oxford University Press.

Heritage, J. (1984a). *Garfinkel and ethnomethodology*. Cambridge: Polity.

Heritage, J. (1984b). A change-of-state token and aspects of its sequential placement. In J. M. Atkinson & J. Heritage (Eds.), *Structures of social action: Studies in conversation analysis* (pp. 299–345). Cambridge: Cambridge University Press.

Heritage, J. (2002). Oh-prefaced responses to assessments: A method of modifying agreement/disagreement. In C. E. Ford, B. A. Fox, & S. A. Thompson (Eds.), *The language of turn and sequence* (pp. 196–224). New York: Oxford University Press.

Heritage, J. (2010). Questioning in medicine. In A. Freed & S. Ehrlich (Eds.), *"Why do you ask?": The function of questions in institutional discourse* (pp. 42–68). New York: Oxford University Press.

Heritage, J. (2011). Territories of knowledge, territories of experience: Empathic moments in interaction. In T. Stivers, L. Mondada, & J. Steensig (Eds.), *The morality of knowledge in conversation.* Cambridge: Cambridge University Press.

Heritage, J. C., & Clayman, S. (2010). *Talk in action: Interactions, identities, and institutions.* Chichester, UK: Wiley-Blackwell.

Heritage, J., & Lindström, A. (1998). Motherhood, medicine, and morality: Scenes from a medical encounter. *Research on Language and Social Interaction, 31,* 397–438.

Heritage, J., & Raymond, G. (2005). The terms of agreement: Indexing epistemic authority and subordination in assessment sequences. *Social Psychology Quarterly, 68*(1), 15–38.

Heritage, J., & Raymond, G. (forthcoming). Navigating epistemic landscapes: Acquiescence, agency and resistance in responses to polar questions. In J.-P. De Ruiter (Ed.), *Questions: Formal, functional and interactional perspectives.* Cambridge: Cambridge University Press.

Heritage, J., & Sefi, S. (1992). Dilemmas of advice: Aspects of the delivery and reception of advice in interactions between health visitors and first time mothers. In P. Drew and J. Heritage (Eds.), *Talk at work: Interaction in institutional settings.* Cambridge: Cambridge University Press.

Heritage, John (2002). *Oh*-Prefaced Responses to Assessments: A Method of Modifying Agreement/Disagreement. In Ceci Ford, Barbara Fox and Sandra Thompson, (Eds.) *The Language of Turn and Sequence.* Oxford, Oxford University Press: 196–224.

Herlin, I. (1998). *Suomen kun* [Finnish kun]. Helsinki: Finnish Literature Society.

Hobson, P. (1993). *Autism and the development of mind.* Hove, UK: Erlbaum.

Hobson, P. (2002). *The cradle of thought: Explorations of the origins of thinking.* London: Macmillan.

Hochschild, A. R. (1979). Emotion work, feeling rules, and social structure. *American Journal of Sociology, 85,* 551–75.

Hochschild, A. R. (1983). *The managed heart: Commercialization of human feeling.* Berkeley: University of California Press.

Hokkanen, M. (2008). Tosiaan-partikkeli ja toisto keskustelussa: vahvistaminen ja palaamisen funktiot keskustelussa [The particle *tosiaan* and repetition in conversation]. (Unpublished Pro gradu [master's] dissertation). University of Helsinki, Finland

Holt, E. (1993). The structure of death announcements: Looking on the bright side of death. *Text, 13*(2), 189–212.

Holt, E. (1996). Reporting on talk: The use of direct reported speech in conversation. *Research on Language and Social Interaction, 29*(3): 219-245.

Holt, E. (2000). Reporting and reacting: Concurrent responses to reported speech. *Research on Language and Social Interaction, 33*(4), 425–54.

Holt, E. (2010). The last laugh: Shared laughter and topic termination. *Journal of Pragmatics, 42,* 1513–25.

Holt, E., & Clift, R. (Eds.) (2007). *Reporting talk: Reported speech in interaction.* Cambridge: Cambridge University Press.

Hopkins, D., Kleres, J., Flam, H., & Kuzmics, H. (Eds.) (2009). *Theorizing emotions: Sociological explorations and applications.* Frankfurt: Campus.

Howlin, P., & Rutter, M. (1987). *Treatment of autistic children.* New York: Wiley.

Hurme, R., Malin, R.-L., & Syväoja, O. (1984). *Uusi suomi–englanti suursanakirja* [Finnish–English General Dictionary]. Helsinki: WSOY.

Hutchins, E. (2006). The distributed cognition perspective on human interaction. In N. J. Enfield & S. C. Levinson (Eds.), *Roots of human sociality* (pp. 375–98). Oxford: Berg.

Iacoboni, M. (2008). *Mirroring people: The new science of how we connect with others*. New York: Farrar, Straus, & Giroux.

Irvine, J. (1982). Language and affect: Some cross-cultural issues. In H. Byrnes (Ed.), *Contemporary perceptions of language: Interdisciplinary dimensions* (pp. 31–47). Washington, DC: Georgetown University Press.

Irvine, J. (1990). Registering affect: Heteroglossia in the linguistic expression of emotion. In C. A. Lutz & L. Abu-Lughod (Eds.), *Language and the Politics of Emotion* (pp. 126–85). Studies in emotion and social interaction. New York: Cambridge University Press.

Jaffe, A. (2009a). Introduction: The sociolinguistics of stance. In A. Jaffe (Ed.) *Stance: Sociolinguistic perspectives* (pp. 3–28). New York: Oxford University Press.

Jaffe, A. (Ed.) (2009b). *Stance: Sociolinguistic perspectives*. Oxford: Oxford University Press.

James. W. (1884). What is an emotion? *Mind, 9,* 188–205.

Jefferson, G. (1978). Sequential aspects of storytelling in conversation. In J. Schenkein (Ed.), *Studies in the organization of conversational interaction* (pp. 219–48). New York, Academic Press.

Jefferson, G. (1979). A technique for inviting laughter and its subsequent acceptance declination. In G. Psathas (Ed.), *Everyday language: Studies in ethnomethdology* (pp. 79–96). New York: Irvington.

Jefferson, G. (1980). The analysis of conversations in which "troubles" and "anxieties" are expressed. End-of-grant report, HR 4805/2. London: Social Science Research Council.

Jefferson, G. (1981). The abominable "ne?": A working paper exploring the phenomenon of postresponse pursuit of response. Occasional Paper 6, Department of Sociology, University of Manchester.

Jefferson, G. (1984a). On stepwise transition from talk about a trouble to inappropriately next-positioned matters. In J. M. Atkinson and J. Heritage, (Eds.), *Structures of social action: Studies in conversation analysis* (pp. 191–221). Cambridge: Cambridge University Press.

Jefferson, G. (1984b). On the organization of laughter in talk about troubles. In J. M. Atkinson & J. Heritage (Eds.), *Structures of social action: Studies in conversation analysis* (pp. 346–69). Cambridge: Cambridge University Press.

Jefferson, G. (1985). An exercise in the transcription and analysis of laughter. In T. A. van Dijk (Ed.), *Handbook of discourse analysis*. (Vol. 3) *Discourse and dialogue* (pp. 25–34). London: Academic Press.

Jefferson, G. (1988). On the sequential organization of troubles talk in ordinary conversation. *Social Problems, 35*(4), 418–42.

Jefferson, G. (2002). Is "no" an acknowledgement token? Comparing American and British uses of (+)/(-) tokens. *Journal of Pragmatics, 34,* 1345–83.

Jefferson, G. (2004a). Glossary of transcript symbols with an introduction. In G. Lerner (Ed.), *Conversation analysis: Studies from the first generation* (pp. 13–31). Amsterdam: Benjamins.

Jefferson, G. (2004b). A note on laughter in "male–female" interaction. *Discourse Studies, 6,* 117–33.

Jefferson, G. (2010). Sometimes a frog in your throat is just a frog in your throat: Gutturals as (sometimes) laughter-implicative. *Journal of Pragmatics, 42,* 1467–84.

Jefferson, G., Sacks, H., & Schegloff, E. A. (1987). Notes on laughter in the pursuit of intimacy. In G. Button & J. R. E. Lee (Eds.), *Talk and social organisation* (pp. 152–205). Clevedon: Multilingual Matters.

Jefferson, G., &. Lee, J. R. (1981). The rejection of advice: managing the problematic convergence of a "troubles telling" and a "service encounter". *Journal of Pragmatics, 5,* 399–422.

Jefferson, G., &. Lee, J. R. (1992). The rejection of advice: Managing the problematic convergence of a "troubles telling" and a "service encounter". In P. Drew & J. Heritage (Eds.), *Talk at work: interaction in institutional settings*, 521–48. Cambridge: Cambridge University Press.

Jefferson, Gail (1984). On the Organization of Laughter in Talk About Troubles. In J. Maxwell Atkinson and John Heritage, (Eds.) *Structures of Social Action*. Cambridge, Cambridge University Press: 346–369.

Kagan, J. (1981). *The second year: the emergence of self-awareness*. Cambridge, MA: Harvard University Press.

Kahri, M. (in preparation). Regulation of emotion in infant-caretaker interaction: a conversation analytic perspective. (Unpublished doctoral dissertation). University of Helsinki, Finland.

Kangasharju, H. (2009). Preference for disagreement? A comparison of three disputes. In M. Haakana, M. Laakso, & J. Lindström (Eds.), *Talk in interaction: Comparative dimensions* (pp. 231–53). Helsinki: Finnish Literature Society.

Kappas, A. (2008). Psssst! Dr. Jekyll and Mr. Hyde are actually the same person! A tale of regulation and emotion. In M. Vandekerckhove, C. von Scheve, S. Ismer, S, Jung, & S. Kronast (Eds.), *Regulating emotions: Culture, social necessity and biological inheritance* (pp. 15–38). Oxford: Blackwell.

Kaye, K. (1982). *The mental and social life of babies*. Hemel Hempstead, UK: Harvester Wheatsheaf.

Katz, J. (1996). Families and funny mirrors: A study of the social construction and personal embodiment of humour. *American Journal of Sociology, 101*(5), 1194–237.

Katz, J. (1999). *How emotions work*. Chicago: University of Chicago Press.

Kemper, T. D., & Collins, R. (1984). Power, status, and emotions: A sociological contribution to a pscyhophysiological domain. In K. Scherer & P. Ekman (Eds.), *Approaches to emotion* (pp. 369–83). Hillsdale, NJ: Erlbaum.

Kemper, T. D., & Collins, R. (1990). Dimensions of microinteraction. *American Journal of Sociology, 96* ,32–68.

Kendon, A. (1992). *Conducting interaction: patterns of behaviour in focused encounters*. Cambridge: Cambridge University Press.

Kendon, A. (2009). Language's matrix. *Gesture, 9*, 353–72.

Kidwell, M. (2003). "Looking to see if someone is looking at you": gaze and the organization of observability in very young children's harrassing acts toward a peer. (Unpublished doctoral dissertation). University of California at Santa Barbara.

Kidwell, M., & Zimmerman, D. (2006). "Observability" in the interactions of very young children. *Communication Monographs, 73*, 1–28.

Kielitoimiston sanakirja. [New dictionary of modern Finnish] (2006). Helsinki: Kotimaisten kielten tutkimuskeskus.

Klatt, D. H. (1976). Linguistic uses of segmental duration in English: Acoustic and perceptual evidence. *Journal of the Acoustinc Society of America, 59*(5), 1208–21.

Kohler, K. J. & Niebuhr, O. (2007). The phonetics of emphasis. *Proceedings of the 16th ICPhS, Saarbruecken, Germany*, 2145–8.

Kurhila, S. (2008). Ymmärtäminen, vuorovaikutus ja toinen kieli. [Understanding, interaction and second language.] In T. Onikki-Rantajääskö & M. Siiroinen (Eds.), *Kieltä kohti* (pp. 105–27). Helsinki: Otava.

Kurth, E., Spichiger, E., Stutz, E. Z., Biedermann, J., Hölsi, I., & Kennedy, H. P. (2010). Crying babies, tired mothers—challenges of the postnatal hospital stay: An interpretive phenomenological study. *BMC: Pregnancy and Childbirth, 10*(21).

Kärkkäinen, E. (2003). *Epistemic stance in English conversation: A description of its interactional functions, with a focus on I think*. Amsterdam: Benjamins.

Laakso, M. (1997). *Self-initiation of repair in conversations of fluent aphasic speakers*. Helsinki: Finnish Literature Society.

Labov, W. (1972). The transformation of experience in narrative syntax. In *Languages in the inner city. Studies in the black English vernacular* (pp. 354–97). Philadelphia: University of Pennsylvania Press.

Labov, W., & Fanshel, D. (1977). *Therapeutic discourse: Psychotherapy as conversation*. New York: Academic Press.

Lamoureaux, E. (2010). Presenting depression. Unpublished paper. Department of Sociology, University of California, Los Angeles.

Larsen, R. J. & Diener, E. (1992). Promises and problems with the circumplex model of emotion. In M. Clark (Ed.), *Review of personality and social psychology* (Vol. 13, pp. 25–59). Newbury Park, CA: Sage.

Laury, R. & Seppänen, E.-L. (2008). Clause combining, interaction, evidentiality, participation structure and the conjunction-particle continuum. The Finnish että. In Ritva Laury (Ed.), *Crosslinguistic studies of clause combining: The multifunctionality of conjunctions* (pp. 153–78). Amsterdam and Philadelphia: Benjamins.

Leech, G. N. (1983). *Principles of pragmatics*. London: Longman.

Levinson, S. L. (2006a). Cognition at the heart of human interaction. *Discourse Studies*, 8(1), 85–93.

Levinson, S. L. (2006b). On the human "interaction engine". In N. Enfield & S. Levinson (Eds.), *Roots of human sociality: Culture, cognition and interaction* (pp. 39–69). Oxford: Berg.

Levinson, S. L. (forthcoming). Action formation and ascription. In T. Stivers & J. Sidnell (Eds.), *Handbook of conversation analysis*. Oxford: Wiley-Blackwell.

Lindström, A. (1995). Addressing relevance in talk-in-interaction: The case of the Swedish "or":-constructed inquiry. Paper presented at the annual meeting of the American Sociological Association, Washington, DC.

Lindström, A. (1997). Designing social action: Grammar, prosody, and interaction in Swedish conversation. (Unpublished doctoral dissertation). University of California, Los Angeles.

Lindström, A. (2005). Language as social action: A study of how senior citizens request assistance with practical tasks in the Swedish home help service. In A. Hakulinen & M. Selting (Eds.), *Syntax and lexis in conversation: Studies on the use of linguistic resources in talk-in-interaction* (pp. 209–30). Amsterdam: Benjamins.

Lindström, A., & Mondada, L. (Eds.) (2009). Assessments in social interaction [Special issue]. *Research on Language and Social Interaction*, 42(4).

Lindström, A., & Sorjonen, M.-L. (in press). Affiliation in conversation. In T. Stivers & J. Sidnell (Eds.), *Handbook of conversation analysis*. Oxford: Wiley-Blackwell.

Linehan, M. M. (1997). Validation and psychotherapy. In A. C. Bohart & L. Greenberg (Eds.), *Empathy reconsidered: New directions in psychotherapy* (pp. 353–92). Washington, DC: APA Press.

Linell, P. (2009). *Rethinking language, mind, and world dialogically: Interactional and contextual theories of human sense-making*. Charlotte, NC: Information Age Publishing.

Linell, P., & Bredmar, M. (1996). Reconstructing topical sensitivity: Aspects of face-work in talks between midwives and expectant mothers. *Research on Language and Social Interaction*, 29(4), 347–79.

Lohmann, H., Tomasello, M., & Meyer, S. (2005). Linguistic communication and social understanding. In J. Astington & J. Baird (Eds.), *Why language matters for theory of mind* (pp. 245–65). Oxford: Oxford University Press.

Local, J. (1996). Conversational phonetics: Some aspects of news receipts in everyday talk. In E. Couper-Kuhlen & M. Selting (Eds.), *Prosody in conversation: Interactional studies* (pp. 177–230). Cambridge: Cambridge University Press.

Local, J., & Walker, G. (2008). Stance and affect in conversation: On the interplay of sequential and phonetic resources. *Text & Talk*, 28, 723–47.

Local, J. K., Kelly, J., & Wells, W. H. G. (1986). Towards a phonology of conversation: Turn-taking in urban Tyneside speech. *Journal of Linguistics, 22*(2), 411–37.

Lutz, C. & White, G. M. (1986). The anthropology of emotions. In B. J. Siegel, A. R. Beals, & S. A. Tyler (Eds.), *Annual review of anthropology* (pp. 163–246). Palo Alto: Annual Reviews.

Lutz, C. A., & Abu-Lughod, L. (Eds.) (1990). *Language and the politics of emotion*. Cambridge: Cambridge University Press.

Lutz, T. (2001). *Crying: A natural and cultural history of tears*. New York: Norton.

Manstead, A. S. R., Bem, S., & Fridja, N. (Eds.) (2000). *Emotions and beliefs: How feelings influence thoughts*. Cambridge: Cambridge University Press.

Manstead, A. S. R., Frijda, N., & Fischer, A. (Eds.) (2004). *Feelings and emotions: The Amsterdam symposium*. Cambridge: Cambridge University Press.

Manzo, J., Heath, R. L., & Blonder, L. X. (1998). The interpersonal management of crying among survivors of stroke. *Sociological Spectrum, 18*, 161–84.

Matoesian, G. (2005). Struck by speech revisited: Embodied stance in jurisdictional discourse. *Journal of Sociolinguistics, 9*(2), 167–93.

Matsumoto, D., & Ekman, P. (2009). Basic emotions. In D. Sander & K. R. Scherer (Eds.), *The Oxford companion to emotion and the affective sciences* (pp. 69–72). Oxford: Oxford University Press.

Maynard, D. W. (1985). How children start arguments. *Language in Society, 14*, 207–23.

Maynard, D. W. (1997). The news delivery sequence: Bad news and good news in conversational interaction. *Research on Language and Social Interaction, 30*, 93–130.

Maynard, D. W. (2003). *Bad news, good news: Conversational order in everyday talk and clinical settings*. Chicago: University of Chicago Press.

McIntosh, J. (1986). A consumer perspective on the health visiting service. University of Glasgow, *Social Paediatric and Obstetric Research Unit*.

Merleau-Ponty, M. (1964a). *Sense and non-sense*. Evanston, IL: Northwestern University Press.

Merleau-Ponty, M. (1964b). *The primacy of perception*. Evanston, IL: Northwestern University Press.

Mesquita, B., & Albert, D. (2007). The cultural regulation of emotions. In J. J. Gross (Ed.), *Handbook of emotion regulation* (pp. 486–503). New York: Guilford Press.

Miller, P., & Sperry, L. (1988). Early talk about the past: the origins of conversational stories of personal experience. *Journal of Child Language, 15*, 293–315.

Mills, S. (2010). Impoliteness. In P. Griffiths, A. J. Merrison, & A. Bloomer (Eds.), *Language in use: A reader* (pp. 59–68). London: Routledge.

Mulkay, M. (1988). *On humour: Its nature and its place in modern society*. Oxford: Polity.

Müller, K. (1992). Theatrical moments: On contextualizing funny and dramatic moods in the course of telling a story in conversation. In P. Auer & A. Di Luzio (Eds.), *The contextualization of language* (pp. 199–221). Amsterdam: Benjamins.

Murphy, K. M., & Throop, C. J. (2010). Willing contours: Locating volition in anthropological theory. In K. M. Murphy & C. J. Throop (Eds.), *Toward an anthropology of the will* (pp. 1–27). Stanford: Stanford University Press.

Nesse, R. E. (2009a). Evolution of emotion. In D. Sander & K. R. Scherer (Eds.), *The Oxford companion to emotion and the affective sciences* (pp. 159–64). Oxford: Oxford University Press.

Nesse, R. E. (2009b). Evolutionary and proximal explanations. In D. Sander & K. R. Scherer (Eds.), *The Oxford companion to emotion and the affective sciences* (pp. 158–9). Oxford: Oxford University Press.

Newman, J. D. (2007). Neural circuits underlying crying and cry responding in mammals. *Behavioural Brain Research, 182*, 155–65.

Niemelä, M. (2010). The reporting space in conversational storytelling: Orchestrating all semiotic channels for taking a stance. *Journal of Pragmatics, 42*, 3258–70.

Norrick, N. (1993). *Conversational joking: Humor in everyday talk*. Bloomington: Indiana University Press.

Nummenmaa, L. (2010). *Tunteiden psykologia* [Psychology of emotions]. Helsinki: Tammi.

Nykysuomen sanakirja [Dictionary of modern Finnish]. (1951–61). Porvoo: WSOY.

Ochs, E. (1988). *Culture and language development*. Cambridge: Cambridge University Press.

Ochs, E. (Ed.) (1989). Introduction. The pragmatics of affect [Special issue]. *Text, 9*(1), 1–5.

Ochs, E. (1992). Indexing gender. In A. Duranti & C. Goodwin (Eds.), *Rethinking context* (pp. 335–58). Cambridge: Cambridge University Press.

Ochs, E. (1996). Linguistic resources for socializing humanity. In J. J. Gumperz & S. C. Levinson (Eds.), *Rethinking linguistic relativity* (pp. 407–37). Cambridge: Cambridge University Press.

Ochs, E., Graesch, A. P., Mittmann, A., & Bradbury, T. (2006). Video ethnography and ethnoarchaeological tracking. In M. Pitt-Catsouphes, E. E. Kossek, & S. Sweet (Eds.), *Work and family handbook: Multi-disciplinary perspectives and approaches* (pp. 387–410). Mahwah, NJ: Lawrence Erlbaum.

Ochs, E., & Schieffelin, B. (1989). Language has a heart. *Text & Talk, 9*, 7–25.

Ochs, E., & Solomon, O. (2005). Practical logic and autism. In C. Casey & R. B. Edgerton (Eds.), *A companion to psychological anthropology* (pp. 140–67). Oxford: Blackwell.

Ogden, R. (2006). Phonetics and social action in agreement and disagreements. *Journal of Pragmatics, 38*, 1752–75.

Ogden, R., & Routarinne, S. (2005). The communicative function of final rises in Finnish intonation. *Phonetica, 62*(2–4), 160–75.

O'Neill, D. (2005). Talking about "new" information: the given / new distinction and children's developing theory of mind. In J. Astington & J. Baird (Eds.), *Why language matters for theory of mind* (pp. 150–72). Oxford: Oxford University Press.

Panksepp, J. (2004). *Affective neuroscience: The foundations of human and animal emotion*. Oxford: Oxford University Press.

Papoušek, M., & Papoušek, H. (1989). Forms and functions of vocal matching in interaction between mothers and their precanonical infants. *First Language, 9*, 137–57.

Park, R. E. (1927). Human nature and collective behavior. *American Journal of Sociology, 32*(5), 733–41

Parkinson, B., Fisher, A. H., & Manstead, A. S. R. (2005). *Emotion in social relations*. New York: Psychology Press.

Parsons, T. (1951). *The social system*. Glencoe, IL: Free Press.

Peräkylä, A. (2002). Agency and authority: Extended responses to diagnostic statements in primary care encounters. *Research on Language and Social Interaction, 35*(2), 219–47.

Peräkylä, A. (2004). Making links in psychoanalytic interpretations: A conversation analytic view. *Psychotherapy Research, 14*(3), 289–307.

Peräkylä, A. (2008). Conversation analysis and psychoanalysis: Interpretation, affect and intersubjectivity. In A. Peräkylä, C. Antaki, S. Vehviläinen, & I. Leudar (Eds.), *Conversation analysis and psychotherapy* (pp. 100–119). Cambridge: Cambridge University Press.

Peräkylä, A., Antaki, C., Vehviläinen, S., & Leudar, I. (2008). Analysing psychotherapy in practice. In A. Peräkylä, C. Antaki, S. Vehviläinen, & I. Leudar (Eds.), *Conversation analysis and psychotherapy* (pp. 5–25). Cambridge: Cambridge University Press.

Peräkylä, A., & Ruusuvuori, J. (2006). Facial expression in an assessment. In H. Knoblauch, B. Schnettler, J. Raab, & H.-G. Soeffner (Eds.), *Video analysis: methodology and methods* (pp. 127–42). Frankfurt am Main: Peter Lang.

Peräkylä, A., & Vehviläinen, S. (2003). Conversation analysis and the professional stocks of interactional knowledge. *Discourse and Society, 14,* 727–50.

Peräkylä, A., Voutilainen, L., Henttonen, P., Ravaja, N., & Sams, M. (2010, December 10). Emotion in interaction: Expression, regulation and psychophysiology. *Workshop on affect and interaction, Max Planck Institute for Psycholinguistics,* Nijmegen, Netherlands.

Peter, M., Vingerhoets, J. J. M., & Van Heck, G. L. (2001). Personality, gender and crying. *European Journal of Personality, 15,* 19–28.

Planalp, S. (1999). *Communicating emotion: Social, moral, and cultural processes.* Cambridge: Cambridge University Press.

Poder, P. (2008). The political regulation of anger in organizations. In M. Vandekerckhove, C. von Scheve, S. Ismer, S. Jung, & S. Kronast (Eds.), *Regulating emotions: Culture, social necessity, and biological inheritance* (pp. 291–311). Oxford: Blackwell.

Pomerantz, A. (1975). Second assessment: A study of some features of agreement / disagreement. (Unpublished doctoral dissertation). University of California, Irvine.

Pomerantz, A. (1978). Compliment responses: Notes on the co-operation of multiple constraints. In J. Schenkein (Ed.), *Studies in the organization of conversational interaction* (pp. 79–112). New York: Academic Press.

Pomerantz, A. (1984a). Pursuing a response. In J. M. Atkinson & J. Heritage (Eds.), *Structures of social action: Studies in conversation analysis* (pp. 152–63). Cambridge: Cambridge University Press.

Pomerantz, A. (1984b). Agreeing and disagreeing with assessment: Some features of preferred / dispreferred turn shapes." In J. M. Atkinson & J. Heritage (Eds.), *Structures of social action: Studies in conversation analysis* (pp. 57–101). Cambridge: Cambridge University Press.

Potter, J. (2006). Cognition and conversation. *Discourse Studies, 8*(1), 131–40.

Potter, J., & Hepburn, A. (2010). Putting aspiration into words: "laugh particles," managing descriptive trouble and modulating action. *Journal of Pragmatics, 42,* 1543–55.

Potter, J., & Wetherell, M. (1987). *Discourse and social psychology: Beyond attitudes and behaviour.* London: Sage.

Rae, J. (2008). Lexical substitution as a therapeutic resource. In A. Peräkylä, C. Antaki, S. Vehviläinen, & I. Leudar (Eds), *Conversation analysis and psychotherapy* (pp. 62–79). Cambridge: Cambridge University Press.

Raevaara, L. (1989). *No*—vuoronalkuinen partikkeli [No—a turn initial particle]. In A. Hakulinen (Ed.), *Suomalaisen keskustelun keinoja 1,* Kieli 4 (pp. 147–61). Department of Finnish, University of Helsinki, Finland.

Raymond, G. (2003). Grammar and social organisation: Yes / no interrogatives and the structure of responding. *American Sociological Review, 68,* 939–67.

Reber, E. (2008). *Affectivity in talk-in-interaction: Sound objects in English.* (Unpublished doctoral dissertation). University of Potsdam, Germany.

Reber, E., & Couper-Kuhlen, E. (2010). Interjektionen zwischen Lexikon und Vokalität: Lexem oder Lautobjekt? [Interjections between lexicon and vocalization: Lexeme or sound object?]. In A. Deppermann & A. Linke (Eds.), *Sprache intermedial. Stimme und Schrift, Bild und Ton* (pp. 69–96). Berlin: de Gruyter.

Reilly, J., & Seibert, L. (2003). Language and emotion. In R. J. Davidson, K. R. Scherer, & H. H. Goldsmith (Eds.), *Handbook of affective sciences* (pp. 535–59). Oxford: Oxford University Press.

Roach, P. (1983). *English phonetics and phonology: A practical course.* Cambridge: Cambridge University Press.

Robinson, J. (1982). *An evaluation of health visiting.* London: Council for the Education and Training of Health Visitors.

Rogers, C. R. (1957). The necessary and sufficient conditions for therapeutic personality change. *Journal of Counseling Psychology*, *21*, 95–103.

Routarinne, S. (2003). *Tytöt äänessä. Parenteesit ja nouseva sävelkulku kertojan vuorovaikutuskeinoina* [Girls talking: Parentheses and rising intonation as narrator's interactional devices]. Helsinki: Finnish Literature Society.

Russell, J. A., & Fernández-Dols, J. (1997). *The psychology of facial expression*. Cambridge: Cambridge University Press.

Rutter, M., & Bailey, A. (1993). Thinking and relationships: Mind and brain (some reflections in theory of mind and autism). In. S. Baron-Cohen, H. Tager-Flusberg, & D. Cohen (Eds.), *Understanding other minds: Perspectives from autism* (pp. 481–504). Oxford: Oxford University Press.

Ruusuvuori, J. (2005). "Empathy" and "sympathy" in action: Attending to patients' troubles in Finnish homeopathic and general practice consultations. *Social Psychology Quarterly*, *68*(3), 204–22.

Ruusuvuori, J. (2007). Managing affect: Integrating empathy and problem solving in two types of health care consultation. *Discourse Studies*, *9*, 597–622.

Ruusuvuori, J., & Lindfors, P. (2009). Complaining about previous treatment in health care settings. *Journal of Pragmatics*, *41*, 2415–34.

Ruusuvuori, J., & Peräkylä, A. (2009). Facial and verbal expressions in assessing stories and topics. *Research on Language and Social Interaction*, *42*(4), 377–94.

Saarni, C. (1979). Children's understanding of display rules for expressive behavior. *Developmental Psychology*, *15*, 424–29.

Saarni, C. (1999). *The development of emotional competence*. New York: Guilford Press.

Saarni, C., Campos, J., Camras, L., & Witherington, D. (2006). Emotional development: Action, communication and understanding. In N. Eisenberg (Ed.), *Handbook of child psychology* (Vol. 3, pp. 226–99). New Jersey: Wiley.

Sacks, H. (1974). An analysis of the course of a joke's telling. In R. Bauman & J. Sherzer (Eds.), *Explorations in the ethnography of speaking* (pp. 337–53). Cambridge: Cambridge University Press.

Sacks, H. (1980). Button button who's got the button. *Sociological Inquiry*, *50*, 318–27.

Sacks, H. (1984a). On doing "being ordinary". In J. M. Atkinson & J. Heritage (Eds.), *Structures of social action: Studies in conversation analysis* (pp. 413–29). Cambridge: Cambridge University Press.

Sacks, H. (1984b). Notes on methodology. In J. M. Atkinson & J. Heritage (Eds.), *Structures of social action: Studies in conversation analysis* (pp. 21–7). Cambridge: Cambridge University Press.

Sacks, H. (1992). *Lectures on conversation* (Vols. 1 & 2). (G. Jefferson, Ed.; introduction by E. A. Schegloff). Oxford: Blackwell.

Sacks, H., Schegloff, E. A., & Jefferson, G. (1974). A simplest systematics for the organization of turn-taking for conversation. *Language*, *50*, 696–735.

Safran, J. D., Muran, J. C., Wallner Samstag, L., & Stevens, C. (2001). Repairing therapeutic alliance ruptures. *Psychotherapy*, *38*, 406–12.

Sander, K., & Scheich, H. (2005). Left auditory cortex and amygdala, but right insula dominance for human laughing and crying. *Journal of Cognitive Neuroscience*, *17*, 1519–31.

Sandlund, E. (2004). Feeling by doing: The social organization of everyday emotions in academic talk-in-interaction. *Karlstad University Studies*, *2004*(36).

Schacter, S., & Singer, J. E. (1962). Cognitive, social, and physiological determinants of emotional state. *Psychological Review*, *69*(5), 379–99.

Scheff, T. J. (1997). *Emotions, the social bond, and human reality*. New York: Cambridge University Press.

Scheff, T. J. (2000). Shame and the social bond: A sociological theory. *Sociological Theory*, *18*, 84–99.

Scheflen, A. (1973). *Communicational structure: Analysis of a psychotherapy transaction.* Bloomington: Indiana University Press.

Schegloff, E. A. (1980). Preliminaries to preliminaries: "Can I ask you a question". *Sociological Inquiry*, *50*, 104–52.

Schegloff, E. A. (1996a). Confirming allusions: Toward an empirical account of action. *American Journal of Sociology*, *102*(1), 161–216.

Schegloff, E. A. (1996b). Turn organization: One intersection of grammar and interaction. In E. Ochs, E. A. Schgeloff, & S. A. Thompson (Eds.), *Interaction and grammar* (pp. 52–133). Cambridge: Cambridge University Press.

Schegloff, E. A. (2007). *Sequence organization in interaction: A primer in conversation analysis* (Vol. 1). Cambridge: Cambridge University Press.

Scherer, K. R. (1989). Vocal correlates of emotional arousal and affective disturbance. In H. Wagner & A. Manstead (Eds.), *Handbook of psychophysiology: Emotion and social behaviour* (pp. 165–97). London: Wiley.

Scherer, K. R. (1996). Emotion. In M. Hewstone, W. Stroebe, & G. M. Stephenson (Eds.), *Introduction to social psychology: A European perspective* (2nd ed., pp. 279–315). Oxford: Blackwell.

Scherer, K. R. (2003). Vocal communication of emotion: A review of research paradigms. *Speech Communication*, *40*, 227–56.

Scherer, K. R. (2004). Feelings integrate the central representation of appraisal-driven response organization in emotion. In A. S. R. Manstead, N. Frijda, & A. Fisher (Eds.), *Feelings and emotions: The Amsterdam symposium* (pp. 136–57). Cambridge: Cambridge University Press.

Scherer, K. R. (2009). Emotion classifications. In D. Sander & K. R. Scherer (Eds.), *The Oxford companion to emotion and the affective sciences* (pp. 140–41). Oxford: Oxford University Press.

Schieffelin, B. (1990). *The give and take of everyday life: Language socialization of Kaluli children.* Cambridge: Cambridge University Press.

Schieffelin, B., & Ochs, E. (Eds.) (1986). *Language socialization across cultures.* Cambridge: Cambridge University Press.

Schumann, J. H., Crowell, S. E., Jones, N. E., Lee, N., Schuchert, S. A., & Wood, L. A. (2004). *The neurobiology of learning: Perspectives from second language acquisition.* Mahwah, NJ: Lawrence Erlbaum.

Sefi, S. (1988). Health visitors talking to mothers. *Health Visitor*, *61*, 7–10.

Selting, M. (1992). Prosody in conversational questions. *Journal of Pragmatics*, *17*, 315–45.

Selting, M. (1994). Emphatic speech style—with special focus on the prosodic signaling of heightened emotive involvement in onversation. *Journal of Pragmatics*, *22*, 375–408.

Selting, M. (1996). Prosody as an activity-type distinctive cue in conversation: The case of so-called "astonished" questions in repair initiation. In E. Couper-Kuhlen & M. Selting (Eds.), *Prosody in conversation: Interactional studies* (pp. 231–70). New York: Cambridge University Press.

Selting, M. (2010a). Affectivity in conversational storytelling: An analysis of displays of anger or indignation in complaint stories. *Pragmatics*, *20*, 229–77.

Selting, M. (2010b). Prosody in interaction: State of the art. In D. Barth-Weingarten, E. Reber, & M. Selting (Eds.), *Prosody in interaction* (pp. 3–40). Amsterdam: Benjamins.

Selting, M., Auer, P., et al. (2011). A system for transcribing talk-in-interaction: GAT2. (E. Couper-Kuhlen & D. Barth-Weingarten, Trans.) *Gesprächsforschung—Online-Zeitschrift zur verbalen Interaktion* Retrieved from.http://www.gespraechsforschung-ozs.de/heft2011/px-gat2-englisch.pdf (November 2011).

Shantz, C. (1987). Conflicts between children. *Child Development, 58,* 283–305.

Shearman, J. (1992). *Only connect: Art and the spectator in the Italian Renaissance.* Princeton: Princeton University Press.

Sieben, B., & Wettegren, Å. (2010). Emotionalizing organizations and organizing emotions—our research agenda. In B. Sieben & Å. Wettegren (Eds.), *Emotionalizing organizations and organizing emotions* (pp. 1–20). Basingstoke: Palgrave Macmillan.

Smith, III, A. C., & Kleinman, S. (1989). Managing emotions in medical school: Students' contacts with the living dead. *Social Psychology Quarterly, 52* 56–69.

Smith, D. (1978). K is mentally ill: the anatomy of a factual account. *Sociology, 12*(1), 23–53.

Smith-Lovin, L. (1995). The sociology of affect and emotion. In K. S. Cook, G. A. Fine, & J. S. House (Eds.), *Sociological perspectives on social psychology* (pp. 118–48). Boston: Allyn and Bacon.

Sorjonen, M.-L. (2001). *Responding in conversation. A study of response particles in Finnish.* Amsterdam and Philadelphia: Benjamins.

Steensig, J., & Drew, P. (Eds.) (2008). Questioning and affiliation / disaffiliation in interaction [Special Issue]. *Discourse Studies, 10*(1).

Stern, D. (1985). *The interpersonal world of the infant.* New York: Basic Books.

Stern, D. (2004). *The present moment in psychotherapy and everyday life.* New York: Norton.

Sterponi, L. (2004). Construction of rules, accountability and moral identity by high-functioning children with autism. *Discourse Studies, 6,* 207–28.

Stets, J. E. (2003). Emotions and sentiments. In J. Delamater (Ed.), *Handbook of social psychology* (pp. 309–35). New York: Kluwer Academic/Plenum.

Stivers, T. (2005). Modified repeats: One method for asserting primary rights from second position. *Research on Language and Social Interaction, 38*(2), 131

Stivers, T. (2008). Stance, alignment, and affiliation during storytelling: When nodding is a token of affiliation. *Research on Language and Social Interaction, 41*(1), 31–57.

Stivers, T., & Rossano, F. (2010). Mobilizing response. *Research on Language and Social Interaction, 43*(1), 3–31.

St. James-Roberts, I. (1988). Persistent crying in the first year of life: A progress report. *Newsletter of the Association for Child Psychology and Psychiatry, 10,* 28–29.

Streeck, J. (2009). *Gesturecraft: The manu-facture of meaning.* Amsterdam: Benjamins.

Stribling, P. (2007). Interactional competencies in children with autistic spectrum disorders. (Unpublished doctoral dissertation). Roehampton University, UK.

Sy, T., Côté, S., & Saavedra, R. (2005). The contagious leader: Impact of the leader's mood on the mood of group members, group affective tone, and group processes. *Journal of Applied Psychology, 90*(2), 295–305.

Szczepek Reed, B. (2006). *Prosodic orientation in English conversation.* New York and Basingstoke, UK: Palgrave Macmillan.

Szczepek Reed, B. (2011). *Analysing conversation: An introduction to prosody.* New York and Basingstoke, UK: Palgrave Macmillan.

ten Have, P. (2002). Ontology or methodology? Comments on Speer's "natural" and "contrived" data: A sustainable distinction? *Discourse Studies, 4,* 527–30.

ten Have, P. (2007). *Doing conversation analysis: A practical guide* (2nd Ed.). London: Sage.

Terasaki, A. K. (2004 [1976]). Pre-announcement sequences in conversation. In G. H. Lerner (Ed.), *Conversation analysis: Studies from the first generation* (pp. 171–225). Amsterdam: Benjamins.

Thompson, R. A., & Meyer, S. (2007). Socialization of emotion regulation in the family. In J. J. Gross (Ed.), *Handbook of emotion regulation.* New York: Guilford Press.

Tinbergen, N. (1963). On the aims and methods of ethology. *Zeitschrift für Tierspsychologie, 20,* 4410–63.

Tomasello, M. (1999). *The cultural origins of human cognition.* Cambridge: Harvard University Press.

Tomasello, M. (2008). *Origins of human communication.* Cambridge: MIT Press.

Toskala, A., & Hartikainen, K. (2005). *Minuuden rakentuminen: Psyykkinen kehitys ja kognitiivis-konstruktiivinen psykoterapia* [The construction of selfhood: Psychic development and cognitive-constructivist psychotherapy]. Jyväskylä: Jyväskylän koulutuskeskus.

Trigg, R. (1970). *Pain and emotion.* Oxford: Oxford University Press.

Trommsdorff, G., & Rothbaum, F. (2008). Development of emotion regulation in cultural contexts. In M. Vandekerckhove, C. von Scheve, S. Ismer, S. Jung, & S. Kronast (Eds.), *Regulating emotions: Culture, social necessity, and biological inheritance* (pp. 85–120). Oxford: Blackwell.

Tulbert, E., & Goodwin, M. H. (2011). Choreographies of attention: Multimodality in a routine family activity. In J. Streeck, C. Goodwin, & C. D. LeBaron (Eds.), *Embodied interaction: Language and body in the material world* (pp. 79–92). Cambridge: Cambridge University Press.

Tulving E. (1984). Precis of elements of episodic memory. *Behavioural and Brain Sciences, 7,* 223–68.

Turner, J. H. (2000). *On the origin of human emotions: A sociological inquiry into the evolution of human affect.* Stanford: Stanford University Press.

Turner, J. H., & Stets, J. E. (2005). *The sociology of emotions.* Cambrdige: Cambridge University Press.

Uhmann, S. (1996). On rhythm in everyday German conversation: Beat clashes in assessment utterances. In E. Couper-Kuhlen & M. Selting (Eds.), *Prosody in conversation: Interactional studies* (pp. 303–65). Cambridge: Cambridge University Press.

Valsiner, J. (1987). *Culture and the development of children's action: A cultural-historical theory of developmental psychology.* Chichester, UK: Wiley.

Vandekerckhove, M., von Scheve, C., Ismer, S., Jung, S., & Kronast, S. (Eds.) (2008). *Regulating emotions: Culture, social necessity, and biological inheritance: An interdisciplinary perspective.* Oxford: Blackwell.

Vehviläinen, S. (2003). Preparing and delivering interpretations in psychoanalytic interaction. *Text, 23*(4), 573–606.

Vilkuna, M. (1997). Into and out of the standard language: The particle *ni* in Finnish. In J. Cheshire & D. Stein (Eds.), *Taming the vernacular: From dialect to written standard language* (pp. 51–67). London: Longman.

Vingerhoets, A. J. J. M., & Becht, M. C. (1996). *Adult crying inventory (ACI).* Unpublished questionnaire. Department of Psychology, Tilburg University, Netherlands.

Visapää,. L. (2010). Infinitives revisited: A cognitive and interactional approach. Manuscript. Department of Finnish, Finno-Ugrian and Scandinavian Studies, University of Helsinki, Finland.

Vöge, M., & Wagner, J. (Eds.) (2010). Social achievements and sequential organization of laughter. Studies in the honor of Gail Jefferson [Special issue]. *Journal of Pragmatics, 42.*

vom Lehn, D., Heath, C. C., & Hindmarsh, J. (2001). Exhibiting interaction: Conduct and collaboration in museums and galleries. *Symbolic Interaction, 24,* 189–216.

Voutilainen, L., Peräkylä, A., & Ruusuvuori, J. (2010a). Recognition and interpretation: Responding to emotional experience in psychotherapy. *Research on Language and Social Interaction, 43*(1), 85–107.

Voutilainen, L., Peräkyla, A., & Ruusuvuori, J. (2010b). Professional non-neutrality: Criticising third parties in psychotherapy. *Sociology of Health and Illness, 32*(5), 798–816.

Voutilainen, L., Peräkylä, A., & Ruusuvuori, J. (2010c). Misalignment as a therapeutic resource. *Qualitative Research in Psychology*, 7(4), 299–315

Ward, N. (2006). Non-lexical conversational sounds in American English. *Pragmatics & Cognition*, 14(1), 129–82.

Warner, M. A. (1997). Does empathy cure? A theoretical consideration of empathy, processing, and personal narrative. In A. C. Bohart & L. Greenberg (Eds.), *Empathy reconsidered: New directions in psychotherapy* (pp. 125–41). Washington, DC: APA Press.

Whalen, J., & Zimmerman, D. H. (1998). Observations on the display and management of emotion in naturally occurring activities: The case of "hysteria" in calls to 9-1-1. *Social Psychological Quarterly*, 61, 141–59.

Wierzbicka, A. (1995). Emotion and facial expression: A semantic perspective. *Culture & Psychology*, 1, 227–58.

Wierzbicka, A. (1999). *Emotions across languages and cultures: Diversity and universals*. Cambridge: Cambridge University Press.

Wilce, J. M. (2009). *Language and emotion*. Cambridge: Cambridge University Press.

Wilkinson, S., & Kitzinger, C. (2006). Surprise as an interactional achievement: Reaction tokens in conversation. *Social Psychology Quarterly*, 69, 150–82.

Wootton, A. (1981). The management of grantings and rejections by parents in request sequences. *Semiotica*, 37, 59–89.

Wootton, A. (1984). Some aspects of children's use of "please" in request sequences. In P. Auer & A. Di Luzio (Eds.) *Interpretive sociolinguistics* (pp. 147–63). Tubingen: Verlag.

Wootton, A. (1994). Object transfer, intersubjectivity and third position repair. *Journal of Child Language*, 21, 543–64.

Wootton, A. (1997). *Interaction and the development of mind*. Cambridge: Cambridge University Press.

Wootton, A. (2002/3). Interactional contrasts between typically developing children and those with autism, Asperger's syndrome, and pragmatic impairment. *Issues in Applied Linguistics*, 13(2), 133–59.

Wootton, A. (2005). Interactional and sequential configurations informing request format selection in children's speech. In A. Hakulinen & M. Selting (Eds.) *Syntax and lexis in conversation: Studies on the use of linguistic resources in talk-in-interaction* (pp. 185–208). Amsterdam: Benjamins.

Wootton, A. (2007). A puzzle about "please": repair, increments and related matters in the speech of a young child. *Research on Language and Social Interaction*, 40, 171–98.

Wootton, A. (2010). "Actually" and the sequential skills of a two-year-old. In H. Gardner and M. Forrester (Eds.), *Analysing interactions in childhood* (pp. 59–73). Chichester, UK: Wiley.

Wright, M. (2005). Studies of the phonetics–interaction interface: Clicks and interactional structures in English conversation. (Unpublished dissertation). University of York.

Wright, M. (2007). Clicks as markers of new sequences in English conversation. *Proceedings of the 16th International Congress of Phonetic Sciences*, Saarbrücken, Germany, 1069–72.

Yaeger-Dror, M. (2002). Register and prosodic variation, a cross language comparison. *Journal of Pragmatics*, 34, 1494–536.

Zahavi, D. (2011). Intersubjectivity. In S. Luft & O. Overgaard (Eds.), *Routledge companion to phenomenology*. London: Routledge.

Zajonc, R. B. (1980). Feeling and thinking: Preferences need no inferences. *American Psychologist*, 35, 151–75.

Zhu, J., & Thagard, P. (2002). Emotion and action. *Philosophical Psychology*, 15(1), 19–36.

INDEX

Accountability, 137–38, 196, 207, 209, 220–21
Accounts, 6, 9, 30–36, 57–58, 86, 94, 106, 114, 125, 147, 153, 191, 196, 201, 207–8, 220, 246, 250, 258, 261, 264, 267, 269–71, 286
  second pair part, 33
Adelswärd, 184
Adjacency pairs, 10, 198
Affiliation, 4–7, 10–11, 13, 65–66, 75–80, 88–90, 147, 156, 163, 168–69, 236, 239, 242, 257
  and complaint stories, 113–45
  dis-, 65–66, 88
  empathic, 148, 257
  emotional, 257
  in institutional settings, 11, 235–55, 280
  non- , 113–44, 246–50
  pursue of, 13, 246–50
Agency, 26
Agreement, 27, 47, 60–61, 106, 108–9, 121, 124, 126, 145n7, 205, 207, 236, 243–45, 254, 260–62, 264–67, 269
  pro forma, 121, 264
Alignment, 5, 8, 16, 23, 38–39, 52, 61, 66, 83, 93, 100–103, 112n10, 113–14, 145n13, 152, 159, 168, 204, 222, 224, 226–27 232, 237, 252, 257, 261
  of the bodies, 8
  co-, 33
  congruent, 22–23, 40
  embodied, 21–23
  of the face, 220
  nongranting, 52
  oppositional, 22, 40
  re-, 92, 224
Anger, 5, 8, 13, 17, 20, 58, 60, 90, 93, 106, 112n15, 113–17, 121–32, 136, 139, 140–44, 245, 255, 278, 280

  communication of, 42
  display of, 42, 114, 122–26, 131
  expression of, 92, 277
Appeals, 30–34, 41n10, 79
Asperger's syndrome, 55
Aspiration 14, 199, 201 (*see also*, inbreath)
  marked, 31
  transcription of, 174, 199
Assessment, 6, 8, 9, 66, 88, 92–112, 114, 124, 145n7, 145n18, 145n20, 146n31, 148, 159–64, 166, 171, 184, 264–65
  agreeing, 4, 7, 106
  congruent negative, 13, 108, 125–26, 132, 137, 142, 144
  congruent, 124–26
  lexical, 100–107
  negative, 138, 142
  oh-prefaced, 101
  parallel, 145n18
  positive, 100–107
  postannouncement, 94
  responsive, 7
  second, 106, 241
  sequence of, 7, 84
  subjunctive, 145n18
  of valence, 159

Bailey, A., 57–58
Bateson, G., 17–18
Becker, H., 93
Beebe, B. 91, 145n21
Bell, N. 176, 193n4
Besnier, N., 41n3, 147
Blonder, L. 196, 208
Blum-Kulka, S., 26
Body, 8, 16–19, 21–23, 34–40, 110, 225, 278, 282, 284, 287
  positions, 8
  postures, 8, 12, 16